Reviews from Amazon.com Readers of Previous Editions

"...My productivity has increased tenfold."

⭐⭐⭐⭐⭐ **This really works**, September 30, 2007
Beancounter

"I have been using Michael Linenberger's system for about 3 months now and my productivity has increased tenfold. With this system, I have a way to track important tasks and I feel that I am on top of my job."

⭐⭐⭐⭐⭐ **This book changed my life!,** December 19, 2010
Julie Davis (Darwin, NT Australia)

"I cannot tell you how grateful I am to Michael Linenberger for writing this fantastic book. I was constantly on the look out for how to become more efficient, pack more into each day, stop missing deadlines and reduce stress in my everyday work life - and this book has dealt with all of those issues. For the very first time in 18 years, I left work to go on holiday leave at a reasonable time (5.10pm) instead of working until 2am to get everything under control before I left. I cannot tell you how this had changed my life. Not only did I leave work at a reasonable time but I left feeling confident that I had completed all my important and urgent tasks and that all other tasks were in my task list dated appropriately and would be done in an orderly and timely manner when I returned. Working hard and working long hours is simply not enough in our current working environments. Michael Linenberger has changed my life for the better and I cannot recommend this book highly enough to anyone needing to get control of the myriad of tasks that come your way on a daily, if not hourly basis. I have bought 2 more copies to give to my friends who I know will benefit greatly from the systems that Michael recommends."

⭐⭐⭐⭐⭐ **Best and most practical book on managing your workflow**, August 18, 2009 Amy M. Leschke-Kahle

"I've read many many books and attended way too many classes on "time management" only to wonder what I was doing wrong when I couldn't sustain writer's magic method. That was until I found Total Workday Control. Michael Linenberger has finally developed a practical, real-world approach to managing the workday. It's clear that he gets how today's world in the office works. "

⭐⭐⭐⭐⭐ Everything I hoped it would be...and more, March 19, 2010
Antone M. Goyak (Wisconsin, USA)

"What I appreciate about Michael Linenberger's approach is that it is simplistic, yet very powerful. I felt like my workday was not as effective and productive as it could have been - mainly because of the way I approached the planning and tasks that came with each new day. What excites me about this process is that you do not have to use everything in the text to be effective - it is not an all-or-nothing venture. I have utilized a few key aspects and have seen immediate results. I have learned how to competently organize my day, all while staying current with emails and tasks. Michael's thought process and approach to tasks and emails is getting the job done for me. Along with the crucial basics, I am now learning some of the finer aspects of workday management in later chapters so that my thinking is getting transformed along with my actions. I feel like my day is not disjointed anymore and that I am able to tackle what is most important and not let the menial tasks fill my day. What I received for the price of the book has been remarkable. Kudos to Michael for a text that is well-written, fully illustrated, and easy to read."

⭐⭐⭐⭐⭐ I Love This Book, July 2, 2009
R.D. (New York)

"I have a demanding job and get more mail than I can process every day, and I've often wished that I had some better strategy to deal with all of my incoming mail. One day I declared I would have a clean inbox, and then I just moved all of my mail out of my inbox... just to see some space in it. But after a day or two, I had an out of control inbox again... after a few weeks... I was basically back where I started and I was frustrated. When I first saw this book, I was intrigued. But what dragged me in was the clarity with which Linenberger seemed to understand modern workday problems. I found myself nodding my head over and over again and saying "this guy speaks the truth!" His language is direct, clear and concise, and he seemed to really understand what I had to go through every day. So I kept reading until I just had to buy the book..."

⭐⭐⭐⭐⭐ Second most lifechanging book ever, January 12, 2007
Cynthia Choi (Albany, NY)

"This book is the second most lifechanging book I've ever read. Completely awesome. His system is not overly cumbersome and lightweight enough to be realistic to use every day. Project managers can read the book and learn the system in one afternoon and have your inbox cleared from 800 down to zero by the next day."

★★★★★ **Kudos to you, Michael!,** August 3, 2009
Mark B. Logan "marklogan"

"I don't say this often, but it is well deserved... reading this book and implementing its recommendations has been nothing short of life changing. I've been using the techniques and framework as outlined in the book and immediately recognized the benefits and realized significant time-saving and stress-reducing results. What a great feeling it is to zero out my inbox on a daily basis!"

★★★★★ **OUTSTANDING!!!,** April 28, 2009
Adam S. Farrah (Middletown, CT)

"Hands down the best Outlook book ever. What makes it so good is that Michael teaches a system of thinking and using Outlook within that system. If you just "learn Outlook" you'll be better with Outlook but not much better at managing your day and to-dos. Michael and his system (Manage Your Now) gives you a WAY to manage your days that uses Outlook as the platform. Michael shows you how to completely reconfigure Outlook AND use it's inherent power. Outlook is a great program - once you unleash its true potential using Michael's book!"

★★★★★ **Great Productivity Tool,** September 20, 2009
L. Krolik "L. Krolik, More Time For You" (Palo Alto, CA)

"I found the 1st edition very helpful, but this one is much more in tune with how our world works today. It's very difficult if not impossible to keep up with all that we need to do in a single day. Total Workday Control helps you achieve that goal and the Manage Your Now strategy is very easy to implement and maintain. I work with so many clients who have e-mail overload and task lists that are endless. This book teaches a GREAT prioritization system and I like its use with Getting Things Done: The Art of Stress-Free Productivity philosopshy. The book is an easy read and although it seems rather large, you put the system into play after reading the first 4 chapters. Michael gives instructions as to when to skip sections if you are an experienced Outlook user, or if you have read the 1st edition, or if certain things do not apply to you. All in all it's a great book and system for making Outlook the productivity tool it was intended to be."

★★★★★ **Delighted with this book!,** March 17, 2010
LeaRae Keyes "cabin stuff creator and nurse e... (Minneapolis, MN USA)

"I have been delighted to have found the book "Total Workday Control Using Microsoft Outlook (Second edition)" by Michael Linenberger. Mr. Linenberger identifies common problems experienced by Microsoft Outlook users such as important tasks not getting done, having a full email inbox, and feeling overloaded and overwhelmed. Prior to reading this book I knew that using my inbox as a place to store email was not a way to use Outlook correctly, but I didn't understand how I could reasonably handle all the email I receive in a day. It is not unusual for me to receive over 200 emails per day. When I began reading this book I had over 1000 emails sitting in my inbox. Now I am down to less than 200 and expect that in less than a week I will be down to zero emails in my inbox. I feel as though a heavy weight has been lifted…"

★★★★★ **Total Workday Control Works**, August 3, 2007
W. Parks (Wilmington, DE)

"A colleague of mine recommended I get the book TOTAL WORKDAY CONTROL USING MICROSOFT OUTLOOK. I help operate 5 companies and found that the recommendations in this book are terrific in terms of integrating tasks along with the calendar function. The techniques eliminate paper post-it notes, organize tasks so that they prompt at the proper time, and yet keep the Microsoft Outlook Calendar clear of non-appointment type items. These techniques really do help personal productivity. I strongly recommend reading this book and trying its suggestions."

★★★★★ **Great book - Easy system you will actually use**, November 4, 2006
Garafano (Massachusetts USA)

"Terrific book. I spent a few hours with Michael's system and the results were amazing. I have cleaned out my inbox and have a working, viable task management system that is showing some big results. It doesn't take weeks of studying or a massive effort to use. It is casual, simple, and really allows you to focus on the information rather than the system. I use it in combination with Clear Context and I couldn't be any happier."

★★★★★ **Well worth its weight in gold!**, August 14, 2007
Dr. Eric G. Kassel "ekpharmd" (Shorewood, Illinois United States)

"I read David Allen's GTD and struggled to incorporate into my e-World. I then read TWC and eagerly jumped on board. It was exactly what I needed and in 1/2 a day I was reconfigured and recategorized with an inbox that read zero. I am a convert and preacher. I recently had Michael come in to address my group of 60 field scientists who often are challenged with email, follow up and loosing their drive. I am still getting compliment and people are excited to get back to work. EXCITED! To get back to email! Well worth the book, the live session…"

★★★★★ **Total Workday Control**, October 3, 2007
A. Ames (New Mexico)

"This book is a great way to learn how to manage your Outlook e-mail in an easy to follow, step-by-step methodology. I had taken David Allen's seminar, Getting Things Done, and this book really helped to close the loop on implementation. Well worth the time and money spent."

★★★★★ **Outstanding Book!**, October 2, 2007
David R. Drake (Iowa City, IA USA)

"I am a professor at a major research university in the US. I have struggled with dealing with multiple tasks and emails for years... until I have embraced the fantastic system described in this great book. If you use Outlook as your major portal for email and tasks, you MUST read this book. The approach here is logical and work for you. It is that good."

★★★★★ **Helped me on day 1**, December 15, 2007
JDM "I Have Too Much E-mail" (Houston, TX)

"I picked this up when I was browsing the business section and the description of the problems that we all have with too many tasks and e-mail fit myself and my co-workers exactly. I followed the instructions for reconfiguring the way I use Outlook tasks and it started helping me get organized right away. I have only had the book for a week and I am getting ready to try the e-mail organization using categories. I am definitely recommending this to all of my co-workers."

★★★★★ **Finally! A 'Real World' Implementation of Outlook that really works!**,
September 22, 2007   Timothy Seward "ROIRevolution.com"

"I TOTALLY agree with all of the 5 star reviews... after struggling with [other systems] for 6-9 months I finally found what really works.

In this book you'll get an actual implementation that works--meaning a regularly empty inbox (and I deal with hundreds of emails a week), a fantastic way to organize and systematically get dozens of tasks (including those you delegate to others with a perfect way to close open loops) w/ a corresponding sense of accomplishment and feeling of being on top of it that is incredible.

"I have done it all: Day Timer, Covey's system, used Palm Pilots/Treo's, etc and nothing has ever even come close to Michael Linenberger's system.

"I have already implemented this with two of my direct reports and they are ecstatic with the fact that they too have a empty inbox, no more sticky notes, etc."

★★★★★ **Great Book—It Works**, August 9, 2007
William M. Stabler (Albuquerque, NM USA)

"I thought I knew most of the tricks on making my day productive. But Michael's book was a great eye opener. The book is well written, easy to follow and provides simple but practical methods to make your Outlook life easier. This is a definite read for anyone who is in the corporate world and gets lots of email. Thanks!"

★★★★★ **Project manager**, January 15, 2007
Mark Marker (Chicago Illinois Area)

"Superb guideline. Even if you don't follow it line for line... it distills a task mentality in your daily work habits. It causes one to stop and take a moment to plan out the day. If you feel like you have 10 pounds of work in a 5 pound bag then this book will be of great help."

★★★★★ **A book I return to over and over again**, August 27, 2007
Barry J. Kurtz "Business Process Master" (New Jersey USA)

"As a person who practically lives in Outlook, this book has provided me with many tips and ideas on how to use the product better. Outlook has many capabilities hidden from the person who does not have the time or desire to study every technical nuance of the software. This book distills a lot of useful information into easily digestible chunks that you can make use of directly or build upon to suit your personal needs. If you use Outlook to help manage your computer-based life, this book should be on your desk."

★★★★★ **Getting Control of My Work Day**, July 20, 2007
Jon M. Ahrens (San Francisco, CA, USA)

"Prior to reading and using the tools and techniques introduced in this book, my desk, PDA and laptop were covered with notes, reminders, and post-its as a means to keep ahead of my demanding job and schedule. Now, each day I track my tasks and meeting schedules quickly and easily, and I have control of my work day. This book provides the tools, and the discipline, to keep me ahead of the game. Most importantly, my colleagues have noticed the difference, and have picked up a copy of Michael Linenberger's book to improve their hectic schedules."

★★★★★ **Chock Full of Good Advice**, July 18, 2007
J. Lushinski (Ashburn, VA)

"This is a great book for anyone that uses Outlook. There are great tips in here whether you're a basic user or someone who has been using it for years. The writing is easy to follow and remember. You won't get this kind of advice from anyone else. I'm constantly coming back to it and finding new tips. I'm sure this will be a valuable asset on your desk."

★★★★★ **No More Gridlock in Outlook!**, July 18, 2007
A. J. Rachele

"I have always been the type of person who gradually accumulates up to 2,000 messages in my In-Box and continually wastes valuable work time looking for key e-mails that are buried somewhere in that mess. Trying to organize all that has always seemed an impossible task ("wasting" even more of my work day) so I have simply surrendered to E-mail Gridlock and considered it an unavoidable irritation. Until now. This book gave me the steps to clean out my inbox without losing valuable information and to keep it clean on an ongoing basis. The task that seemed so impossible proceeded easily on a step by step basis. Now I'm able to keep the contents of my inbox to a day or so of e-mail on an ongoing basis and develop a workable list of "to-do's" that actually get done every day!"

★★★★★ **By far the best system I've ever used... you should get this book**, July 14, 2007
K. Vickers (Washington DC)

"I've tried them all and the thing about Michael's approach is that it not only works with a product I'm already familiar with and use extensively every day (Outlook) but it's also a system I can use without major disruptions to my work life—it just works. By implementing this approach I've gone from well over 1,000 emails in my in box to the point where I can now leave at the end of the day with less than 10. I'm also much more relaxed knowing that I have a handle on all the items I need to work on... In short, this approach has transformed my work life..."

Total Workday Control Using Microsoft® Outlook

Third Edition

By Michael Linenberger

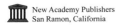 New Academy Publishers
San Ramon, California

Third printing 2012

ISBN-13: 978-0974930466
ISBN-10: 0974930466
Library of Congress Control Number: 2011923201

Visit the publisher's website at www.MichaelLinenberger.com for additional information.

The following trademarks appear throughout this book: Microsoft, Windows, Windows XP, Microsoft Windows Vista, Microsoft Windows 7, Windows Mobile, Microsoft Office, Microsoft Outlook for Mac 2011, Microsoft Office Outlook 2010, Microsoft Office Outlook 2007, Microsoft Office Outlook 2003, Microsoft Outlook 2002, Franklin-Covey, ClearContext, ToodleDo, Master Your Now!, Now Horizon, Over-the-Horizon tasks, Now Tasks, Critical Now, Opportunity Now, Target Now, Defer-to-Do, Defer-to-Review, FRESH Prioritization, Getting Things Done, GTD, X1, Yahoo Desktop Search, Google Desktop Search, Windows Desktop Search, Palm, GotVoice, Jott, Simulscribe, CallWave, Maxtor One Touch, Acronis True Image, Retrospect.

Cover photograph of Michael Linenberger by Joe Burull

Preface to Third Edition

A Major Update

With this third edition you now have an improved productivity system, and a significant set of updates that integrate Outlook 2010 and Outlook for Mac 2011 into the MYN (Master Your Now!) system.

In this edition I've also dropped support of Outlook 2002 to make room for the new versions. Outlook 2002 is being used by very few companies and individuals anymore, so I felt confident that dropping it was the right decision. However, if you or your colleagues still need support for 2002 (or 2000), the second edition of the book will remain on sale for some time to come.

Here is the full list of major changes in this edition, compared to the second edition.

Book and System Changes in the Third Edition

▶ Outlook 2010 support has been added. Compared to Outlook 2007, the new Outlook 2010 brings some fresh features and changes to many existing one. It replaces the menu bar with the Ribbon, which leads to new command sets. It has a greatly improved Instant Search interface, and many other controls have changed. All modifications in 2010 that impact MYN are covered in this book. I have an article about 2010 changes at this URL: www.myn.bz/Win2010.htm.

▶ Outlook for Mac 2011 support has been added. Nearly every lesson except for Lessons 10 and 12 have changed extensively to incorporate Outlook for Mac 2011. The Mac version is fairly comparable to Outlook 2010 in many ways except for tasks, where it has, by comparison, a greatly reduced feature set. Because of its tasks limitations, users of the

MYN system need to take a quite different approach on the Mac, and that's thoroughly covered in this book. Also, with a reduced task toolset, 2011 inevitably gets less overall coverage than the Windows versions. I have an online introduction to Outlook for Mac 2011 here: www.myn.bz/mac2011.htm.

▶ Because of the Mac's weak task module, I've also indicated another task software option for Mac users. In Lesson 6 a non-Outlook version of MYN is identified and discussed for any of you that may need to move away from Outlook tasks. It's a versatile task software package called ToodleDo that can be used with any e-mail system. Links to additional ToodleDo documentation and a free MYN version are provided.

▶ Outlook 2002 has been removed from the book. Removing this version simplified much of the book since 2002 functioned so differently. For example, Lesson 8 on filing e-mail is now much simpler, as is Appendix B on archiving. The second edition is still for sale should you need support for Outlook 2002 (or Outlook 2000, which is very similar).

▶ The Significant Outcomes concept has been added. This was a tool introduced to MYN in my 2010 book *Master Your Workday Now!* to provide focus on higher-level actions. It is covered in this book in Lesson 6 and it brings many benefits to those using the MYN system.

▶ The Mobile Systems section in Lesson 6 has been greatly expanded and now includes solutions for the BlackBerry, iPhone, iPad, and Android (smartphones and tablets). You can now take the MYN system just about anywhere on just about any device.

▶ Appendixes A and B, on Outlook folder systems and archiving, have been extensively updated.

▶ The name of the system has been adjusted slightly; it's now called *Master Your Now* (still MYN). The word *master* speaks well to the outcome of using the system. And that word aligns this book more with my 2010 book *Master Your Workday Now!* which covers similar material applied outside of Outlook.

▶ I added a Quick Start chapter at the front of the book to get readers moving on the system within minutes.

That's the list for the third edition. If you are moving to this third edition directly from the first edition, note there were a long list of changes between the first and second editions that you should be aware of. In fact, the MYN system was totally redesigned. I've listed those next to help you make the transition.

Book and System Changes Between the First and Second Editions

Here are the changes made to the book and the MYN system between the first and second editions. These are included for historical reference and to help any readers who may be jumping right from the first edition to this edition.

▶ Starting in the second edition, the system is now based on a new theory of task management that describes how knowledge workers typically model urgency in their work. That model and theory is presented in Lesson 1; I think you will find that it is intuitive and compelling. Knowledge of the model provides a clear structure to better explain the steps you take when using the system every day.

▶ In the second edition I introduced the name *Manage-Your-Now!* or MYN for short. This name, while perhaps sounding a bit esoteric, very accurately describes what the system accomplishes—full control over your most intense work period, the work you are doing right *now*. (In this edition I have adjusted that name again, this time slightly, to *Master Your Now*).

▶ The concept of daily tasks, a core component of the original system, was replaced in the second edition with "Now Tasks"—a much better approach and a more appropriate terminology. The idea is that the main tasks you display on your TaskPad or To-Do Bar are tasks eligible to do now, that need to be in your awareness right *now*. Specifically, they are tasks that fall within your Now Horizon (fully explained in Lesson 1). Making this definition part of your task system helps you keep your task list focused and even relieves anxiety about work. It does this by maintaining a clear delineation between *current* and *deferrable* actions.

▶ Master tasks, another core component of the original system, were removed in the second edition. They are no longer used as the primary way to store tasks you want to remove from your main list. The master tasks list was replaced in the second edition with a new methodology called Strategic Deferrals. Strategic Deferrals are used to handle lower-priority tasks, tasks that you wish to keep out of sight but well managed. A redesigned Master Tasks view is optionally available (Windows only) for those who prefer that structure but, in general, master tasks have retired.

▶ Miniprojects as a way to manage multistep tasks were replaced with a new *series tasks* structure. This is much simpler and more effective.

▶ Goals and projects can be tracked via new optional Outlook custom view definitions, and an optional Outlook Categories method is provided for linking them to tasks (Windows only).

► Microsoft Office Outlook 2007 support was fully incorporated in the second edition, with several system changes to take advantage of new Outlook 2007 features. Explanations of difficult-to-understand aspects of Outlook 2007 related to tasks, including use of flagged mail, were included.

► The Outlook Start Date, instead of the Due Date, was introduced in the second edition as the primary date field. This matches the original system intent for dated tasks better and works better technically with Outlook 2007 (and beyond). New configuration instructions are provided to incorporate that change.

► An optional Deadline column was added to improve tracking tasks that have true hard deadlines (Windows only).

► My recommended location for the Processed Mail folder changed in the second edition: I now recommend placing it (for most users) as a sub-folder of the Inbox instead of in a Personal Folders group, though that remains one option. This is to make the system easier for beginners and more usable with mobile devices and Outlook Web Access. In Appendix A I provided various other setup scenarios to meet a wide variety of storage and mail access needs.

► In the second edition I introduced a new system of TaskPad/To-Do Bar prioritization, called FRESH Prioritization, which clarifies how to sort and order tasks in your to-do list.

► I divide e-mail management into two steps: emptying the Inbox and optionally using topic-based filing (like Outlook Categories). If the first step is used alone, e-mail search tools are now emphasized as the primary way to find mail.

► I teach a new optional way of identifying and notating what I call the *intrinsic importance* of tasks. This important concept provides a way to advance and track *important but not urgent* tasks.

► The appendix on archiving has been completely rewritten to provide much better archive solutions; manual archiving is among the methods covered.

► Optional Outlook add-in software called ClearContext is highlighted wherever its benefits are important, including as an alternative way to tag-file mail.

► The book now uses lesson-oriented chapters, with core "getting started" material presented in the first five lessons. Users can now get started quickly on the system and enjoy major benefits early.

A Very Powerful New Edition

Those are the major changes to the system. If you are an existing user, I think you will find the system changes to be very powerful, so I encourage you to get started immediately.

Enjoy the new edition, and do not hesitate to contact me with feedback. Contact information is on my website: www.MichaelLinenberger.com.

Michael Linenberger
February 2011

▪   ▪   ▪

Acknowledgments

Deep thanks go to the following individuals for their assistance in preparation of this book and earlier editions: Mary Calvez, Rob Tidrow, Ruth Flaxman, Mark Rhynsburger, Brad Meador, Linda Halley, and Amy Leschke-Kahle.

xiv   Total Workday Control Using Microsoft Outlook

Contents at a Glance

Contents

PART II: Maturing the System .115

Total Workday Control Using Microsoft® Outlook

Third Edition

MYN Quick Start

Before plunging into the main lessons in this book, Windows Outlook users should consider using this optional Quick Start section to get going with the Master Your Now (MYN) system right away. Here, in about 15 minutes, you will learn an abbreviated version of the system—enough to give you an immediate solution for many of your current workday-control issues.

Macintosh users, my apologies; due to the design of the Outlook 2011 tasks system, there are no easy quick steps for you. Instead, please go directly to the Introduction or to Lesson 1.

Finding Your Windows Outlook Version Year

The steps in this Quick Start vary depending on your version year of Outlook. The Quick Start covers 2003, 2007, and 2010. Here's how to find your version.

First, if you have a large set of tabbed icons at the top of your Outlook window with these tab names: File, Send/Receive, Folder, and more, then you are using Outlook 2010; that's Microsoft's latest version of Outlook for the PC (as of this writing).

If instead you see a set of menu names at the top labeled File, Edit, View, and more, then there's one more step to determine the version. Click on the Help menu, and choose the About Microsoft Office Outlook menu item; then look at the date at the very top of the small window that opens. That date is your version year; you are looking for either 2003 or 2007. Eligible versions are discussed more in Lesson 2.

A video version of this Quick Start is also available at the following links:

▶ For Outlook 2007 or Outlook 2010, go to: www.myn.bz/QS-2007-10.htm

▶ For Outlook 2003 go to: www.myn.bz/QS-2003.htm

The MYN Task List in Outlook

The central tool in the MYN system is the MYN task list, which is a powerful control panel for managing your work. In this Quick Start, you are going to create a simplified version of the MYN task list. I also call this list the Workday Mastery To-Do List; it's the same thing.

As a first step, let me show you the task area in Outlook that you're going to work with to create the task list. Note, you're *not* going to use Outlook's main tasks folder yet; rather you're going to use a smaller task list that is more convenient. Where you find that smaller task list depends on your Outlook version.

Outlook 2007 and 2010

In Outlook 2007 and 2010, the task list to use for MYN is the one in the To-Do Bar. The To-Do Bar is a large pane that usually (but not always) occupies the right side of your Outlook window. You can recognize it by the mini-calendars at its top (see Figure 1). If you don't see it on the right side of your screen (or are not sure), go to your View menu or tab, choose To-Do Bar, and then choose Normal from the submenu—that will open it. Note that the To-Do Bar has a list area at the bottom—that's the task list we're going to modify for use in MYN.

The first modification is this: if the task list is too short, as in Figure 1, right-click the very top of the To-Do Bar, just above the mini-calendars, and clear the check mark next to the Date Navigator. That will make the task list bigger. If your To-Do Bar seems too narrow, drag the left edge to make it wider.

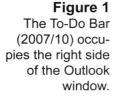

Figure 1
The To-Do Bar (2007/10) occupies the right side of the Outlook window.

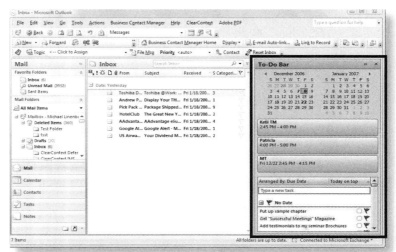

To make this task list into a Quick Start version of the MYN task list, I recommend that next you clear any view settings you may have applied to this
To-Do Bar task list—so we can start with a clean slate and so the settings
below will work. Here's how. At the top of that list, right-click the header
phrase Arranged By (or Arrange By, or Task Subject). In the resulting shortcut
menu, choose Custom… or Customize Current View… or View Settings…
(you will see one of those three). Then, in the dialog box that opens, click the
button in the lower left corner that says Reset Current View. If that button is
dimmed, your settings are already in default mode and you need to do nothing. In either case, click OK to close that window.

Now, the next step—the only real MYN setting you need to make in this
Quick Start—is simple. Just left-click (normal-click) the Arrange By (or
Arranged By) label at the top of the task list, and, from the shortcut menu,
select Importance. That's it!

Look at your task list; it may be currently empty, or it may have a few tasks,
or may have tens or hundreds of tasks listed in there. If it has lots of tasks—
tasks that you may not remember entering—they are probably virtual copies
of old mail that you flagged in the past. Outlook displays flagged mail here
to remind you that they may need action. If there are lots of them, you should
clean this list up by removing flags from that old mail. You can do that now
or wait till Lesson 2 where I'll show you how to clean those out in bulk. Also,
ignore the red color you might see on tasks—we'll fix that in Lesson 3.

At this point, Outlook 2007 and 2010 users can jump to the section farther
below called Adding Tasks to Your Task List.

Outlook 2003

In Outlook 2003 the task list we are going to use is in an optional pane called
the TaskPad. It's only visible in the Calendar view, so navigate to your Calendar view now by clicking the word Calendar in the lower left-hand corner of
your Outlook window. Next, look on the right side of the Calendar window
to see if you have that pane—one that shows a list area with one or more
mini-calendars at above it—it's labeled TaskPad (see Figure 2). If you do not
see that pane, then from the View menu, choose TaskPad; that should open it.
If that does not open it, then skip ahead to Lesson 2 and find the section called
Five Ways to Find a Hidden TaskPad; use those instructions to reveal it.

Next, if the TaskPad is very narrow, grab the left edge of it and drag it to the
left an inch or two so that it is wide enough to work with easily. It widens in
jumps, so drag the mouse a full inch or two to get it to open more.

Let's set the TaskPad up for MYN. To do that, find the word TaskPad at the
top of the list and right-click it. From the very bottom of the shortcut menu
that opens, choose the item labeled Customize Current View…. Then, in the
window that opens, I recommend you click the button in the lower left corner
that is labeled Reset Current View; this is to clear any settings you may have

Figure 2
The TaskPad (2003) occupies the lower right corner of the default Calendar folder view.

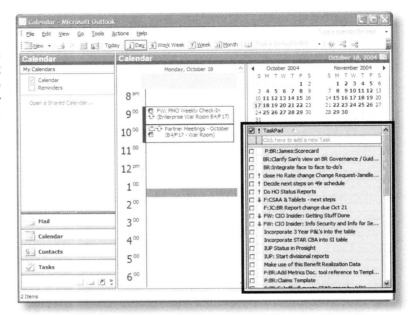

applied to the current TaskPad task list (perhaps without knowing you did that). If that button is dimmed then your settings are already in default mode and you need to do nothing.

Next, click the Fields… button at the top left. In the Show Fields dialog box that opens you should see three fields listed on the right. In the scrolling list on the left, select Priority and click the Add-> button in the middle so that Priority gets added to the list at right. Then drag that Priority item up or down within that list so that it is the second item from the bottom, just above Subject. Make any other adjustments needed to create these field names in this order: Icon, Complete, Priority, and Subject. Click OK, and then OK again.

Back at the TaskPad, you'll now see a black exclamation point in the header at the top of the task list. Right-click it and from the shortcut menu choose Group By This Field. After that, any tasks in your TaskPad will be grouped by priority (High, Normal, and Low). If you do not have tasks, you'll see no groups yet—but next we'll add some tasks so you can. Ignore the red color you might see on any previously existing tasks—we'll fix that in Lesson 3.

Adding Tasks to Your Task List

For all versions, to enter a task, just type in the row near the top of the list—it's labeled Type a New Task. After you type a task name, press the ENTER key, and the task will drop into your task list into the top of the group labeled Normal. You have just entered your first task; congratulations!

Next, make sure you have at least a few tasks in each of the three priority groups (High, Normal, and Low). So, enter more tasks and set a few at each priority level. Here's how to set the priority: After you create a task, double-click it in the list and, in the middle of the dialog box that opens, you'll see the Priority drop-down menu; set it there. Ignore the date fields and other controls; we'll talk about start dates, due dates, and much more in later lessons. Click Save & Close in the upper left corner of the task dialog box.

Using the MYN Urgency Zones

Now you are ready to apply a few MYN principles. Once you have a few tasks entered at each of the three levels, you'll clearly see the three priority-labeled groups in your task list (see Figure 3). These three groups correspond to three *urgency zones* in the MYN tasks system. The key teaching of MYN is that tasks in each urgency zone require a different level of attention. If you place tasks in the correct zones and then apply your work intensity appropriately, you'll greatly reduce your stress level and you'll get your tasks well under control. Let's see how to do that.

The first urgency zone is called Critical Now, and we'll use the High priority group in your task list for these (see top of Figure 3). These are tasks that are absolutely due today. You should list tasks here only if they are so critical for today that you would work late into the evening were they not complete; you should have no more than five tasks here each day, hopefully fewer. You'll

Figure 3
The Quick Start version of the MYN Tasks List (Outlook 2010 shown; other versions similar)

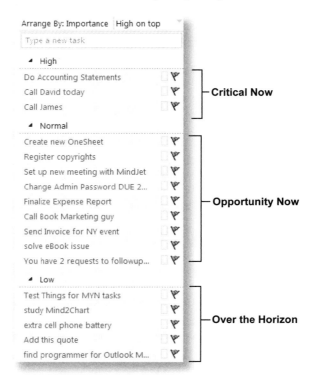

want to check this list often, perhaps even once per hour, to see what might get you in trouble (or keep you late at work) if not completed by end of day. It is very refreshing to have this list clearly delineated and well controlled.

By the way, make sure the High priority group is always at the top of your task list. If the entire group is at the bottom, you can fix that as follows: In 2003 click the black exclamation point at the left end of the task list header; in 2007/10 click the small arrow (triangle) at the right end of the header.

The next urgency zone is called Opportunity Now, and this corresponds to the Normal priority group in your task list (see middle of Figure 3). Place tasks here that you would work on today *if you had the opportunity*, but that you could let slide up to ten days or so. Plan to review this complete list at least once per day to see if anything there has jumped in importance and needs to be done today. The main rule here is this: you should have no more than about 20 items in this list. If you have more than 20, drag the lowest priority items to the third zone, covered next.

The third and final urgency zone is called Over the Horizon, and it corresponds to the Low priority group in your task list (see bottom of Figure 3). Place tasks here that you can ignore for longer than ten days; perhaps much longer. Then plan to review this list *once per week*; I recommend every Monday morning—but the actual day is up to you. If on review anything looks like it has become more important, drag that item to one of the higher priorities.

Converting E-mail to Tasks

To avoid losing tasks in your Inbox, and to keep the Inbox under control, do this: When you get an e-mail that has an action for you to do, drag that e-mail from the Inbox list and drop it on top of the Tasks icon at the bottom left of the Outlook window; that icon looks like a clipboard with a check mark in it. When you drop it there, a task window will pop open (like the one you saw earlier when you double-clicked a task). Immediately change the subject line to be the task action and set the priority level as appropriate; ignore the dates and other controls and click the Save and Close button on the task. You'll see it appear in your MYN task list. Then work these in priority order off your task list—don't try to use your Inbox as a task management system.

Converting e-mails to tasks like this is very important; it prevents you from losing important action requests, it enables you to work incoming requests in priority order, and it allows you to file mail out of your Inbox more easily.

Next Steps

That's it—that's the most critical portion of the system in a nutshell. If you like, use this for a while before proceeding with the rest of the book; put all your tasks in this task list using the urgency zone rules described above to sort tasks into each priority. And don't forget, allow no more than five tasks in High and no more than twenty in Normal—everything else goes into Low.

Then, start reviewing each section of the list as I instructed above — check the High-priority section once an hour; Normal once a day; and Low once a week. Use this as your single place to look for everything you do. Once you start using this regularly, you'll feel the stress draining off your day and you will come to realize you now have all major things under control.

Obviously, the configurations and principles above represent only a small portion of what you'll learn in the rest of the book. So when ready, read the Introduction and then move to Lesson 1, which will help you understand the urgency-zone theory behind the MYN system.

Introduction

The First Time, Task, and E-mail Management System That Will Work for You

This book is not just about how to use Microsoft Outlook. It is about how to combine Outlook with a set of easy-to-use principles that will get your workday under control. It presents a complete step-by-step system, allowing you to get ahead of your to-do's and e-mails and helping you feel much less stressed about your busy day. Its main focus is your to-do or task list: how to create and manage one in Outlook using powerful, newly developed time and task management principles. And it shows you how to keep it small, well managed, and well executed.

Equally important are the techniques for getting e-mail under control, primarily by identifying the action components of e-mail and managing them systematically as tasks. And I show you principles that allow you to easily empty your Outlook Inbox every day.

In learning all this, you will learn the true potential and power of Microsoft Outlook. It will finally become the tool that you always hoped it would be, a tool to truly help you manage your very busy workday.

A Totally New, Guilt-Free To-Do System, Called *Master Your Now!*

There are lots of to-do systems available today — Day-Timer®, Franklin-Covey®, Getting Things Done®, Day Runner®, Circa® — more than we can keep track of. A few of them offer ways to use Outlook, supposedly to get ahead of your to-do's. So, does the world really need *another* to-do or day organizer system applied to Outlook? I say emphatically, yes, we do. And when the first version of this system came out several years ago with the first edition of this book (then called the Total Workday Control system, or TWC for short), it quickly became the best-selling Outlook volume on the market because readers found it really worked. That was followed by the second edition, which updated the system itself in significant and powerful ways. So significant were the updates that I gave the system a new name: "Manage-Your-Now!" or MYN for short.

In this third edition, I am adding support for Outlook 2010 and for Outlook for Mac 2011. I am also changing the system name to "Master Your Now!" — still MYN for short. This lines it up better with my 2010 book *Master Your Workday Now!* a book that elaborates on the underlying theory and provides a way to use the system on paper. The word *master* also captures better the outcome of using the system.

Why a New To-Do System

The reason I developed and am teaching this to-do (and e-mail) management system is that I am convinced most popular to-do systems available today are wrong. I have tried and worked with all the major ones. And while some are okay, they all fail in the long run.

The main problem with most of them is that they are based on *guilt*, and over time, positive-minded people like you and me give up on guilt-based systems; they do not feel good or right to us and are actually unnecessary. Systems also fail due to lack of appropriate automation. Some are just dated. Most have no integrated solution for e-mail, which is a major source of office inefficiency these days.

Instead I developed and teach the Master Your Now! system, which I like to say is *guilt-free,* and uses the best and latest features of Outlook. The system is fully automated and based on solid theory described fully in Lessons 1 and 9. In fact the name itself, Master Your Now! was carefully picked and describes the theory well; it is a system to successfully **master** the overload of work that you have on **your** plate right **now**. It truly does help you master that period of time you tend to be most anxious about: your *now.* It helps you choose what tasks to do now, what e-mail to focus on now, what not to worry about now. You gain confidence that the important tasks are attended to, which greatly lowers any anxiety you might have about your workday. Based on feedback from thousands of users, it just might be the first task (and e-mail) management system that consistently works for you.

But before describing that system, let's look at some of the current approaches out there and why they do not work very well, starting with typical guilt-based systems.

Outlook's Default Task System

The system built into Outlook, unmodified, is guilt-based and, as is, I do not recommend it. On the positive side, at least it is automated, which is good.

But the problem with the unmodified Outlook task system is it places the oldest, most overdue tasks at the top of your TaskPad or To-Do Bar task list and marks them in bright red, which is bad. Why? Because that ends up emphasizing only *very old, very dead* tasks. All the recent, energized tasks will be scrolled down to the bottom of the task list, way out of sight. The message seems to be this: "If you have not completed your oldest, least interesting tasks, you are a bad person, and so these are what I am going to show you first; don't do anything else until you complete these." That's a very discouraging message.

And when you upgrade to Outlook 2007 or 2010, the installation does something even more discouraging. It takes every e-mail you have ever set a follow-up flag on (perhaps years' worth, perhaps thousands) and copies them as tasks into the to-do task list, also marked in a bright "you are a bad person" red. No wonder so few people use the standard Outlook task system for very long.

The good news is that the Outlook task system is configurable, and in the Master Your Now! system we change those configurations for the better, making Outlook a very useful and powerful tool. You'll do those changes in Lesson 3.

Note: *While the Windows version of the Outlook task system is completely configurable, the Mac version is less so and has fewer features. Because of that, the Mac version may not be your best MYN task solution; other software may be better. While this book shows you how to use Outlook for Mac 2011 with MYN, I also discuss alternative software in the mobile section of Lesson 6. Or see the Software page of my website at the following link: MichaelLinenberger.com/Software.html.*

Paper-Based Task Systems

I actually think the old paper-based task systems many of us use, both formal and informal, work better than an out-of-the-box Outlook task system. At least with paper-based systems, as you turn the pages and copy important tasks forward to the new days, you can leave the older, less energetic tasks behind, keeping your list fresh. And with paper systems you can make sure your highest-priority tasks, even new ones, are at the top and circled, underlined, starred, or otherwise dramatized.

However, there are two problems with most paper systems. First, you need to apply effort and discipline to copy older important tasks forward; as a result, tasks often get inadvertently dropped or missed. Lack of automation hurts here. Second, and more critical, due to the limits of paper, you quickly ge a point where even your "important" tasks become too numerous to m So out of practicality you need to decide either to completely abandon ing many tasks or to try to work with an overly large list. The proble if you abandon lots of tasks, you may feel guilty or that you've faile you do not abandon them, you feel overwhelmed. Neither feels g new Master Your Now! system replaces this double jeopardy with a clean and manageable solution. It prevents your task list from getting too big by putting lower-priority tasks out of sight but "in the loop" for future scheduled reviews. You'll learn how ahead.

Action-List Systems

Too many tasks building up is also a problem with popular action list systems, whether automated or paper. These emphasize a generalized to-do list, action folder, or sometimes a next-action list, but they do not offer a well-designed prioritization system or a clean way to shorten the action list other than deleting. As a result these lists grow too large and they become unusable. More on that later.

Any System That Claims Everything Must Have a Due Date Will Ultimately Fail

You have probably heard the expression: "Put a due date on every task or it won't get done." This approach ultimately fails. Why? Again, it is guilt-based and our psyche ultimately rejects this over time, especially when the system does not deliver. The reason it doesn't deliver is that artificial due dates just don't work; we adjust to them. We can smell a fake due date a mile away, and in the heat of the busy workday we just skip over a task with such a date. Worse, this actually leads to *missed deadlines*, because on those rare occasions when we *do* have a true hard deadline, we may ignore it, since we have become so accustomed to ignoring most of our other due dates. More on this below.

A number of systems out there claim to have the task-management processes optimized. Over my many years in professional life I have studied nearly every system on time and task management there is and used them in my own work, first as an engineer, then as project manager, manager, senior executive, and consultant. Most helped a little but not enough. The two systems that I have used the most are the FranklinCovey® system and David Allen's Getting Things Done® system, and these two are the best. All systems borrow from one another or from past time management books, and in that spirit I have also borrowed a few elements from these and other systems (and give credit in the book where I have). But mostly this solution is entirely new and distinct.

The *Master Your Now!* System Is an Entirely New Solution

The MYN system is distinct in at least five ways:

► **The MYN system uses a new kind of to-do list called the Workday Mastery To-Do list,** or MYN task list for short. As you will see in Lesson 1, it is based on managing urgency and clearing the grip that out-of-control urgency has on so many of us. That way you can focus on your most important work with much less stress.

▶ **The MYN system integrates e-mail in a way no other system does**, recognizing that many of our new tasks arrive by e-mail. MYN states that good task management is the solution to out-of-control e-mail, primarily by converting e-mails to tasks. No other system puts so much emphasis on an integrated e-mail solution.

▶ **It is optimized for guilt-free to-do list management.** It is probably the first system that recognizes that you, as a busy professional, will nearly always think of more things to do than you can possibly do—and it consider that a *good* thing. It is good because as professionals we should be constantly reaching for more. So this system does not punish or wrongly nag you when lower-priority or aged items are not complete. Rather, it gives you a unique, *trademarked* approach for creating a short, usable daily action list, and it adds scheduled solutions for the overflow items that have dropped in relative priority. This approach uses two key techniques called *Defer-to-Do*™ and *Defer-to-Review*™ to keep uncompleted lower-priority tasks out of sight but attended to responsibly. It does this in a scheduled, no-regrets, successful way. With this—finally—there is a positive approach to a busy professional's natural overload, one you can feel good about that doesn't drive you into frustration. Coverage of these two approaches is in Lesson 9.

▶ **It is the only system that emphasizes a start date, not a due date, as the primary management date.** As described above, the idea that every task should have a due date or it won't get done is just plain wrong and actually risky, as it leads to missed deadlines. The Master Your Now! system is the first and only to identify the *start date* field as the key task management field. With start dates you control when you see tasks and when you want to think about tasks. It does not *ignore* deadlines, but rather emphasizes deadlines only when they are actually present. This is a much more positive, realistic, and *natural* approach to task management. This is introduced in Lesson 4.

▶ **It is optimized for the strengths of Microsoft Outlook.** While many systems have been bolted onto Outlook, this one, from top to bottom, has been designed with Outlook in mind. It started and grew entirely in Outlook, over five generations of software versions. And you can apply the system without adding new software to Outlook; you just make some simple configuration changes (Lesson 3). That said, helpful software add-in options are available that support the Master Your Now! system, and these are discussed in the book. But again, since the system was designed from the ground up in Outlook, you will find that the methods and Outlook features work hand in hand.

Note: While this system has been designed for Outlook, many of the Master Your Now! principles can be applied to other formats, like paper. See my 2010 book Master Your

Workday Now! *for non-Outlook implementations of the underlying system. Also see Lesson 6 of this book, where alternate software is discussed.*

The result is that the Master Your Now! system really works for nearly everyone who tries it, and so it just may be the first to-do (and e-mail) management system that really works for you. Over 40,000 people are using elements of this system successfully. You can too.

Getting Started

Let's begin this story by describing the problem and then some elements of the solution. I think this will help convince you that taking the time to learn the system is worthwhile. However, if you are ready to start now, feel free to skip to Lesson 1.

The Problem Is Rampant

I have seen this in many places where I have consulted. Staff routinely complain of being overloaded with tasks, of putting in long hours to try to finish their work.

Managers complain that assigned tasks are not getting done. It's as if individual work assignments are deposited into a black hole, and the only way they get done is through repeated nagging by the task assigner.

And staff seem too busy to reply to or act on most of the e-mails they get. Important e-mails with requests for a reply are ignored. E-mails with clear requests for action get buried in the recipient's Inbox.

In some cases the root cause of these problems is that staff really are assigned too many tasks. But in most cases the problem is lack of an effective task and e-mail management system. Tasks are never really incorporated into an effective system for getting them done and focusing on the highest priorities first. And how to manage e-mail effectively is left to each individual to figure out.

Finding a Solution Is Important

Solving this problem so that you can get the most important work done at a reasonable pace is important. If struggling staff try to "do it all" by rushing through the day at 200 mph, they become even more inefficient. Dr. Edward M. Hallowell, in a January 2005 *Harvard Business Review* article, describes a near-clinical mental condition staff and managers can reach when they try to push through their out-of-control workday at a near-panic pace. When under this type of stress, the human brain functions differently, less effectively, displaying Attention Deficit Disorder (ADD)–like symptoms. The degraded functionality can grow worse, month after month.

Or staff can mentally "give up" and divest from work goals, showing up physically but without spirit.

Either way, the results can be devastating to productivity. As task and e-mail management gets out of hand, individual productivity plummets. Perhaps worse is that team productivity suffers. Team collaboration suffers because teammates cannot trust each other to complete tasks they have agreed to, or to reply to simple requests for assistance. When team members cease collaborating and team collaboration becomes ineffective, the goals of the organization suffer.

You Know the Symptoms

► You work late and feel you have far too much to do.

► You have a sense that there is no time in the day to get things done.

► You leave important tasks uncompleted.

► You focus only on the work that is right in front of you and rarely plan tasks in advance.

► You may have a number of loose task lists, but you have them spread around and they are generally out of control.

► Rather than controlling your e-mail, you find yourself just barely reacting to e-mail.

► You know that buried in your e-mail are many requests for action and you regret not getting to them quickly.

► If you are a manager, you find yourself practicing *reactive* management, acting only on the emergencies as they arise around you.

► You find yourself reacting to visitors, phone calls, and immediate needs but you rarely gain a sense of completion of important tasks.

► You have a sense of forgotten or misplaced tasks.

► People are often reminding you of things you promised that are not yet complete.

► You consistently leave work knowing something important is not finished.

Unmanaged Tasks and E-mail Derail Work Effectiveness

While you may in fact have too many required tasks, it is more likely that your problems stem from *unmanaged* tasks. The fact is we all will always have too many tasks; the secret is in managing them. Unmanaged tasks can derail your work effectiveness because:

► You spend too much time on low-priority tasks.

▶ You drop important tasks and actions in e-mails and they then become emergencies that require inefficient activity to fix.

▶ You do no planning of synergies, which leads to inefficient task completion.

▶ You are forced into too much wheel spinning, rehashing of tasks, and rereading of e-mails.

▶ You have a sense of being out of control, leading to a poor attitude; you really do not expect to get to assigned tasks, to get to all your e-mail.

Ambiguity Is One Problem

One problem with casual task and e-mail management approaches is ambiguity:

▶ We are not sure where task lists are and which are up-to-date.

▶ We are unsure how to plan and prioritize action on tasks.

▶ We are vague about what to do with items like e-mails that have tasks implied in them.

▶ We do not know how to handle an overflowing task list.

Benefits of the Master Your Now! System

Increased Efficiency and Productivity

Getting tasks and e-mail organized with a system that finally works (and this one does) goes a long way. Having your tasks clearly organized and prioritized in a usable system helps you work on the most important tasks first. When properly organized, tasks that you postpone or drop due to lack of time are usually the least important ones. Having a way to translate into your task system tasks embedded either explicitly or implicitly in e-mails will bring your e-mail under control.

Having your tasks and e-mail organized and under control makes you more efficient at accomplishing them or responding to them; you actually spend less time finishing more activities. Why? Because when all your important tasks are clearly in front of you, you can multitask in meetings. You can take advantage of chance encounters with people and places. You can, during unexpected free slots of time, see and pounce on your most important tasks and get many of them done. You can organize your day to attack tasks in optimum order. And you can ensure that only the lowest-priority tasks are dropped if you run out of time at the end of the day.

And with a smooth system of processing e-mail, you will spend much less time in your Inbox. You will greatly reduce Inbox churn, where you reread many messages looking for items you left in the Inbox. You'll spend less time processing new mail because you will learn how to immediately convert action mail to tasks and move on.

As a result, in my surveys of seminar participants who stick with the system (same content as this book), most users say they gain back at least 25 percent of their week; many say much more, some say up to 45 percent.

Reduced Stress and an Improved Attitude

But perhaps just as important is this: having your tasks and e-mail under control in a usable system reduces your workday stress and improves your attitude. If you are like me, you probably tend to carry uncompleted tasks with you in your subconscious throughout the day (and sometimes night!). This stress is exaggerated when tasks are not well organized.

Our Mental Limit for To-Do's

Malcolm Gladwell in his book *The Tipping Point* describes long-standing research that shows the human mind cannot clearly remember more than six or seven items at once. This is called the channel capacity of the brain. This commonly known limit has, among other things, led to early phone numbers being limited to seven digits. It applies to tasks as well. Once your mental task list exceeds that count you forget what's on the list. Uncontrolled and forgotten tasks tend to nag us. We carry a sense of being behind the game, of being on the wrong side of the curve. A sense of something that we should do, something we have been remiss about. Not only is this very stressful, but it's often what drives us to work late nights with the thought: "If I work more hours I'll get it all done and this feeling will go away." However, usually it is exhaustion that finally quenches the feeling instead, along with the thought: "I have worked far more hours than is reasonably expected; surely I can go home now." Unfortunately, without a good task and e-mail management system, fate will curse us to stay late night after night. Eventually, many workers just do not expect to complete their tasks, even important ones, and they carry that expectation as an attitude that sabotages their success.

Burden Lifted

Once you get your tasks and e-mail controlled correctly, as done in this system, you lift this burden. It is such a relief to know you have identified and organized everything on your plate. It is a relief to clearly identify what is most important (and to work on it first) and to know what can wait and how to defer it with appropriate follow-up. It is such a relief to be able to say to yourself: "That's all of it; I've got it all in sight, and there is nothing hanging out there that will bite me later." Achieving this organized state usually reveals that the critical portion of your list is much shorter than you think, and it allows you to get the critical items done first. Therefore it enables you to know that you can leave the office guilt-free at the end of the workday without dropping key responsibilities. Your mind is free and clear to enjoy the evening at home or the weekend out and about.

When your mind is free from the subconscious message "I am out of control," you can more effectively execute activities. You can plan to get at tasks before they become emergencies. When you accomplish tasks in nonemergency mode, they fall into place more cleanly and easily and with less expenditure of energy.

You May Even Find This System *Enjoyable*

I've said a number of times: this is not a guilt-based system. This is not a list of "shoulds" that you hope to find time to do but know you probably will not. Rather, I think you will find that you may even *enjoy* doing most of the steps in this book.

Really? you say. *Actually* enjoy *the steps*? Let me demonstrate this by asking you whether you feel bad about the following:

► Stepping into a nice warm shower every morning when you clean up?

► Setting the table in a pleasing way before a good meal is brought out?

► Frosting a cake for your child's birthday?

► Closing the garage door when you drive away from your house in the morning?

These are all small efforts we make that we feel good about because they are mostly effortless, they keep our life tidy, and they lead to a more rich experience in life, and many are fun in the process. In the same way, once you get past a few setup activities, the steps in this system are all simple, effortless, and actually enjoyable in most cases, primarily because as you do them you feel satisfaction. The results are a richer, more satisfying work experience.

So give this system a try.

■   ■   ■

Designed for a Quick Start

After Part I You Are Ready to Go

This book is presented as lessons. My intention is that this will be a smooth and compact learning experience for you. I have tried to keep theory at a minimum and practical application at a maximum. I have also carefully organized the book so you can quickly get started and then learn increasingly advanced material lesson by lesson.

To that end, I provided a Quick Start chapter (just prior to this one), that gets you started with the system within minutes.

And to make the next level of commitment easy, the rest of the book is divided into three parts that each nearly stand alone. By the end of Part I, which is approximately the first 100 pages of the book, you will be using almost the full system and benefiting greatly; you could even stop at the end of Part I if you wanted to. Part II takes you to the next level by teaching more about tasks and filing e-mail. And Part III covers advanced system practice.

In general you should plan to do the lessons in order because they build on one another. In some places I invite you to skip ahead to particular lessons if interested, but that is the only exception. Once you get to Part III, however, feel free to skip around as much as you like, as all lessons there are optional.

Here are details of what is in each part of the book.

Part I: The Basic MYN System

Part I teaches the basic MYN system. It starts by teaching you in Lesson 1 the underlying theory and an overview of the system. You can skip that lesson if you'd like to accelerate starting the system, but I think you will find it very interesting.

In Lesson 2 you learn how to navigate across the various task tools Outlook offers and the basics of entering tasks. I also show you brief introductory coverage of an important skill: how to convert e-mails to tasks. In Lesson 3 you get clear instructions on how to quickly configure Outlook for the MYN tasks system. In Lesson 4 you'll learn the core principles of the MYN system, those for guilt-free, effective task management. And then in Lesson 5 you'll learn how to clear your Inbox and enjoy the bliss that experience brings. By the end of those five short lessons you'll be using the system and gaining great benefits in your workday. You could even put the book down after these lessons and feel satisfied that you learned all you need to learn.

Part II: Maturing the System

Part II is about maturing your usage of the system. In Lesson 6 you drill down on which tasks are best to put in Outlook and how you use them in this system. Mobile systems are covered there as well. In Lesson 7 you get the complete coverage of converting e-mails to tasks, an essential portion of the system and the cure to Inbox stress. In Lesson 8 you learn e-mail filing techniques that really help you get ahead of too much e-mail. And in Lesson 9 I revisit the underlying theory of the system and use that as a basis for explaining the very important topic of Strategic Deferrals. If after a few weeks or months of using the system you find your task list has grown unbearably large, Strategic Deferrals will solve that for you. By the end of Part II you will be totally proficient at converting e-mails to tasks, you will have a sophisticated e-mail filing technique under your belt, and you'll be managing tasks effectively.

Part III: Mastering the System

Part III is all about mastering the system in an advanced way. In Lesson 10 you will focus on techniques for assigning and managing delegated tasks. In Lesson 11 you will find a discussion of time management and time-saving approaches that add efficiency to your day. In the final lesson, Lesson 12, I give you advanced ways to use the system to track high-importance tasks as well as ways to track projects, goals, deadlines, and other extensions of the system. There I teach you how to create several optional Windows Outlook views that will help you get the most out of the system.

Appendixes

Appendix A is about Outlook folders and how to use them. I also explain some difficult-to-understand enhancements of Outlook 2007/10 and 2011. There I explain how to use the Navigation Pane and some of the oddities introduced by Outlook 2007/10 flagged-mail tasks.

In Appendix B I teach you strategies for archiving the Outlook e-mail you store using the MYN system. I show strategies both for manual archive and for using Outlook AutoArchive. I think you'll find that appendix to be a highly valuable explanation of this difficult topic.

Appendix C is a list of resources you may find useful when further exploring the topics of this book. I also provide a few "tear out" quick guides for use on your desktop.

Getting Started

But what is most important is that you get started immediately on using the system and gaining relief from your out-of-control workday. At minimum, take Lessons 1 through 5 and enjoy the benefits of the system for a while. Then come back to the book to complete the other seven lessons.

Book Website and Newsletter

I encourage you to go to my website now to see if there are any updates to this book, which will be posted free. I also recommend that you sign up for my free monthly e-mail newsletter while there. In that newsletter I announce system enhancements and changes and give tips on system usage. The website is www.MichaelLinenberger.com.

PART I

The Basic MYN System

Lesson 1:
Managing Your Now in Outlook— Theory and Overview

Introduction

Before moving into the Master Your Now! (MYN) system implementation, and creating the Workday Mastery To-Do List in Outlook, let me show you some of the underlying MYN theory that guides this system and give a brief overview of its key components. That way you know why you are doing the upcoming Outlook configurations and why you are learning the new workday processes. This is interesting material and I think you will like it.

However, reviewing this theory is not a prerequisite to success with the system, so if you are eager to get going on implementation and want to skip this, feel free to jump to Lesson 2 now. For readers of the first edition of this book that for some reason never read the second edition, I encourage you to read the theory below so you can understand how and why the new system is different. And readers of my 2010 book *Master Your Workday Now!* can skip ahead to the section in this lesson called The Workday Mastery To-Do List in Microsoft Outlook.

Master Your Now—The Theory

Solving Two Harsh Realities of Today's Workday

The MYN system of task management is largely based on solving two harsh realities of today's typical workday. In fact, a blunt recognition of these realities is what allows the system to work so well. You see, this is not an idealized system that works only for those who do everything just right and commit to a new organized life. Rather, it recognizes your workday is currently overwhelmed and probably a bit out of control, and starts from there. The system is based on modeling such an overwhelmed work life and then attending to it. Most people when they learn the theory behind this system say, "Yes, that's my workday!" I think you will too.

First, here are those two harsh but absolutely true conditions of today's work-day experience that are dealt with up front in the MYN system.

▶ You, as a busy professional, cannot possibly get it all done. You will think of, and be handed, way more tasks (and e-mail) than you can possibly act on fully. The MYN system acknowledges that and teaches you how to deal with it in a positive and productive way.

▶ While you know that your *goals and values* should rule your activities, usually it is *urgency* that rules what you do at work every day. So the MYN system starts with an urgency-based model. MYN teaches you how to manage the urgency in your current work life; later you will learn to insert goal- and value-driven tasks as you mature the system.

These two simple realities guide the theory behind the system. After using it awhile, as your workday comes nicely into control, I think you will find these realities no longer so harsh.

The Now Horizon Model of Work

A Time- and Urgency-Based Mental Model

Let's talk more about how prominent urgency is in guiding most people's work activities. As busy professionals we all collect a very large number of near-term responsibilities and tasks. In a busy office we tend to focus first on immediate emergencies if any exist. Next, we focus on urgent things due soon, and then on slightly less urgent things that are due a little farther out, and so on. In the midst of that are meetings, interruptions, and diversions, and hopefully some importance-based tasks. In general, though, our focus is based on time and urgency. In fact one can describe this time and urgency focus in terms of a *mental model* of our workload, which I believe most of us unconsciously structure our work around. This model diagrams how we tend to interpret, mentally and emotionally, various levels of urgency. It helps explain our feeling of overload as well as define a solution to the overloaded workday.

An Exercise to Identify Your Now Horizon

To define that model, consider this. If someone (not your boss) tried to insert a half-day project into your currently very busy schedule, giving you no permission to drop other items, and then asked you to complete it *tomorrow*, I am pretty sure you would say, "No, I am too busy right now." However, even with the same workload, if that request were due, say, two months from now (and you had some interest in it), you would probably say "fine." Somewhere in the range between tomorrow and two months is what I call your Workday

Now Horizon, or Now Horizon for short. It is the date after which you stop feeling too busy, as you mentally gaze into the future.

The Workday-Now Horizon helps define the mental model of your current workload. It delineates which commitments you consider when you think about what is on your plate *now*. Most very busy people, when they think about work inside that horizon, feel anxious or stressed about their workload. When they consider work beyond that horizon, however, they usually mentally relax, even if there is no change in their job or commitments.

Typical Now Horizon Periods

Interestingly, across all the busy knowledge workers I have interviewed, that period is usually around 1 to 1.5 weeks. There are exceptions of course and it varies by industry and job type; for example, it is longer for senior managers, shorter for administrative staff. But 1 to 1.5 weeks is a typical average.

Consider the exercise above for a moment, and determine your Now Horizon. Keep that in mind as you continue reading.

A Model of Near-Term Work

Horizon as a Sight Limit

Think of what the word *horizon* means. If you imagine yourself standing on a flat beach and gazing out over the ocean, the horizon is that line on the ocean where you can see no further. So your Now Horizon is that time edge of work beyond which you do not mentally see your future work clearly.

Combined Model: Conveyor Belt or Treadmill

Let's combine the horizon concept with another mental model that many people think of when they think of work. Factory workers often work next to a conveyor belt in which physical objects are brought to them, perhaps machine parts they need to assemble or pack. Their speed of work is often controlled by the speed of the conveyor belt.

Knowledge workers who work in offices do not have a physical conveyor belt, but their work life is often described in a similar way, like being on a *treadmill*.

Combining all the above, here is a useful model. Imagine a man or woman walking in place on the left end of a moving treadmill-like conveyor belt that stretches to the right a far distance; for simplicity of discussion we'll assume it is a man for now. He is facing and walking toward the right end at a speed that just keeps him in place above the left end of the moving belt (see Figure 1.1).

The Flow of Work

Coming toward him on the belt are workday tasks and meetings that he needs to do and keep up with in order to "do his job." Those things immediately in front of him are what he is working on now or that are due now; as he accomplishes these he tosses them into his mental "accumulated accomplishments" pile shown in Figure 1.1 and moves on to the next item in front of him. A little beyond his immediate tasks are things that are going to impact him soon and that he may need to get ready for. And beyond that are less urgent things, but they are still in his awareness. Typically, the man works on tasks as they arrive to him on the belt. But occasionally he reaches out and picks items farther ahead, to get them done ahead of time, either because he wants to be proactive and get ahead of his work or, more likely, because the timing of related circumstances might be right to get them done now.

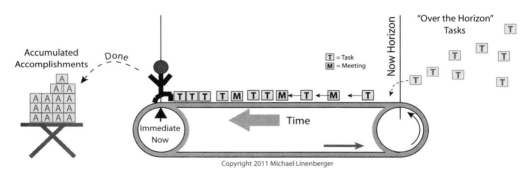

Figure 1.1   Now Horizon conveyor belt workload model. Ideal state.

Now Horizon = End of Conveyor

At the far right end of the conveyor belt is the limit of what he can easily see coming. It is the Now Horizon we described above. It is not that no work exists beyond that horizon; it is just that work beyond that point is out of sight and therefore out of mind, and so the man is not anxious about it and probably does not think much about it.

This is a good model for your workload. You tend to put all your attention on your work inside (to the left of) the Now Horizon. You tend to get most anxious about work due soon; it is only logical.

Rate of Work

If the rate of work entering and the completed work leaving your Now Horizon is the same (as in the picture above) you feel good. If you complain about being overloaded with work, you are most likely complaining that the rate is too high and pileups of work are occurring inside the Now Horizon. If the pileup is too great, you start to miss opportunities and deadlines, and that leads to your sense of regret or anxiety about work (see Figure 1.2).

Again, whether overwhelmed or not, you still do not think much about work outside, or "over," the Now Horizon.

Your Urgency Zones

You'll soon see that you can define what I call "urgency zones" within this model. Identifying these zones is extremely useful since doing so provides a way to manage within them. It gives you a way to apply work intensity appropriately. To identify the zones, let's add a bit of detail to this model.

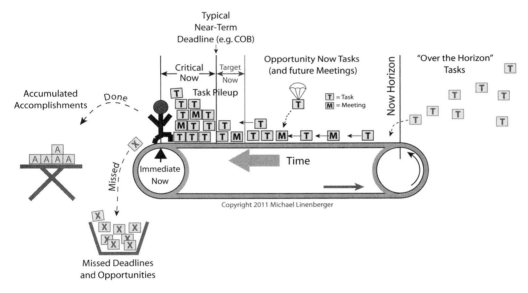

Figure 1.2   The Now Horizon model showing various "urgency zones," and an overloaded state.

Critical Now Tasks

Draw a line just to the right of where the man is standing on the conveyor belt, about one-fifth of the way across the belt, as shown in Figure 1.2. This line represents the typical deadline for things the man is currently working on or worried about. For most knowledge workers in most industries, this typical deadline is at the close of the current business day (COB); but it varies across industries. I call that time period, from the immediate now to the end of the typical deadline, the Critical Now. Naturally, tasks *due* inside that time frame have most of the man's attention and urgency. They probably have most of his anxiety as well. It is here where the typical task pileup occurs, which leads to missed deadlines and opportunities. Tasks due inside the Critical Now period I call Critical Now tasks.

Opportunity Now Tasks

Tasks to the right of the Critical Now deadline, but to the left of the Now Horizon, are tasks that the man is aware of and knows he needs to do soon or as soon as is practical, but he'd only do them *now* if the right opportunity were presented to him. For example, say the right person came by, or he had an inspired moment, or he completed all his urgent work. In those cases he might do these tasks, therefore he wants them in his awareness just in case. I call tasks in this zone of the conveyor belt Opportunity Now tasks.

Target Now Tasks

The man may also have tasks inside the Opportunity Now period he would *like* to do now but that are not urgently due. Getting them done now might make a client happy or ease the timing on downstream tasks, but he would not work late to get them done. I call these tasks Target Now tasks. You can see that in Figure 1.2 as well.

Over the Horizon Tasks

And finally, any tasks to the right of the Now Horizon, beyond the man's current consideration, are called Over-the-Horizon tasks. By definition, he is not very concerned about them. There are exceptions, of course; there might be a big event a month out on his calendar that captures part of his attention. But regarding day-to-day responsibilities, these are tasks he does not think much about.

Again, all these task types are shown in Figure 1.2 above.

In my book *Master Your Workday Now!* I showed you how to combine these zones into one paper list I called the Workday Mastery To-Do List, and how to use it to manage your day. Here, I show you how to create that to-do list in Outlook—providing a much more powerful way to use this system.

The Workday Mastery To-Do List in Microsoft Outlook

Most people who see this model find it matches their work experience. That fact is encouraging because it appears we have the situation well defined. Defining a problem is only half the solution, however; the rest comes when steps are provided to manage within the model. I do that by mapping components of the Outlook task system into this model, and by providing processes to manage within the model using Outlook. This is the Workday Mastery To-Do list applied in Outlook. You'll also see it referred to as the MYN task list throughout the book.

Grouping Outlook Priorities

The first part of the solution comes in Lesson 3. There I will show you how to configure Outlook to group your tasks by the Outlook Priority field. Let me explain. If you have used the Outlook task system at all already, you may know that built into Outlook are three levels of priority: High, Normal, and Low. Any task must be set to one of these, with Normal being the default setting. At the end of Lesson 3, tasks in your Outlook tasks list will be visibly grouped by each priority. In Windows Outlook, all groups will be in the same list with High being the top group, as shown in Figure 1.3. On the Macintosh, each group will be in its own folder as shown in Figure 1.4.

Figure 1.3
How the Workday Mastery To-Do List will look in Windows Outlook's task list, once configured in Lesson 3.

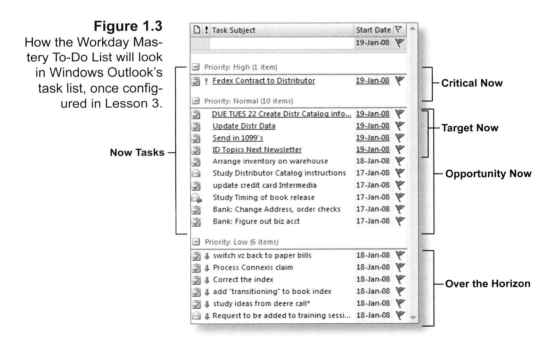

Figure 1.4
How the Workday Mastery To-Do List will look in the Outlook for Mac 2011 task list, once configured in Lesson 3.

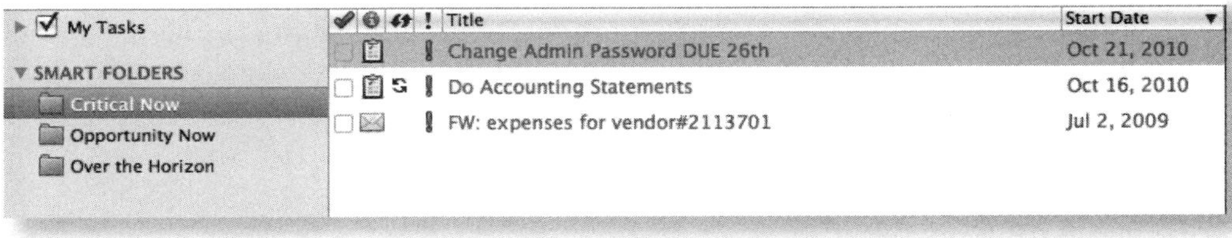

In terms of applying the Now Horizon work model, each of the Now Horizon urgency zones is going to map to these Outlook priority groups. Here is how.

Critical Now Tasks Use the "High" Priority of Outlook

The Critical Now tasks in this new model are going to be mapped to the High priority in Outlook tasks; so Critical Now tasks represent the top section of the list in Figure 1.3 (Windows), and the top folder at the left of Figure 1.4 (Mac). The deadline for these tasks is today in this system. You will see later in the book a process that helps you identify those tasks early, track them all day, and get them done on or ahead of time. This greatly eases the tension of the day and enables you to leave work on time more often.

Opportunity Now Tasks Use the "Normal" Priority of Outlook

Tasks in the Normal (medium) priority section of Outlook tasks will correspond with the Opportunity Now tasks on the Now Horizon conveyor belt model above. You can see these in the middle of the list in Figure 1.3 and the middle folder at the left of Figure 1.4. From now on, Normal priority Outlook tasks will be used for items not due today but that may impact you soon, and that you want to keep in daily sight to work on when possible. You do them when and if you have the opportunity, but you allow them to defer to the next day if you do not. Having this list well defined gives you a practical "short list" that you can scan as you plan your workday and during any gaps in the day when you can get more work done. I provide a number of principles to help you manage that portion of the list in the lessons ahead.

Target Now Tasks Are at the Top of the "Normal" Priority Section of Outlook

The Target Now tasks list represents the upper portion of the Normal (medium) priority section of Outlook. In other words, they are your most important Opportunity Now tasks. I'll discuss later how to indicate these and how to manage them; delineating them represents an *optional* part of the MYN system for now. See the underlined tasks at the top of the Opportunity Now section in Figure 1.3. These are not shown in Figure 1.4, but Mac users will see these tasks sorted to the top of the Opportunity Now Smart Folder once it is open (however, no underlining will be seen).

Over the Horizon Tasks Are in the "Low" Priority Section of Outlook

Tasks over the Now Horizon will be stored primarily in the Low priority section of Outlook. You will learn how and when to toss low-priority tasks over the Now Horizon to manage down the size of your Now Tasks list. This is an effective and legitimate way to improve your focus and decrease your workload anxiety. As you progress through the book and mature your usage of the system, you will see a few variants of that, including a way to schedule review and "reentry" of these tasks back inside the Now Horizon. More on that below in the section called MYN Strategic Deferral, and then again in later lessons in the book. See the bottom tasks in Figure 1.3 and the bottom folder in Figure 1.4.

Critical Now Tasks + Opportunity Now Tasks = Now Tasks List

Combining the two main Now Horizon groups (Critical Now and Opportunity Now) together conceptually is useful. Together they make up what I call your Now Tasks list. On the conveyor belt model, they represent everything inside (to the left of) the Now Horizon line. By their definitions, you can see that Now Tasks are tasks you either must do now or would *consider* doing now if you could. These tasks are listed, visibly, in the upper two priority sections of your Outlook tasks list, once it is reconfigured in Lesson 3 (see the upper portion of Figure 1.3 and the top two Smart Folders in Figure 1.4). I explain these further at the start of Lesson 4.

The Now Tasks List is a hugely powerful list. It becomes your active to-do list. Managed as taught in this book, it places everything you need to worry about in a relatively short collection of items. And you can take comfort that you do not need to worry about anything *not* on the list. Having that clearly delineated and managed down to a reasonable size quickly leads to a reduction of stress in your workday. This Now Tasks list, along with your daily calendar and Inbox, places everything you need to know about your Workday Now in one control panel in Outlook.

■   ■   ■

Managing in the Now Horizon

The ultimate goal of applying this Workday Mastery To-Do List is that your workday will start to look like Figure 1.1, at the start of this lesson. This is a smooth workday flow where tasks and e-mail processing are paced appropriately for your workday and you experience mainly the satisfaction of accumulating new accomplishments every day.

To get there, in addition to reconfiguring Outlook in Lesson 3, you will mainly be learning new MYN task and e-mail management principles in Lesson 4 and beyond. Here is an overview of those new MYN task and e-mail management principles that you will learn in this book.

Prioritization

Must-Do-Today Tasks

The identification and management of Critical Now tasks as your highest-priority daily tasks is an essential part of this system. These are also called Must-Do-Today tasks, defined as any tasks that you would not leave work on a given day without completing. Just having a discipline to separate these out and draw fairly consistent attention to them during the workday goes a long way toward getting your workday under control. You'll learn tips and processes to make using this technique a powerful part of your daily practice in Lesson 4.

FRESH Prioritization System

Inherent in any task management system should be a way to prioritize all tasks. Above you've seen the primary, urgency-based priority system applied in MYN Workday Mastery To-Do List. One layer below this is how to prioritize *within* the Opportunity Now tasks list. This list tends to get big, so an approach is needed to keep that list well managed. To do that I teach you a new prioritization method called FRESH Prioritization. This guilt-free method recognizes that task importance wanes over time. In today's fast-paced work environment, newer tasks tend to hold a higher priority since they reflect the latest company priorities and urgencies, while older tasks tend to lose importance.

The FRESH Prioritization system allows older tasks to scroll lower in the list and eventually scroll off the page and out of sight if you let them. It also allows you to move tasks back to near the top of the Opportunity Now list. One way to state this is: older tasks need to *earn* their position near the top of your list. That is what this system accomplishes, and it leads to a self-cleaning capability, something sorely needed in an automated task system that never forgets, like Outlook. It is also what distinguishes this system from most other task systems that are guilt based and that *promote* older tasks to the top of the list. I explain the FRESH Prioritization system thoroughly in the latter half of Lesson 4. The configurations in Lesson 3 are designed to support the FRESH Prioritization system.

All Tasks in One Place

In Lesson 6 you will see I recommend you place *all* ad hoc tasks in your new Outlook Workday Mastery To-Do List. Otherwise, if you need to look in multiple places, you will not have confidence that you know everything on your plate. You will not be able to easily prioritize. And you will not be able to leave work at the end of the day with confidence that all important tasks are complete, that nothing is hanging out there at risk. Strategies for placing all tasks in Outlook are delivered in Lesson 6.

Deadlines, Start Dates, and Follow-up Tasks

Part of managing the priority of tasks is managing deadlines and when to do tasks. This is another place where many other task systems abuse our common sense. The old bromide that you must place a due date on a task or it will not get done is no longer appropriate in today's business world. We get just too many tasks and too many new priorities every day to constantly be recalculating artificial due dates on tasks. We quickly reach the point that we ignore all due dates if we do this. Instead, I teach you to put a *start date* on every task and to use a deadline only on tasks with true hard deadlines.

Using a start date in this system allows a mechanical way to keep your Now Tasks list relatively short by hiding tasks until their start date arrives. Using a start date also gives you more fluidity when managing a constantly changing set of priorities, since starting a task past its original start date does not imply a missed deadline; deadlines are managed separately and only when needed. Using start dates is covered fully in Lesson 4.

One place I do often recommend hard due dates is on follow-up tasks. These are tasks you set to track promises and progress on activities. Such tasks are quick to achieve and using them regularly helps keep your work streams on track. You'll see how to create and use these in Lesson 6 and again in Lesson 8.

E-mail Management

Converting E-mails to Tasks

As you progress through this book, you will soon find that successful e-mail management is largely accomplished through intelligent *task* management. At the very end of the Lesson 2, I show how to convert e-mails to tasks. And then all of Lesson 7 will drill down more on that critical skill. I hope you take the time to study and practice that, because you are going to find this skill is *the* fundamental step to getting e-mail under control.

Here's why this is so important. Converting e-mails to tasks allows you to remove the tension from the Inbox by moving unreconciled actions into the task system. There they can be prioritized, scheduled, delegated, worked, or deferred, all with appropriate tools to do so effectively. Using this skill allows you to speed through your Inbox by giving you a way to process action e-mails without dwelling on them.

Emptying the Inbox

Converting e-mails to tasks also allows you to achieve something that I find is very important and blissfully satisfying: an empty Inbox. You really want to get the Outlook Inbox back to a receiving-only function where it is emptied every day; otherwise the Inbox becomes hopelessly cluttered. A cluttered Inbox represents a congestion of unattended responsibilities. Emptying the Outlook Inbox every day relieves that congestion in a very noticeable way. It also makes you more efficient, because without clearing your Inbox you'll be constantly glancing through old mail in search of passed over to-do's and unfiled information. Emptying the Inbox helps prevent responsibilities buried in e-mail items from getting away from you. It saves you time because it allows you to clearly delineate between mail that needs further processing and mail that you no longer need to read.

In Lesson 5, I teach a simple, no-brainer way of emptying the Inbox, using a single storage folder called the Processed Mail folder. This straightforward technique allows you to create a workflow in which you first extract tasks, and then drag all mail from the Inbox, every day. I also show you how to use a variety of search tools to find mail in that folder at a later time. Students of mine who use this approach find the empty Inbox experience incredibly satisfying and useful.

Filing E-mail by Categories

While you could stop with Lesson 5 and just use a search tool to find mail and perhaps accomplish all of your e-mail filing needs, many people need more. Many people need a true topic-based filing system. So in Lesson 8, I discuss topic filing, including using multiple folders. I am not a big fan of using multiple folders, however, so I also emphasize a more complete e-mail filing system based on tagging mail by topic, primarily using Outlook Categories. Outlook Categories are an extremely useful way to file mail because they allow you to keep all mail in a single date-sorted folder (the Processed Mail folder); such a single-folder approach is a good way to find recent mail. You can also sort by sender in such a folder, grouping all mail from the same person together, and find mail that way. More important, using Outlook Categories allows you to view your mail in folder-like category groups. You can even assign more than one category to an e-mail, and the item will show up in both places. If you need true topic-based filing, I strongly encourage you to give this method a try.

MYN Strategic Deferral

Once you start using the task system to manage your e-mail and tasks for a while, you will be recording in Outlook more tasks than ever before. Most of those will not be critical; they will be Opportunity Now tasks, as described above. Since Opportunity Now tasks are discretionary they tend to build up over time. As your Opportunity Now tasks list grows in size you'll be faced with a quandary; you'll have way more tasks recorded than you have time to do. Keeping the Now Tasks list to a reasonable number is important.

The typical way to manage excess tasks in any system is by using the "three D's"—Delete, Delegate, or Defer. In my experience, it is very hard for the average knowledge worker to delete or delegate many tasks. Rather, they need to *defer* activities in a strategic way, keeping their business well focused on a few important priorities while keeping track of the deferred ones, and over time deleting those whose usefulness has finally expired. That's what the MYN Strategic Deferral process does. Referring to the model above, I teach users how to toss lower-priority tasks over the Now Horizon, so they sit just out of sight and do not contribute to workload anxiety. I then show how to schedule these deferred tasks for review so they are not lost. Each task can get its most appropriate review date assigned. The review process is nearly automatic and does not distract from the primary task system.

This MYN Strategic Deferral process is a very powerful component of this system, and one that maps well to what you may be already doing now when you ignore tasks you have no time to do; however, I suspect you are not doing that in a very organized or satisfying way. MYN Strategic Deferral adds structure and a scheduled process to postponing lower-priority tasks, and it lets you relax knowing they are being managed in a timely fashion.

Note: *For those of you who used the master tasks concept in the first edition of this book, Strategic Deferral replaces most of its function of hiding low-priority tasks.*

I discuss a simplified manner of doing Strategic Deferrals in Lesson 4 and reserve complete coverage to Lesson 9. The Outlook configurations in Lesson 3 support all the Strategic Deferral processes and review steps.

Optional Components of the System

A number of other components of the system come into play in the latter part of the book. You might call these optional, depending on the role you play at your workplace. For example, if you have staff you delegate to, you'll definitely want to read Lesson 10 on delegation; otherwise it is optional. If you manage projects, read Lesson 12. Here are some highlights from this more discretionary portion of the system.

Delegation

If you have a number of staff to delegate to, you may be frustrated by lack of a clean way to manage delegated tasks. Failures with delegation often stem from lack of good systems to assign, track, and follow up on delegated tasks; they are not usually because of irresponsible subordinates.

What is often missing is a logical assignment and tracking system, so you can see what tasks are assigned and know when to check in on given tasks and when not to. Key to accomplishing this is setting follow-up tasks to yourself to track delegated assignments and to time contact with subordinates to check on assignments. I teach a simple task nomenclature and timing system to help you do this. The complete process steps are to identify a need, gain buy-in from your staff, and then enter an automated follow-up cycle until the task is done. Lesson 10 is devoted to this important process.

Time Management

When people say they need to learn time management, I find they usually need to learn *task* management. You can meet most of your time management needs by following the task management principles in the MYN system. You will use your time much more efficiently and effectively. As I mentioned in the introduction, most users of this system say they gain back at least 25 percent of their workweek; many say much more.

Beyond the task management principles taught in this book, however, a few simple time management techniques are, in fact, part of this system.

First, if your day is mostly full of appointments, you'll need to set some time aside to work your tasks. I encourage those using this system to schedule general task time right on their calendar. That is discussed in Lesson 11.

Second, you may need to make sure that your time spent working your task list is kept well focused. In Lesson 11, I provide a number of techniques to ensure that. I also provide a simple process for identifying clearly whether you really are overloaded with high-importance tasks or just working inefficiently; identifying that helps lead to a solution.

There are also a large number of things that you can do to make your use of Outlook and this system quicker and more efficient; all those are listed in Lesson 11 as well.

Intrinsic Importance

I promised above that once you have brought order to your workday chaos and your work life is generally under control, the system will then allow you to track and manage intrinsically important tasks. What do I mean by *intrinsic importance*? Tasks that link strongly to your values or goals are tasks that I say have high intrinsic importance.

I show in Lesson 12 a way to delineate and track such tasks. I think you will find this optional lesson provides a very useful way of identifying these tasks and integrating them into your daily workflow.

Goal and Project Linkage

One useful way of prioritizing ad hoc tasks is to identify where they come from, why you are doing them, and what larger outcome they support. Once you have tasks well under control, doing this exercise can help to add structure and may identify tasks that should be reprioritized. The main way to accomplish this exercise is to map ad hoc tasks to your *goals and projects*.

You can link tasks to goals and projects in a variety of ways. The simplest way is to create a goal and project list and keep that list in mind as you create daily tasks. In other words, as you plan out your day look at your list of goals and projects and make sure you add tasks to your Now Tasks list, or appointments to your calendar, that support these higher-level priorities. To this end, I show a new way in Lesson 12 to build the master tasks list (a tool from the first edition of this book) that serves as a good place to list and review projects and goals.

A more elaborate solution is to actually link specific Outlook tasks to goals and projects; that way you can see what tasks already on your list are contributing to a specific outcome. In Lesson 12, I show one way to do that in a new Outlook custom view using Outlook Categories. And the Outlook add-in software ClearContext, which I highlight throughout this book, provides a strong linkage between projects and tasks.

Beyond that, for more sophisticated goal and project management, I emphasize using other tools. Specifically for project management, once you reach a need to show clear linkages between dependent tasks, it really is time to move up to a tool like Microsoft Office Project. For planning hierarchical relationships between goals, projects, and tasks, a tool like Mindjet's MindManager Pro is highly recommended. That said, I do show some ways to build Goal→Project→Task hierarchies in Outlook 2007/10 and Outlook for Mac 2011. Lesson 12 puts all of this into perspective.

■ ■ ■

Summary of System Theory and Key Components

So that's the Master Your Now! system in a nutshell. As a final overview, below is a summary of the theory and major components of the system that you have just learned. All components are detailed in the following lessons.

▶ The system is based on an urgency model of a typical workday called the Now Horizon, which shows how nearly all our attention is placed on near-term tasks. This model provides a structure to manage those tasks.

▶ You will configure Outlook to map to the "urgency zones" in that model into a unified approach called the Workday Mastery To-Do List, or MYN task list for short. You will then learn ways to manage within each zone of that list.

▶ The Critical Now and Opportunity Now zones together make up what I call your Now Tasks list; these are tasks inside the Now Horizon—tasks you consider each day.

▶ After using the system for a while you will want to take advantage of MYN Strategic Deferral—tossing low-priority tasks over the Now Horizon and scheduling reviews on them. This will keep your Now Tasks list at a reasonable size.

▶ You will learn two methods of prioritizing tasks, including the FRESH Prioritization system, which by default gives higher priority to newer tasks and uses start dates rather than due dates to guide task completion. Deadlines are used only when needed.

▶ Converting e-mails to tasks, and then managing those actions in your new MYN tasks system, is the number one way to get ahead of out-of-control e-mail.

▶ Emptying the Inbox every day will provide relief from the tension of unreconciled responsibilities buried in your Inbox. You will learn a simple way to do that.

▶ For people who need topic-based filing of e-mail, I recommend and teach a system of category-based tagging of Outlook mail, all within one folder, and then show how to apply a custom view to display them in folder-like groups. Other options are discussed.

▶ The latter part of the book covers optional but important topics such as delegation, time management, intrinsic importance, and goal and project management. Consider exploring those topics after you have mastered the core skills of the system.

Next Steps

As I said above, the ultimate goal of applying this model and corresponding management principles is that your workday will begin to look like Figure 1.1. This is a smooth workday flow where tasks on your list are paced appropriately for your workday, and you experience only the satisfaction of accumulating new accomplishments every day.

Using the task management system in Outlook is a key first step of doing that. So in the next lesson, Lesson 2, I show you basics of the out-of-the-box Outlook task management system. I then teach a simple version of the important skill of converting e-mails to tasks.

Then, in Lesson 3, I show you how to reconfigure the Outlook tasks system to match MYN principles. Detailed MYN principles to manage the task list and e-mail start in Lesson 4 and continue to the end of the book.

So get started now on Lesson 2, and you will soon have your tasks, e-mail, and workday well under control.

Lesson 2:
Yes, You Can Gain Workday Control Using Outlook

Introduction

Yes, Microsoft Outlook can solve your out-of-control workday. In fact I am willing to wager that you have for some time suspected that if you just took a little effort to learn Outlook more thoroughly, you could gain big benefits in getting your workday organized.

Well, that's partially true; learning Outlook features will help, but merely learning more about Outlook is not sufficient. The real key is learning and applying a powerful new methodology, or system, of task and e-mail management, one that is optimized for today's rapid work pace and for today's huge volumes of e-mail. There is real power in applying that methodology to Outlook.

In This Lesson

To start that journey, in this second lesson I want you to learn the out-of-the-box task system in Outlook, and how to navigate it. I'll show you a few different ways to enter tasks in Outlook. I'll show you some of the new task features of Outlook 2007 and 2010 if you have those versions. I'll show you how to clean up the results of an upgrade to Outlook 2007 or 2010. And if you have the Macintosh version (2011), I'll describe how it is different. At the end I'll show you a quick way to convert e-mails to tasks in all versions, which is a core element of this new system.

For the more advanced Outlook users, some of the material in this lesson may seem basic, but stay with me. I suspect you will learn some new things. For the rest of you, this lesson is a core building block for using the MYN system.

If You Have Tried the Outlook Task System Before and Given up, Please Try Again

Most people I know who have tried the Outlook task system have given up on it quickly. I did too the first couple of times I tried it. However, do not let past failures with the task system stop you from trying again now. Let me tell a story that explains why.

Some time ago a company I worked for adopted Microsoft Outlook as its e-mail system, so it was natural at that time for me to try Outlook's task-management system. This was not the first time I had tried to manage tasks with an automated to-do list like the one in Outlook. I'd attempted this with many other automated packages, including Palm handheld software synchronized with the desktop version of the Palm software. I had also tried task software on a BlackBerry synchronized with Outlook.

However, in the past, and again this time, I found that within a few weeks the automated to-do list quickly got out of hand, and invariably I stopped using it. What happened was that a large list of tasks built up. These were tasks that I intended to get to but that I was unsure when I needed to complete them. Not wanting to lose sight of these tasks, I did not delete them from the task list, and the task list grew to a size that I found either psychologically overwhelming to look at or just impossible to scan through. I had trouble deleting tasks because even the lower-priority ones seemed significant once on the list. Of course, I tried assigning priorities to tasks, but then I ended up with a large number of high-priority tasks, most of which were important but not important for any given day. Therefore, while they remained sorted high on the task list I constantly skipped them as I used the list. So due to the overwhelmingly large size of the list, even the high-priority portion of the it, the list became weak and useless. Outlook did not seem to solve the problem for me.

What finally changed this was when I developed some task and e-mail management methodologies that worked in Outlook. They involved reconfiguring Outlook in various ways to show only pertinent tasks, to provide ways to defer tasks, and to provide new approaches to task prioritization that work in today's business environment. Once the methodologies were applied, and the configurations of Outlook changed, Outlook worked splendidly for managing tasks and e-mails.

The moral of this story is that while the tool was in place, a usable process or *methodology* was not. So even if you have tried and given up on Outlook tasks, give the task system another try now. You now have a powerful new system to work with that will make it shine, especially if you use Windows Outlook. The Mac version has a much weaker task system, but you can still use it.

Next, let's discuss what versions of Outlook work with this system.

Outlook Versions Supported in this Book

Not all versions of Outlook are supported in this book—versions older than 2003 just didn't make the "cut." Specifically, here is what *is* supported.

Microsoft Outlook for Mac 2011

In late 2010 Microsoft released Outlook for Mac 2011, its first Outlook version for the Macintosh in many years, and the only one discussed in this book. The earlier Microsoft product, Entourage, is not supported in this book.

Windows Outlook Versions 2003, 2007, and 2010

This book supports Windows Outlook versions 2003, 2007, and 2010. In reality, all versions of Windows Outlook, starting with 2000 and later, are adequate for use with the system taught in this book. But if you have Outlook version 2000 or 2002 (2002 is also called Outlook XP), please purchase the second edition of this book where they are directly described. Note that Outlook Express is not supported in any edition.

Also note that among the supported Windows Outlook versions—2003, 2007, and 2010—there are many differences, so it is important that you know which of these you have; I tell you how to determine that next. Service packs, dot releases, and so on are not important in making this determination.

By the way, starting with the 2003 version, Microsoft changed the name from *Microsoft® Outlook 2002* to *Microsoft® Office Outlook® 2003*. The newer 2007 was named in this manner as well; but then they seemed to drop that nomenclature in 2010. But, for brevity in this book, I will refer to all the different Windows versions merely as Outlook 2003, Outlook 2007, and Outlook 2010. And I frequently lapse into just stating the version year.

Identify Your Windows Outlook Version

Here is how to determine what version of Windows Outlook you are using. If you have a tabbed Ribbon menu at the top of Outlook, you are using Outlook 2010. If not, go to the Help menu, and choose About Microsoft Outlook (or it may say About Microsoft Office Outlook). At the very top left of the window that opens, you will see the full name of the software in small lettering. As described above, the version year is embedded in the name. If it is labeled Outlook XP (or indicates it is part of Office XP) then you have Outlook 2002 and, again, it is not supported in this third edition; use the second edition instead.

One more caveat. I also assume you are mostly using the desktop or laptop version of Outlook rather than accessing Outlook through your web browser. The features of the web browser version of Outlook (called Outlook Web Access and recently Outlook Web App; or OWA for short) are powerful, but OWA lacks a few features needed to fully implement the methods in this book. Certainly, OWA can be used periodically to supplement access to your main copy, when away from your desk.

Impact of Version Differences in This System

All versions of Outlook covered in this book can be used with MYN principles described throughout the book. However, how you mechanically apply the principles varies across the versions.

Outlook for Mac 2011

The new Macintosh version of Outlook treats tasks quite differently than any of the Windows versions. For that reason I describe it separately in many of the instructions. It also is not as powerful and has far fewer features amenable to MYN than the Windows versions. For that reason, you will see less coverage of it throughout the book. And because of the weaknesses, I think some of you may be better off using a different software product for managing tasks per the principles in this book. I discuss an alternative in Lesson 6 called ToodleDo; you can read about it there or go to my website for more information: www.myn.bz/ToodleDo.html.

Windows Outlook

Windows Outlook 2003 provides everything you need to implement the system. Outlook 2007 and 2010 are even better, and the two are nearly identical for MYN purposes. Because of that, in most cases ahead I will refer to them together as Outlook 2007/10.

Microsoft, starting in 2007, made major changes to the small task pane called the TaskPad, which in previous versions sat next to the Calendar; in 2007/10 the TaskPad is now called the To-Do Bar. Outlook 2007/10 also added a new type of task called the flagged-mail task. All these changes offer a number of advantages for the Master Your Now! system, and I will cover them extensively throughout the book. The changes do complicate things a bit, however, so you will see more details on Outlook 2007/10 than on any other version.

Navigating Through Outlook (Windows and Mac)

Okay, let's get started with some Outlook basics. I want to show in particular how to navigate among various Outlook folders, since you will be doing that as you use this system. Most of what follows applies to both the Windows and Mac versions; but I will call out some differences. If you are an experienced Outlook user, you can skip this section on Outlook folders and navigation and jump ahead to the section below called Learning Outlook Task Basics.

Data Types

Both Windows and Mac Outlook have five different data types, some of which you are probably familiar with. They are Mail, Calendar, Contacts,

Tasks, and Notes. Outlook Windows has one more: Journal. Which data type is selected defines how a particular item behaves. When you create a new e-mail item, for example, you are simply creating a new instance of a Mail data type. And all data types exist within corresponding folders.

Folders

Data types are stored inside Outlook folders; folders are simply specific collections of these Outlook data-type items. If you currently use Outlook as your primary e-mail system, you are using Outlook folders. Every time you view your calendar, your e-mail, or your contacts, you are choosing to open a specific type of Outlook folder and view the items inside. You can create as many folders of each type as you want, although Outlook usually starts out with one folder of each type (except for Mail, which has several delivered out of the box).

No matter how many folders you have, each Outlook data type has only one *default* folder at any given time. It is that default folder that you end up opening when you click one of the major banner buttons in Outlook labeled with those data types. So for instance if you click the Contacts banner button, you are probably opening the default contacts folder. If you want to open any other contact folders (assuming you have created additional ones), you will need to use a *folder list* to find them and open them. A folder list always allows more detailed navigation than using just the banner buttons or icons at the bottom left of the screen. Note that the banner buttons are the wide labeled bars near the bottom, while the icons are smaller and arranged horizontally along the very bottom of the Navigation Pane. Later I explain how to convert banner buttons to icons and vice versa.

Choosing Folders Using the Navigation Pane

The left side of all windows is dominated by a large navigation structure called the Navigation Pane. See Figures 2.1 and 2.2 for Windows and Figure 2.3 for Mac. If the Navigation Pane shown in those figures is not visible on your screen, open the View menu or tab and click Navigation Pane. In Outlook 2007/10 that will open a submenu from which you should choose Normal to open the Navigation Pane. In Outlook 2003 and 2011 simply clicking Navigation Pane will open it. Note, however, that in Outlook 2003 you may need to click the Expand button (shown below) found at the bottom of the menu list to display the Navigation Pane choice.

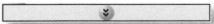

The Navigation Pane is a powerful tool, but in many ways it is confusing; I provide a complete explanation of the Navigation Pane near the end of Appendix A. However, for now, follow this simplified two-step approach: start by using the banner buttons and icons in the lower portion of the Navigation Pane to select the data-type mode (see Figure 2.1 or 2.2); this will open

Figure 2.1
The Navigation Pane occupies the left side of the Outlook Window (2007 shown here).

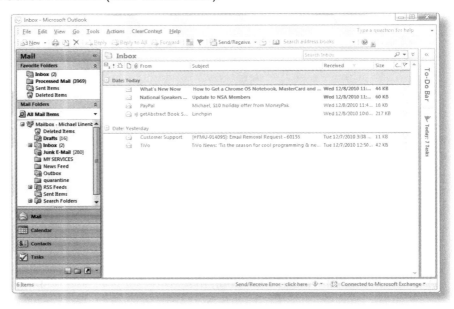

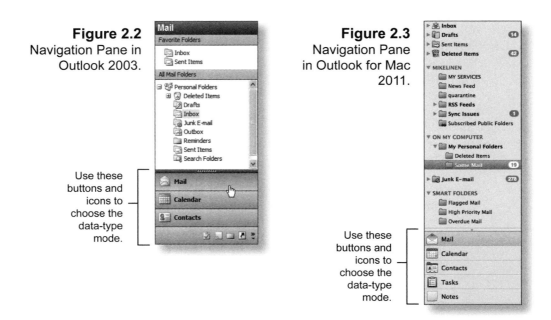

Figure 2.2
Navigation Pane in Outlook 2003.

Use these buttons and icons to choose the data-type mode.

Figure 2.3
Navigation Pane in Outlook for Mac 2011.

Use these buttons and icons to choose the data-type mode.

the current default folder and will display the complete folder list for that data type. Then if needed, click in the upper portion of the pane to open other folders of that type.

If in Outlook 2003 or 2007/10 you want to use a complete folder list that includes *all* data types (mail, contacts, tasks, and so on), sorted by where they are stored, then instead click the Folder List banner button or icon at the bottom of the pane (see samples below). That opens a larger folder tree in the Navigation Pane that can be very useful. This Folder List choice is not present in Outlook for Mac 2011.

Folder List icon

As mentioned, there is much more to understanding the Navigation Pane, and that is discussed near the end of Appendix A.

Learning Outlook Tasks Basics

Now that you know how to navigate among the various Outlook data types, let's focus on one specific data type: Tasks. Outlook tasks are at the core of getting your workday under control and at the core of the MYN System, so take some time to learn how to use them.

Accessing the Outlook Tasks System

There are two primary ways you can access the tasks system in Outlook: by using the Tasks folder (all versions) and by using the TaskPad/To-Do Bar (Windows only).

Using Tasks Folder(s)

As described above, you select a Tasks folder by clicking the Tasks icon or button in the Navigation Pane on the left side of the Outlook window. This opens a full window depiction of tasks in the Outlook task system.

As you will see later, in the Tasks folders you can also configure and save various additional *filtered* views. These configurable views can be useful to us, and I will cover how to create and use them in Lesson 12.

We'll use the Tasks folder rarely on Windows, using the TaskPad/To-Do Bar instead on most occasions in MYN. On the Macintosh the opposite is true; we'll use the Tasks folders exclusively for all our task work on the Mac since no equivalent exists there for the Windows TaskPad or To-Do Bar. To describe the latter, most of the next pages focuses on Windows Outlook.

Using the TaskPad and To-Do Bar (Windows)

The most important place to access Tasks on Windows is in the TaskPad (2003) or the To-Do Bar (2007/10) (see Figures 2.4 and 2.5).

The TaskPad and To-Do Bar task lists are abbreviated depictions of Outlook tasks. Out of the box, they show *simpler* columns of task information than the complex views within the Tasks folders mentioned above, making them a good quick-review location for tasks. And you will further configure these task tools to show tasks in a way specific to the MYN system. Once configured, the TaskPad or To-Do Bar will become your primary task input and review facility, so you will want to become familiar with them. By the way

Figure 2.4
The TaskPad (2003) occupies the lower right corner of the default Calendar folder view.

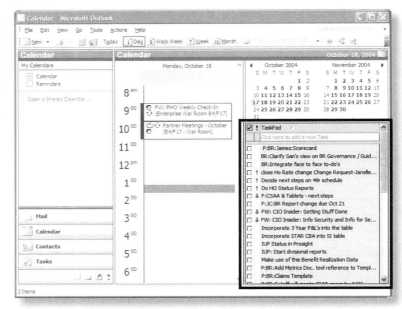

Figure 2.5
The To-Do Bar (2007/10) can occupy the right side of every view in Outlook (Normal mode shown).

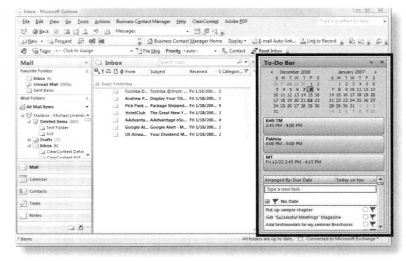

do not get the To-Do Bar confused with the To-Do List, which is in the Tasks folder views. Let me show you now how to find the TaskPad and To-Do Bar.

Note: Outlook 2003 users can skip the next section if you are already using the TaskPad. However, Outlook 2007/10 users, even if you are using the To-Do Bar now, you may want to read the 2007/10 section below because you will very likely learn some new things.

Viewing and Resizing the TaskPad (Outlook 2003)

The primary Calendar folder is where you are able to see the TaskPad in Outlook 2003. Navigate to your primary Calendar folder using the techniques you learned above. Once there, you should see the TaskPad in the lower right corner. If you do not see the TaskPad within your default Calendar folder view as in Figure 2.4, open the View menu at the top of your Outlook window and choose TaskPad from that menu to insert the TaskPad into your Calendar folder view.

Five Ways to Find a Hidden Outlook 2003 TaskPad

That should do it, but if not, try activating the Day view of the Calendar, by clicking Day at the top of the Calendar window. If still hidden, there are a couple of possible reasons. First, make sure you are in a standard Day/Week/Month view. You do that by going to the View menu, choosing Arrange Views, and then the Current View submenu; then ensure that Day/Week/Month is chosen. If it is, yet you still cannot see the TaskPad, two more conditions might be hiding the TaskPad, described next.

If all you see is the mini-calendars section on the right side of your Calendar window, in that case you need to select the bottom border of the mini-calendar section and drag it up to expose the TaskPad. The other condition is if you see no mini-calendars at all on the right side of the Calendar window (rather than just the hourly information in the main Calendar, Day view). In that case

Ignore the TaskPad View Submenu

Outlook 2003 has a number of specialized TaskPad views that you can choose from the View menu, under the TaskPad View submenu. However, other than starting with the default view called Today's Tasks (which you will modify), none of these specialized views are useful once you start using the MYN system. The reason is once you customize the TaskPad view in any manner, the choices in the TaskPad views submenu become void: choosing any of them displays your same modified TaskPad view the way you currently customized it. So, essentially, you should ignore the TaskPad View menu and its submenus.

you need to select the border just inside the right edge of the Outlook window and drag to the left, exposing the TaskPad and mini-calendars.

If you still do not see the TaskPad, ensure that you are using the primary Calendar folder; the TaskPad is only visible in that. Look to see if you have any other Calendar folders in the Navigation Pane on the left, and try the steps above on each of them.

Resizing the TaskPad

You can resize the TaskPad to your liking by dragging its top border up or down, or its left edge right or left. Note when dragging left and right that the TaskPad resizes in "jumps"; it will not resize at first, but then as you drag more, it will jump to a new size.

At this point, Outlook 2003 users can skip to the section below called Entering Tasks, past the long section on Outlook 2007/10 below.

Viewing and Resizing the To-Do Bar Task List (Outlook 2007/10)

There is a lot more to the task system in Outlook 2007/10, so this section is much longer than the one above for 2003.

Features of the To-Do Bar

The To-Do Bar in Outlook 2007/10 replaces the TaskPad of previous Outlook versions. If you used Outlook 2003 or earlier, you probably know that the older TaskPad, which sits to the right of the appointment calendar, is a key view for tasks. The new To-Do Bar continues that tradition. But the new To-Do Bar also introduces some new behavior compared to the TaskPad, new behavior you may like.

Probably the most important new behavior is that the To-Do Bar can be kept visible on the right side of *any* Outlook folder and view. That's hugely important, as it elevates the stature of tasks in Outlook, something I felt for some time was needed. Once you open the To-Do Bar in the various views, it will be there when you come back. You can quickly arrange so you never lose sight of your important daily tasks, and thereby increase the probability of working them consistently. Let's discuss in detail how you open it, as this may be a little confusing.

Viewing the To-Do Bar

The To-Do Bar has three display states: Normal (fully opened), Minimized (a narrow vertical bar at the right side of Outlook screen), and Off (totally hidden). You may choose these states from the main Outlook View menu (2007) or Ribbon View tab (2010) as shown in Figure 2.6.

Another way to change the display state once the bar is open is to use the small button(s) on the top right of the To-Do Bar. This varies between 2007 and 2010. For example, to minimize you can click the small right-pointing

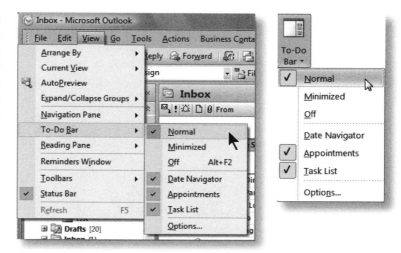

Figure 2.6
Controlling the
To-Do Bar states
from the View
menu (2007 is on
left and 2010 is
on right)

arrow in the upper right corner of the To-Do Bar as shown in Figure 2.7. In 2007 that is a double arrow (a chevron) and in 2010 it is a single arrow.

Once minimized, the To-Do Bar looks like Figure 2.8.

To fully open a minimized To-Do Bar, click the left-pointing arrow at the top of the minimized To-Do Bar; this opens it back to the Normal or fully opened state. By the way, in Outlook 2007/10, this same minimize behavior is applied to the Navigation Pane (again, the Navigation Pane is the folder list that occupies the left side of the Outlook application window).

Closing the To-Do Bar

Now, to remove the open To-Do Bar completely, in 2007 you click the Close button (x) next to the chevron as shown in Figure 2.7. Closing it like this only removes it from the current data type, by the way (Mail, Calendar, Contacts, Tasks, and so on). In 2010 that Close button does not exist; you'll need to go to the View tab to fully close it.

Once you've clicked that Close button, or closed it from the menu, there are no buttons you can click to bring the To-Do Bar back for that data type, so to reactivate the To-Do Bar you'll need to go to the View menu or tab, choose To-Do Bar, and choose Normal. These activation decisions are specific for each of the data types (Mail, Calendar, Contacts, Tasks, and so on). So if you close the To-Do Bar in any of the Calendar folders or views, when you navigate to any of the Mail folders or views it may still be open. And if the To-Do Bar is closed for all major data types, and you want it open for all, you'll need to open it one at a time while in each data type, using those View menu or tab commands again each time.

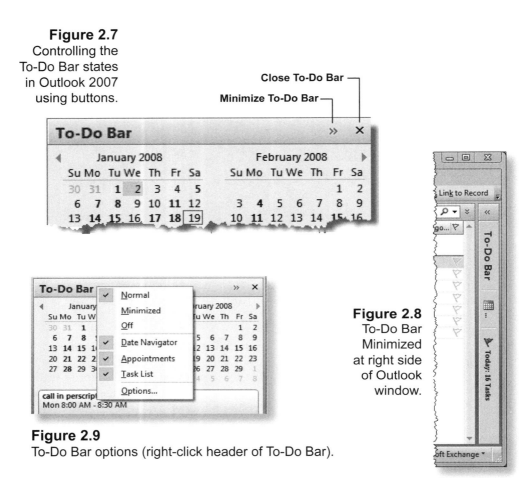

Figure 2.7
Controlling the To-Do Bar states in Outlook 2007 using buttons.

Close To-Do Bar

Minimize To-Do Bar

Figure 2.8
To-Do Bar Minimized at right side of Outlook window.

Figure 2.9
To-Do Bar options (right-click header of To-Do Bar).

Temporarily Opening the To-Do Bar

There is actually a fourth view state for the To-Do Bar that I call "popped open." Let me explain. Normally, when the To-Do Bar is fully open, it resizes whatever window is to the left of it smaller, to make room, collapsing the width of columns as needed to keep them all in view. Figure 2.5 shows an example of this.

In contrast, the *popped open* state causes the To-Do Bar to pop open *on top of* the Inbox without collapsing column widths, *actually covering* the right columns. You achieve this state by clicking in the lower portion of the minimized To-Do Bar, (for example, by clicking the rotated text "To-Do Bar" in Figure 2.8). The resulting To-Do Bar display truly is a temporary popup; if you click anywhere else in Outlook, this overlaid To-Do Bar will minimize again.

Why do this? If your screen is a bit small and you periodically want to take a quick peek at your to-do list, you would use this method. And this explains why the To-Do Bar seems to disappear sometimes when you are using it; you probably opened it in the popped-open mode without realizing it. This popup behavior is also available on the Navigation Pane.

Resize the Outlook 2007/10 To-Do Bar Tasks List to See More Tasks

By now you have noticed that the new To-Do Bar is not a one-to-one replacement of the older TaskPad. The old TaskPad only included a tasks list, while the new To-Do Bar also incorporates a new area that lists upcoming appointments. And on a bit more subtle note, the monthly mini-calendar row (called the Date Navigator; you may have hidden it in the Quick Start) above the task list in all versions is in 2007/10 now technically part of the To-Do Bar construct (in older versions of Outlook that item was actually separate from the TaskPad). So by default, the task list in the new To-Do Bar really only occupies about the lower third of the To-Do Bar (see bottom right of Figure 2.5).

If you have a small screen, the task list portion of the To-Do Bar may seem too small. The main reason is that the future appointments section can take up a fair amount of space on the To-Do Bar. If you have limited screen space, you'll need to decide if you really want to show this future appointments section. The same holds for the Date Navigator since it takes space as well.

If you agree that the tasks portion seems too short on your screen, the way to remove that Appointments or Date Navigator section is by right-clicking the To-Do Bar header, and in the shortcut menu that appears, clear the check mark next to the Appointments item, and/or the Date Navigator item, as shown in Figure 2.9.

Figure 2.10 shows how it looks once you clear just the Appointments section. Or to make just a little more room, you can simply configure the Appointments section to show fewer upcoming appointments. To do that in 2007, use the Options… item in that same shortcut menu and specify a smaller number of appointments. In 2010 simply drag the top edge of the task list up.

Resize the Width of the Outlook 2007/10 To-Do Bar

Regarding the size of the To-Do Bar, there is one other new feature compared to the TaskPad. By default, the task list in the To-Do Bar has two modes of view depending on how *wide* you make it. Currently I assume your task list looks something like Figure 2.10: one wide column and two narrow ones, and no column titles. But now try this: drag the left edge of the To-Do Bar to the left to widen it and see what happens to this column layout. Figure 2.11 shows how mine looks after I widen it quite a bit.

See all the new columns? So what's happened here? By default, the task list is configured to show a compact layout mode when the width is less than 80 characters, and that's what you see out of the box. Once you drag it wider,

Figure 2.10
To-Do Bar, compact layout
and no Appointments section.

Figure 2.11
Same To-Do Bar in noncompact
layout.

the *actual* column configuration is displayed. So what you are seeing while it
is narrower is a special simplified configuration. It hides many columns, and
combines some columns together. It is an abbreviated view that only shows
task subject, category color, and flag status. Try dragging the left edge of the
To-Do Bar to the left and right to see this reconfiguration happen.

For the average task user, I think this compact view is a nice design. However, for the beginning MYN user it hides some important fields, so I have
you remove this compact view in Lesson 3. Then in Lesson 12 after you
become more adept at the system, I'll show you an optional way to use the
compact view as part of the MYN system again.

Note: *You may want to move the Reading Pane in the Inbox to the bottom once you open
the To-Do Bar. Go to the View menu or tab, select Reading Pane, and choose Bottom.*

Entering Tasks

Windows Outlook: Two Methods of Task Entry

There are two primary methods of entering tasks in Windows Outlook, and
you can use either method according to your preferences and the needs of the
moment. Both work whether you are working from the TaskPad/To-Do Bar,
or from one of the Tasks folder views, but as you will see I recommend using

Figure 2.12
TaskPad
New Item
row.

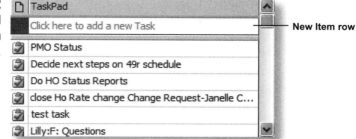

New Item row

the TaskPad/To-Do Bar for nearly all your task management activities. The two entry methods are the *quick entry method* and the *full entry method*. You will normally access both methods by clicking in the New Item row, which is located at the very top of the TaskPad/To-Do Bar, and Tasks folder. Note the blank line in Figure 2.12 labeled Click Here to Add a New Task; that's it. In the Outlook 2007/10 compact layout it will say Type a New Task, as in Figure 2.10. Clicking once there starts the quick entry method and clicking twice there (double-clicking) starts the full entry method. If that row is not present on your TaskPad or To-Do Bar, see the sidebar discussion below.

Quick Entry Method of Creating Tasks

To use the quick entry method, simply single-click anywhere on the New Item row and that line will become editable. I prefer to click in the Subject box, the wide box in the middle, because it then is selected for editing, and this is normally the first piece of information I will be entering in a new task. I then type in the name of my task. If a date field is visible, tab over and enter a date (enter today's date for now). You can type the date by hand, or better, click once in the field and use the date drop-down list. I then press ENTER or just click off the task line, and the new task is saved.

Figure 2.13
Outlook
Task dialog
box in 2003
(2007/2010
are similar).

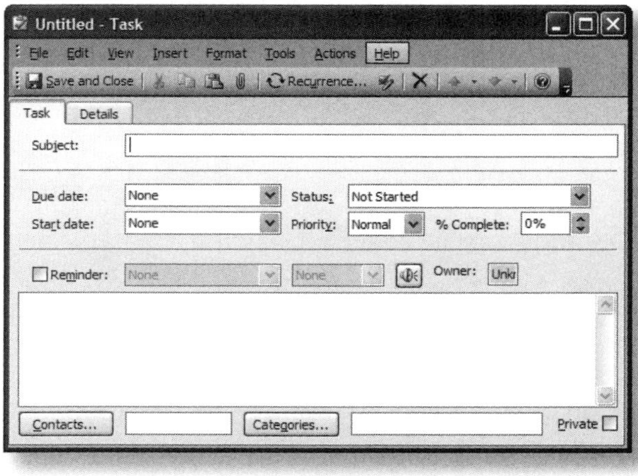

Full Entry Method of Creating Tasks

To use the full entry method, instead of single-clicking the New Item row, double-click that row. This brings up the standard Outlook Task dialog box. (See Figure 2.13.) Enter a Subject and Start date, and then click Save and Close.

Note: *This double-click method of opening the Task dialog box also works on existing tasks, if you want to edit them. More on that below.*

When to Use Each Method

So which method of creating new tasks do I use? I nearly always use the quick method from within the TaskPad/To-Do Bar. It is just quicker and

Showing the New Item Row (Windows)

If the New Item row is not visible in your TaskPad/To-Do Bar, or in your Tasks folder, do this:

1. Right-click any column heading of the TaskPad/To-Do Bar, or the Tasks folder view, and from the shortcut menu choose Customize Current View... (it may say Custom... or in 2010 it may say View Settings...)

2. A dialog box will open labeled Customize Views (called Advanced View Settings in 2010). In that dialog box, click the Other Settings button on the middle left.

3. A dialog box labeled Other Settings will open, the top of which is shown below. Select the Allow In-Cell Editing check box near the top right of the dialog box, and then select the Show "New Item" Row check box just below it; both are shown below, middle right.

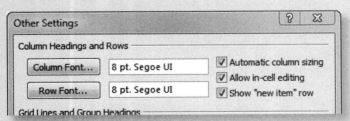

4. Click OK and then OK again to close the configuration dialog boxes.

The second check box is necessary so that you can edit your tasks in place within the TaskPad.

Once you are sure the New Item row is configured to be visible, you can start using the quick method of task entry.

Figure 2.14
Setting the Priority box in the
Task dialog box.

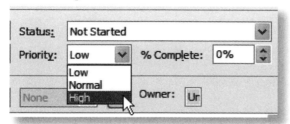

Figure 2.15
Setting the Priority box in
the TaskPad or To-Do Bar.

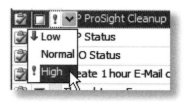

easier. However, if you have any detailed text to enter in the body of the task, you will need to use the full entry method. That is really the only thing the full method adds in this system.

Using the New Button or Keyboard Shortcuts (Windows)

In Outlook 2003 and 2007 you can use the New button to open a new task window; just click the drop-down arrow next to it and choose Task. If one of the task folders is active, rather than click the drop-down arrow next to the New button, click the button itself; it will have a task icon embedded in it if it's ready for that operation.

In Outlook 2010 the button is labeled New Items; clicking it allows you to choose Task. And if a Tasks folder is open, a New Task button is also visible.

In all Windows versions, you can use a keyboard shortcut. If a task folder is active, use CTRL+N. If a task folder is not active, use CTRL+SHIFT+K.

How to Set Outlook Priorities on Tasks (Windows)

With a Task dialog box open, use the Priority box to select one of three priority levels in Outlook. (See Figure 2.14.)

In Lesson 3, I will show you how to add a Priority column to the TaskPad/ To-Do Bar list view. Once enabled, you merely click the task's Priority box (the column space with the ! label above it) and the three Outlook priority choices will pop up; choose one of them and your task Priority box is set. (See Figure 2.15.) However, prior to Lesson 3 your views do not yet display that column, so for now set it from within the Task dialog box by using the Priority box.

Entering Tasks in Outlook for Mac 2011

Outlook for Mac 2011 has fewer ways to create new tasks. There is no quick method like that on the Windows versions—all new tasks are created in the full Task dialog box. To open a blank new dialog box, from any folder you can click the New button at the left of the Home tab on the Ribbon. And from the Tasks folder you can click the Task button at the left end of the same

Figure 2.16
Outlook Task
dialog box in
Outlook for
Mac 2011.

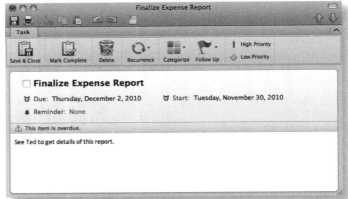

Ribbon. While the Tasks folder is active you can also use the following keyboard shortcut: CMD+N.

Once the Task dialog box is open you should set a subject for the task by clicking on the phrase New Task in the middle left of the dialog box—that opens a text box that you can type into. To enter a due date or start date, click on the phrase No Date next to each of the Due or Start labels. Figure 2.16 shows how this looks after entering some values.

How to Set Outlook Priorities on Tasks (Mac 2011)

Inside an open task, at the right end of the Ribbon, you will see a High Priority and Low Priority button (see top of Figure 2.16). Clicking either one highlights the button and sets that level. New tasks are set to Normal (medium) priority by default (neither button is highlighted). Once you set a priority to High or Low, simply clear that same button to set the task back to Normal (click it to remove the highlighting).

You can also set the priority level from the Tasks list view. At the top of the list view in the middle of the Home tab of the Ribbon, you'll see the same two High and Low Priority buttons. Select a task in the list and use those buttons the same way you did within an open task. You can also set the priority by CTRL-clicking the item in the list and choosing a priority from the Priority submenu.

Practice Entering and Editing Tasks Now (Windows and Mac)

Entering Tasks

If this is your first time using Outlook for task management, you might want to practice entering a few tasks now. Both Mac and Windows users, try using the New or New Items button and keyboard shortcuts described earlier to enter a number of tasks. For this practice, put a start date and due date of *today*. Windows users, try using the quick method—find the New Item row, click once, and enter the subject or action there. Do the same using the full entry method (double-click), and practice setting the priority there. Again, this is just for practice; I will go over proper use of these boxes and fields later, so don't get carried away yet.

Editing Tasks

Windows and Mac users, you can edit in the full Task dialog box by double-clicking the task in the list view.

Windows users note that you can also edit existing task information right in the task list; for example, you can change the text in the subject line by clicking once on the subject text and retyping. And if date fields are shown, you can edit them by clicking them.

While Mac users cannot edit in the task list like that, as just mentioned, they can CTRL-click an item and reset the priority from the submenu. And Mac users can use the Follow Up command on that menu to reset the dates.

Marking Tasks Complete

Later, once you complete working on the task and no more effort on that task is required, you should mark the task complete.

The easiest way to mark a task complete is to do it from one of the list views of Tasks, but how to do that varies with version and view. In the Mac version, in the Outlook 2003 TaskPad, and in many Tasks folder views in those same versions, you mark a task complete by checking the box in the Complete column at the left edge of the task in the list (see Figure 2.17). In the To-Do Bar of Outlook 2007/10, with out-of-the-box configurations, you mark a task complete by clicking the flag at the right edge of the task (see Figure 2.18). This flag is discussed more in a coming section. Or you can add the Complete box to 2007/10 if you prefer that (in Lesson 3).

Depending on your configurations, once you mark a task complete, it will either disappear from the list view, or it will remain visible but turn gray (and in Windows it will have a line through it).

You can also mark tasks complete from within the full task dialog box. In Windows, find the Status box and change it to Completed. Notice there are many other status values available there, none of which you'll use in this system. In the Mac version, there is a completed check box inside the task window itself, just to the left to the task title, which you can click (see Figure 2.19). Or you can click the Mark Complete ribbon item (also in Figure 2.19).

Finding Completed Tasks

If you mark a task complete by accident, and (depending on settings) it disappears from your list view, you can always use the Undo command to restore it quickly (CTRL+Z in Windows; CMD+Z in Mac).

Complete column

Figure 2.17
In Outlook 2003, checking the box in the Complete column changes the status of the task to Completed.

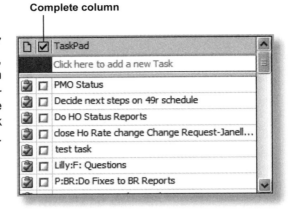

Flag Status column

Figure 2.18
In the Outlook 2007/10 task list, clicking the flag at the right of a task marks it complete.

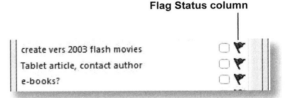

Figure 2.19
In Outlook for Mac 2011, two other ways to mark a task complete.

Mark Complete button

Completed Check Box

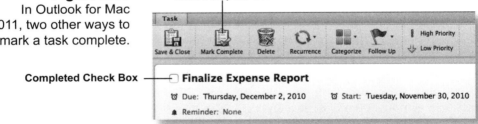

Or later, you can find the completed task and reverse its completed status. How you view completed tasks depends on the Outlook version.

Showing completed tasks in Mac 2011 is easy. From within the Tasks folder just open the Home tab on the Ribbon and click the Completed check box at its right end; this adds completed tasks to the list.

In Windows, displaying completed tasks in the Tasks folder can be a little harder since a number of specialized views are available and many of them hide completed tasks; so you need to activate a view that displays them. To do that, first open the Tasks folder. Then, in Outlook 2003 and 2007, look in the middle of the Navigation Pane and click a view name like Simple List or Detailed List; that will display all tasks including completed ones.

Outlook 2010 users, once at the Tasks folder, go to the View tab on the Ribbon, and at its left end click the Change View button. Then click either the Simple List or Details List view; that will display all tasks including completed ones.

All versions, once you find the task in the list there you can remove the check mark. This will restore the task within your Tasks folder or the TaskPad/To-Do Bar.

■   ■   ■

Using Other Fields in the Task Dialog Box (Windows and Mac)

Within the Task Dialog Box you will see other fields you may want to use. Some appear in both the Windows and Mac versions, and others in Windows only.

Reminder Check Box

About half of the way down on the left of Figure 2.13 you will see a small item labeled Reminder. In case this is new to you, reminders are small Outlook message boxes that pop to the front of your screen when an item is due (often with a beep). Using this box is how you activate a reminder on a task. However, I do not engage reminders on tasks and I recommend you don't either; I explain why in the Lesson 4 section on deadlines. In fact in Lesson 3, Outlook 2003 users will remove the Outlook setting that makes this the default.

Large Text Field

Perhaps 10 percent of the time, I enter text in the large text field at the bottom of the Task tab (see Figure 2.13). This is a very good place to put task details and, most commonly, it is where you will see the text of an e-mail that generated the task (you will see how to do that at the end of this lesson). Or I may copy notes from my notebook, notes that I collected when the task was assigned to me in a meeting.

Status, Percent Complete, and Owner Fields (Windows)

I ignore the % Complete field in Figure 2.13. Later you will learn that tasks entered in this system are generally small, next-step style tasks; these tasks should be relatively discrete and not subject to partial completion. That's also why I do not use the various values available in the Status field such as In Progress, Deferred, and Waiting on Someone. While these status values are used extensively in other systems, there are other ways in Outlook that you will use to indicate these status values, in a much more useful way.

I also ignore the Owner field. This and many of these other fields are more useful when integrating Outlook tasks with other Microsoft products such as

Microsoft Project, or if using the formal Assign Task button described in the Delegation lesson, Lesson 10.

Categories Button (Windows and Mac)

At the bottom of the task entry dialog box in Outlook 2003 you'll see a Categories button (see Figure 2.13). In Outlook 2007/10, and in Outlook for Mac 2011, that button, renamed Categorize, is in the Ribbon near the right end of the Task tab (as in Figure 2.16). Clicking that button brings up a dialog box or menu in which you can assign a category to the task. Why might you want to do this? Outlook allows you to filter on category types when you view tasks in any of the task views. However, initially you will probably not use Outlook Categories with *tasks*. In the pages ahead, you will see that there are many better ways to accomplish what Categories achieves for tasks in other systems. I do introduce using Categories for tasks in Lesson 12, to track projects and goals. And I *do* use Outlook Categories extensively with e-mail in this system; I discuss this quite thoroughly in Lesson 8.

Details Section (Windows)

The second section in the task entry dialog box is the Details section. This is opened by clicking the Details tab in Outlook 2003 (see Figure 2.20), or the Details button on the Show group within the Ribbon in Outlook 2007/10 (see Figure 2.21). I completely ignore the Details section when working with tasks. This is another case where fields are useful only when integrating Outlook with other Microsoft applications such as Microsoft Office Project, or perhaps when tracking billable time against a task.

Figure 2.20
Details tab on Outlook 2003 Task dialog box.

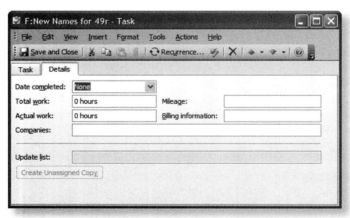

Figure 2.21
Details button, Outlook 2007/10 Task dialog box.

Using Flags in Outlook (Windows and Mac)

Flagging E-mail

Ever since early versions of Outlook, a flag field has been present in all e-mail list views. It's called the Follow Up Flag, or the Flag Status field. The meaning of that field has evolved over time. Prior to Outlook 2003, clicking the flag simply turned it red—it was a way to highlight an e-mail (for whatever purpose you may want). In Outlook 2003 Microsoft added a choice of bright colors to choose from—it was a way to classify mail in a variety of ways, with each color representing something different (those meanings were up to you).

With Outlook 2007 Microsoft introduced a totally new philosophy on what flags on e-mail were for, and this has continued through versions 2010 and 2011. Flags on mail in these versions indicate that the mail needs *action*. In other words, these flagged items represent a kind of *task*. And the wide range of bright colors in 2003 are gone—now only shades of red are available.

Note: In Outlook 2007/10 and 2011, you can still classify mail with various bright colors by using Outlook Color Categories; we'll cover Color Categories quite extensively in Lesson 8.

You can set dates on the flags you set on e-mail, and the entire e-mail will turn red when that date arrives (indicating the action is overdue). You can even set reminders to trigger an alarm on those dates (though I do not recommend that). In fact, I recommend that you generally avoid using the Follow Up Flag tool for now as a way to convert e-mails to tasks. Later in this lesson, and in Lesson 7, I show a better way to convert e-mails to tasks. However, there *are* appropriate times to flag e-mails. But since these flags create task-like qualities in Outlook 2007/10 and 2011, you will want to learn more before doing that; they are a bit tricky and they will impact your use of Outlook tasks greatly. Flags also come in handy when using some mobile devices. For those reasons, the next section covers flags in more detail, and Lesson 7 covers them even more extensively.

In Outlook 2003 they are less important, so 2003 users feel free to skip to the section at the end of this lesson called Introduction to Converting E-mails to Tasks. We'll come back to Outlook 2003 flags in Lesson 7.

Flagged-Mail Tasks in Your Task Lists (Outlook 2007/2010, 2011)

Since flagged mail represents a certain kind of task, Microsoft took this a step further. Starting in Outlook 2007, certain views in the Tasks folder (and all views in the To-Do Bar in Windows versions) display flagged mail in the task list. What this means is that when you set a flag at the right edge of an e-mail message, a virtual copy of the mail item is added to your Tasks folder and to the To-Do Bar task list. In prior versions of Outlook, setting a flag added color to the flag on that mail item, and allowed some optional reminder capability. But it was not until Outlook 2007 and beyond that the flagged mail item actually appeared in the task list. This enhancement adds a huge new utility as it provides a very quick way to convert e-mails to "tasks," which I will cover more at the end of this lesson and in Lesson 7. But it can also clutter the task list and it introduces some challenges.

To create a flagged-mail task in Outlook 2007/10, and 2011, you can left-click the flag, which by default sets it to a red flag with a start and due date of today. See the flagged e-mail at top right of Figure 2.22. Or you can right-click the flag, which gives you a shortcut menu with a choice of preset dates and other operations, as shown in the lower right of Figure 2.22.

Once it is flagged, the e-mail stays in the Inbox, and in Windows it also appears in the To-Do Bar task list. In all versions you can find it in the Tasks folder (in Windows, it's in the To-Do List folder within the main Tasks data type). With default Outlook settings, flagged-mail tasks look just like regular tasks in these lists. In Lesson 3, after you reconfigure the To-Do Bar task list, the item icons will be displayed, and then you can see the difference in the list by seeing a different icon for flagged-mail tasks.

One other thing. When you look at the To-Do Bar in Outlook 2007 and 2010, you might also think that only the items in the To-Do Bar task list with flags at the right edge are flagged-mail tasks, but as mentioned above, *all* items in the To-Do Bar task list have flags, whether they are flagged e-mails or tasks. More on that below in the section "Understanding the Flags…"

Figure 2.22
Flagging mail in Outlook 2007.

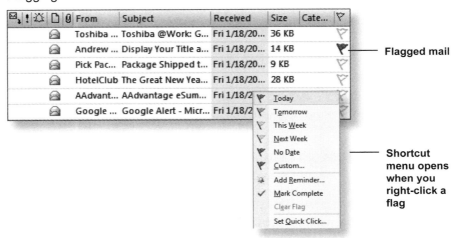

Cleaning Up Flagged-Mail Tasks (Outlook 2007/2010, 2011)

As described above, adding a flag to a mail item in Outlook 2007/10 or 2011 creates a task-like entry called a flagged-mail task in your task list. A somewhat unfortunate side effect of this is that if you have used flags on mail in the past, and then more recently decided to start using the task system, your task system will appear overloaded with these. These accumulate even if the mail is stored away in older folders, even from years ago.

Clearly this is not something you want, given how old these items are, and if you have a lot of them it can make the task list almost unusable. So you will want to clean this up, either by filtering them out, or by clearing them.

To filter them out of Window Outlook, see this article: www.myn.bz/FlagFilter.htm; it shows you settings you can make to filter Inbox flagged mail out of the To-Do Bar.

Alternately, you can clear the flags. You can clear them one at a time just by clicking each flag. Or you can SHIFT-select a number of the messages in the task list at once, right-click the flag, and choose Clear Flag (in Windows if you select more than one, the right-click choice will be Clear Flag/Delete Task—it leads to the same outcome). Clearing flags preserves the original mail and removes the item from the task list, so it could be just what you want. If the old mail still has meaning to you, consider applying a color category to that mail as a way to mark it for later search. If there is some action still due on the flagged mail, you may even want to convert the e-mail to a task per the instructions at the end of this chapter.

If you have hundreds of these scattered among hundreds of real tasks, then scrolling and selecting these can be hard to do. So better is to group all the flagged-mail tasks together and clear the flag on all of them at once, in bulk. Here is how.

How to Do a Bulk Flagged-Mail Task Cleanup:

1. Go to your Tasks folder. Once there, Windows users be sure the To-Do List folder is selected in the upper left of the Navigation Pane.

2. At the top of the list view, click the header of the Item Type Icon column; it's usually the column at the far left. On Windows its symbol looks like a dog-eared document; on the Mac it looks like a tiny i inside a circle. Again, click that symbol in the header at the top of the column—this sorts all items on that column.

3. Scroll the task list to find the top of the icons that look like an envelope and then use the SHIFT key to select all these (select the top item, scroll to the bottom item, press and hold the SHIFT key, then click the bottom item). You've just selected all your flagged-mail tasks. If you were flagging e-mail recently to indicate tasks, then leave unselected any new flagged tasks you may have created on purpose.

4. Then, Windows users, right-click the flag column on any one of them, and choose Clear Flag/Delete Task from the shortcut menu. Mac users, find the Follow Up flag button in the Home tab of the Ribbon menu, click the small down arrow at its right, and choose Clear Flag from the shortcut menu.

Those steps will clear out your old unwanted flagged-mail tasks from your task lists, but will retain the original e-mail. It will also remove the flags from all those mail items in whatever mail folder they are stored in.

Windows users who recently upgraded from Outlook 2003 will most likely find that all that mail has a corresponding color category still assigned. Decide if you want to remove that as well.

Some cautions: do not simply delete these items using the DELETE key, since that will delete the corresponding e-mails. And do not select any of the true tasks during step 3, as those really will be deleted. And finally, remember, if you have been purposely creating flagged-mail tasks for a while before reading this book, do not clear those out.

Understanding the "Flags" at the Right Edge of All Tasks in the Outlook 2007/10 To-Do Bar

By now you have noticed that the To-Do Bar displays a flag at the right edge of every task in the task list there (see Figure 2.18). That flag looks just like the flag you see at the right edge of flagged mail items in the Inbox, which may make you think these are indicators of the new flagged-mail tasks described above. Not so. Rather, *all* items in the To-Do Bar task list have flags, whether they are flagged e-mails or true tasks. These flags are here for a different reason—to provide a shortcut way to set task dates and status.

This can be really useful—for example, when changing dates on many tasks at once. Let's say you want to delay starting several tasks one day; to do that, you can select them all, and then right-click one of them and choose Tomorrow, and they are all redated to tomorrow.

Note: *There are subtleties to this. For example if you select Next Week from that menu, the Start Date field is set to next Monday and the Due Date field is set to next Friday; that can lead to some issues in MYN, so avoid the Next Week selection.*

If you want to set a date different from the preset list, use the Custom… choice and you can set any dates you want. Unfortunately the Custom… choice is not available when selecting a group of items.

One caution when using this flag in the To-Do Bar is that, as mentioned earlier, it is also used to mark tasks complete. If you *left*-click an item in the To-Do Bar (a normal mouse click) it marks the item complete and in most cases *removes* the item from the To-Do Bar. This can be a bit disturbing if you're not used to it; you are probably accustomed to left-clicking flags on mail items *without* having the item disappear. You will get accustomed to this

Figure 2.23
Figure 2.23
Daily Task List at
bottom of the
Outlook 2007/10
Calendar.

Daily Task
List

after a while. You can easily restore tasks you accidentally mark complete by
selecting Undo Flag from the Edit menu (not present in 2010), or use the keyboard shortcut, CTRL+Z (CMD+Z on the Mac). Or, you could go to the Tasks
folder and clear the check mark from the Completed check box for that task;
see the section above called Finding Completed Tasks for more information.

Daily Task List below the Calendar in Outlook 2007/10

There is one other task feature of Outlook 2007/10 that I need to mention
briefly. In the default Calendar data-type view, if you view by day or by
week, you may see tasks listed under each day as in Figure 2.23. Ignore this
task list for now. It is another way to view the same task database you have
been working with so far, but because of how it is configured, it is not very
useful to MYN system users. You can read more about that at the very end of
Appendix A.

My Day Window in Outlook for Mac 2011

In Outlook for Mac 2011 there is another task view called My Day. It's a small
vertical separate window that looks somewhat like the To-Do Bar in Windows Outlook 2007/10. But because of how it is configured, the tasks list on it
is not useful to MYN system users.

That said, My Day does show your appointments for the day, so take a look
at it and see if it that makes it useful to you. You access it by clicking the
Tools tab (look at the left edge of that Ribbon) or by selecting it from the Tools
menu. In fact, My Day is a separate application that you can launch without
even opening Outlook, which makes it a possible quick-launch view of your
appointments. Look in the Office folder for the icon to launch it.

Introduction to Converting E-mails to Tasks (All Outlook Versions)

There is one last skill I want you to learn before you complete this lesson, and that is a simple introduction to how to convert e-mails to tasks. Converting e-mails to tasks is at the core of the MYN system. If you learn one thing, it should be this skill. In fact I have an entire lesson on this topic, Lesson 7. The steps below will get you started with an easy approach. If you like what you see here, and you want to skip ahead to do Lesson 7 now, feel free to do that. Just come back and start Lesson 3 after you are done.

Windows Outlook

Windows users, try this now. Look in your Inbox and find an e-mail that has notified you of some action you need to take, either explicitly or implicitly. Find one without an attachment for now to practice this easy approach. Once you find one, close the e-mail (if you opened it) and do these steps:

1. From within your regular e-mail list view, click the e-mail item (a regular left-click) and drag it over to the Tasks folder icon or banner button in the Navigation Pane.

2. Once you drag it there, release the mouse, and a new task window will open, just like the window you saw above when you used the Full Entry method to create a new task. The beauty of this approach is that the new task window will contain the entire e-mail text, and the task name will equal the subject name of the e-mail. That means you have very little typing to do to complete the conversion. But you should at a minimum do the following steps immediately:

Note: Outlook 2010 sometimes displays odd behavior when doing this; the new task window may flash for a moment and then disappear behind the main Outlook window. This happens if you linger your mouse for more than a second over the Tasks folder icon or banner button prior to dropping the e-mail there. To avoid this, drop the item quickly once your mouse passes over the Tasks folder icon or banner button.

3. Change the subject of the newly created task to a title that describes the action needed. This is an essential step; you must extract from the e-mail text the core action it requires of you and write that into the subject line, overwriting the old e-mail title.

4. Set the start date and due date for this task to today for now; do not leave it at None. Ignore the task priority for now.

5. Click Save and Close in the upper left corner of the new Task dialog box.

That's it! Your task has been saved in the task database inside Outlook. You might be able to see the new task appear right in your TaskPad/To-Do Bar now—go take a look. However, if you have lots of other tasks in there it might be buried under other tasks. Don't worry if you cannot find it; in the next lesson you will clean up the configurations of the TaskPad/To-Do Bar such that newly converted tasks will jump to the top of your task list.

As I mentioned earlier, avoid for now using the Follow Up Flag tool as a way to convert e-mails to tasks. Even though this places the e-mail in the tasks list, there are many disadvantages to doing that. I discuss at length in Lesson 7 the right and wrong ways to use flagged-mail tasks.

Outlook for Mac 2011 – Use AppleScript

Regrettably, converting e-mails to true tasks in Outlook for Mac 2011 is not as easy or flexible as in Windows; it's just not built into the software design. However, Microsoft added an AppleScript to enable the missing capability, and it works well. It's not really a command in Outlook; rather it's an add-in script that should be automatically installed when you install Outlook 2011. Here's how to find and use it.

With a message selected in Outlook for Mac 2011 (either in the message list or as an open message), open the AppleScript menu at the far right end of the Outlook menu bar at the top of the Macintosh screen (it's a small icon that looks like a scrolled document) and choose Create Task from Message from the drop-down menu. A new task opens with the e-mail title as the task name, and e-mail body in the body of the task. Rename the task to be an action-oriented phrase; then be sure to set the start date, priority, and other fields, and save it.

Note: *If the Create Task from Message command is missing from your script menu, go to this link: www.myn.bz/MacScript.htm to learn how to install it.*

As with Windows, avoid for now using the Follow Up Flag tool as a way to convert e-mails to tasks. Even though this places the e-mail in the tasks list, there are many disadvantages to doing that. I discuss at length in Lesson 7 the right and wrong ways to use flagged-mail tasks.

Summary

Congratulations, you have completed the first step of your journey toward workday control. You now know where to find the task system in Outlook and how to enter tasks. Outlook 2007/10 and 2011 users have learned some of the new tasks features in those versions and have cleaned the flagged-mail tasks associated with old mail out of your task list. Macintosh users have learned the different way Outlook 2011 displays and treats tasks. And you now know an easy way to convert e-mails to tasks in all versions.

Next Steps

I suggest that as you start using the system after the next lesson, you begin converting important e-mails to tasks immediately. You will find such tasks are much easier to keep track of in the task list than in the Inbox. However, do not go through your whole Inbox yet because this was just a brief lesson on the topic, intended only to get you started early. I devote an entire lesson to this topic in Lesson 7; there you will learn, for instance, how to include attachments with your converted tasks (Windows only).

In the next lesson you will change the configurations of the task lists to prepare them for using the core MYN task management methodology.

Lesson 3:
Configuring Outlook for
MYN Task Management

Introduction

Now that you know how to use the task system in Outlook, let's fix it. As I mentioned in the Introduction to this book, the out-of-the-box task configurations for Outlook are unfortunately poorly configured for use in today's business world. That's because those configurations, like those in many other task systems, assume a guilt-based task management methodology, one that ends up emphasizing old, dead tasks. Systems like that become unusable quite quickly in a busy office environment.

That was not Microsoft's intention, of course. They've merely used the same approach that nearly every other system today uses, an approach that sorts the oldest uncompleted tasks to the top of the task list, and marks them in bright red. That might still work in a home system, where tasks accumulate slowly and all chores are eventually done. But in today's business world where priorities change nearly every day, and high volumes of business e-mail can deliver us tens of new action requests per day, our business task systems need a vastly different approach. This lesson teaches the core configurations for that new approach, the Master Your Now! (MYN) system.

One great strength of Windows Outlook is that it is an extremely flexible application that can be reconfigured in numerous ways. Outlook for Mac 2011 has far less configurability, but can still be modified in useful ways. This lesson walks you through a simple reconfiguration of Outlook for use in the MYN system. In the next few pages you'll learn how to fix your copy of Outlook so you can start applying the MYN best practices of task management. The core of those best practices will be covered in Lesson 4.

Configuring Outlook for MYN

For this early lesson in the book you will reconfigure key Outlook tasks lists to represent the Workday Mastery To-Do List. In Windows Outlook, that means you will be configuring the TaskPad (2003) or the To-Do Bar (2007/10); in the Mac version it will be the main Tasks folder. If you did the Quick Start configurations in Windows, the ones here will go well beyond those.

As defined in Lesson 1, the Workday Mastery To-Do List, or the MYN task list for short, is a way of displaying tasks sorted by urgency zones. To create this list in Outlook, you will be applying a custom filter to the tasks lists and adding some custom columns, formatting, and sorting. When done, your Windows TaskPad/To-Do Bar will look roughly as shown in Figure 1.3 in Lesson 1. The Mac Tasks folder will look considerably different but still serve the purpose. In either case, the configuration steps below take about 30 minutes to complete (working slowly). In future lessons, you will be optionally making additional configuration changes; but this is enough for now.

I'll start with the complete Windows Outlook configurations; if you are configuring a Macintosh, skip ahead to the section titled Configuring Outlook for Mac 2011, which starts about two-thirds through this Lesson.

Configuring Windows Outlook for MYN

Sitting adjacent to your main Outlook views, the TaskPad (Outlook 2003) or the To-Do Bar (Outlook 2007/10) will be the primary command post for the tasks you use and look at several times a day. Ahead you will customize the TaskPad/To-Do Bar so that it will:

▶ Show only tasks with a start date of today or earlier.

▶ Filter out completed tasks.

▶ Show the Start Date column and a few additional task columns.

▶ Group on priority and sort on start date descending.

▶ Display some custom formatting.

▶ Clear two default settings in Outlook: one that turns all "old" tasks red, and one in 2003 that forces all dated tasks to start with a reminder set.

Note: *In case you followed the first edition of this book, but not the second edition, two major changes started in the second edition that you should be aware of. First, I am now emphasizing the Outlook Start Date rather than Due Date field. And second, Master Tasks are no longer emphasized in this system. In fact, the new TaskPad/ To-Do Bar configuration below will make your previous Master Tasks view no longer usable. Lessons 9 and 12 provide new options for this functionality, and a newly designed Master Tasks view is shown in Lesson 12, in case you still want to use that. For more discussion, see the Preface and also see the Note at the end of this lesson.*

Outlook Add-in Software ClearContext

The same Windows Outlook configurations made manually here are built into the MYN Special Edition of the Windows Outlook add-in software called ClearContext, available through a link on my website. Should you install that software now instead of doing the configurations below? Doing so will not really save you setup time, since the software installation steps themselves take time, and you'll need to learn how to use the software. And most corporate environments discourage adding software (though ClearContext is usually not blocked even in locked-down environments). The primary reason to consider this software is that the paid version adds many optional but useful new features to Outlook, features that simplify some MYN functionality described in this lesson and lessons ahead. I'll make notes in the book where advantage can be gained from the software; you can decide later if you want to install it. If you do, be sure to access the special version from my website; other software options may be available on my website as well. And be sure to sign up for my newsletter when you visit my website so you will be notified of software option changes. The website is www.MichaelLinenberger.com.

Before You Start, Log Off Any Other Open Copies of Outlook

Before you start these configurations, if you are in an Exchange Server environment and logged on to more than one computer, exit Outlook on all other computers first. Reason: all settings you are about to make are saved first in the Outlook client, and then in the Exchange Server profile; if you have multiple Outlook clients running, Exchange can get confused about which client's settings take precedence in the central profile.

Also, if you get halfway through the settings and need to pause, I recommend you save the progress of the configurations. Do this by closing whatever view you are working on (by clicking OK all the way out of the configuration screens), and then exit Outlook and come back in. That saves the settings.

All these precautions are to prevent you from losing the configurations you make.

Start the Configurations by Opening the TaskPad/ To-Do Bar Customize View Controls

It's now time to get started. Almost all configurations are started from one primary Outlook configuration dialog box, which you will see below.

1. Outlook 2003 users recall you are starting at the Calendar folder to see the TaskPad (see Lesson 2 if needed). Outlook 2007/10 users are configuring the To-Do Bar at the right of the Outlook window. *Note: You are*

not editing the Tasks folder, or the To-Do List, a common mistake here since the steps look the same. Make sure you are in the TaskPad or To-Do Bar.

2. Right-click anywhere on the TaskPad/To-Do Bar task list heading bar (the bar with the heading TaskPad, or Task Subject, or Arrange By on it). Choose Customize Current View… from the shortcut menu. It might say Custom… instead, and in Outlook 2010 it might say View Settings…. The following dialog box will open. You are going to set a few of the View attributes in this dialog box.

Note: In most figures in this lesson, I will show Outlook 2007 images. I will call out any important differences from other versions if they exist. For example, the dialog box below is identical in Outlook 2003; in Outlook 2010 it is also essentially the same, but called Advanced View Settings instead. Also, in 2010, the Fields button at the top is called the Columns button (but it does the same thing). We'll be returning to this dialog box frequently, and since that name varies so much across versions, from now on I'll affectionately refer to it as "the large stack of buttons."

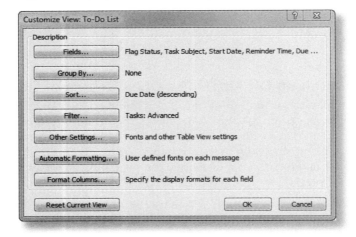

Adding Some Fields (Columns)

1. Start by clicking the Fields… button (called Columns… in 2010), which opens the Show Fields (Show Columns) dialog box.

2. Use the Add and Remove buttons to create a new field list in the right side of that dialog box; what you put in that list depends on your version of Outlook, as indicated below. If you need to add fields, select them first on the left and click Add; to remove fields select them on the right and click Remove. See comments at the end of this step in case you have difficulty finding these fields in the list on the left.

For Outlook 2007/10 create this list: Icon, Priority, Task Subject, Start Date, Flag Status (match the right side of figure below).

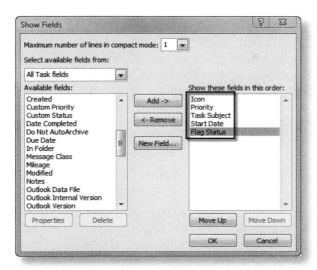

For Outlook 2003 create this list (shown below): Icon, Complete, Priority, Subject, Start Date (match the right side of figure below).

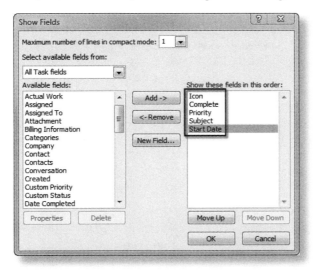

Use the Move Up and Move Down buttons to place them in the right order; or simply click the field name and drag it to the desired position.

Note, you must match these names exactly; some may look similar. If you have any trouble finding any of the field names above in the list on the left, try selecting All Task Fields in the list box titled Select Available Fields From, and then look again at the scrolling field list. That should display the fields you need, with two exceptions. The Task Subject and

Flag Status fields in Outlook 2007/10 (should you need to re-add them) are located in the All Mail Fields list.

3. Once you have all the fields and they are in the correct order in the right side of the dialog box, click OK and return to the large stack of buttons shown at the start of these steps.

Group by Priority

A core principle of the MYN configurations is to have High priority tasks sort and group at the top of the TaskPad/To-Do Bar. To enable this:

1. Back at the large stack of buttons, click the Group By... button, which opens the Group By dialog box (see below).

2. If checked, clear the check box in the upper left corner that says Automatically Group According to Arrangement.

3. Choose Priority from the Group Items By list box. Ensure that Show Field in View is checked, and ensure that Descending is selected to the right. See figure below. Then click OK.

Note: If you cannot find the Priority item, try selecting All Task Fields in the Select Available Fields From box at the very bottom of the window.

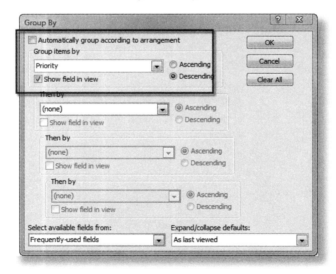

Sort by Start Date

Once you have set the Group By, you return to the large stack of buttons. You now want to have medium priority tasks with newer due dates sort to the top of the medium group of tasks. To enable this:

1. Click the Sort... button, which opens the Sort dialog box.

2. Choose Start Date from the Sort Items By list box. Ensure that Descending is selected to the right. See figure below. Then click OK.

Setting the Filter

Once you have set the Sort, you return to the large stack of buttons. You are now going to create a somewhat complex filter to ensure that you see only certain tasks.

1. On the large stack of buttons click the Filter... button.

2. The Filter dialog box opens; click the Advanced tab. Outlook 2007/10 users should see two filter conditions in the upper part of this window already. Leave those there if so; if they are not present you will add them in steps below. Previous users of this system who configured Outlook using the first edition (but not the second edition) may have a Due Date filter in there; if so remove that.

Note: *The rest of these instructions assume you do not know how to create an Outlook filter, and so the steps are very detailed. If you **do** know how to set a filter, just examine the figures below, and match them according to your Outlook version.*

3. Start by clicking Field in the middle left of this dialog box.

4. From the Field list, choose Date/Time fields, and from its submenu choose Start Date.

5. From the Condition list choose On or Before.

6. Type "Today" in the Value box; there is no Today list choice.

7. Then click Add to List to place this condition in the criteria list at top middle of the dialog box. This filter ensures that future dated tasks are hidden from view.

8. Leave this dialog box open (do not click OK); you are going to create some more queries.

9. Click Field in the middle left of the dialog box again.

10. From the Field list, choose Info/Status fields, and from its submenu choose Status.

11. From the Condition list, choose Not Equal To.

12. In the Value box select Completed.

13. Then click Add to List to add this condition to the criteria list in the middle of the dialog box. This filter removes completed tasks from view; otherwise they will clutter your list.

14. Click Field in the middle left of the dialog box again.

15. From the Field list, choose Date/Time fields, and from its submenu choose Start Date.

16. From the Condition list, scroll to the bottom and choose Does Not Exist. This filter allows tasks to stay in the list even if you forget to set a date for them; otherwise they will be hard to find.

17. Do not use the Value box (it is dimmed). Click the Add to List button. Your filter should look like Figures 3.1 (2007/10) or 3.2 (2003). The top two items in Figure 3.1 may not be present; if not, 2007/10 users should add them in the same way as above. Note that to do that you will find the Flag Completed Date item under All Mail fields (one of the sub-menus you will see after you click the Field button). If you like, you can read in Lesson 12, in the section called Outlook 2007/10 To-Do List Tasks Folder, why these two filters are needed.

18. Click OK, and return to the large stack of buttons.

Adjusting the Other Settings

You want to ensure that you can enter tasks directly into the TaskPad/To-Do Bar and that you can see all fields. To enable this, do the following steps.

1. From the large stack of buttons click Other Settings…; you will see the dialog box in Figure 3.3.

2. Ensure that the three check boxes in the upper right corner are checked, as shown in Figure 3.3.

3. In the lower portion of the box, under Other Options, clear the check box next to Use Compact Layout in Widths Smaller Than… (this will say Use Multi-line Layout in Widths Smaller Than… in Outlook 2003).

4. Just below that, ensure that Always Use Single-Line Layout is selected.

5. Click OK.

Figure 3.1
Outlook
2007/10
To-Do Bar
filter.

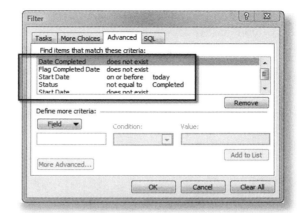

Figure 3.2
Outlook 2003
TaskPad filter.

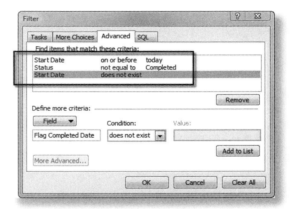

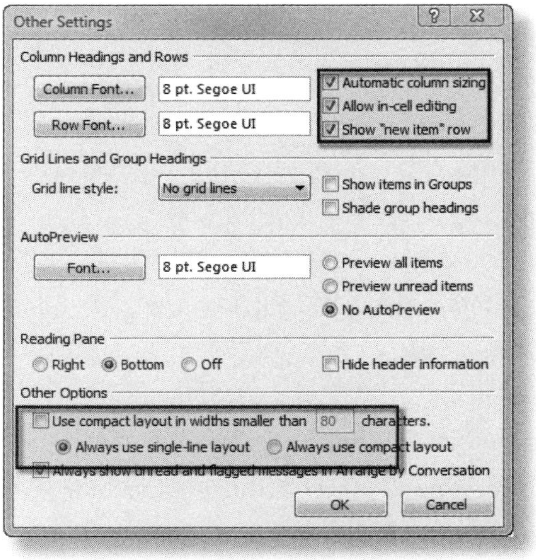

Figure 3.3
Adjust Other
Settings.

The above configurations represent the primary changes needed to the Task-Pad/To-Do Bar. Now for some final formatting.

Disabling the Overdue Tasks Rule, and Formatting Tasks Due Today

1. In the large stack of buttons click the Automatic Formatting… button (it's called Conditional Formatting… in Outlook 2010), and you will see the following dialog box open.

2. Clear the check box next to the Overdue Tasks rule in the middle of the dialog box. This prevents tasks with an old Due Date field from turning red, which does not make sense in our system.

3. Click Add to create a new rule and type Start Date Today in the Name field.

4. With the new rule selected, click Font…, and in the Font dialog box select the Underline check box, then click OK.

5. Click Condition… on the left side of the dialog box, then click the Advanced tab of the Filter dialog box.

6. Click Field in the middle left of this dialog box.

7. From the Field list, choose Date/Time fields, and from its submenu choose Start Date.

8. From the Condition list choose Today. Ignore the Value box.

9. Click Add to List. The filter should look like what you see below.

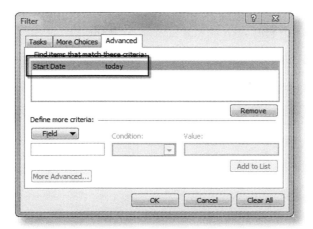

10. If it matches the image above, click OK. Click OK again, and then again, to close all configuration windows and return to the newly configured TaskPad/To-Do Bar.

Your configurations are now mostly done. Next, you will run a few tests to confirm they were done correctly.

. . .

Confirming that the Windows Configurations Are Correct

You should stop and check that the configurations are correct. Do the following checks; if any fail, repeat the configurations.

1. Examine the column labels of your TaskPad/To-Do Bar header, left to right, and ensure that they match the figures below, according to your Outlook version:

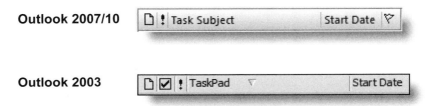

Note: in Outlook 2010, if using the Black color scheme, the symbol labels at the top may be invisible. To fix that, go to the File tab, choose Options, and at the top of the General option, change the Color Scheme to Silver.

2. Create a new task and set the start date to today, priority equal to Normal. When you save it, that task should appear near the top of your Priority:Normal section, underlined.

3. Create a new task and set the start date to today, priority equal to High. When you save it, that task should appear in a separate Priority:High section, near the top of the TaskPad/To-Do Bar. It will be underlined.

4. Create a new task and set the start date to tomorrow, priority equal to Normal. It should disappear from the list when you save it.

5. Create a new task and do not set any date, priority equal to Normal. It should appear near the bottom of your Priority:Normal group, with None in the date field.

6. Create a new task by using the Task dialog box. Set the start date and due date both to yesterday, priority equal to Normal. When you click Save & Close, that task should appear in your Priority:Normal group, below the underlined items. It should not be red.

The reasoning behind many of these settings will be explained in Lesson 4.

Once all the above are confirmed, there are a few more optional formatting step to take, below.

Formatting the Date Column in Outlook 2003 and 2007/10

1. In Outlook 2003 and 2007/10 you can fine-tune the formatting of columns in the TaskPad/To-Do Bar. I like to reset the date format to use a narrower scheme. This is purely optional, so feel free to skip this step.

2. Right-click anywhere on the TaskPad/To-Do Bar task list heading bar (the bar with the heading TaskPad, or Task Subject, or Arrange By on it). Choose Customize Current View… from the shortcut menu. It might say Custom… instead, and in Outlook 2010 it might say View Settings…. The dialog box with the large stack of buttons will open.

3. Choose the Format Columns… button near the bottom of the list on the left. The dialog box shown below opens.

4. Select Start Date in the list at left.

5. In the Format box at right, select the format shown below (study the *format* below, the date itself will be different). So an example is 15-Apr-11.

6. Select Best Fit in the Width section. Click OK, and then OK again.

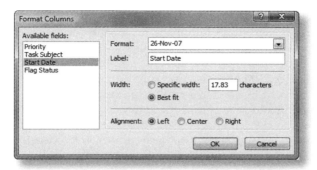

Adjusting the Width of the TaskPad/To-Do Bar and Start Date Column (All Windows Outlook Versions)

Finally, back at the TaskPad/To-Do Bar view, drag the left edge of the Task-Pad/To-Do Bar to widen or narrow it if needed. Recall that in Outlook 2003, the left edge of the TaskPad moves in "jumps," so you may need to drag it some distance before it seems to adjust. Next, you will probably want the Start Date column a different width; simply drag the left edge of the column *in the header* to the right or left until you can see just enough of the date to read it.

That's it for the TaskPad/To-Do Bar.

Turning Off the Task Reminders Default Setting (Outlook 2003)

Next, in Outlook 2003, you are going to configure the Reminder check box on the task entry dialog box so that it starts out unchecked when creating new tasks. You make that reconfiguration by doing the following:

From the Tools menu, select Options, Preferences tab, and then click the Task Options button, and clear the bottom check box: Set Reminders on Tasks with Due Dates as below. This setting is clear by default in Outlook 2007/10 but sometimes turned on by the user; turn it off if so.

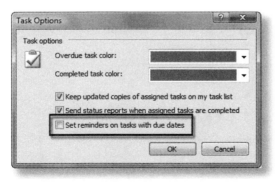

Here is why you did this. In case this is new to you, reminders are small Outlook message boxes that pop to the front of your screen, often with a beep. These are very useful when assigned to calendar appointments for reminding you when an appointment is about to start (and this configuration will not change that default). However, the opposite is true for tasks, given the way you will be using your task list; reminders for tasks will only be a nuisance. They are distracting and serve no purpose if they pop up in the middle of other activities. And there are technical problems with using them, all discussed in Lesson 4. Instead, using this system, as you find available time to work on tasks, you will develop a habit of reviewing your tasks list several times per day; this eliminates the need for a task reminder. If a task needs to be done at a particular time of day, make an appointment, not a task, and apply the reminder to it.

■ ■ ■

Configuring Outlook for Mac 2011

Because of a unique design compared to Windows Outlook, setting up the Macintosh version is quite different. The main difference is that you'll be making all the configurations in the Tasks folder, not a separate smaller view (there is no configurable To-Do Bar). And due to sorting limitations, you cannot show all MYN tasks in one list; rather you will be creating three different lists, one for each priority. To do that, you'll use an Outlook for Mac 2011 feature called Smart Folders.

Set Filter Check Boxes

To get started, first, you'll go to the Tasks folder (click on the Tasks banner button or icon in the lower left of the Outlook window). Next, click on the Home tab of the Ribbon, and look at the right end of that tab. You'll see three check boxes as below—these are the filter check boxes. Please select and clear those check boxes so they match the ones shown below.

Select and Reorder the Task Folder Columns

Next, with the Outlook window active, click the View menu in the menu bar at the top of your Macintosh screen, and choose Columns. You'll see a submenu like the one shown below—this controls which columns appear within the Tasks folder. Use that submenu a number of times to clear and add check marks to match the list in the image below.

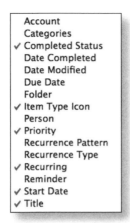

Next, you are going to reset the left-to-right order of those columns at the top of the tasks list. To do that, click and drag the column headings as needed to place them in the order shown in the figure below. Also, while there, confirm that all the column icons and names shown below appear at the top of your tasks list; if not, redo the step above. Adjust the width of the Start Date column as needed by dragging the edge of the column header.

Sorting on Start Date Descending

Next, click the Start Date header as highlighted in the figure above, to force a descending sort; the arrow will point down and the newest start dates should be at the top.

Note: *This sorting will apply to the Smart Folders that you will create next. Once set as above, I recommend you avoid changing the sorting of any columns in those Smart Folders; i.e., don't click the header of any column within the Smart Folders. If you do, due to a bug in Outlook 2011 (present at the time of this printing), you'll lose the descending start date sorting and you will not be able get it back while the Smart Folder is open. You can in fact get it back, but you'll need to navigate back to the main Tasks folder (click the Tasks icon at the top of the Navigation Pane) and re-sort it there to get the newest start dates back at top — then reenter the Smart Folder.*

Creating the Three Smart Folders

To group on task priority, you will be using a feature in Outlook for Mac 2011 called Smart Folders. You will create three separate Smart Folders to view each of the three urgency zones we use in the Workday Mastery To-Do List described in Lesson 1: a folder for High (Critical Now), a folder for Normal (Opportunity Now), and one for Low (Over the Horizon).

Note: *I'd rather you could do this in one folder like you can in Windows Outlook, but three separate folders are needed since sub-sorting on the start date, a key part of the MYN system and present in Windows Outlook, is not an available feature of the Outlook 2011 Tasks folder.*

To create a new Smart Folder you have to first do an Outlook search and then save the search criteria. You do that as follows:

1. In the Tasks folder, click on the Tasks icon in the top of the Navigation Pane. Then click once in the search box in the upper right of the Outlook window (labeled Search This Folder); that activates the Search Ribbon (shown below) — you may have to click on the purple Search tab title to truly activate it.

2. Click the Advanced button at the right end of that tab (shown below); once you do, you'll see an Item Contains button appear below the Ribbon menu.

3. Click the Item Contains button and change it to Start Date in the popup. In the new button that appears to the right, select Within Last. And in the field to the right of that enter 10,000 (this is simply a very large number to include all tasks with the past few years; feel free to change that if you like to include more or less). All this is shown below.

4. Click the plus sign (at the far right end of that search line) to start a new search line.

5. Using the principles above, create the next two search lines, duplicating exactly what you see in the image below (Priority; Is; High; and Is Incomplete; Is Incomplete).

6. To turn this into a Search Folder, click the Save button that sits just to the left of the Advanced button in the Search tab. When you do that, a new Smart Folder appears in the Navigation pane at the far left with an Untitled name selected. Type over the word Untitled with the phrase Critical Now and press the Return key. Your first Smart Folder is done.

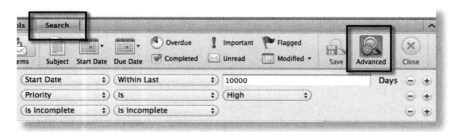

7. Create another Search Folder by repeating steps 1-6 but when you get to step 5, change the Priority values in the priority search line (the second line) to be Moderate. And in step 6 title the folder Opportunity Now.

8. Create the third Search Folder by repeating steps 1-6 but when you get to step 5, change the Priority values in the priority search line (the second line) to be Low. And in step 6 title the folder Over the Horizon.

9. I suggest you delete the remaining predelivered Smart Folders so your three priority folders stand out by themselves; you delete a folder by CTRL-clicking it and choosing Delete.

The left side of the figure below shows how your new Smart Folders list will look in the Navigation Pane. You can now click any of those folders to review your tasks in the three urgency zones. In the figure below, the Critical Now Smart Folder is selected, displaying all Critical Now (High priority) tasks to its right. Notice the exclamation points in the 4th column from the left—that indicates these are all High priority.

Due to the "smart" nature of these three Smart Folders, they will automatically populate based on task date and priority. For example, if you change a task's priority to High in any folder, it will move to the Critical Now folder. If you set the start date to the future it will disappear, and then reappear on its date.

Clicking the general Tasks folder icon above the Smart Folders (labeled My Tasks below) will show you future dated tasks. If you want to include completed tasks, you'll need to toggle the Completed filter check box you cleared in the Filter steps above. In the next chapter I'll show you how to use these folders.

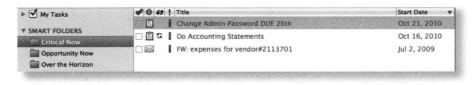

■   ■   ■

Confirming Your Outlook for Mac 2011 MYN Configurations Are Correct

You should stop and check that the configurations are correct. Do the following checks; if any fail, repeat the configurations.

1. Create a new task and set the start date to today, priority equal to Normal (i.e., no priority set). When you save it, that task should appear near the top of your Opportunity Now Smart Folder.

2. Create a new task and set the start date to today, priority equal to High. When you save it, that task should appear near the top of your Critical Now Smart Folder.

3. Create a new task and set the start date to today, priority equal to Low. When you save it, that task should appear near the top of your Over the Horizon Smart Folder.

4. Create a new task and set the start date to tomorrow, priority equal to Normal. It should not appear in any of the three Smart Folders after you save it (you will see it appear tomorrow in the Opportunity Now folder).

5. Create a new task and set the start date and due date both to yesterday, priority equal to Normal. When you save it, that task should appear in your Opportunity Now Smart Folder, below the items dated today. It will appear red (we will ignore that red color; there is unfortunately no way to turn off that setting in the Mac version of Outlook).

Exit Outlook and then Restart Outlook

That completes all the configurations you will make in this lesson. After you have completed these settings, exit Outlook and then restart it. That saves the settings. Do that immediately because Exchange Server update events can (in rare cases) clear these settings unless you save them first by exiting Outlook before waiting too long.

Next Steps

Your tasks system is now configured; you are ready to apply the MYN processes to manage your tasks in an intelligent and effective way. You just need to learn how to use these new configurations.

The core processes for using these new configurations are all presented next, in Lesson 4. After that lesson, you will have all you need to manage tasks in a basic way. Subsequent lessons will expand on those skills.

Note: *For Windows Outlook users who configured their Outlook per the first edition of this book, but did not update to the second edition of this book, you will see by adding the configurations above that all your old master tasks will now be visible in the TaskPad/ To-Do Bar; that's because undated tasks now appear there. Here's what to do next. First, assign a priority of Low to all tasks with no dates, to clean up the High and Medium portions of your list. Then read Lesson 4 all the way through, especially the section titled Converting Tasks to Over-the-Horizon Tasks. If you previously had a very large number of master tasks, and the Low priority section is now overwhelmed, I suggest you jump immediately to Lesson 9 to learn the Defer-to-Review method, which replaces the Master Tasks view approach. If, after reading all this, you decide you still prefer using a Master Tasks view, study the Lesson 12 section on building a new Master Tasks folder and view which is compatible with this new edition of the book.*

There is one other update procedure that has to do with recurring tasks. Any recurring tasks created under the configurations of the first edition now need to be deleted and recreated, this time making a point of saving the task with a start date set (by default Outlook often leaves that field blank, which is why you need to recreate these tasks). Do not just try to edit an existing recurring task and add a start date; that will not work. You need to completely delete and recreate all your recurring tasks.

Lesson 4:
A New Approach to Managing Tasks in Outlook

The Master Your Now! Methodology: How to Take Control of Your Tasks in Outlook

All the configurations in Lesson 3 were done for a reason: to set up a task list to match the principles described in Lesson 1, so you can succeed at managing tasks in Outlook. I call the resulting task list the Workday Mastery To-Do List; or you can also call it the MYN task list. The next step is to start applying the MYN system best practices of task management that this new task list supports. Let's go over those now.

The Now Tasks List

Tasks You Would Consider Doing Now

The first and perhaps simplest of these best practices of managing tasks in Outlook is this: from now on, the tasks you place in the High or Normal (medium) priority sections of your MYN task list should be *tasks you would consider working on now*. These tasks I label together as *Now Tasks*; they were first described in Lesson 1. I repeat a figure from that lesson below (Figure 4.1). It shows where Now Tasks sit on your newly configured TaskPad/To-Do Bar in Windows Outlook (the Mac shows urgency zones separately as shown in Figure 4.2 ; you cannot view the Now Tasks list in one list).

What I mean by "consider working on now" is this: they are relevant for current goals, events, and priorities and can be acted on now as stand-alone tasks. They include typical to-do's that need to be done as soon as possible; tasks from yesterday you did not complete; and High priority tasks that must be done today. The only thing stopping you might be time or perhaps circumstance: you do not have enough time to do them now, or you might need to

Figure 4.1
The MYN task list
and urgency zones
in Windows Out-
look, once config-
ured in Lesson 3.

Now Tasks

Full MYN Task List

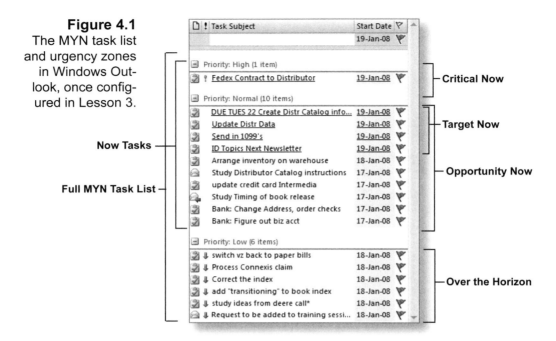

Figure 4.2
On the Mac, the three MYN urgency zones correspond to three
named Smart Folders shown at left, as configured in Lesson 3.

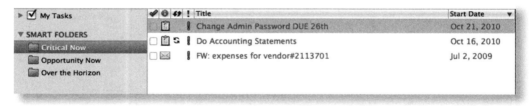

see someone to do the task. But any one of these tasks should be eligible to do
now given enough time, the right location, or the right person.

As a contrasting example, you would not list all the tasks leading up to the
future completion of a project, because many are dependent on other actions
happening first, and so you cannot act on them now. Those dependent tasks
would just clutter the list. Instead, use a separate way to plan and schedule
future project tasks (see the section titled The MORE Task in Lesson 6 for one
way). What you *would* put on the Now Tasks list is the very *next* step of that
project that you *can* take action on *now*.

Note: *More discussion of next steps and next actions is provided in Lesson 6. And more
discussion of project management is provided in Lesson 12.*

No More Daily Tasks in MYN

In the first edition of this book, the task list simply showed what I called "Daily Tasks." This was a terminology relatively consistent with many other systems. However, starting with the second edition, I no longer use that term. A couple of things happened to change my terminology and approach:

▶ The term Daily Tasks in most other systems means tasks you *intend to do today;* but that is not what the Now Tasks list represents. While Now Tasks include those, Now Tasks also include tasks you would only like to *consider* doing today but you know you may not get to until later this week or early next. This is a subtle but very important distinction that matches better how we work.

▶ Also, Microsoft coopted the term Daily Tasks in Outlook 2007/10. In those versions, at the bottom of the Calendar, Outlook displays a task list called Daily Tasks. However that list does not contain MYN Now Tasks; see Appendix A for an overview of Outlook 2007/10 Daily Tasks.

No Christmas Trees in August

Similarly, you would not display tasks on your Now Tasks list that only make sense to do on some future date, tasks that you would never consider doing now. You would not display "Decorate the Christmas Tree" on the list in August. More realistically, you would not place "Write the Friday status report" on the list the previous Monday. Tasks like this would only clutter the list and weaken it. You *would* include tasks you did not complete from previous days, if they still make sense to do now. Again, *Now Tasks are tasks currently eligible for action now* (I will discuss future-dated tasks below).

Figure 4.1 shows how Outlook's three built-in priorities for tasks — High, Normal, and Low — map to the Now Horizon urgency zones discussed in Lesson 1. Tasks in the first of those priority sections, the High priority section, are called Critical Now tasks. Let's talk about that priority and how best to manage tasks there.

Critical Now (Must-Do-Today) Tasks: Identify Them Early, Do Them Early

In this system there is a lot of emphasis on High priority Outlook tasks. This is important because, in this system, a High priority setting indicates what I call *Critical Now* tasks, as explained fully in Lesson 1 (in the first edition they were called Must-Do-Today tasks, a term still viable today).

One of the first things you will notice in Windows Outlook, when you start adding tasks to the newly configured TaskPad/To-Do Bar, is that High priority tasks pop to the top of the task list, in their own group. That's to

Fixing the Priority Group Sort Order (Windows)

If after using the TaskPad/To-Do Bar with the Lesson 3 configurations you find your Priority:High group is not above the Priority:Normal group, the priority group sort order is off. This is easy to disturb, since clicking anywhere on the TaskPad/To-Do Bar header will re-sort the list. To fix it, click once on the black exclamation point (!) at the left end of the header of the TaskPad/To-Do Bar task list (see figure).

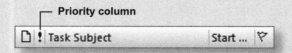

Clicking that black exclamation point should move the Priority:High group to the top. Be careful not to arbitrarily click that header bar from now on. If you do, however, a few well-placed clicks on the header should fix it.

emphasize their critical importance. In the Mac they have their own Smart Folder.

Note: If setting priorities on Outlook tasks is new to you, review the Lesson 2 section entitled How to Set Outlook Priorities on Tasks.

You Can Shorten Your Workday

This High priority group is enormously useful. Establishing and using a Critical Now (Must-Do-Today) tasks list will actually *shorten your workday*. Why? Because it helps prevent a common problem that many very busy people experience, the working late syndrome. Let me explain this by sharing how it first helped me.

In 2002, just before I developed this system, I moved from a consulting role in a large company called Accenture into the role of Vice President of Technology for a new Accenture spin-off company. At that company I found myself consistently putting in 12-hour workdays, and I was not happy about that. After a little self-analysis I found one root cause was that I tended to start work on important actions only after I got out of all my daily meetings, usually around 5 p.m. Before 5 p.m., I did not really know all that was due *that day*. It was not until I finally examined my meeting notes, my sticky notes, my various to-do lists (and maybe my Inbox) that I usually discovered a number of critical deliverables for the day. As a result, a major portion of my workday actually *started* at 5, and I had to work late nearly every day to get those tasks done. Of course I wrote this off to the reality of all the meetings a senior executive tends to have. But actually, that was not the core problem.

Virtual Assistant

One way to illustrate the core problem is this. If I had an assistant who chased me around all day and collected my commitments, and then reminded me throughout the day of some key things I promised to complete that day, I probably would complete those tasks earlier. Knowing and seeing the list early and consistently, I would make the time to ensure that my promises were completed before my preferred departure time.

What I recognized is that without clear focus, I became a bit lazy about working tasks during the day. Instead I just went to meetings, reacted to phone calls and interruptions, and attended to my BlackBerry or e-mail, all day long. I consistently expected I would dig out of my task commitments later, after the hustle and bustle of the day had ended. By doing this, however, I was letting lower-priority items rule my day and ignoring my high-priority commitments. And I was extending my workday.

Without an assistant, how might I have ensured a more appropriate focus? This sort of focus on current important commitments for the day is exactly what the Critical Now process and configurations give you: a way to clearly record and easily see at a glance what your critical list for today is and to facilitate getting items on that list done early. I cannot emphasize enough how useful this is.

The Critical Now (Must-Do-Today) Process

The Critical Now process is simple, deceptively so. From prior days, and then early in this day and throughout the day, identify urgent things that absolutely must get done today. Enter them as tasks in Outlook (configured as in Lesson 3), and mark them with a High priority and today's date in the Start Date field. Reserve the High priority only for these items. Then, throughout the day, glance at that list often, perhaps even hourly, and ensure that you get all High priority tasks done as early as possible. To work those tasks, use either dedicated task time or gaps in your day. If necessary, use part of your lunchtime or time freed up by skipping a low-value meeting. Just try to get them done early. That way, when the normal end of your workday arrives, your critical commitments are done. If you decide to stay late at that point, you do so only to work on *discretionary* tasks, not because you *have* to stay. With this new process, you will likely be able to leave work on time most days of the week, if you so choose.

Knowledge that using the system will get me out early is what makes this aspect of the system self-sustaining for me; when I look at my Critical Now task list I think to myself, "If I get these done I can leave work on time today." It is incredibly motivating. This also motivates me to find and write these tasks down; I become somewhat obsessive about identifying them since I know these are what may sabotage a reasonably timed exit later in the day.

By the way, when you do get these tasks done early, you have a sense of being ahead of the curve, which is a very nice feeling to have. It changes your whole work attitude and greatly reduces your level of stress at work.

Also, by creating this list early in the day and managing it throughout the day, you should be able to tell early if your critical list really will exceed your capacity to complete it that day. That gives you time to reach out to stakeholders early and get permission to extend their deadlines, or reach a compromise on the delivery. This avoids the sickening anxiety that can occur when the day's true deadlines tumble down on you late in the day, and it prevents an angry line of stakeholders from forming at your desk when you are trying to leave.

Do Not Abuse

But be sure not to abuse this High priority category. It is easy to move items into the High priority section just because you are enthusiastic about them. This category is only for urgent items that must be completed today. Here is a simple test. Ask yourself, "Would I work late tonight to complete this item if it is not complete by the normal end of the workday?" If the answer is "no," then do not mark it High priority. Instead, mark it Normal (medium) priority. I'll explain use of the Normal and Low priority sections in a moment.

Again, be conservative when using High priority. If a High priority task remains in that section for two or more days straight, what does that tell you about how seriously you are taking the phrase "must do today"? I usually have only two or three items in that section, perhaps occasionally up to five. If you have more I suspect you have lost the point of the Critical Now section.

Task Importance

Maintaining the count small in the High priority section is essential; overloading it artificially will destroy its utility. One reason many new users load up the High priority section with too many tasks is they confuse the must-do-today concept with the thought "This is important to me." Unless it is time-critical for today, keep it out of the High section.

Some tasks are important but not urgent, however, and that's good to know too. In this system those tasks are described as having high *intrinsic importance*. They link strongly to your goals and values. I have other ways to treat those, explained fully at the very beginning of Lesson 12; you'll get there soon enough. But for now, unless tasks have an urgent deadline of today, keep them out of the High priority section of the MYN system.

Critical Now Next Actions

Another reason people load up nonactionable items in their Critical Now section that linger from day to day is they fail to delineate a task's next action, and thereby they put too large an item in the High section. You'll learn more about next actions in Lesson 6, but for now know that it is better to define for today only the small portion of a large task that you know you can and need to get done today. So instead of writing Quarterly Report Project, write Send E-mail to Team about Quarterly Report. That task you can knock off quickly and it really may be the only part of the project that is urgent for today. Again, Lesson 6 will teach you more about this concept.

Most Tasks Do Not Have Deadlines

Now that you have done the configurations in Lesson 3, note that the Due Date field is not shown in the MYN task list, just the Start Date field. "What's up with that?" you might ask. Here's why that configuration is used.

Somewhere during the history of task management training, someone created a rule that says, "If you do not assign a due date to a task it won't get done." That rule sounds good, doesn't it? It sounds so *proactive*. That is why nearly all automated task systems include a due date field. But as I mentioned in the Introduction, this is not a good rule. Why? Because the way the rule is usually used, which is to set *artificial* due dates on most tasks, it is an attempt to trick yourself, and you are not so easily tricked. It reminds me of the people I once knew who set their wristwatch ahead ten minutes thinking it would help them be on time to meetings. In reality, it only worked for a couple days and then the person just mentally adjusted and started being late to meetings again. You do the same with artificial due dates; you just start to ignore them.

Also mentioned in the Introduction is that artificial due dates can actually lead to more missed deadlines, because as you start to skip deadlines that you know are false, you suffer from the "cry wolf" phenomenon. Since most of your tasks have fake due dates you get used to skipping them, and then you may not recognize a true due date when you see it, and you may skip it. Like Little Red Riding Hood, you get eaten alive, but in this case by missed deadlines.

That does not mean you should not apply a true deadline to those tasks that really have them, particularly those imposed from the outside (from your client or boss for example); there *are* appropriate times to set true deadlines. But you will not be using the Outlook Due Date field to do so; you will use other approaches. I will show you how to do that just ahead. For now, note that the kinds of tasks you should put on your Now Tasks list are small, next-step or next-action tasks. These are small actions toward larger goals, and these kinds of intermediate-step tasks usually do not have hard deadlines; so please don't set them artificially. Instead, use the next technique: set a *start date*.

Always Set a Start Date

While most next-step style tasks do not have hard deadlines, most *do* have approximate time frames for when they are best acted on. As part of this system I want you to use the *Start Date* field in Outlook to indicate that approximate time frame, and that's why the Start Date field is exposed on the MYN task list in this system. In fact, I want you to apply a start date to *all* Now Tasks; do not leave any tasks on the MYN task list with a date set to None.

There are two good reasons to put a start date on all Now Tasks:

► To tell you when to *first start considering* the task, so you can approximately schedule it to appear on your Now Tasks at the right time.

► To support something I call the FRESH Prioritization approach to Opportunity Now (Normal priority) tasks.

Using the Start Date Field versus the Due Date Field

Readers of the first edition of this book may recall I previously used the Outlook *Due Date* field to indicate the date I wanted to consider doing the task. That worked also, and the reason it worked is, in spite of the name "due date," I instructed readers *not* to treat it like a hard deadline. I asked them to treat it like a start date, just as described above. That is also how I taught it in my seminars. That old usage is effectively the same as described above. It really doesn't matter which field you use as long as you treat it as a start date. It actually worked better at that time because it made it easier to convert daily tasks to master tasks, which were emphasized in that system. However, master tasks are no longer factored into this new system, at least not in the same way.

Here's another reason. In the older version of the book I was trying to help readers who were FranklinCovey users transition from the FranklinCovey software, which focuses on the Due Date field, and I wanted to keep it consistent. But I am no longer concerned about that.

So if they can be used in the same way, why switch to the Start Date field? Over the years since that first edition, I have found the Start Date field actually works better in Outlook. Here's why. First, the name of the Start Date field more closely matches what I intend that date to be used for; it is a date to *start considering* the task. So it is less confusing to teach it that way and easier for students of MYN to understand it that way. The Outlook Start Date field also works better, *technically*, with the preset date selector controls built into the new flag tool in Outlook 2007/10 (shown in Lesson 2). For example, if you defer a task to Next Week using those flag controls, the Start Date field is set to next Monday, as you would expect. However the Due Date field is set to *Friday*; if the Due Date field were your guiding field, this would definitely *not* be what you wanted. So with Outlook 2007/10, the Start Date field now is the best field, both technically and with regard to meaning. And it also works fine as the key date field in earlier Outlook versions.

Those two factors are where the most value in dating tasks comes from. I'll talk about the first of these immediately below; the FRESH Prioritization technique is addressed in its own section further below.

Decide When to Start Considering a Task

I wish I could do most tasks immediately when I think of them, and I would, if only I had infinite available time. Why do I like to do tasks immediately? There is an energy associated with a task the moment I think of it that helps define it, that helps me start it, and that helps me complete it. If I put the task off, I lose that momentum. And like many people, I enjoy instant gratification; I want to do it now. But while *sometimes* I can do tasks as soon as I think of them, *usually* my workday world doesn't support that sort of spontaneity. Rather, I have promises to keep that day, or higher-priority items to do first, and so I need to focus on those. Instead I put the new, inspired task on my task list for later action. Or maybe the task was imposed by someone else and I really do not want to do it now, so I mark it for later action. On the task list I indicate approximately when I hope or intend to get to it. Sometimes it's later today, but usually it is some later day or week.

By "when I hope or intend to get to it," I usually mean the day I want to consider doing it, or first start thinking about doing it. Wording it that way recognizes this: I am not committing to doing it on that day. It's not that I am afraid of commitments; rather, I feel commitments should be used only with true deadlines. I don't make a firm commitment on a task like this because I know I cannot "do it all." I know I'll always think of more to do than I can do, I will always bite off more than I can chew. I expect your world is like that as well. As professionals and dynamic individuals, that is natural. And as a result, you will often be delaying nondeadline tasks to later, as other more important or more inspired items drop in ahead of them. I feel it is okay to delay tasks without hard deadlines; priorities and inspirations change and you should react accordingly to the new priorities. Feel no regrets when you delay such a task (again, I'll discuss how to schedule tasks with true hard deadlines in a moment; these are treated differently in this system).

Note: *Once you enter a date in the Start Date field I recommend you ignore the Outlook Due Date field. In all cases Outlook will populate it automatically, behind the scenes; the MYN system just ignores that. And again, please do not try to use the Due Date field as a hard deadline field; since it always auto-populates, there is no way to tell that you purposely entered a date there. Other techniques are shown below.*

So from now on when you create a task, think of approximately when you would like to consider doing the task, and write that in the Start Date field. This is when the task will appear on the Now Tasks list, which means this is when the task will be included in the list of tasks you consider that day. Then when you work your tasks that day you will weigh it against the other things on your list and see if, given the shifting priorities and urgencies of the day, it makes sense to do it. If not, it will forward on to the next day.

The Growing Opportunity Now Tasks List

As I said earlier, in an environment with constantly changing priorities, it is likely that when the day comes that you want to work a task (the start date), other urgent events may take over part or much of your day and you will not get it done, and that is okay. In our Lesson 3 configurations, tasks not completed automatically forward to the next day. This is expected; it happens a lot in real life, and so it is an important design element in this system. That's why it is best to think of the start date not as the day you *must* do the task, but rather think of it as the day you want to *first consider* doing the task, knowing that it is likely to forward on after it appears. Remember, this is a guilt-free system.

Of course, as uncompleted tasks remain on your list from day to day, and you add new tasks each day, your list will grow. Particularly once you start converting action e-mails to tasks, your list will grow very rapidly. You will quickly reach a list size that is larger than what you can possibly consider in a given day. And that is good, to a point. It is good because you want your Opportunity Now list to be a reasonably large-size list of tasks that you can pick from using your business intuition about what is best to do that day. Having a choice like that increases the chance that you are picking the highest-priority things to do that day. This works well as a way to allow you to get the most important work done each day, by having your prioritized list of top *candidate* tasks visible at all times and reviewed daily.

But you do not want your Opportunity Now list to get *too* large. If you have too many tasks there, you will not scan the whole list every day and some important tasks may get dropped. And you may find the large size demoralizing. You need to keep the size of that list reasonable enough that it is not impossible to review and consider in one brief scan. I think 20 tasks is the ideal upper limit for an Opportunity Now list.

Prioritize by Keeping Your Opportunity Now List at a Reasonable Size

So that raises a question. Once I reach 20 items do I stop adding tasks? No, absolutely not; you have to keep moving forward in life, keep the momentum of new ideas and passions going. So instead of stopping new tasks and ideas, you now need to start prioritizing your current and new tasks so that the 20 items left on your Opportunity Now list are your *best* ones, given current work priorities. You need to shorten it back down to 20 or so. Comprehensive strategies to keep it at about 20 are discussed in Lesson 9 about Strategic Deferrals. A simple approach to use now is this: Delete, Delegate, Defer.

Deleting Tasks

If a task has lost all life, certainly delete it. But don't spend a lot of time fretting over whether it is dead or not. If you cannot decide, keep it. I do not delete tasks unless I am confident they are dead.

Delegating Tasks

Obviously, if you have staff or team members to delegate to and can do so, take advantage of them as a way to lighten your workload and reduce your effort on large tasks. But note this, you still need to track delegated tasks and you are ultimately responsible for them, so delegating does not really remove an entry from your list, it just reduces the amount of work you need to expend on it. Techniques for tracking delegated tasks are discussed in Lesson 10.

Deferring Tasks: Setting Task Start Dates in the Future (Simplified)

A key part of the system configurations you just made in Lesson 3 is this: if you set a start date in the future on a task, the task will disappear from the MYN tasks list and remain out of sight until that date arrives. This is a great way to keep your Now Tasks list small, focused, and doable. Just schedule into the future those tasks that you can postpone to a day best suited to work them. The task will appear at its appropriate date. I call this Strategic Deferral and it is fully covered in Lesson 9. For now, a simplified version of this is to set the start date ahead for any task you know is best worked on a *specific* future date, keeping the priority at Normal or High. You change the start date by editing the date in the Start Date field.

Note: Right-clicking the Follow Up flag at the right edge of any task in the Outlook 2007 To-Do Bar can be used as a quick way to set the defer date on a task.

Windows: Viewing Future-Dated Tasks

Once you defer a number of tasks, you may at times want to view what's coming in the future. Unfortunately you cannot see them by clicking a future date on the mini-calendar above the TaskPad/To-Do Bar; that changes the calendar view but not the tasks list view. Rather, if you want to see future-dated tasks, go to the Tasks folder (to a default view there), and sort on Due Date by clicking Due Date in the header. You can see all tasks there, and the due date is usually equal to the start date, so this is a good estimate. However, it is not entirely accurate and the view is a bit messy, so I provide instructions for a custom view in Lesson 12 that is better and uses the Start Date field; it's called MYN All Now Tasks.

Note: For now, if you know how to add fields, feel free to add the Start Date field to the default Tasks folder view, called Simple List.

Mac: Viewing Future-Dated Tasks

On the Mac, the way to see future-dated tasks is to simply click on the Tasks icon in the Navigation Pane above the Smart Folders section. Then sort on the Start Date field by clicking the header of that column.

Why the Underlined Tasks in Windows

By the way, when a deferred task's start date arrives and it appears on your list, it appears at the top of its priority section and in Windows it is *underlined*. This is a result of the configurations you did in Lesson 3, when you stipulated that all tasks with a start date of today should be underlined. One reason for that configuration is this: when a deferred task pops into your list, you might not notice it. By underlining all tasks with a start date of today, you are more likely to notice a deferred task that pops in fresh that day. There are additional reasons for that underlining rule, and I will describe those in Lesson 9.

Don't Defer Too Many High or Medium Tasks

You do not want to defer all excess tasks to the future as High or Normal (medium) priority tasks, as they will just catch up with you then and load up your Now Tasks list again. Reserve this approach only for tasks that have a fairly firm day when they will become important or more easily done. That won't be too many, so you need another way to get tasks out of the medium-priority section. That way, for now, is to convert them to Over-the-Horizon tasks using the Low priority setting.

Converting Tasks to Over-the-Horizon Tasks

Using the "Low" Priority Section

Another form of deferral is to convert tasks to Over-the-Horizon tasks (long term tasks) for periodic review as a group. In the first edition of this book I instructed readers to use a *master tasks list* to do that. As you will see in Lesson 9, I now teach a number of other processes to accomplish the same goals that are much better. But before you get there, for now, I want you to use the *Low priority section* of the MYN task list to store long-term, Over-the-Horizon tasks. Use that section as a way to indicate a task that you do not need to think about for a while, one without a specific future action date. Referring to Lesson 1, this is the same as tossing the tasks over the Now Horizon. And you'll see in Lesson 9 this is pretty close to the remainder of the Strategic Deferral process, but not quite; this is simpler and sufficient for now.

Over-the-Horizon Task Process

Here is how you do this. When your Normal priority list (the Opportunity Now list) gets too long, identify a few tasks in the Normal section that you do not need to think about again for a week or two or more, and move them down to the Low priority section. Due to the FRESH Prioritization system, described ahead, these are likely the tasks at the bottom of your Normal priority section.

Later, every week or so, review the Low priority list to see if anything in that section needs attention. This means that the Low priority section should be *reserved* for such tasks; don't put tasks you intend to work today or this week there.

This process should serve you well for a while, but it is really a temporary solution. Eventually the Low priority section will become too large to easily review weekly. No worries. You'll replace this process when you get to Lesson 9.

Summary of Managing Your TaskPad/To-Do Bar Task List

Here is a summary of the steps you will take as you add to and edit your Now Tasks list.

► Place only those tasks on the Now Tasks list (the High and Normal priority sections) that you could consider working on now. That usually means tasks with a deadline of today (High priority, Critical Now tasks) and tasks you would like to consider working but know you may not get to for up to a week or so (Normal priority, Opportunity Now tasks).

► If the Now Tasks list (the High and Normal priority list) gets too large, try deleting or delegating first. If that is not possible, defer any with logical specific future dates by setting the start date ahead. Move tasks without specific future action dates (probably most of them) that you can put off for a week or two (or more) to the Low priority section (just reset the priority; they will move automatically). Do that until you have 5 or fewer High priority tasks, and 20 or fewer Normal priority tasks.

► Review Critical Now tasks every hour or so. Review Opportunity Now tasks at least once a day. And review the Low priority section once a week. Low priority tasks are your Over-the-Horizon tasks, tasks tossed over the Now Horizon so they are out of sight most of the time. But you do need to check in weekly to see if their importance has increased.

Moving excess tasks to the Low priority section is also a key part of the FRESH Prioritization approach, covered next.

■   ■   ■

The FRESH Prioritization System

Prioritizing within the Opportunity Now Section

High priority or Critical Now (must-do-today) tasks always take precedence and presumably are completed each day, so they do not tend to build up. In contrast, Normal (medium) priority tasks (also called Opportunity Now tasks) are discretionary and *do* tend to build up from day to day, and that's okay as long as you keep that list to about 20 tasks total, using the techniques above. Even with a list of 20, you probably need a way to indicate which ones are most important so you know which ones to do first. And if you let your list grow longer, you definitely want to prioritize it, so you know which ones to remove first. That is where the FRESH Prioritization system comes in — to prioritize the Normal priority or Opportunity Now section of your task list using a system that keeps newer, fresher, more energized tasks at the top of your list. In fact, the word FRESH spells out this approach: Fresh Requests Earn Sorting Higher. More on that below.

As you will see, the FRESH Prioritization system is nearly automatic; there is very little for you to do. But it is what makes the system usable and successful day after day, week after week. And it is one thing that helps keep this system guilt-free. Here is how it works.

Two Uses of the Start Date

I stated earlier that one reason I want you to put a start date on all tasks is because of the system's FRESH Prioritization approach. In this system, the start date, if in the future, is used to determine when the task appears on your list. However, once a start date arrives and a task shows up on your Now Tasks list, the start date's role completely changes. Now the date's purpose is to show you how *old* the task is, and to allow older tasks to sort lower in your list. I am going to discuss this at length because it works so well.

Newer Tasks Sort Higher

By sorting older tasks lower in the Normal (medium) priority section you end up directing most of your attention to your newer tasks, the ones at the top of the list. This keeps the task list fresh, energized, and relevant to your latest priorities.

As I have stated earlier in the book, nearly all other systems place the *oldest* tasks at the top of the list. Those tend to be dead, unconnected to recent priorities, and guilt-laden. And while a case might be made that "if you wrote it down you should do it, even if it is old," that is not how you, as a dynamic individual, really work. Rather, as a professional and busy person, you know by now that you will never get it all done; that you or your boss will always think of more to do than you can possibly do. You live in an environment with constantly shifting priorities, interests, and preferences. This abundance of new things to do is a good thing. It keeps life dynamic, interesting, and active (and as an employee it keeps you employed).

Your newer tasks tend to reflect those latest priorities and interests. You move and advance beyond old ideas quickly, and so your older tasks tend to become less meaningful. One way to say this is that the half-life of a task is very short, and you need to recognize that.

Paper Systems Are Self-Cleaning

While finding lots of new tasks can be good, the trouble with *automated* task systems like Outlook's is that they never forget the *old* tasks, and that can lead to an overloaded task list. One good aspect of *paper* journal systems is that old tasks you lose interest in disappear into the old pages of the journal. As a result, those systems are essentially self-cleaning. But the computer never forgets. Combine your constantly expanding appetite for new things with a system that never forgets, and you have a dangerous result. The task list of an automated system just gets bigger and bigger, and quickly impossible to manage. You need a system that is essentially self-cleaning, like the old paper systems.

Older Tasks Sort Lower

The FRESH Prioritization approach is that system. It allows older tasks to scroll lower in the list and eventually scroll off the page and out of sight. You could stop prioritizing at that step if you really wanted, working from the top of your list down, but some of those old tasks are probably still important. So as part of the system I ask you to scan your whole list every day or two, and if you see anything important that has scrolled too low, set the start date back to a recent date. That will move it back to near the top. One way to state this is: older tasks need to *earn* their position near the top of your list. That is what this system accomplishes.

Note that even after prioritizing a task higher like that, as new tasks are added, it will start to drift down again. That's a good thing. It causes you to re-ask how important that old task is. Eventually you may decide to move it to the Over-the-Horizon tasks list (the Low priority section), especially if you have 20 items that seem more important. This system allows the task list that you look at daily to be time-tested as to its real value.

That's it. That is the FRESH Prioritization approach. It is simple, powerful, and effective. Study the Normal priority section of Figure 4.1 to see this in action.

Why It Is Hard to Delete Tasks

Sometimes I get this question about this method of prioritizing tasks: Why not just ask people to delete tasks they do not want? Well, the answer to that is simple: deleting is good but not sufficient as a strategy to keep your list short.

Sure, you should delete old, useless tasks. But ask someone to identify tasks that are "no longer important and are ready to delete," and I guarantee you that they will find very few.

Why? As responsible adults, we all tend to feel that if something was important enough to write down, it is important enough to do. We have trouble letting go of written tasks, even old ones. So with FRESH, you are not asked to admit that most old tasks are no longer important and to delete or downgrade them (hard to do). Rather, you are merely asked to recognize which tasks in your list are the *higher* priorities, and the rest sort themselves down and finally out of our daily view, almost by themselves, as they age.

Give this FRESH Prioritization approach a try; I think you will like it. The configurations you did earlier in Lesson 3 already support it.

Keep a Date-Sorted Task List

There is one thing you need to do to support this FRESH Prioritization approach. You need to ensure that your MYN task list remains *date sorted*, with newest start dates at top. Unfortunately, this sorting is easy to mess up, especially in Outlook 2003 and 2011; all you need to do is accidentally click the task list header bar and the sorting is gone.

To demonstrate, try this, as an example.

In Outlook 2003, in the task list header in the TaskPad, click the word TaskPad. Now look at the dates, and notice that date sorting is gone. What you just did was sort your task list (within the priority groups) alphabetically on task name.

In any Outlook version, try this: click Start Date in the task list header, and notice that the sorting reverses, with oldest dates on top, within a given priority group.

What this demonstrates is how easy it is to mess up the sorting on Outlook's task lists.

To fix misplaced sorting, click Start Date in the header once; that will re-sort on the start date. You might need to click a second time to ensure that the newest dates are at top. You can do that in any list on Windows Outlook. But on the Mac, due to a bug present as of this writing, you'll need to click on the main Tasks icon first and then click the Start Date column header to sort it.

On Windows, one way to determine, at a glance, if your sorting is correct, is to notice whether your underlined tasks are at the top of each section. If not, the sorting is off, and you should fix it by clicking the Start Date field header. You will get in the habit of noticing this, and after a while you will make a habit of avoiding stray clicks on the task list header bar. Also ensure that the High priority group is always at the top. If it is not, click on the black exclamation point in the task list header.

Managing Deadlines

How to Indicate Tasks with True Hard Deadlines

As discussed above, most small, next-step tasks do not have hard deadlines; they are intermediate steps to larger goals or projects, and it's those larger end points where the deadlines usually reside. And short of making a formal project plan, say in Microsoft Office Project, which maps out detailed task dependencies and dates for each, I have not found much value in trying to identify firm deadlines for small independent next-step tasks. The start date system described above usually works best.

But occasionally a task needs to be entered on your list that does have a firm deadline. How should you show that? Well, you might think that since you are not yet using the Due Date field, that field would be available for showing these hard deadlines. Unfortunately, for technical reasons, once the start date is set, there is no way to leave the Due Date field empty in Outlook. If you do not populate it, it always self-populates anyway with whatever is in the Start Date field. The result is there is no way to distinguish when the populated due date means something. Furthermore, if you were to ever change the start date, the due date value would automatically change by the same interval, whether your deadline moved or not. So the Outlook Due Date field is not used in this system—it's ignored.

Five Ways to Indicate Hard Deadlines

Instead I teach five alternate ways to indicate hard deadlines; pick one that works best for you and each task.

1. If the deadline is today, just set the Priority field to High; after all, the definition of a High priority task in this system is that the task must be done today. If the deadline is in the future and you do not need to start work on it till that day, set the start date to the future and mark it High.

2. If the deadline is some day in the future, but you want to start work on it before the deadline day (say you want to see it on your task list starting today), do this. Enter today's date in the Start Date field, and enter the deadline day or date at the beginning of the text in the subject line, with the word DUE in all caps. So, for example, if a final year-end report is due Friday of this week, enter "DUE FRI Final Year-End Report." If due a few weeks out, enter: "DUE Dec 26 Final Year-End Report" as shown below. Set the start date to today so you can start working on it now; in the sample below the start date is December 19.

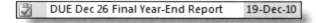

While this may seem like a rather low-tech method, it works surprisingly well as a way to keep the deadline in sight. If the deadline is this week or early next, this should be all you need to do. However, if the deadline is farther out, do this *and* consider the following.

3.   Occasionally, using the above method alone could be problematic — especially if the deadline is several weeks or more away. That's because that task may scroll off the bottom of the task list and out of sight as newer tasks fill in on top, and you may miss the actual deadline. So in these cases, in addition to doing option 2 above, try adding this optional bit of insurance: create a duplicate task with the Start Date field set to the deadline, and the Priority field set to High. Here's how this looks. First, as above, set a Normal priority task set to start today (Dec 19) with the Due date inserted in the text; see below:

Then, set a High priority task to appear on the deadline (Dec 26) as shown here:

| 🗓 ❗ Final Year-End Report | 26-Dec-10 |

This second task causes a task to pop into your Critical Now section on the day of the deadline. It is a fallback in case you lose track of the first task.

Note: *In case the task has a lot of text or attachments and you do not want to create it from scratch again, in Windows Outlook there are two quick ways to create a duplicate task in the TaskPad/To-Do Bar: (1) in Outlook 2003 and earlier, press CTRL and drag, dropping the task within the TaskPad. Or (2) in all Windows versions: right-click and drag the original task from the TaskPad/To-Do Bar to the Tasks icon on the left side of your Outlook window; choose Copy from the shortcut menu that pops up when you drop it. In both cases you'll see the duplicate task appear in the TaskPad/To-Do Bar.*

4.   The above three options, used together, are sufficient for the rare times that you need to set deadlines. But if you tend to have a lot of next-action tasks with deadlines, the above actions will start to feel like a lot of steps, particularly having to create duplicate tasks. In that case, Windows Outlook users should add the optional Deadline field to the TaskPad/ To-Do Bar, per my instructions in Lesson 12. This field does not have the problems of the Due Date field. Here is how that looks once added.

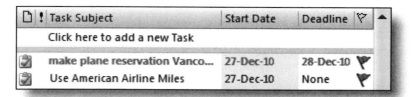

This makes life much simpler, but I only recommend doing so if you have lots of true deadlines, because it occupies valuable screen real estate. Unfortunately, Mac users cannot add this field.

5. And finally, if the deadline is a major one, you might want to place the task as an entry on your Outlook calendar. You can do this one of two ways. Make it an all-day, nonblocking appointment (use Show Time As: Free), so it sits at the top of the day for that day on the Outlook calendar but does not block out your day for other appointments (see the Finish Quarterly Report task below).

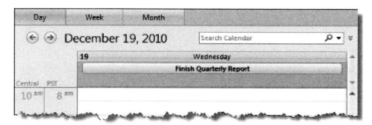

Or, if you think you might need an hour or two (or more) of final action to wrap the task up, schedule it as a blocking appointment on your calendar and label it something like: "Finalize Year-End Report." That way you have time locked in for final actions.

Feel free to use an Outlook reminder on these appointments.

These are the best ways to indicate hard deadlines for Outlook tasks. Do not use the Outlook Reminder feature on tasks to mark such deadlines; it is okay to use it on appointments. See the next section for reasons why.

Note: *One word of caution, use the word DUE as described in step 2 above only if the date is a true deadline. If the date is merely a soft deadline, or a preferred date, or a date that would be nice to meet but that you might let slip when it arrives, do not use the word DUE. Otherwise you may get into a "cry wolf" routine again, and end up watering down the meaning of the word DUE; you might start ignoring it. Instead, I recommend you enter the word TARGET as text in front of such dates, using options 2 and 3 above in the same way. The word TARGET matches the meaning of our Target-Now tasks described in Lesson 1, and described more fully in Lesson 9.*

Do Not Use Reminders on Outlook Tasks

You might be tempted to use the Reminder capability of Outlook to emphasize *task* deadlines. It is good to use Outlook reminders on Outlook calendar
appointments but not on Outlook tasks — they cause problems in tasks.

*Note: That's why, in the Lesson 3 Outlook 2003 configurations, I had you turn off the
default reminders setting for new tasks.*

Reminders cause an alert window to pop up on your computer screen on
a specified day at a specified time. "What could be wrong with that?" you
might ask. Well, while reminders work well on Outlook appointments, here's
the problems they cause with tasks:

▶   The reminder date is not stable. If you try to use it to indicate a hard
deadline, this usage might fail, because unfortunately if you later change
the start date, the reminder date will change by the same interval, and
you will miss your deadline. As you recall, I encourage you to change the
start date frequently as a way to prioritize Now Tasks.

▶   It's not the right approach anyway. Reminders should only be for time-of-
day-specific items like appointments. The idea behind using a task list is
that items on that list should be worked when the right moment, energy,
situation, people, and so on, present themselves in the day. Having an
alert pop up in the middle of other activities does not make that moment
the right time to do the task. It is likely that you will ignore it anyway. At
a minimum, the reminder distracts you from other things you might be
doing. Instead, work your tasks off your list, when you have time to work
tasks, using the start date system described above. If an activity is very
time sensitive, make an appointment out of it, and set a reminder on the
appointment, as in option 5 above.

■   ■   ■

Summary: Your Task Management Steps

The long description above explains the theory and practice of how you
should manage tasks in the days ahead, now that you have configured your
MYN task list per the MYN System principles. Let's put this all together into a
clear set of steps and rules.

From now on, as you create tasks in your task list, from e-mail or other
sources, do this:

1.   Assign a High and Normal priority only to tasks you must do or would
consider doing now. These are your Now Tasks. Give must-do-today
tasks a High priority (your Critical Now tasks), and all other tasks a Normal (medium) priority (your Opportunity Now tasks).

2. Set the Start Date field of all tasks to the day you would like to start see-ing the task on your MYN task list. If it is in the future, the task will not appear on your list till that day. Do not leave any tasks with a start date of None.

3. Do not set Outlook reminders on tasks (*do* set them on appointments).

4. Set to a High priority any task due today; that means any task you would not leave work today without completing. Keep that list to five or fewer items. Work those tasks early.

5. If a task has a future deadline, but you'd like to start work on it before that deadline, set the start dater earlier, use a Normal priority, and enter DUE and the deadline date in front of the task title. Consider creating a duplicate High priority task with the start date equal to the deadline. Or use the Deadline field taught in Lesson 12 instead of either of these.

6. Complete all your High priority (Critical Now) tasks by end of day.

7. Review your Critical Now tasks about once an hour; review your Oppor-tunity Now tasks once a day; and review your Over-the-Horizon tasks once a week.

8. When reviewing your Normal priority (Opportunity Now tasks) section, if you find tasks near the bottom of the list that are important and need to be emphasized, set their start dates to a date near today. That will move them to near the top of the list. This is the FRESH Prioritization approach in action.

9. Keep the Opportunity Now section of your MYN task list no larger than about 20 items. If it gets much larger than 20, first try deleting or delegat-ing. If that is not possible, set some tasks to a future date, or better, move tasks to the Low priority section by setting their Outlook priority to Low; this is the same as tossing them over the Now Horizon as described in Lesson 1. Review your Low priority section once a week in case any tasks there become more important over time.

That's it! You have learned the core task management principles of the Master Your Now! system. Follow these principles and you will find your workday starting to come under control.

You may want to review this lesson a week from now, to make sure all the principles have "stuck."

■   ■   ■

Exercises

Create in your TaskPad/To-Do Bar four types of tasks as described below, paying attention in particular to start date and priority. Item number 4 will require more than delineating just start date and priority.

1. Enter a task you would like to start today.

2. Enter a task absolutely due today.

3. Enter a task you would like to start working on tomorrow.

4. Enter a task absolutely due next Wednesday that you'd like to start working on today.

Exercise Solutions

1. Enter a task you would like to start today: *Start Date equals today, Normal priority.*

2. Enter a task absolutely due today: *Start Date equals today, High priority.*

3. Enter a task you would like to start working on tomorrow: *Start Date equals tomorrow, Normal priority.*

4. Enter a task absolutely due next Wednesday that you'd like to start working on today: *Enter "DUE Wed" at beginning of subject line, and set Start Date field to today, Normal priority. Optionally, create a duplicate task with the Start Date equal to next Wednesday, and a High priority. Or instead of either of these, use the Deadline field added in Lesson 12. Or place it on your calendar for next Wednesday (and set a reminder).*

■   ■   ■

Next Steps

Start entering tasks in Outlook now, both by converting e-mails to tasks (as taught at the end of Lesson 2) and by entering them manually, say from tasks received in meetings. If you have written task lists from an older paper system, start copying them into the Outlook task system now. In general, I encourage you to start using the MYN task system; you have learned all the basics. Review this chapter as needed to keep the processes fresh as you enter and use tasks.

In the next lesson, I will focus on e-mail and on how to empty your Inbox.

Lesson 5:
The Bliss of an Empty Inbox

Introduction

I am about to describe an action, the benefits of which are almost magical. I say magical because, whenever I do it, I cannot really explain why it works so well, but it always leaves me in awe. This magical thing is emptying my Outlook Inbox. Even today, every time I do it, I am left feeling amazed. Amazed at what a difference it makes. Amazed at the refreshed feeling I experience each time, the reduction in Inbox stress, and at my resulting eagerness to move forward with my work and even to get new e-mail.

All that joy really does not make sense. After all, all I am doing is dragging a group of e-mail en masse from one folder to another. I usually don't even classify or file it into different folders. I really haven't done anything with that mail, other than having previously extracted tasks from it when I first read it, and making one last scan of titles to ensure that I didn't miss anything.

And yet a remarkable change occurs as soon as I drag the mail. All the tension and uncertainty associated with e-mail I've been getting all day instantly disappears. Questions like Have I read it all? Did I forget to reply to anyone? Is there a time bomb in here? Am I leaving something undone? All those are gone when I glance at my empty or near-empty Inbox. It clears my psyche by clearing one big block of my day's open ends.

That is such a refreshing feeling, to know there is nothing lurking in there. Emptying the Inbox provides that very clear, almost symbolic statement: "I am done with it all, and I can move on."

The Real Purpose of the Inbox

There is some history here. There is a reason why Microsoft called the place where Outlook stores your incoming mail the "Inbox." You may recall the old two- or three-level tray systems office workers used on their desks to process incoming paper mail. Some still do. While these systems varied, the top box was always called the "In Box" or "In Tray." And the meaning of this box was simple: it was where new, unprocessed paper mail and memos were placed. And the rules of most of the systems were this: as soon as you picked up and read an item from the In Tray, it never went back to the In Tray. Rather, it was filed, or disposed of, or placed in one of the lower boxes indicating that the item was "in process" or "ready to be filed." There was great value to these systems and they generally worked well if you knew how to use them.

This idea of using the Outlook Inbox in a similar way, as a place only to receive new unread items, has unfortunately been lost by most users of e-mail. The Inbox now not only has that receiving function but has also become the place to store previously read "in-process" mail that you have additional actions in mind for, as well as being a bulk filing location for old mail. No wonder the Inbox has become so useless for so many people. You just cannot mix all these functions together and hope to make sense of your e-mail.

As I stated in Lesson 1, you really want to get the Outlook Inbox back to the receiving-only function; otherwise the Inbox becomes hopelessly cluttered. A cluttered Inbox represents a congestion of unattended responsibilities. Emptying the Outlook Inbox every day relieves that congestion in a very noticeable way. It also makes you more efficient, because without clearing your Inbox you'll be constantly glancing through old mail in search of passed over to-do's and unfiled information. Emptying the Inbox helps prevent responsibilities buried in e-mail items from getting away from you. It saves you time because it allows you to clearly delineate between the mail that needs further processing and mail which you no longer need to read.

Note: Having less mail in your Inbox also helps when later using a mobile device, since it synchronizes faster and leaves you less mail to scroll through when finding new mail.

Four Ways to Empty the Inbox

There are four ways to empty the Inbox daily, only one of which I will cover in this early lesson.

▶ The first is to toss it all. This most likely is not an option for you, but I mention it for completeness and because for many people it is a partial solution.

▶ The second is to do what most people who file do, and that is to distribute mail among multiple topic-named Outlook folders. It is neat, logical, and matches what we do when we file physical papers in manila file folders.

▶ The third is to file all mail, in bulk, into one other location, either ignoring topics or optionally applying topic-like "tags" to the mail in that location. Doing the first part of this is the focus of this lesson. The latter I save for Lesson 8.

▶ And the fourth is a combination of some or all of the above.

Focus on Filing in Bulk

In this early lesson, I am only going to teach you the third of these methods, and only the first part of that: how to file in bulk. I feel this is the simplest and most practical way to empty the Inbox. Filing in bulk is a method that nearly everyone can do, and it is the quickest way to empty the Inbox every day. It also can be combined with topic filing into multiple folders, the method that many of you are doing now. And in Lesson 8, I'll show you a different topic approach that uses topic-named Outlook tags added to the bulk-filed mail. But that comes later. The very first step is simple: how to empty your Inbox every day, and declutter your life.

If You Are Already Filing Mail

If you have an existing filing system and it is working for you, *and you are emptying your Inbox every day*, you can skip the rest of this lesson and begin reading Lesson 6. You should be proud that you have mastered this and you should stick with it—there is no need to change.

Unfortunately though, many people with seemingly good filing systems in fact find it nearly impossible to empty their Inbox daily, usually because the system takes too long to do it. So if you are unable to empty your Inbox every day using your filing system, I encourage you to read on and give this new approach a try. The benefits of achieving that empty Inbox every day are just too good to pass up.

A Very Simple System: Drag All Mail to the Processed Mail Folder

A Simple Solution

The first step of the Master Your Now! (MYN) e-mail filing system, the step covered in this lesson, is so simple it is almost silly. It is just this: create one folder called Processed Mail, and every day, after you have extracted all tasks from mail in your Inbox (more on that later), and read or replied to those you want to, drag all of your mail from the Inbox to that folder. That's it! I'll discuss how to create the folder below.

In its simplest form that really is it; you merely leave all the mail in the Processed Mail folder, and you are done. There are exceptions and complications of course, which I will mention below and in Lesson 8, but they are not so bad. For most users, what I just described—simply dragging all mail to one folder—is all you need to do. It is a very quick and simple system. Now let me explain why this is so powerful.

▶ It's simple and easy to do. This ensures that you will do it every day.

▶ It gets you quick results. As you can tell, I am passionate about an unclut-tered Inbox and I want you to be able to get there quickly one or more times a day.

▶ When you leave all your old mail in the Processed Mail folder, you have all the benefits of a single date-sorted storage location for your e-mail, just like the Inbox (more on that ahead).

▶ It sets you up well for filing or tagging topics, covered in Lesson 8.

▶ And best of all, your Inbox is freshly emptied, one or more times a day (this is worthy of repeating).

Three Other Reasons to File Mail

Let's step back a moment. I have emphasized filing mail out of the Inbox pri-marily to achieve a clean and refreshed Inbox and to enjoy the benefits of that. Here are three additional reasons to file mail:

▶ To encourage you to do final processing of your Inbox every day. This is important. Just before I file my mail into the Processed Mail folder, I take one last scan of my e-mail titles. I do this to see if I missed anything; when I read new mail on and off during the day it is easy to skip some and I often do. This scan prevents me from dropping important items, whether task conversions, important replies, scheduling events, or anything else important that might arrive by e-mail. The bliss of an empty Inbox is dependent on that scan, so I make certain to do that scan.

▶ To solve any space limitations you may be reaching in your Inbox. This is the reason most people want to file or toss mail.

▶ To make it easy to find the mail you file, if you need to see it again. This is the reason most people get serious about choosing a good filing sys-tem; otherwise they would just toss away all their previously read mail. Let's talk more about this point—finding mail after it is filed—as it's a big topic.

Five Ways of Finding Mail After It Is Filed

I am a pack rat; I tend to save all my business e-mail. My theory on saving most mail is this: storage space is much cheaper than the time it takes me to confidently decide that I can throw an e-mail away. Sure, if the mail is obviously spam or junk, I delete it immediately. But if I have any hesitation about tossing a business-related item, I retain the mail and move on. My time is just too valuable, and I suspect yours is too.

This means when I go looking for mail I have quite a bit of mail to sort through. However, using the Processed Mail single-folder system, I can actually *find mail easier*. With this single-folder system, there are five different ways you can find your mail:

1. You can find it the same way you find mail now when you leave it in your Outlook Inbox: visually. One great advantage to the Processed Mail folder system is that it gives you one long list of all your mail, just like the Inbox, so you can visually scan down your e-mail list, searching backward in time. This is not such a bad way to search for mail, particularly for mail less than two or three weeks old, which is the mail you are most likely to search for on any given day. You can use dates and adjacent e-mail titles to reconstruct events and determine approximately when the mail arrived, and usually find it fairly quickly. Or you can sort on the From column (just click the column header) and search for all mail sent by a sender; that's another way we often search for mail.

   The utility of a single list of mail is one reason why I think many people do not file mail out of their Inbox. Even if they want to file it, they unconsciously know leaving it in the Inbox is a pretty good means of keeping recent mail searchable (it is just a bad place to leave mail for other reasons). Losing the power of a single list is also the main reason multiple topic-named folders for filing mail is not my preferred method; they preclude me from doing these sorts of visual one-stop searches (I list other disadvantages of using multiple topic-named folders in Lesson 8).

2. In addition to doing a visual search, you can use Outlook's search engine on the Processed Mail folder. If you use Outlook 2007/10 or Outlook for Mac 2011, this approach is excellent. In those versions, Microsoft integrated a fully indexed search engine into Outlook (called Instant Search in Windows and Spotlight in the Mac). What this means is that searches can be made blindingly fast. But even earlier versions of Outlook's search engine work adequately, albeit slowly, if you're searching in only one mail folder, as here.

3. Use a third-party, fully indexed search engine. If you are using Outlook 2003, which has a slower built-in search engine, add-in software tools are available that enable fast, fully indexed searches of your e-mail. Software like Windows Desktop Search, Google Desktop Search, and Xobni are all excellent and most are free. Or consider a high-end commercial product like X1. However, many organizations will not allow you to install third-party software on your issued corporate computer, so be sure to check with your technical staff.

4. If you are solidly set on using multiple topic-named folders, you can periodically file out of the Processed Mail folder into those folders, and

you can later search visually within those folders. Presumably you will know exactly which folder to go to when you need to.

5. Finally, if you know you need to file by topic, I hope you will consider using the Outlook Categories filing system I teach in Lesson 8 as an alternative to using multiple topic-named folders. Using this, you essentially "tag" mail items in the Processed Mail folder with topic-named categories. The categories system allows you to keep all your mail in one Processed Mail folder, thereby maintaining the visual date-based or sender-based searches described above. But it also allows you, when needed, to view all mail in virtual category groups that you can open and close, as if they were in a folder system. And you can store one e-mail item in multiple categories. To view this mail in category groups you merely click the Categories column heading. You will learn all this in Lesson 8. Other tagging options are presented there as well.

More on Topic-Based Filing

Two of the options above for finding mail rely on topic-based filing, that is, identifying a keyword to associate each mail item with, and either filing it in a folder with that name or tagging it in a bulk location. But remember that filing by topic is optional. And given the large ratio between the time consumed filing mail by topic and how often you probably search for mail, I think topic-based filing all your mail is of questionable value for most users. Given the power of e-mail search tools, especially the newer ones discussed above (and again later in this lesson), I think most people can get by with just dragging all their mail to one folder (the Processed Mail folder) and then using a search tool on it as needed. This saves a huge amount of time, time otherwise spent on topic-categorizing all the mail you get; some people spend an hour a day filing their mail, which just doesn't make sense. And in case you need help using these search tools, I'll show you how to use a few of them at the end of this lesson.

But some people or organizations need topic-based filing. And there are ways to speed up topic-based filing and make it more practical, at least for some of your mail. You can use Outlook rules to automatically tag e-mail with categories based on, for example, sender, subject, or body text keywords. And add-in software can do more intelligent tagging and filing, allowing you to auto-file entire "conversations," for example. All of that I describe in Lesson 8.

And if perhaps you like to store only a small portion of your mail by topic, by all means do that filing either before or after you store the rest of the mail in the Processed Mail folder. That can be a good compromise for those of you who have just a few key topics that need special attention. Again, that too is discussed in Lesson 8.

Emptying the Inbox—Step 1: Creating the Processed Mail Folder

But we are jumping ahead of ourselves. The purpose of this early lesson is to teach the simple art of emptying the Inbox every day. I really want you to experience that simple pleasure before you worry too much about how you are going to use topics, if at all.

The first step in emptying your Inbox is deciding where to create the Processed Mail folder. For now I suggest you make it a subfolder of your Inbox so it looks like this:

Here are the steps:

Windows Outlook

1. Go to the Navigation Pane and click the Mail banner button or icon.

2. Right-click the Inbox.

3. Choose New Folder from the shortcut menu.

4. In the dialog box that opens type "Processed Mail" as the folder name. Leave all other settings as is, and click OK.

Outlook for Mac 2011

1. Go to the Navigation Pane and click the Mail banner button or icon.

2. If you have a small arrow to the left of your Inbox, toggle it so you can see account names or locations below. Find your main account (it's probably the top one) and use it in the next step. If no account names are below the Inbox, then focus on the Inbox itself in the next step.

3. CTRL-click the item in step 2.

4. Choose New Folder from the shortcut menu.

5. A folder is created with the name Untitled selected; replace that with the name "Processed Mail" and press ENTER or RETURN.

Note: Windows and Mac, if you have many other Inbox subfolders, consider placing an underscore in front of the P, to drive it to the top of the list: "_Processed Mail." Or use some other symbol.

The above is a quick way to get started on using the Processed Mail folder. For advanced users or those with more time, I invite you to read a full discussion of Outlook folders in Appendix A. There you will find complete coverage of strategies for the best place to put your Processed Mail folder, ones that include getting mail off the Exchange system to beat any space issues you might have there. But try this quick solution for now and start emptying your Inbox into the Processed Mail folder per the points below. I think you will like it. You can always study Appendix A later. And if you currently have Exchange space issues, see the Note after step 6 in the next section; that may work for now.

Next, you need to copy mail into this new folder. Here's how.

Step 2: Filing into the New Processed Mail Folder

The workflow for sending mail to the Processed Mail folder follows.

As you read mail in your Inbox:

1. If the mail is obviously junk, delete it. If not junk, just save it; your time is too valuable to spend much time deciding.

2. If the mail has an action (or appointment) associated with it, copy it to a task (or appointment). You saw a quick way to do that at the end of Lesson 2. I cover it more fully in Lesson 7. If the action is quick (under a minute), like a quick reply, just do it now instead.

3. Repeat the above every time you read new mail throughout the day; optionally categorize and drag the mail to the Processed Mail folder.

Then, at the end of the day, process any remaining mail:

4. Optional: if you are using Outlook Categories (Lesson 8), apply categories to mail remaining in the Inbox.

5. All users, take one more scan through your e-mail titles to make sure you did not miss anything important.

6. Drag remaining mail to the Processed Mail folder.

That's it, your mail is filed, and your Inbox is empty! Do this every day. I do it several times a day.

Note: *Since for this introduction you created the Processed Mail folder as a subfolder of the Inbox, here's an important point: if your Exchange mailbox has size limits you will periodically need to drag mail from the bottom of the date-sorted Processed Mail folder to some off-server location; perhaps create a folder there called Older Processed Mail to drag into. Do this just as you are doing now for your Inbox. Or read Appendix A to explore more complete alternatives.*

Start Storing Mail in the Processed Mail Folder Now

I cannot emphasize enough how important and powerful emptying your Inbox every day is. Get started on this today. If after doing that you are eager to include a topic filing system, feel free to skip ahead to Lesson 8 now to learn how to use Outlook Categories as your topic-based filing system within the Processed Mail folder. You can also read about other approaches there. Then come back and study the rest of this lesson.

If instead you want to save time and use a search tool approach within the Processed Mail folder (my current favorite method), read on; I explain those below. Or if you already know how to use the search tools built into Outlook and are happy with them, you can skip the remainder of this lesson and move on to the next.

Assuming you do want to use this single-folder filing system (with or without categories), how do you transition from what you are doing now?

Transitioning

From a Multiple-Folder-Based Filing System

If you are already using a multiple-folder-based filing system for e-mail, you may wonder what my recommendations are for transitioning to a single folder–based system. My primary recommendation is this: start fresh. There is no reason you cannot add a Processed Mail folder to your existing multiple-folder system and start using it with mail that is currently in your Inbox. Then retain your current system for the old mail you have already filed.

I realize this splits your stored mail for a while, but note the useful life of most old mail passes fast; in no time the only old mail that you'll be looking at will be the mail filed in the Processed Mail folder, and your old multifolder-based filing will be a rarely touched system. At some point you will feel confident to archive that system and refer only to your Processed Mail folder.

From No Filing System

If you do not have a filing system, chances are good that your Inbox is quite overcrowded with months of old mail. How do you get started? Do you need to commit to extracting tasks from all of your months of old mail before dragging it to the Processed Mail folder? My answer is no.

Again, what I recommend is to take a fresh start. In this case, I recommend picking a date one week ago and dragging all mail older than that to the Processed Mail folder immediately. Mail newer than that you should commit to processing into your Processed Mail folder immediately, extracting tasks as you do so. Now you have an empty Inbox! Make a note of that processing cutoff date.

Then, as time allows in the days ahead, dip into the older mail in the Processed Mail folder and extract more tasks, doing at least one full day at a time, and note the date on which you stop again each day, so you can start below that the next time you come back to this task.

But doing this additional processing is purely optional; it is likely that embedded tasks older than a few weeks have diminished in importance anyway, or have been communicated again.

These steps enable what is most important: that you empty your Inbox quickly, start extracting tasks, and start experiencing the benefits of an empty Inbox. Then keep emptying the Inbox every day.

One last point. If you are going to process much of your older mail, you might want to skip ahead and study Lesson 7 completely before spending too much time. There you will find thorough coverage of all the various ways to convert action e-mails to tasks. Also, study the end of that lesson for more transitioning suggestions. But first, read on below to see how to *search* your newly filed mail.

Using Search Tools with the Processed Mail Folder

I discussed above the five ways to find mail once you store it in bulk in the Processed Mail folder. For most of us, using a search tool will be all you need to know. The tool built into Outlook 2007/10 and 2011 is nearly perfect. So in the rest of this lesson, I am going to describe how to use Outlook's built-in search tools: Instant Search (Outlook 2007/10) and Spotlight (Outlook for Mac 2011). If you already have a search tool in use, and are happy with it, you can skip the rest of this lesson.

I am also going to cover Find for Outlook 2003. But if you are using Outlook 2003, I hope you can and will add a third-party indexed search tool like I mentioned earlier. Here is a list of popular ones for your reference; sources for each are listed in Appendix C:

Third-Party Tools for Outlook 2003 Search

► X1 (paid)

► Windows Search (free)

► Google Desktop (free)

► Xobni (free and paid version)

Still, if due to company policy you cannot install such software, using the Find search tool built into Outlook 2003 may do the job for you.

Using the Outlook 2007/10 Instant Search Tool

Let's start with my favorite, the Outlook 2007/10 Instant Search tool. Mac and Outlook 2003 users, note this section on Outlook 2007/10 is long, so skim ahead until you find the write up for your version.

History of Windows Outlook 2007/10 Instant Search

A little history on this tool is in order. Microsoft introduced Instant Search as a totally new Outlook search engine in Outlook 2007. Actually, it was not completely new since it was based on the same search engine used in Windows Desktop Search, which came out well before Outlook 2007. Windows

Desktop Search was an optional add-in to the older PC operating system Windows XP. It is still available under the name Windows Search, and it enables searching all files and e-mail on your Windows XP computer. Before Outlook 2007 and Vista came out, I used Windows Desktop Search regularly, and it worked relatively well, but I never really liked the user interface. In Outlook 2007 and 2010, however, Microsoft has integrated the e-mail portion of that search engine very effectively into Outlook. Microsoft also integrated the file search portion of Windows Desktop Search into Vista and Windows 7. In fact, these days it's all one tool again; the indexing service engine built into later versions of Windows is used by Outlook for its searches. And in the midst of this evolution, Microsoft also improved the user interface considerably. You will now see search boxes throughout the latest versions of Windows and a search box inside the latest versions of Outlook, and they are really the same indexed search tool, just searching for different things. And with the unified interface they are now a pleasure to use.

Note: *While Instant Search is included with every Outlook 2007/10 package, in some circumstances it must be activated. Look for the command Click Here to Enable Instant Search just below the Search box in Outlook. If it's not there, and you see no search box, or if the extra fields described in the section ahead called Narrowing Your Search are grayed out, then check with your IT department to fully activate it. Also note that if you are using Windows XP and try to activate Instant Search in Outlook 2007/10, you may be directed to install Windows Desktop Search first, since it provides the core indexing engine in XP. Vista and Windows 7 users, make sure you have not turned off Indexing Service on your computer for some reason; that will disable Outlook Instant Search.*

How to Use Windows Outlook 2007/10 Instant Search

In Outlook 2007, the tool sits inconspicuously to the right of the folder name at the top of the current folder contents; you might not even notice it is there. In Figure 5.1 it is the box with the words Search Inbox inside.

In Outlook 2010, Instant Search sits above the current folder contents, and depending on how wide your Outlook window is, it can occupy the full width of that space (see Figure 5.2).

Like all good modern search engines, the tool works by first indexing your mail, which means it builds invisible tables of the locations of every word in every e-mail; that's why searches are so fast. Building this table ahead of time takes time, so when you first install the program it will spend hours working in the background doing this indexing. Mine took almost a day to complete, since I save so much old mail. Don't worry, this will not slow your computer significantly, and it automatically stops when you start using the computer. After it is complete, as you add more mail, it indexes only the new mail as it comes in, almost instantly. However, if you rearrange all your folders one day, it will take quite a while to re-index everything in their new locations.

Instant Search box

Figure 5.1
Outlook 2007
Instant Search
box.

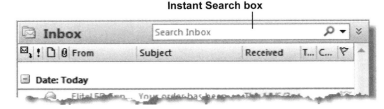

Instant Search box

Figure 5.2
Outlook 2010
Instant Search
box.

Using Instant Search for Basic Searches in Windows Outlook 2007/10

Once you click inside the search box, the entire folder header lights up in orange, indicating the search tool is ready for you to use. And in Outlook 2010, the Search Ribbon tab becomes visible. Type your search term in the box, and depending on the settings (discussed below), the results either show up immediately when you pause typing, or when you click the magnifying glass icon at the right end of the search field. The results *replace* the mail previously displayed in the folder. To clear the results and see all your mail again, click the Close button (**x**) that replaces the magnifying glass after a search; the orange coloring goes away to confirm that you are back to your full folder contents again.

Changing the Index Settings

If you have lots of old mail in many different Personal Folders groups, one thing you may want to do is expand or restrict the personal folders being indexed. Restricting it can save time during the initial installation, which can help you get started on searching more quickly that day. And it reduces subsequent indexing efforts if you move folders around.

To do that in Outlook 2007, first click the drop-down arrow at the right edge of the search box, and the menu shown in Figure 5.3 appears. This is the main Instant Search menu. From that menu choose Search Options… and a dialog box called Search Options opens. At the top of that dialog box (in the section called Indexing) you can control which data files are indexed. This will list your Exchange mailbox if you have one, and then any personal folders file

groups you might have. It may even include SharePoint servers if your organization has those. Select or clear the check boxes to suit your search needs,
keeping them to the smallest set you may need.

In Outlook 2010 it's more complicated. First, click once in the Instant Search
box to activate the Search tab in the Ribbon, and then click the Search Tools
drop-down menu at the right end of the tab as shown in Figure 5.4. From that
menu select Search Options… and in the window that opens click the Indexing Options button. This opens an Indexing Options dialog box that applies to
all of Windows. Select Microsoft Outlook in the list and then click the Modify
button near the bottom of the window. In the next window toggle the arrow
to the left of Microsoft Outlook, and then add or remove check marks next to
the file stores you want to index. Click OK all the way out when done.

*Note: After you confirm which check boxes are selected and click OK, Outlook may ask you
to restart Outlook before continuing.*

The Outlook 2007/10 Search Options control described above is also where
you can turn on and off the "search while typing" feature (look for the check
box with that phrase). Experiment selecting or clearing that check box to
see whether you like it. I find that given all my old mail, if I include too
many data stores in my scope of search (described below) I don't like having the search-while-typing feature on — it makes the search a bit "jumpy."

Figure 5.3
Outlook 2007
Instant Search
main menu and
Search Options.

Figure 5.4
Outlook 2010
Search Tools
menu and Search
Options.

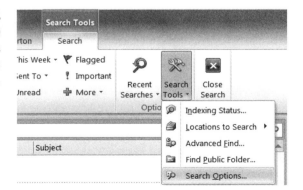

Particularly when using More fields in 2010 (discussed ahead). But with simple, one-folder-at-a-time searches, it is usually fine.

Controlling Scope of Search

Selecting a wide *index* scope as described above does not mean that all files are automatically searched at once when you actually do a search. By default, Instant Search only searches the currently open folder. This default is perfect for our MYN Processed Mail folder system, where all mail is stored in one folder.

If you do not find what you are looking for and want to search beyond the current folder, once the search is complete, Instant Search gives you an option to expand the search to more items (you'll see the phrase Try Searching Again in All Mail Items—click it to expand the search).

Instead of indicating which folders to search, another way to control the scope is to indicate which data stores and data types you want to search selectively. Here's how.

Controlling Scope of Search in Outlook 2007

In Outlook 2007 you control which data stores and types are searched using a control installed near the top of the Navigation Pane. It is separate from the main search box, so you may not notice it. Figure 5.5 is how it looks when Mail is the active data type in the Navigation Pane; note the All Mail Items banner in the middle of that figure.

That may look like a label, but it is actually an Instant Search control. Also note the magnifying glass icon to its left; that's how you know this control is associated with Instant Search. The label of this control changes when you change which data type is active in the Navigation Pane. If you want to search across all Outlook data types (Mail, Contacts, Calendar, and so on), click the Folder List button at the bottom of the Navigation Pane; doing so will change the mode of the Navigation Pane to show all Outlook data types. *Then* click that new control; it will now be labeled All Outlook Items. If you want to search on all contacts (only), click the Contacts banner button or icon first in the lower portion of the Navigation Pane to enter Contacts mode, and so on. For a discussion of the Navigation Pane and its various data type modes, see the second half of Appendix A.

This Instant Search scope control bar in the Navigation Pane also lights up in orange when you start using Instant Search. Note as soon as you click this control, whether you open it or not, you immediately expand the scope beyond the currently active folder, and your search speed will slow noticeably if you have lots of other mail. That also changes the title at the top of the search results window on the right (for example, to All Mail Items if the Navigation Pane is in Mail mode), reminding you of your search scope.

If you click the solid arrow at the control's right edge in the Navigation Pane, the list of data stores is exposed, and you can select or clear those you want included in the upcoming search (see Figure 5.6). If you do this *after* running a search, it will start the search again and update the search results in the search window.

If you find this a bit complicated, I agree. In Outlook 2010 Microsoft simplified these controls greatly.

Controlling Scope of Search in Outlook 2010

In Outlook 2010 all the search scope controls are located in the Search tab in the Ribbon menu. For simple control, look a the left edge of the Search tab and find the Scope group (see Figure 5.7). The selection there defaults to Current Folder; but you can change it in individual searches by selecting the other choices: All Subfolders, All Mail Items, or All Outlook Items. The phrase All Mail Items changes depending on whether you are in a mail, tasks, contacts, or calendar folders. Selecting All Outlook Items searches across all those data types. This is a major improvement over the Outlook 2007 interface.

If you know you always want to search all folders within a given data type (and do not want to wait until after the first search attempt to expand your search), then open the Search Options dialog box (using the menu shown in

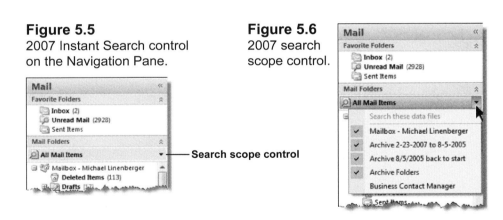

Figure 5.5
2007 Instant Search control on the Navigation Pane.

Figure 5.6
2007 search scope control.

Figure 5.7
2010 Search tab

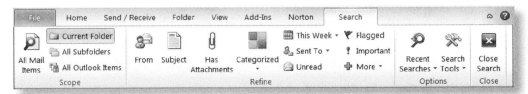

Figure 5.4) and change the Include Results Only From setting to All Folders. From now on all searches will start with a search of all folders.

To selectively change which data stores are searched do the following. From the Search tab click Search Tools, and then select Locations to Search… and then add or remove check marks against the various data files or accounts listed there. Those settings are permanent until you reset them later.

Next, I want to cover how to enhance the logic of the item terms you are searching on.

Narrowing Your Search

If all you do is type a word or phrase in the search box, you can get a pretty wide search with too many hits. If you want to narrow the logic of the search, you need to use additional controls.

In Outlook 2007 you narrow your search by opening the Query Builder; you reach it by clicking the down-pointing chevron at the right of the search box — that results in Figure 5.8. Here you can limit the search by entering additional search terms specific for various e-mail fields. For example, in the search in Figure 5.8, I want to find all mail with "Intermedia Exchange" anywhere in the message, and I want the word "Intermedia" to be in the Subject field. The default field list you see may be different from that in Figure 5.8; you control that either by using the Add Criteria button at the bottom, or by changing the title of any existing field using the drop-down arrow next to each. I recommend you play around with this query tool and teach yourself how to search on various field combinations; it's fairly intuitive.

In Outlook 2010 you can narrow your search by using the commands in the Refine group on the Search tab (see Figure 5.7). There you can limit the search to certain senders, subjects, date ranges, and so on, but you need to edit the values in the search box and that can be confusing. I prefer using the older Outlook 2007 interface that gives you a separate box for each search criterion (as in Figure 5.8); you can get to that in Outlook 2010 by clicking the More button at the lower right of the Refine group on the Search tab. Click that More button as many times as needed to add fields to narrow the search. If you use More fields a lot in Outlook 2010, I recommend turning off the "search while typing" that was discussed above, as that feature can lead to frustrating behavior when entering field values (if you pause too long, the cursor jumps out of the box you are entering).

Note: *If you preferred the Advanced Find interface of Outlook 2003 for this type of query creation, it is still available for use with the indexed search engine in 2007/10. To access the old interface in Outlook 2007, on the Tools menu choose Instant Search and then Advanced Find…. In Outlook 2010, on the Search tab of the Ribbon choose Search Tools and then Advanced Find…. Note, however, that using this interface you can only search one data store at a time.*

Figure 5.8
Instant Search Query
Builder.

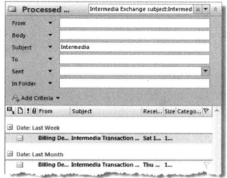

Figure 5.9
Query syntax, sample
documentation.

Type this	To find this
bobby	Items containing *bobby*, *BOBBY*, *BoBby*, or any other combination of uppercase and lowercase letters. Instant Search is not case sensitive.
bobby moore	Items containing both *bobby* and *moore*, but not necessarily in that order.
bobby AND moore	Items containing both *bobby* and *moore*, but not necessarily in that order. Note that logical operators such as AND, NOT, and OR must be in uppercase letters.
bobby NOT moore	Items containing *bobby*, but not *moore*.
bobby OR moore	Items containing *bobby*, *moore*, or both.
"bobby moore"	Items containing the exact phrase *bobby moore*. Note the use of double quotes so that the search results match the exact phrase within the quotes.
from:"bobby moore"	Items sent from *bobby moore*. Note the use of double quotes so that the search results match the exact phrase within the quotes.

In Outlook 2007/10, narrowing the search as described above (using Query builder in 2007, or the More fields in 2010) actually edits the search phrase itself in the search box. You'll see a phrase like "iPad received:this week" where iPad is the search term, Received refers to the date field, and This Week is the date value. What you are doing is building a text-based query; the various fields and controls you click are just helping you do that. You can then edit that query directly. In fact, you could build that full query manually, just by typing the query directly in the search box, using the Instant Search query syntax. I cover that next.

Outlook 2007/2010 Instant Search Query Syntax

In case you are an experienced search-tool maven and are starting to think the interface described above seems a little lightweight, know that you can make your searches as elaborate as you want by using a very sophisticated query syntax. Rest assured you can, if you study, find a way to find almost anything. You will want to study Microsoft's documentation on search syntax to understand all the possibilities. Figure 5.9 shows the first seven commands in one of the query syntax documentation sets; the full list of commands stretches to nearly five pages in length, so there is a lot of power here if you want it. To find this documentation, open a Google Internet search and enter "query searches in Outlook"; find the article titled "Learn to narrow your search criteria for better searches in Outlook." Other documentation exists as well.

Using Search in Outlook for Mac 2011

The indexed search capability in Outlook for Mac 2011 is based on Spotlight — the search tool used throughout the Macintosh. Compared to Outlook 2007/10, the user interface is much simpler in Outlook for Mac 2011, but just as powerful.

To start a search in Outlook for Mac 2011, click the Search This Folder box shown at the top right of Figure 5.10. Once you stop typing, the results are

Figure 5.10
Outlook 2011 Search tab is activated after clicking in the search box.

Figure 5.11
Narrow your 2011 search by choosing a column name just after typing.

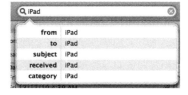

Figure 5.12
Outlook for Mac 2011 Advanced Search.

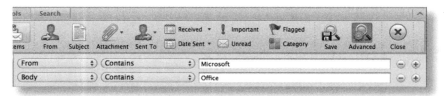

displayed in place of the current folder contents. Then, by clicking a choice in the popup shown in Figure 5.11, which automatically appears after you type the search term, you can narrow that search to a particular Outlook column name; or ignore the popup.

You can get more control over those column name searches if you click the buttons in the middle of the Search tab (see From, Subject, Sent To, and so on, in Figure 5.12). Each time you click one, you add a line to the Advanced Search panel just below the Ribbon as shown in Figure 5.12. You can also add or remove lines in that section by clicking the minus and plus signs at the right end of each search line. And you can change the search logic by changing the values in the popup column names and search verbs; the latter usually defaults to Contains. You can show and hide that entire Advanced section by clicking the Advanced button at the right end of the Search tab in the Ribbon.

Controlling the scope of the search is possible as well. By that, I mean controlling what folders or Outlook data types are searched. You do that by using the four buttons at the far left of the Search tab. For example, if you choose All Mail, the search expands to multiple mail files or mail accounts (should you have those). If you choose All Items, Outlook searches through mail, tasks, contacts, calendar, and notes for your search term.

Like Outlook 2007/10, you can gain even more search control by typing complex search criteria directly into the Search box. Do a Google Internet search on "Spotlight Search Syntax" to find documentation on available commands.

Using Find in Outlook 2003

The search tool in Outlook 2003 is called Find, and it has gained a bit of a bad reputation. That's primarily because it can search only one data store at a time and because it is slow. I know in the past I avoided using this tool due to its slow speed. But if you cannot use an add-in indexed search engine, take another look at it; it's better then spending hours filing your mail.

How slow is it? Here is a worst-case example. Searching three years' worth of my saved mail (14,000 items in one Processed Mail folder) on the word "Outlook" (I get a lot of mail with that word in it), it took about two minutes to search titles only; three minutes when I included all text in all messages. Two to three minutes is a long time to wait, but again, this is a worst-case example.

It can be much faster. In a typical corporate environment where the Exchange mailbox is limited in size, if you search only your Processed Mail folder there, your searches will be much faster. And even with large folders, in Outlook 2003 I found that once I did any search, if I searched again during the same Outlook session, the subsequent searches were dramatically quicker, even for different words. For example, my second search of the same 14,000 items, full text of messages, on the word "Microsoft" took only 13 seconds (and the same if I searched on the word "Outlook"); this is pretty reasonable, and no doubt faster for smaller collections. I suspect a temporary index of some sort is built during the first search and reused on subsequent searches.

As to the data-store scope limit, again, if you limit your searches to the Processed Mail folder, you should be fine.

So give this tool a second try if you have given up on it in the past due to speed or scope limits; you may find it quite usable once you start using a single folder filing system and get past the first search of the day. And compared to hunting through long lists of mail, or spending hours per week filing mail by topic, it has got to be better.

There are two modes of this search tool, Simple Find and Advanced Find; people who use this nearly always use Simple Find.

Simple Find (Outlook 2003)

Simple Find is activated by clicking the Find button on the main Outlook 2003 toolbar, or by selecting Find from the Tools menu. This places a toolbar-like row of commands and fields at the top of the currently open folder (see Figure 5.13).

Using that toolbar, just type your search term into the Look For box at the left and click Find Now in the middle, and the results replace the mail in the folder below. Watch the small document and magnifying glass icon at the left end of the toolbar (not shown in Figure 5.13). If it is moving and circling, the search is still in progress; when it disappears the search is complete.

By default Simple Find looks in the currently selected folder. You can expand that by first clicking the drop-down arrow next to Search In. There you can select All Mail folders. Better though, given speed issues, is to click the Choose Folders item and carefully select only those folders you need to search from the Select Folder(s) dialog box, shown in Figure 5.14. Note that subfolders are not automatically included when you select parent folders in this dialog box.

After the search is done, to clear the search results, click the Clear button on the Find toolbar; or click the Close button (x) at the right side of the Find toolbar, which also closes the Find toolbar.

Advanced Find (Outlook 2003)

Advanced Find is activated by clicking the Options drop-down on the Find toolbar, and selecting Advanced Find; or from the Tools menu, click Find, and then Advanced Find. That opens the dialog box in Figure 5.15.

You can see you have much more flexibility in building search criteria here, but understanding this dialog box can be a bit daunting, especially under the Advanced tab.

Advanced Find also looks in the currently selected folder by default. To expand that scope click the Browse… button, and the same Select Folder(s)

Figure 5.13
Outlook 2003 Simple
Find.

Figure 5.14
Select Folder(s) dialog
box in Simple Find.

Figure 5.15
Advanced Find.

dialog box used in Simple Find opens, from which you can include more folders to search.

That's all I am going to say about Find. For more features and functions information about Find, I recommend studying any of the excellent Outlook reference books available, listed in Appendix C.

Summary

▶   Emptying your Inbox every day is an important way to increase workday control because it clears unattended responsibilities that may otherwise haunt you. It removes clutter from an important area of daily focus. It signals you are ready to move on to new work.

▶   The easiest way to empty the Inbox is to first extract tasks and then drag everything to one folder (called the Processed Mail folder), which for now I recommend you create as a subfolder of the Inbox.

▶   If you'd like to get started quickly, drag all mail older than a week from the Inbox to this folder now. Then immediately process the mail left in the Inbox into the Processed Mail folder as well, extracting tasks as you go. Make a note of the cutoff date, and when you have time later, extract tasks from mail older than that date. If you are in an Exchange Server environment with tight mailbox size restrictions, you will now be emptying your older mail from your Processed Mail folder as you reach your limits.

▶   Consider studying Appendix A for other Processed Mail folder location suggestions (such as using a local folders file).

▶   Try using Outlook's built-in search functionality as your way to find older mail in the Processed Mail folder. If you are using Outlook 2003, the one version covered in this book that does not have a fast indexed search engine, install one of the powerful add-in indexed search engines if your IT department will permit that. Many such search tools are available but I recommend X1. If you cannot do that, then give the Outlook Find tool a try; it can work better with a one-folder search.

Next Steps

Congratulations on finishing Part I! You are now using all components of the system in a basic way. You can stop here if you like, and start to enjoy the fruits of your labor. This book was designed so you can do just that: get a relatively speedy start, and then take a break from study if desired.

But better is, if you have time, to plunge ahead into Part II. You have more to learn. For example, if you intend to empty a relatively full Inbox now and extract tasks, you may want to skip ahead and take Lesson 7, which is the full lesson on converting e-mails to tasks. That way your task creation will be most productive. And if you are eager to apply topic-based filing to the mail stored in your Processed Mail folder, feel free to jump ahead and take Lesson 8 now as well. In both cases come back to Lesson 6 to complete your core training. Lesson 6 will help you understand task management even more.

PART II

Maturing the System

Lesson 6:
When and Where to
Use Outlook Tasks

Introduction

You've come a long ways on learning how to use tasks. In Lesson 2 you learned how to use the basic task system in Outlook and learned a quick way to convert e-mails to tasks. In Lesson 3 you learned how to configure Outlook for the Master Your Now! (MYN) approach to tasks, and in Lesson 4 you learned the MYN best practices for managing tasks. Now, let's step back a moment and think a little more deeply about using tasks in Outlook.

First, let's consider what we really mean by *tasks* and what kinds of tasks are best to place in Outlook; while most belong there, some do not. We'll look at the very important concept of *next actions*. I'll describe the idea of *follow-up tasks* and how they can improve your work life.

As to the "where" in the title of this lesson, I'll discuss taking your tasks mobile with using various approaches. I'll discuss which mobile devices make sense, and what software approaches to consider.

And finally, there are some situations where, even if you use Outlook for e-mail, I do not recommend using Outlook as your task solution—I recommend other products. I'll tell you why and what to use instead.

But first, let's start with the basics—what a task is and why knowing that matters.

What Is a Task?

Tasks versus Appointments

A question I often get is, Should I enter an action in Outlook as an appointment on my calendar or as an item in my task list, and if I put it on my calendar is it still a task? Let's start with defining appointments.

Appointments

Appointments are time-defined events, usually meetings, which have distinct stop and start times. To most, this is obvious: you should manage appointments by placing them on your Outlook calendar. The Master Your Now! system uses Outlook appointments occasionally as a technique to complete tasks, but appointments are only a peripheral focus of this system; virtually all our tasks go into the MYN task list. If there is a specific time of day that a particular task must be done, yes, make an appointment out of it. And, in general, whenever you need to delineate a certain part of a day for an activity (or, say, block off the whole day), use an appointment on the calendar, not a task on the task list.

Tasks

Tasks, then, are activities that do *not* need a specific time of day identified. They are the types of things you would normally write on a to-do list. They may have a specific *day* as a deadline, but as long as they are not *time*-specific, then in general keep them on your task list.

That said, there are times I move a task to the calendar; for example if a deadline is coming up and I want to delineate some specific time to work on it. But that is the exception rather than the rule.

Ad Hoc versus Operational Tasks

The distinction between ad hoc tasks and operational tasks can be important too. A lot of companies have stable operational environments with daily repeated tasks and work steps that are best managed by dedicated workflow systems, either manual or automated. For example, if you process a hundred invoices a day, I hope you are using an invoice management system (a specialized application to process invoices). I do not want you to think I am recommending Outlook's task system for high-volume work processes like this that have better automated systems available.

Note, though, you might be assigned a related task *outside* of such a system. For example, if you are a manager and do not routinely use the invoice management system but occasionally are sent invoice-approval e-mails generated by that system, the Outlook system described in this book *can* be useful for you, to track these one-off requests as Outlook tasks.

The Place for Goals

Do I Need to Identify My Goals First?

Nearly all teachings on time and task management start with a discussion of goals. The general line of thought is this: how can you work on any tasks unless you know what your own goals are? The message is usually that you should not focus on tasks unless you have first mapped out your personal mission, vision, and goals and have ensured that your tasks link to those goals through planning.

This is sage advice. However, my experience is this: most people cannot get even their minimal daily tasks off their plate effectively enough to have time to focus on visualizing and planning tasks to meet their goals. They have no system for doing so. In the heat of the business day, inspired goals are usually the first things that they abandon as they scramble to stay ahead of the freight train of urgent work. There is nothing more frustrating than seeing your favorite goals crushed under the wheels of out-of-control urgency at work.

But goals do have an important place; let me explain where they fit.

The Workday Mastery Pyramid

In my 2010 book *Master Your Workday Now!* I identify three levels of work focus: Control, Create, and Connect, and I show them graphically in a pyramid (see Figure 6.1).

The Control level, at the base of the pyramid, is all about keeping urgency managed, and tracking tasks appropriately so that the right things get done first. It's what this Outlook book is about. The result is you accomplish more with less stress, and your mind is free enough to start focusing on your larger goals.

Figure 6.1
The Workday
Mastery Pyramid

Connecting
Your Work with
Who You Really Are
Connect

Creating Your Outcomes
by Using Now Goals,
and Goal Activation
Create

Getting Control of Your Workday
by Managing Urgency Zones
Control

Goals are what the Create layer is all about—visualizing and managing larger outcomes. You have a different mindset when working at this level, one where your attention is on achieving more in your work and life. This is where you consider the bigger things you want to accomplish and how they pull you forward and even excite you. Broader thinking occurs here in the Create Layer, as does creative thinking and visioning.

After you spend adequate time at the Create layer, then the Connect layer comes next. The Connect layer is all about connecting the entirety of your work to who you really are. It is about deciding that most or all of your work activity should be spent on activities that support your core, higher, motives. It is about seeking work that connects you to who you really are, and it is about constantly expanding toward that in your career. Ultimately, it is creating a career by doing what you are passionate about—doing what you love.

A key premise of this three-layer model is that you cannot rise successfully to the Create or Connect levels until you have the Control level fully mastered—Control is the basis of creating the time and mental space for your higher-level work. If you are constantly distracted by out-of-control urgency, or if you are constantly feeling behind and always fighting fires, you can never reach the more passionate and creative mindset that higher-level goals are based on.

So, while there is a major place for goals in the overall skill of mastering your workday, this book is about mastering the control level first so you can get beyond it. And of course it uses Outlook as the tool to do that. Therefore, you won't find my theories about creating and achieving goals in this book—read my other book, mentioned above, for that emphasis; about one third of that book is all about goals and how to succeed with them.

That said, in Lesson 12 of this book, I do cover mechanical ways to track and work your own goals into your task stream; I show you ways to do that in Outlook.

Do I Put Goals on My Now Tasks List?

The next question I get is, When I do identify my goals, should I place them on my task list? For instance, should I put the statement "Practice an Exercise Program" or "Increase Sales" on my Outlook TaskPad or To-Do Bar? The answer is no; this is too broad a statement to put on your to-do list. There are practical reasons not to. For instance, when you see this on your list in the heat of the business day, you will skip right over it—it is too big to do. And there are logical reasons not to as well; successful goal management requires a much different sort of mindset than task management. Instead, what you should put on your Now Tasks list is some next step or action that you intend to take to reach that goal. For instance, "Make appointment with Jake the personal trainer" is a good task to put there, or "Register for Sales 101 class." I'll talk extensively about the concept of next actions a few pages ahead.

The Place for Projects

Similar to the question above about whether goals should be listed on the Now Tasks list, you might ask if *projects* should be listed there. For instance, should you make an entry like "Rebuild garage" on this list? As before with goals, the answer is no, because this is too broad a task to place on your Now Tasks list; you will skip over a task like this in the heat of a busy day. Rather, once again, any *next steps* due against a project can and should be listed on your Now Tasks list. For example, "Call Jim for an estimate on garage" is a good task to list on your Now Tasks list. Some fine points of this will be discussed in the section about next actions. And a full discussion of making project lists and tracking tasks against projects is provided in Lesson 12.

Significant Outcomes

Finally, there is something that sits between next-action tasks on the one hand, and projects or goals on the other: Significant Outcomes, or SOCs. These are the big things you want to accomplish this week. They aren't as big as goals but they are too big to be called tasks. Since they don't list well on the MYN task list, you need another way to show them. I'll talk more about SOCs later in this lesson.

Put Nearly All Your Tasks in Outlook

What's left is everything else: all ad hoc tasks, all next steps on projects and goals, actions from e-mails, actions from meetings, and actions from phone calls. The very first and most important thing you can do to get ahead of your workday is to track all these ad hoc tasks in this one location. What you should *not* do is try to use Outlook task tools in combination with other formal or informal ad hoc task tracking systems. This applies to obvious external task systems such as paper to-do lists, yellow sticky notes on your computer monitor, journals, and so on. Sure, use those as collection spots while on the move or to plan out projects, but as soon as you are back to Outlook, copy specific tasks into Outlook's task list.

Note: If you have a separate system to track operational tasks, like those described above in the section Ad Hoc versus Operational Tasks, or if you have a system to plan and track future project tasks (like Microsoft Project), continue to use those. I am only referring here to multiple ways to track ad hoc tasks, daily to-do's, or current next steps on projects.

Why One Location Is Important

Why is having one place for all tasks so important? If you don't have one place to look, you will not know where to look for your next-highest-priority to-do. You will not get the benefits of being able, at a glance, to know what is on your list for today (and what isn't). More important, at the end of the day, you won't have a clear picture of whether all your critical tasks are done and whether you can leave the office in comfort. You will gain a huge sense of relief by having one and only one task list that you get in the habit of using.

This can also lead to rather subtle distinctions. For instance, something we all tend to do is leave important e-mails in our Outlook Inbox with the intention of returning to them later to act upon them. By doing this, however, you have created a second home for storing your to-do's. Similarly, we all tend to leave important voice mails in our voice mailbox with the intention of following up later on them as well.

So one subtle but important discipline is to get into the habit of immediately transferring both explicit and *implied* tasks into the MYN Outlook system as soon as you receive them.

Keeping Tasks Out of Your Head

One more place you should not store tasks: your head! All good task management experts recommend getting out of the habit of trying to rely on your memory for tracking to-do's. This was a personal epiphany for me, when I finally accepted this lesson years ago. You may think you have a good memory, and you might, but that is not the point. The point is that until you spread your task list out in front of you visually, it is impossible to adequately prioritize, filter, defer, and dismiss tasks that are bouncing around in your mind all day. You should use your mental cycles for strategic thinking, planning, analysis, appreciating life, and so on—not for constantly tracking and revisiting responsibilities. And if you are currently experiencing any anxiety about the number of tasks you seem to have on your plate, storing them only in your mind will exacerbate that anxiety.

It's the tasks that you cannot remember but you know are there that have the most destructive effect. In the Introduction I mentioned long-standing research that shows the human mind cannot clearly remember a list of more than six or seven items at once. Beyond that items become a blur, and it's that blur that increases mental stress. That nagging feeling that you are ignoring important responsibilities has a negative effect on your attitude, your sense of well-being, and your self-esteem. For some, it can be hard to relax in the evening after work or on the weekend when they sense that they have much work left undone. What a tremendous relief my clients report when they finally get all of their to-do's out of their head and into one visible location.

And if you maintain that approach—recording to-do's immediately in one location as they come up rather than holding them in your head—you will be amazed at the sense of freedom this provides.

Getting Tasks Out of Physical Piles

One of the common sources of tasks is stacks of paper on your physical desktop, bookshelf, cabinet, or in a desk drawer. A primary benefit of implementing an effective task management system is no longer feeling haunted by piles of paper that you know contain things you need to work on. So from now on, as you receive physical documents with things for you to do in them, rather than using a pile as a to-do system, immediately enter the required action in Outlook before you drop the item on your desk. Then when Outlook tells you the time is right to work it, go find the item as required.

If you find you are currently overwhelmed by an out-of-control pile of materials on your desk or an overflowing physical in-basket, David Allen, in his book *Getting Things Done*, has some great techniques to get you past that (see Chapters 5 and 6 of that book). He describes a system that will get rid of your piles and create very simply organized and highly usable file cabinets. His techniques will help you to get those tasks out of your piles, and they dovetail nicely with transferring them into Outlook.

Voice Mail

Think of your voice mailbox as a big pile of paper with buried to-do's in it; it is adding to your sense of your workday being out of control. From now on, whenever you listen to a voice mail, immediately determine the action needed and place that in an Outlook task. Write as many details as possible into the body of the task and delete the voice mail. If the voice mail is too long to write all details down, save it and reference the time and date in your task so you can listen again when you take action. Even better is if your organization has unified messaging, covered next.

Unified Messaging

Regarding work voice mail, one of the greatest recent inventions in voice mail technology is unified messaging. This is an intelligent link between your voice mail system and the Exchange e-mail server, which places entries into your Outlook Inbox for each voice mail you receive. From there you can convert them to tasks as needed using what you learned at the end of Lesson 2 and will learn in Lesson 7. Most systems include a recording of the message attached as a file you can play and listen to on your computer, so when you are ready to work the task, you can listen to the message again right from the task. If your company does not have unified messaging and you receive many voice mail messages, encourage your management to get it.

Note: *Unified messaging is available from a variety of vendors, usually from your corporate voice mail vendor. This is a major upgrade to a company's voice mail and e-mail system, so do not expect this to arrive overnight.*

If you use your cell phone voice mail a lot for business, there are services that will move voice mail out of your cell-phone carrier's voice mail box into your Outlook Inbox or some other text-based system. Some even transcribe the voice mail for you and put it in the text of the e-mail. I describe more below in the section Mobile Voice Mail.

Personal and Work Tasks, Separate or Merged?

I get this question quite often: Should I mix my business tasks with my personal tasks in the same system? Unfortunately the answer is "It depends." If you have a separate Outlook system at home and use it a lot there, I would not want to oblige you to boot up your business system just to look up tasks. Rather, what I commonly do is transfer tasks between the two systems by e-mail. For instance if I am at work and I think of a home task, I'll send an e-mail to my home address with the task in the subject line. Then when I get home I convert that e-mail to a home task. I do the same in the other direction.

If you do not have a home Outlook system, by all means use your business system for home tasks and access it from home. And if you are self-employed, the choice is easy: one system for both.

Summary of Using Outlook for All Tasks

▶ Do not store tasks on paper at your desk: not slips of paper, not notepads, not notebooks, except for initial collection while in meetings.

▶ Do not try to track to-do's by leaving them in e-mails or voice mails.

▶ Do not try to track and work tasks from meeting notes and journals (although you certainly can initially record them there).

▶ Do not try to track tasks in your head.

▶ Do not try to track to-do's in stacks of paper.

▶ Rather, immediately transfer all tasks from e-mail, voice-mail, paper memos, paper slips, meeting notes, journals, incoming physical memos, and your mind into Outlook's task management system.

▶ Consider services that move voice mail automatically into your Outlook Inbox, where converting them to tasks is easy.

▶ Feel free to mix personal and company tasks together or to keep them separate, whichever works best for you.

Going Mobile with the MYN System

iPads, Android tablets, and other tablets are making inroads into the corporate environments. And smartphones are growing in computational power—even Microsoft Office documents are being edited on their small screens. Furthermore, cloud computing, which is a new term for the old concept of working off servers, is gaining steam as a viable work approach—one that makes mobile computing much more feasible. So, you are probably wondering how the MYN system might fit in to this rapidly changing mobile landscape. After all, getting organized and having all tasks and e-mail under control clearly means finding ways to do that while on the road.

In fact, the MYN system plays very well into the growing mobile footprint. But deciding which mobile strategy to use, and even which device to use with MYN, requires some forethought. The right solution really depends on what form your travel takes and the nature of your work when traveling.

First, your form of travel. Is the extent of your mobility walking across the hall into a conference room? Or do you travel to other office locations where you sit and work for extended periods? Or are you often working in transitional locations (an airport gate, an office lobby, or during a taxi ride) where you need to do small, quick, segments of work?

Next, consider how and why you are using e-mail and tasks when on the run. Are you simply reviewing e-mail and perhaps inputting tasks for later work at your desk? Or are you doing the actual task work when on the road?

Finally, consider your connectivity options. Has your IT department enabled access to your company data while on the road such that you can access company servers or documents? In what way have they done that?

All of these considerations help determine which device and approach to use for your mobile solution. With these in mind, let me start with the simplest mobile solution—paper—and work up from there to laptops, tablets, and smartphones.

Printing Your Tasks Instead of Using a Mobile Device (Windows)

I know you may be eager to obtain a sexy new smartphone, tablet, or netbook, but if the extent of your mobility is inside an office building, say, between your desk and a conference room, you can often get by with much less. And if your IT department has not given you appropriate connectivity methods, this may be your only choice.

When I worked in a large corporate office environment years ago, I found I was quite successful with merely printing out my Outlook task list and appointments for the day on one page and taking that to meetings (see Figure 6.2). In my experience, it trumped the complications of a handheld; I found using a full-sized sheet of paper preferable to navigating through the tiny screens on a handheld during a meeting.

If you want to do this, you may wonder how to print your calendar and task list together on one page. In Outlook 2003 it's easy. Just display your calendar in Day view, and choose Print from the File menu; that prints both together. The default layout is quite good (though playing with the configurations can help). In Outlook 2007/10 it is a bit harder; you need to first find the Page Setup dialog box and change the Tasks setting from Daily Task List to To-Do Bar—then print your Day view; go to this URL for more details: www.myn.bz/PrintCalendar.htm

Figure 6.2

How a printed Outlook schedule and MYN task list looks. This is probably your simplest mobile solution.

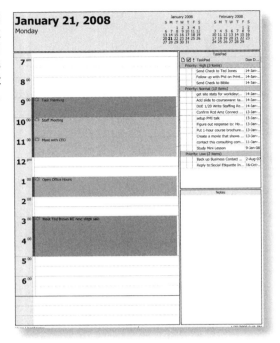

Unfortunately, printing the MYN task list with Outlook for Mac 2011 like this is not currently possible since each urgency zone is in its own folder.

Using this paper approach as my mobile solution worked well in other ways. In meetings I made notes right on the sheet of paper to indicate task changes or additions, and I entered them in Outlook later when back at my desk. And at times I would print a week or month calendar view each morning as well so I could check future appointments when needed in meetings. Because it's so simple, sometimes paper really is better than fancy new technology.

Laptop or Netbook (Windows and Mac)

If you have a laptop or netbook running Windows or Mac OS, and have Internet access to your work servers, then using a full copy of Outlook works beautifully and should not be discarded over using an iPad or Android tablet. If you travel a lot, get a lightweight Mac or PC laptop, netbook, or a full Windows Tablet PC. Make sure you have a good broadband connection. And get accustomed to putting the computer in standby when you close up so you can get in and out of Outlook quickly. Plan to sit for extended moments throughout the day to do some serious e-mail and task management in your full copy of Outlook. Spend some time converting e-mails to tasks and replying to messages.

In this scenario, if you also have a smartphone or added small tablet, I'd plan to use those primarily as a quick way when standing or on the run to *read* e-mail and *view* high-priority tasks, and perhaps make short replies to important messages. Why just that? You will find that even the best new tablets are not as nimble as a laptop with Outlook installed. And most usually allow you to view only a subset of your saved mail and many even have trouble getting at your company servers.

So again, your most powerful solution is to use your laptop with a full copy of Outlook. You want to use the right tools for the right job, and sometimes access to a full copy of Outlook is the only way to go.

By the way, to make this feasible, the laptop or netbook you use needs to be a reasonably updated and light-weight model that you feel good about carrying whenever you travel. Mine weighs 3.5 pounds, launches out of standby in seconds, and has a built-in broadband card that never fails. If instead you are using a ten-pound company-issued monster that crashes a lot, does not handle standby, and has a broadband card that fails half the time, you should demand a new laptop or netbook.

All that said, if you are often in transitional locations where you do work for short bits of time, then a one-pound, instant-on tablet still trumps even the best laptop for quickly checking mail or jumping on a website — there really *are* advantages to these new tablets. And nearly everyone uses smartphones these days. So let's look at how these fit into the MYN system.

Using a Tablet or Smartphone

Beyond laptops, most people when they think of "going mobile" are really thinking of a powerful smartphone like a BlackBerry, an iPhone, an Android or Windows smartphone, or a Palm WebOS phone. And these days, you are likely also thinking of one of the new tablet devices like the iPad or an Android or BlackBerry model. The advantage to all of these over a laptop is they are instant on and very lightweight. Controls are also usually very simple, so you can get at the information you need more quickly.

But using these instead of a laptop means you cannot use a full copy of Outlook. Since no mobile version of Outlook includes a task manager, you'll need to manage tasks another way. You might think a browser version of Outlook for tasks would work in this situation, particularly on a tablet, but it won't; as mentioned earlier, OWA (the web version of Outlook) does not have the task functionality you need to support MYN. Instead, you will want to use native or add-in apps on these devices to access your tasks. So the question is, which apps to use?

Well, if you are using Outlook for all your tasks as I encourage in this book, then only use a mobile task application that allows you to synchronize the tasks easily with Outlook. Do not keep a separate task list on one of these devices — I described above the problems caused by having multiple to-do lists. The best synchronization setup is that available in many corporate settings where the tasks (and e-mail, calendar, and contacts) on your corporate

Outlook Exchange Server synchronize over the air with your mobile devices. And make sure to use an app that can be configured to show the MYN task list.

That's the ideal. But there are currently several barriers to reaching this ideal.

Barriers to Mobile Task Solutions

The first barrier is finding a mobile device that will synchronize tasks with your corporate Outlook servers. iPhones, iPads, and Android devices suffer with this because ActiveSync, the standard Microsoft Exchange interface built into these, is for some reason not enabled for easy *task* syncing on these (mail, calendar, and contacts do sync fine on these; just not *tasks*). Even the new Windows Phone 7, a Microsoft product, as of this writing does not sync Outlook Exchange tasks due to its ActiveSync limitation. This is ironic since task synchronization used to be one of ActiveSync's strong points on Windows Mobile smartphones, which these devices replace. Some workarounds exist for this that I will mention ahead, but choices are limited.

The second issue is, even if your device or app does have task synchronization with your corporate Exchange Server, it is hard to find task software that can be configured to create views anything like the ones you created in Lesson 3. When your mobile devices cannot show those views, it makes it hard to fully use the MYN system from the device. The BlackBerry suffers from this—most BlackBerry devices can sync with Outlook Exchange tasks, but the standard tasks software on the BlackBerry cannot sort or filter tasks flexibly. And they cannot show start dates. Granted, if you have only ten or so tasks in your list, that does not matter. But once you really start using this system, you will likely build up hundreds of short- and long-term tasks (most scheduled to the future), and the poor sorting and filtering in the native BlackBerry task application will make it unusable. Add-in software offers some help here, and I'll describe that ahead.

The third and final barrier to easy use of your Outlook tasks on a mobile device is that you usually cannot easily convert e-mails to tasks on these handhelds—you cannot drag or move your e-mail to the tasks folder in their built-in systems. This is troubling since the primary use of corporate handhelds these days is to check e-mail on the run. Without a good way to convert action e-mails to tasks, you may read an e-mail indicating an important work task for you to do, and then skip to the next message, possibly losing the action as a result. You could stop and enter a new task by hand in the device, but rarely do you have time to do that when on the run. Workarounds exist for this as well; let's get to all those solutions now.

Mobile Solutions

I just painted a fairly bleak picture for mobile devices. But there are workarounds, and even some very bright spots, in the mobile landscape. Let's start with some simple compromise solutions, and then work up to some full-blown MYN mobile solutions.

Monitoring and Entering Outlook Tasks While on the Run

I commonly use my smartphone to see what tasks I can do while on the run. If I am between meetings, I may want to see what my list of Critical Now tasks is, so that I can try to knock some off or plan ahead to do them. And if I am on a plane or in a waiting area and have more time, I may even want to look at lower priority tasks to get some of those done too. So is this possible on most handhelds?

Most corporate-issued smartphones these days have over-the-air sync with your corporate servers for e-mail, calendar, and contacts. BlackBerries and older Windows Mobiles smartphones are unique in that they also sync tasks with standard settings and software; you can see your Outlook tasks imported into the native Tasks application. However, the tasks sort incorrectly in those native applications—you cannot see them in MYN order. But even with these you can usually at least sort the tasks view to show High priority tasks at the top; since High priority represents your must-do-today list, this may be all you need to see when on the run—it may be good enough. To see a true MYN task list, though, you'll need to add software, which I'll cover ahead. And if you do not use a BlackBerry or older Windows Mobile device, you'll definitely need to add software even to see your Outlook tasks; that's because iPhones, Androids, and the newer Microsoft phones do not sync tasks natively with your Exchange Server. I'll show those solutions ahead.

With a synced BlackBerry or older Windows Mobile phone, you can also enter *new* tasks as you get them (just remember to date them and not set a reminder; the defaults may not be right). That way, when you get back to your desk or laptop, you can see them in your Outlook system and handle them appropriately.

Converting E-mails to Outlook Tasks While on the Run

As to converting e-mails to tasks, newer BlackBerry and Windows smartphones allow you to set the Outlook Follow Up flag right on your smartphone. If you are using Outlook 2007/10 or 2011, then back at your desk you'll see the e-mail in your MYN task list as a flagged-mail task. And with Outlook 2003, even though it does not move flagged mail to your task list, just seeing a flagged mail in your Inbox can trigger you to do a proper conversion to a task when back at your desk.

If your device does not have a way to flag e-mail, note that every smartphone allows you to forward mail. So if you get an e-mail with an action in it, you can always forward it back to yourself with the word "TASK:" in the subject line; then when back at your desk, you can do a proper conversion to a task. This works for any device—even those without a task application. In Outlook

2007/10 and 2011 you can also write an Outlook rule that looks for "TASK:" and that will put a Follow Up flag on such e-mails back at your desk, which converts them to a flagged-mail task.

Using Add-in Software for MYN Tasks and Exchange

One reason for the huge success of iPhones, iPads, and Androids is the abundance of third party apps and the ease with which these are installed, updated, and used on your mobile devices. There are lots of third-party *task* applications in this collection too. However, the same issues as above limit greatly what you will be able to use. Most of these apps either do not synchronize with Exchange or do not sort and filter to match the MYN task list. And very few have a good way to convert e-mails to tasks. That said, some do stand out, and I will list those here.

Keep in mind that for each of these, some post-install configuration will be required to make the task list look and act like the MYN task list. And keep in mind this is a rapidly changing environment and my recommendations below may change over time. With that in mind, check my website page to confirm what you read below is still what I consider the best. Go to: MichaelLinenberger.com/software.html.

iPhone and iPad: TaskTask

On the iPhone and iPad, I recommend an app called TaskTask (called TaskTask HD on the iPad). The authors wrote their own interface to Exchange that overcomes the iPhone ActiveSync problems. And its tasks view can be sorted to match the MYN task list. It also recognizes flagged mail tasks in Outlook and displays them in your task list—something very rare to find. With TaskTask, you'll still need to flag or forward e-mails back to yourself as a reminder to convert e-mails to tasks later. See my article on how to configure TaskTask for MYN at: www.myn.bz/TaskTask.htm.

Android: TouchDown

The Android platform (whether a smartphone or a tablet) has the best solution of all the devices listed here; it's an add-in app called TouchDown that interfaces well with Exchange and can display the MYN task list. The product installs a suite of apps including an e-mail client that works well with Exchange. And best of all, it has a built-in command to convert e-mails into tasks (or even into appointments). Again, of all the solutions I have seen on any platform for reaching your Outlook tasks while on the road, the TouchDown solution is the best; to me, this is an excellent reason to migrate to an Android device. See my article on how to configure TouchDown for MYN tasks at: www.myn.bz/TouchDown.htm.

BlackBerry: ToDoMatrix

The BlackBerry is traditionally the most business-focused mobile tool—yet, while they sync tasks with Exchange natively, their task applications are still the most limited from an MYN perspective. A number of BlackBerry add-in task solutions are available. It's just that for those that interface with Exchange tasks, the sorting is usually not right for MYN and they do not include start dates. For those with relatively good sorting, the interface with Exchange is lacking. That said, the application called ToDoMatrix works relatively well and syncs tasks with Exchange. See my article on how to use and configure ToDoMatrix for MYN tasks at: www.myn.bz/TDM.htm.

Windows Mobile 6: Pocket Informant

If you are using the older Windows Mobile 6, you have one of the best solutions available. First of all, the Windows Mobile 6 OS has a full ActiveSync implementation—one that supports task synchronization with Exchange. And equally important, an add-in software application called Pocket Informant is available that offers full MYN task list formatting. I've been writing about using Pocket Informant on Windows Mobile for years; the only reason I don't use it anymore is that I have moved on to newer devices. One thing to keep in mind is this: the Windows Mobile 6 devices are being replaced with Windows Phone 7, so you may have trouble finding one at your wireless carrier store. Go to this link to see instructions for configuring Windows Mobile 6 Pocket Informant: www.myn.bz/PI-Config.htm.

Windows Phone 7: None

Windows Phone 7 is Microsoft's new mobile operating system. Everyone raves about how much easier and better the general user interface is compared to Windows Mobile 6, and I agree. But as mentioned earlier, there is one fatal flaw with Windows Phone 7—its built-in ActiveSync does not sync tasks with Exchange. As of this writing, I know of no add-in software solutions that replace that missing functionality; but check my website in case one was released since this book was printed.

Reasons Not to Use Outlook as your Main Task Solution

The solutions above provide options to take your Outlook-based, MYN tasks mobile. They assume you use Outlook of course, and they also assume you use Exchange server; that's because the connectivity tools in Exchange are the best way to go for over-the-air synchronization of Outlook tasks.

However, in some cases, usually due to the mobile limitations of Outlook, I recommend solutions other than Outlook and Exchange as your main MYN task application. I don't mean to abandon Outlook entirely—Outlook remains my first choice for e-mail, calendar, and other purposes. It's just that there are times when Outlook is not your best *tasks* solution. There are a number of situations where I feel this is the case, and I'll cover each below. Then I'll discuss my recommended replacement.

Here's where Outlook may not be your best task manager:

If you Use a Macintosh

If you are a Mac user, you've noticed by now that Outlook for Mac 2011 provides a relatively weak task solution; and that's true whether you are using it on your main computer or with a mobile solution. I discussed the issues with Outlook for Mac 2011 tasks in earlier lessons, but as a reminder, here are a few again. Since date sorting within priority groups is missing, you cannot see or print one view of your MYN tasks (you need three separate lists). The ability to create custom views is greatly limited. You cannot turn off the red color of overdue tasks, even though we ignore the due date field in MYN. And you cannot attach files to tasks. So you may want to use another task solution, and one that is server based so you can also use it while on the road.

No Remote Exchange Access

To go mobile with Outlook tasks, you need to be able to connect to your Exchange Server tasks from outside your company's firewall. Many companies does not have that connectivity. That's because some companies have not turned on ActiveSync or OWA access, or provided any other remote access suitable for mobile devices. If you lack such connectivity, you'll need another server-based task solution.

No Exchange Server

Or perhaps you are not working in a company with Exchange Server (or a comparable IMAP server with tasks) and so you use Outlook with an Internet mail service. In that case your tasks are stored on your computer's hard drive and you lose the easy over-the-air sync of Outlook tasks with your smartphone. Sure, you can use a local wired or Wi-Fi sync with some smartphones, and there are other solutions, but none are very good if you travel a lot. Rather, my first suggestion is to switch to a hosted Exchange account so you can get all the benefits of Exchange and remote access wherever you go (see Appendix A for a discussion of hosted Exchange). But if that is not practical for you, then using an alternate server-based tasks solution may be your only choice.

Windows Phone 7

As mentioned, at the time of this writing, Windows Phone 7 has no over-the-air Outlook task sync solution; so you'll need some other server-based task solution.

Mixed Mobile Devices

If you use a lot of different mobile solutions, you may have noticed that none of the solutions above work across *all* platforms. Perhaps you have an Android phone, and an iPad tablet, or maybe some other mobile device. If so, a multiplatform task solution may be the best way to preserve a uniform approach.

Recommended Non-Outlook Tasks Solution: ToodleDo

The best way to conquer the mobile limitations described above is to use an Internet server-based (also called cloud-based) task management product that is not limited by platform. That way you can view your tasks in any mobile device that has a compatible app; or use one that has a good Internet browser capability and a screen large enough to read a web page.

The question is which Internet-based task management product to use? Whichever one you choose, it needs to meet the MYN task list requirements. That means it needs to support start dates and it needs to have very flexible sorting and filtering. I have looked at many products on the market and very few meet those requirements. For example, as mentioned above, the web version of Outlook does not pass the test. Another popular product called Remember the Milk does not get close enough either. As of this writing, the only Internet server-based task product that I have found that does the job is called ToodleDo.

ToodleDo is an Internet server-based task application that meets all the task requirements of MYN. And you can also access ToodleDo on just about any device, either from a browser or from a wide range of compatible mobile apps. So, ToodleDo meets MYN mobile needs as well.

Note: Again, since products change quickly, check in with my website to see if other choices have become available. Go to MichaelLinenberger.com/software.html.

ToodleDo's Browser Mode

In its browser mode (its primary mode), ToodleDo can be run on any computer that supports a web browser such as a PC, Mac, Linux, or Chrome OS, as well as most tablet and smartphone operating systems (iOS, Android, BlackBerry, Palm WebOS, and more). The browser solution is ideal for a tablet because of the tablet's large-screen view. A large-screen smartphone works as well.

Note: The preinstalled browser app on some Android phones may not work right with ToodleDo. You can fix that by choosing other browser apps off the Android Market; for example, the Dolphin browser app works great.

ToodleDo Apps

If you don't like using a browser on a smartphone or tablet, there are easy-to-use dedicated apps that connect to the ToodleDo Internet servers and so give you full synchronization of your tasks across all your devices. ToodleDo has created apps for the iPhone and iPad that work great and configure well for MYN. Third party developers are creating apps for Android devices, Black-Berry, and Palm WebOS. For the Android, one stands out called Got To Do since it can be fully configured for MYN. See www.myn.bz/GotToDo.htm to view MYN configuration instructions for Got To Do. To find other MYN compatible apps, go to this URL: www.myn.bz/ToodleDo.html.

ToodleDo Features

ToodleDo has nearly all the features that Outlook has for tasks. And in many ways, once configured for MYN, ToodleDo even goes beyond Outlook tasks. How? As a web application it is well implemented with no task feature degradation across platforms or clients (unlike the web or Mac versions of Outlook, which have limited task capabilities). Furthermore, you can convert e-mails to tasks from any e-mail system on any device, which offers a huge advantage. It uses start dates correctly and it has a correctly implemented due date field (Outlook's due date field is hamstrung once you use the start date), and it has multiple views to track impending due dates. It has newer types of task features that Outlook does not; for example, the iPhone version has location awareness for tasks (e.g., a pending field office task could ring an alarm on your iPhone if you are driving by that office).

So, if you cannot use Outlook for tasks, ToodleDo is the software to use. The company even has a special version of the web software that is preconfigured for MYN. For how to access that, and for how to configure the ToodleDo web version and its mobile apps, go to this link: www.myn.bz/ToodleDo.html.

Paper-Based (Non-Outlook) Solution

And finally, some of you may prefer a nonautomated solution—many people like to use paper for tasks. In my book *Master Your Workday Now!* I show you how to implement the MYN task list on paper, where it uses the same three-urgency-zone approach split across two pages. Read more about this at this link: www.myn.bz/MYWN-Book.htm. And you can download free templates to print out at this link: www.masteryourworkday.com/tooldownloads.

Tasks Received While On the Run

Even with the perfect mobile solution, a number of mobile scenarios complicate collecting tasks in Outlook; they may require some thought to keep them worked into your system. And if you do not have an MYN mobile device like those described above, you may need to get creative. The scenarios below represent common situations where you might receive tasks while between meetings, or away from the office, with some suggestions on how to deal with them. The goal of the points below is to prevent you from falling back into the habit of trying to keep tasks in your head. Many of them rely on the skill you learned at the end of Lesson 2: converting e-mails to tasks.

Entering Tasks on a Mobile Device Directly

In all cases below, if you have a mobile device with synchronized tasks, you can enter a new task that is received on the run directly into the task software. However, I find few people take the time to do that. There is something about needing to stop, open the task software in the handheld device, create a new task, and then type out all the fields in that task that causes people to avoid it. So the solutions below try to find speedier ways.

Entering Tasks on a Mobile Device from E-mail

As mentioned above, if you have an Android device, TouchDown software allows you to convert e-mails to tasks while on the run; it's a simple menu choice. But not many other mobile systems allow that. So, here's the alternate solution I mentioned earlier. If you get an e-mail on your mobile device that has an action for you in it that you cannot do now, just forward the message back to yourself and put the word "TASK:" (all caps) at the beginning of the subject line. That way you will know to convert it to a task when you see it back at your primary computer.

Hallway Conversations

If a colleague or supervisor stops you in the hall and dumps an *unwanted* to-do on you, put the onus back on them by stating: "Hey, could you send me an e-mail on that, otherwise I will forget this." Then, back at your desk, if they have sent it you can convert it to a task. Again, only do this with tasks you'd rather not be responsible for—there is a good chance the person will forget to send it.

Capturing Tasks

For mobile scenarios where you *do* want to remember a task that someone gives you verbally (or if you think up one on the fly), here are some options.

As mentioned above, if you are proficient at entering text into your mobile device and you have it with you, do so (assuming it synchronizes with your main task list). But again, most people never do that. A small pocket notepad that you carry with you is a good option. Alternatively, use the voice recorder built into your smartphone.

Better though is an Internet server-based application called Evernote. It has apps for all smartphone and tablet models and it has a voice note function. This fantastic app drops your voice notes onto its server the moment you stop recording; you can pick them up later from your desktop. Or you can e-mail the recording back to yourself from the smartphone. Either way, you can convert it to a task when back on Outlook. I use it often, especially if I am driving when I think of a task. I also type notes directly into Evernote on my desktop to capture book or newsletter ideas as I am working on other things.

Home Computer

As mentioned earlier, if you are working at your home computer when an office task is identified, you can send an e-mail to your work address with the e-mail title identifying the task. Back at the office, convert the e-mail to a task. I do this a lot and it works great. The reverse is also useful: for things you need to remember to do when you get home, send an e-mail from work.

Mobile Voice Mail

Often you receive and listen to a voice mail on your mobile phone that contains a to-do that you later forget is saved there. There are a couple ways to handle this. You can leave the message in the message queue unsaved. On many phones, this leaves the message icon active; so when you see this icon at your desk, you can listen to the messages again and record it in Outlook. Or after listening to the message, you might leave yourself a voice note in Evernote (described above in section Capturing Tasks).

Sending Your Cell Phone Voice Mail to Outlook

The best solution for voice mail, however, is to use a service that collects your voice mail and sends it into your Outlook Inbox (like unified messaging, described earlier in this lesson). You then later convert these e-mails to tasks. There are several such services. Some provide just the sound file to play at the touch of a button; others transcribe the message into text. Some replace your carrier's voice mail system; others leave your voice mail system as is, but periodically copy messages off it. I provide a complete list in Appendix C. One is worth mentioning now, Google Voice, because it provides a compelling solution and it's free. Google Voice has apps for all smartphone platforms.

Writing Only Next Actions on Your Now Tasks List

Next, let's move away from mobile computing and return to the main topic of this lesson: when to use Outlook tasks and which types of tasks are best to record in Outlook.

To this end, I encourage you to apply the *next-action* concept to your Now Tasks list. This practice I highly recommend because it helps ensure that your tasks actually get done. There is nothing worse than having a task list full of items that sit there without completion; using this technique helps you avoid that and get more tasks done each day.

I first saw this concept in the book *To Do... Doing... Done*, by G. Lynne Snead and Joyce Wycoff. Lynne describes a system of top-down task creation where a small project is planned out as a whole, and then periodically the next action for each project is "time activated" and moved out to the daily tasks list or appointment calendar.

David Allen, author of the book *Getting Things Done*, is probably the most prominent voice for using next actions these days, and his perspectives are worth studying. David attributes his next action ideas to one of his mentors from 20 years back: Dean Acheson (no relation to the former US Secretary of State). Sally McGhee is a productivity writer who also promotes next actions in her books (Sally and David Allen used to work together).

Nearly all writers on next actions emphasize this lesson: examine tasks you have on your to-do list and to ask yourself "What is the very next physical action I need to do to accomplish this task?" They encourage you to identify the most discrete and significant next action possible, and write that down on your task list. This stimulates action more effectively and unsticks tasks that tend to remain uncompleted (more on that below).

Here are some examples of well-written next-action tasks:

▶ Call Fred and ask for new meeting date

▶ E-mail James about proposal

▶ Review Ted's summary notes

Note that each of the examples above has a verb in it; you really want to identify the action, specifically the *next* action needed to achieve an outcome. Make sure the action is as small and discrete as possible.

In contrast, your Now Tasks should not consist of generic nouns such as "James's proposal" or "Ted's notes," because these general descriptions leave you, on cursory review, uncertain of what to do. Reading these poorly written tasks in the middle of the busy day, it may take you a minute or two to decide what the action really is, and that delay can prevent you from acting on the task.

Also, only put the *very* next action task on your MYN task list; don't enter as tasks all sequential steps to a goal. Remember, your Now Tasks list shows only things eligible to do now. So if you list future dependent steps, you will clutter your list with unusable tasks.

The MORE Task

If, once you extract a next-action task, you end up needing more steps to reach the outcome, you now have a multistep task, so do this. Put the first step in the task subject name, and list the subsequent ones inside the *body* of the Outlook task item. Then place the phrase "…MORE" at the end of the subject name, to indicate there is more to this inside the task (see below).

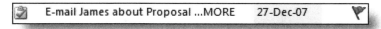

When you complete each step, read the text in the body of the task, and identify the next step, and re-label the item with this new task name (thanks to Don Morgan for this suggestion). This and similar approaches are discussed more in Lesson 12 under the subheading Series Tasks (in the section Tracking Goals and Projects in Outlook).

Next Actions of Projects

The next-action concept applies to projects as well. Plan and manage your projects using whatever project tools you like. Then, to execute specific tasks when their time has come, put *only* the next-action task for each project (or each parallel work stream within a project) on your Now Tasks list. In Lesson 12, I show some ways to use Outlook to track small projects.

Solution to Stuck Tasks

The next-action approach helps you clear stuck tasks. How many times have tasks sat on your to-do list for weeks or months? Many stuck tasks get stuck because you really haven't thought through and identified the very next action needed on the task. Instead, you often end up writing midstream outcomes that in reality require further dependent actions before you can get to them. Or you write higher-level goals with no indications of next steps needed to get there. And so in the midst of a busy day, when you see the item, you get stuck; the task description does not ring true as something that you can do immediately. So it is essential that you clearly think through what the very next action is to achieve a task, and write only that down on your Now Tasks list. This keeps that list action-oriented and focused on the immediate.

Identify the Very Next Action

One way to ensure that you are writing down the *very* next action on a stuck task is to ask yourself several times, "Is there anything else I need to do first?" If you find something, it becomes your very next action. This is also a useful exercise with new tasks, if you have time.

For example, I once received a request to assist the planning department of a client with a project proposal they were developing. I started to write down "Assist planning dept. with project," but then I thought, "No, there's something ahead of that. Of course—I need to call up the planning specialist to discuss the project." I imagined myself doing that and realized I knew nothing about this project and if I got questions during that call, the call would be counterproductive. I knew we had some material on their planned project somewhere, so really the first thing to do was to review the project material. I started to write that down. Then I thought, "Where is the material?" I remembered that Tom last worked on the project and had the file on it. So what I finally wrote down was this: "Call Tom and get planning dept. project file." When I saw that on my list later, it was easily accomplished, and doing it got the project moving. If I had seen my original task "Assist planning dept. with project" in the middle of a busy workday, I probably would have skipped over it. Take a look at your task list now and decide if any of your current tasks can be replaced with more actionable next actions.

However, what I describe above can be a lot of steps. So if you are on the run and don't have time to think this through, get the task recorded as best you can and use the tips I list next to create a placeholder for later consideration.

Helpful Next Action Bridges and Placeholders

Sometimes, when you enter a task, you cannot decide what the next action on a task is or you do not have time to decide. That's okay. Just write "Determine next step for… [task name]." That creates a bridge to further activity when you can later identify follow-up steps. Other useful bridges: "Plan work on… [task name]"or "Start work on… [task name]." Sometimes just getting started on a task allows you to think it through, and by writing it that way you do not commit yourself to a large block that you might skip over when you see it on a busy day. Small-effort tasks like this are often useful as must-do-today (Critical Now) tasks to get you moving on a project that may be stalling out.

Using MYN with Getting Things Done (GTD)

My strong encouragement above to use next actions in your MYN Now Tasks list is about the extent of the obvious overlap between MYN and David Allen's popular Getting Things Done® (GTD®) program. MYN's unique approach to task management is otherwise a quite different system. But if you are a GTD user and are looking for more ways to integrate MYN with GTD, here are some ideas on how to do that.

First of all, the two systems are completely compatible—there is nothing in MYN that conflicts with GTD, and nothing in GTD that I find unusable with MYN. Even better, they are fantastic when used together. In fact, many GTD users say that adding MYN principles on top of GTD solves many issues that come up in GTD if it is not used with care. And MYN's intelligent integration with Outlook provides one way to marry GTD with Outlook, and in a very powerful way.

Here are some points on how to integrate MYN, Outlook, and GTD.

▶   Treat MYN's Now Tasks list (the Critical Now and Opportunity Now lists combined) as your GTD next-action list. MYN's smart way to manage tasks there gives you much more control and solves the common problem of the GTD next-action list getting too long to easily review. Used correctly, MYN gives you the tools to keep the next-action list well controlled and well managed.

▶   Treat the Low priority section (Over the Horizon) as the GTD someday maybe list. Like the GTD next-action list, many GTD users complain their someday maybe list quickly becomes too long to review, and tasks there just disappear never to be seen again. As a result, they stop using the someday maybe list. You'll see in Lesson 9 how MYN's Defer-to-Review process solves that problem quite elegantly. It gives you a very intelligent way of deciding what low-priority entries to review, and when to review them. The result is your GTD weekly review is not overwhelming, and tasks still get the appropriate attention they need. If you are a GTD user, you are going to love the MYN Defer-to-Review process in Lesson 9.

▶   Use the Follow-Up Task process (discussed immediately ahead and in Lesson 7) to replace the GTD waiting-for list. It accomplishes the same thing in a way that I think is easier to use because it places the item right in your Now Tasks list at exactly the right time. It avoids you having one more list to review.

▶ GTD's definition of a project is much different from that in MYN. In GTD, any task that requires multiple steps is defined as a project, so even very small efforts are called projects. In MYN, only large efforts that require formal project management skills are called projects. However, both systems recognize the need to create a project list, and Lesson 12 ahead shows you various ways to make a projects list in Outlook that meets the needs of both GTD and MYN. As with GTD, you can then use the list to feed next-action tasks into the MYN Now Tasks list.

▶ GTD uses the concept of Context to define where and when to focus on particular tasks. It identifies tags like @Computer and @Phone that you can sort on to show you candidate tasks to work on when you are in those settings. MYN does not have a similar concept. In fact, in these days of smartphones, tablets, and other mobile devices, I do not see a strong need for identifying Context. But that said, if you find the Context approach to be useful, you can easily add GTD Context tags to tasks in the MYN system by placing them in Outlook Categories that are then tagged on your MYN tasks. You can then use the skills you learned in Lesson 3 to add a category column to your MYN tasks lists; that way you consider Context when you work your tasks. You can even sort on that column to work similar tasks together.

Those are the obvious ways that GTD and MYN can be used together. I think you will find that MYN solves the common challenges people have with GTD, but still lets you implement all of GTD's principles. And I think you will find that GTD principles help clarify how best to use MYN. Feel free to use as many or as few of the ideas above to merge the two systems.

Significant Outcomes (SOCs)

The recommendation above to put only next-action tasks on your Now Tasks lists may lead to the following question: "How do I show bigger things I am working on?" It could be you are in the middle of a larger effort that you need to focus much of your free time on this week, and just listing next actions doesn't seem enough—you want to give it more prominence.

I call these larger items "Significant Outcomes," or "SOCs" for short. These are usually the bigger deliverables you want to create (for example, a large report) that you are actively working on, in between meetings and other ad hoc tasks. They might also be a less tangible accomplishment (a cleaned-up and organized office, for example) that you would like to get done as soon as possible, and so you want to highlight them somehow on your list.

You often have no specific time you intend to work on them. Rather, you intend to fit some work on them into your schedule when you can. Or you may have smaller tasks on your Now Tasks list that are leading toward the larger outcome, and you want to track that overall outcome.

SOCs Are Smaller than Goals or Projects

SOCs are not significant enough to be called goals—*goals* implies something beyond the task level (see my book *Master Your Workday Now!* for extensive coverage of how to set and manage goals). I do not like calling them projects either—to me the word *project* implies a much bigger activity, often employing formal project management methodologies.

SOCs are just very large tasks, and as with most tasks, typically you focus on these when you have time and it feels right. For example, you may decide, "During this week my major effort between meetings will be to get the quarterly report done." Or you may think, "This week I want to make major progress on designing my new filing system."

It is especially satisfying to complete a few important SOCs each week, as it leads to a significant sense of forward momentum. I call this "knocking your SOCs off" (yes, the pun is intended). So I encourage you to list a few each week and track them.

Deciding how to record SOCs in your task system can be a quandary. Just listing them as Opportunity Now tasks seems too small because they may get lost; you want them in your awareness all week. And they are not Critical Now tasks for any given day, so putting them there does not make sense either. And scheduling specific time for them on your calendar may not feel right either, since you may not be sure when during the week you want to work on them; these are often background activities.

So you need a way to give these Significant Outcomes a general but prominent focus—to keep your attention on doing them during a given week or two.

How to Show SOCs

I recommend two ways to indicate SOCs in Outlook using the MYN system.

First, if you use a monthly or weekly calendar, you can place them as a banner appointment across a period of time, such as a week, or even longer. In Outlook, that means creating a nonblocking banner appointment on the Outlook calendar for the week, and then listing one or more SOCs in that banner appointment. I give it a distinctive color so it stands out. Figure 6.3 is an example of how this might look in the monthly view.

Another way to do this in Outlook is to list it as a Critical Now task with the letters SOC: in front like such as "SOC:Finish Quarterly Report." That way

Figure 6.3 Significant Outcomes (SOCs) in Outlook 2007.

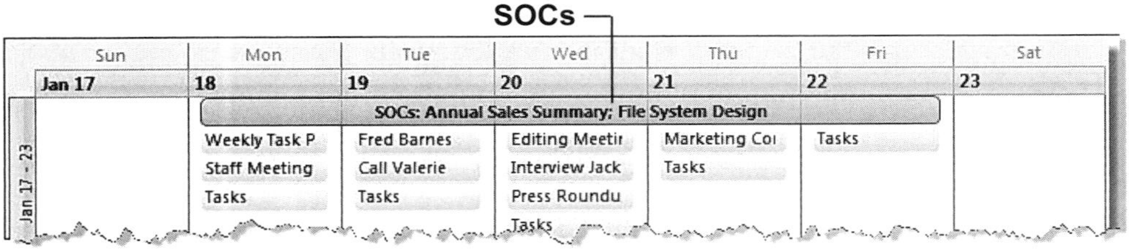

you see it many times a day. This is the only Critical Now item that makes sense to allow to carry over from day to day.

And finally, after you create an SOC, don't forget to also put any appropriate next action tasks for these SOCs right in your Opportunity Now list.

SOCs are Excellent for Deadlines

SOCs are excellent items to put deadlines on. Do you recall how I said that I rarely put deadlines on the typical small next-action tasks I place on my Now Tasks list? That's because they are usually smaller steps on the road to a larger outcome, and the larger outcome is the thing that usually has the true deadline. Well, a SOC is perfect for this because it is usually the larger thing that I am working toward — it is exactly the right place to put the deadline.

Use the deadline approaches I listed in Lesson 4. For example, write the deadline date directly on the SOC subject line: "SOC: DUE Fri Mar 7, Quarterly Report."

Use Follow-Up Tasks for Actions You Are Waiting on Others For

Here is a technique that can protect you from fire drills caused by colleagues or staff who don't deliver. How often in your organization does someone promise to deliver something but never follows through? Perhaps you're in a meeting and a promise is made to fix something. Or you direct someone who works for you to complete some work by a certain date. The trouble is you usually forget that the promise was made until well after the item is due. Then you kick yourself for not doing something earlier to usher the task forward. Whether this is a formal delegation or simply a promise made in a meeting, if you want to make sure it gets done, you need to follow up with the person who promised it at some point before the deadline, to encourage them on. Sometimes people say they will do something and really intend it, but just forget. Other times they say they will do it only to get you off their back. Wouldn't it be nice if you had an automatic way to remind yourself to check in with these people to make sure the promised activity is being done?

Instead of a Waiting-For List

Many task management systems use a "waiting for" list to track items like this. It is one long list of all the things that you are waiting on others to get to you. The idea is to check that list every day or so and then follow up with those items that seem urgent. Outlook has a status value called Waiting On Somebody Else that can be applied to tasks, just to accomplish this.

I don't like using a waiting-for list, and I do not use that Outlook status setting. The problem with this approach is there is no way to tell by examining the list which waiting-for items needs urgent follow-up and which can wait. You need to think about each item, consider when you last checked in on it, decide if now is a good time to do another follow-up, and then move to the next item. I find this way too much work to do every day on a long list. Plus, keeping a separate list to check is one more process you need to remember to do each day.

Create a Follow-Up Task

Instead, my recommended approach to items that you are waiting on is to create follow-up tasks for each item at the time the promise is made; here's how. As soon as someone promises you something, at that point decide when an appropriate time to follow up would be. Then create a task on your own list with a start date of that day. Put an F: in front of the subject line and perhaps the name of the responsible person; for example, "F: Tom–Send me Planning Dept. file." Then, on the date that task pops into your task list, do the follow-up; call the person or write them an e-mail.

This is so much better than a waiting-for list because it removes any ambiguity as to when an action is needed. You decide this when you make the entry, and the actions appear in your task list exactly when needed. Otherwise, examining a waiting-for list can be a painful and uncertain activity. What's worse, you may be examining items that do not need to be followed up on for weeks at a time; this can extend the review unnecessarily and lead you to review less often. The result is that you might miss some important follow-up activities. Follow-up tasks appear right in the same task list you use every day, so you are more likely to do the follow-up. For these reasons, I feel using follow-up tasks is the best method for tracking items that you are waiting for.

Two Types of Follow-Up Tasks

There are two ways to do this. One way I described above: you are in a meeting or have a verbal discussion with someone, a promise is made, and you note the need to track the promise. Just create the task manually in your task list, with a future date. The key here is to select a good follow-up date. If it is a Monday and you need something by Friday, perhaps you should set the follow-up for Wednesday, to give them time to respond to your reminder. When Wednesday comes and the task appears, give the person a call. With tight timing like that, give that task a High priority; that way it appears in your Critical Now list and you do not delay on your follow-up activity.

The other way of creating a follow-up task is useful when you make your original request for action through an e-mail. I have a few tools you can use to automate that process, but you will need to wait to Lesson 7 where I give a much more complete discussion on how to convert e-mails to tasks. And in Lesson 10 I expand on this concept considerably when I cover the topic of delegation.

But for now, start creating future-dated follow-up tasks whenever someone promises an action that you really want completed. I think you'll find this to be very useful.

Summary

So as you can see, there are a wide variety of tasks that you should enter in Outlook. Here are some key points from this lesson:

▶ Make sure you record all your current tasks in one place: Outlook. Do not keep multiple to-do lists.

▶ Use appointments instead of tasks when appropriate, but reserve appointments only for those items that have specific times during the day they need to be done. Otherwise use the tasks list.

▶ Don't list goals or projects on your Now Tasks list, since these broad items are not actionable during a busy workday. Rather, write all your tasks only as next actions; write the next physical action needed to achieve an outcome.

▶ You have many options for viewing your MYN task list on your mobile devices, and for collecting tasks while on the move.

▶ Use Significant Outcomes to track and manage larger efforts that do not warrant formal project management techniques.

▶ Create follow-up tasks when waiting for promises others have made you.

Next Steps

In the next lesson I will enlarge on the technique you learned earlier for converting e-mails to tasks.

Lesson 7:
Cure "Inbox Stress" by Converting E-mails to Tasks

Introduction

Inbox Stress Can Be Cured

You need a cure for what I call "Inbox stress" — that sinking feeling you have when you glance at an overwhelmed Outlook Inbox. It's the stress you feel when you know your Inbox is full of unreconciled requests that will come back to haunt you. It's the dread you feel as you realize you are going to have to sort through and reread weeks or months of mail to find e-mails you promised yourself to come back to or skipped over and never looked at.

Beyond Quick Start and Lesson 2

In the Quick Start and at the end of Lesson 2, I introduced how to convert action e-mails to tasks. The reason I started you so early on this practice was to give you an early taste of how powerful this action really is. When used correctly, it is the solution for Inbox stress. It allows you to remove the tension from the Inbox by moving unreconciled actions into the task system where they can be prioritized, scheduled, delegated, worked, or deferred, all with appropriate tools to do so effectively. It allows you work through your Inbox much more quickly by giving you a way to process action e-mails without stalling on them. And it allows you to fulfill the Lesson 5 steps of emptying your Inbox. If you are doing that now and emptying your Inbox per Lesson 5, I suspect your Inbox stress is nearly cured.

There are some fine points, however, to converting e-mails to tasks that you need to know as you do this more, so I am now going to devote a full lesson to the topic. And in case you have not yet started converting e-mails to tasks, I want to fully convince you here how important this is.

For those who *have* started using this practice on their own Inbox, you probably have noticed how, once you did this, it was much easier to move mail out of your Inbox. Converting e-mails to tasks is the primary enabler of reaching an empty Inbox. In addition, once you do it regularly, you will complete the processing of your Inbox much faster. You will also get important e-mail actions locked into your MYN tasks list where they can be better managed. Ultimately, you will get much closer to being in full control of your workday. Converting e-mails to tasks is in fact the number one most important skill you will learn in this book.

What's in This Lesson

In this lesson you will learn:

▶ More ideas on why converting e-mails to tasks is so critical to getting e-mail and tasks under control.

▶ How the Mac and Windows versions vary in this action.

▶ How to include or access attachments in converted mail so that files you need are at hand when you do the task.

▶ Flagged-mail tasks: what they are and when to use them. They are another way to convert e-mails to tasks.

▶ How to create follow-up tasks from e-mail you send in a way that makes tracking requests much more powerful.

▶ Tips on using the Windows Outlook add-in software ClearContext to automate and improve converting e-mails to tasks.

▶ An e-mail processing workflow, updated from Lesson 5, that incorporates all new elements in this lesson.

Let's start with a bit more background on why this skill is so powerful.

The Trouble with E-mail

Learning how to use e-mail effectively is essential to succeeding in the modern work environment. Why? Because e-mail, which was supposed to *improve* work, actually makes us work *harder*. And I am not referring to just the time it takes to read or respond to e-mail. Rather, the real reason e-mail makes us work harder is that e-mail leads to many more *business interactions* per day than we ever could have with only live phone calls or in-person meetings. Both of those were limited by the hours in the day, but the e-mail Inbox knows no such limits.

Business interactions almost always lead to required action. Think about it. If someone sends you a business e-mail these days, tag, you're it. "I sent you an e-mail on this. Didn't you read it?" You are now on notice, either to process the info or, more commonly, to take some additional action. You can get hundreds of these per day.

And while more business interactions per day can multiply our business success (more sales, more clients, and so on—the upside of e-mail), the added actions represent added work. So yes, we are busier at work, due to e-mail, than ever before. Using e-mail intelligently and managing it efficiently is essential to succeeding in the modern work environment.

Strategies to Fix E-mail in Today's Office

Most people don't think in terms of the potential for greater business success when it comes to e-mail; instead they see an overloaded Inbox and the hours spent thrashing through their mail. People have tried lots of strategies to get around the e-mail problem and optimize its use. For example, some people suggest you control when you read e-mail so as to decrease its impact on your workday. There is even a book titled *Never Check E-mail in the Morning*. And some well-known personalities have posted "e-mail bankruptcy," declaring null and void all old e-mail. A governor of New Jersey several years ago announced to his staff and the world that he was quitting e-mail altogether— he directed them all to other means of communication.

But you do not need to quit e-mail, you just need to be smart in how you use it. The first step to that is to recognize that the problem is not with *reading* e-mail but rather with *doing* e-mail. It is not reading spam or unneeded cc'd mail (colleague spam) that bogs down our ability to get through the Inbox. It is reacting to *meaningful e-mail*, e-mail with potential actions for us to do, that skids us off track. It's this mail that kills a huge chunk of our day. The trouble is, we do not have a natural way to prioritize our reactions to mail like this, so our Inbox and workday spin out of control.

The Solution

The solution is to use the following core principle of my training and this book:

Unless it is time-urgent, don't take significant actions on an e-mail when you first read it. Instead, quickly convert an action e-mail to a prioritized, date-assigned Outlook task, and continue to read or scan all your new mail to the bottom of your Inbox. Then file that mail out of the Inbox, and work tasks off your Now Tasks list.

This is an important, powerful, and *simple to implement* rule. Here's why it's important. What many of us do is try to work action requests as they arrive in the Inbox, thinking we are being proactive. The trouble with this is that these days we all get too much e-mail—way too much to act on everything each day. If we attempt to act on every e-mail as we get it, we miss other important work. By acting on mail as it comes in we are likely working our lowest-priority tasks first. No wonder our important work is not complete at the end of the day. And we'll never get to the bottom of our Inbox that way.

Or some of us completely skip over most e-mail action requests and then spend hours, later, trying to find the important stuff in our Inbox to get caught up on it. This is especially difficult because the titles of e-mail rarely match the request inside. So we are forced to open and reread each e-mail looking for those actions. What a mess and unnecessary churn this creates.

Instead, Speed Through E-mail

Instead, you will speed through your mail by spending only a few seconds converting such action e-mails into *prioritized, dated tasks in Outlook,* without taking action first, and moving on. You will use simple Outlook techniques for converting e-mails to tasks detailed in this lesson. You will then work these tasks later along with your other work, *in priority order,* using the task system you learned in Lessons 1, 4, and 6. As a result, you will end up purposely deferring or deleting many e-mail actions that do not make the priority cut, and that is a good thing in today's overloaded work and e-mail environment. Only the important items get first action.

Shouldn't We Just Use E-mail Less?

Some people say the solution is for organizations to use e-mail far less often for business communication. I disagree. I do believe the Reply All button should be used much more sparingly, as we all suffer from colleague spam as a result of overuse. But mistakes like that should not mean using e-mail less for business communications. E-mail has a huge number of advantages when used and managed correctly:

▶ E-mail can allow batching up of communication processing, which allows you to focus for longer periods of uninterrupted time on dedicated work.

▶ Sending e-mail prevents you from interrupting or distracting yourself and your coworkers with an in-person call or meeting every time you need to pass on information or seek it out.

▶ It speeds communications because you can send a message without starting a live discussion, which usually takes longer.

▶ It speeds communications because you do not need to wait for appropriate times to deliver a communication.

▶ E-mail tracks communications by creating a record of every sent and received e-mail.

▶ It clarifies communications because the well-written word leaves little room for misunderstanding, and the reader can reread a message as often as is needed to fully understand the communication.

All of these advantages, when fully realized, will contribute to the goal of getting your tasks done more quickly and achieving greater accomplishments at work.

So no, don't use e-mail less often. Rather, learn how to use and manage e-mail more *intelligently*. Converting action e-mails into tasks effectively (and sometimes into appointments) and emptying the Inbox daily are two primary ways to do this.

Note: *In Lesson 11, I'll show some other e-mail management tips that will help you and your company or organization become more productive with e-mail, including ways to make the e-mail you send more useful.*

Using Outlook Tools to Convert E-mails to Tasks

When you find an action item in your e-mail, you could create a new task by hand. However, as we've seen, some easy tools are built into Outlook to *convert* e-mail messages directly into tasks. When using these tools, the entire text of the mail is stored in the new task, and the subject line of the task takes on the subject line of the e-mail (which in some cases you can then easily edit). You can optionally include attachments in Windows Outlook. And there is additional Outlook add-in software that makes the conversion even smarter.

Primary Types of Conversion

In the Quick Start, and at the end of Lesson 2, I showed you a simple way to convert an e-mail to a task. But there are really more ways to do this, and many subtleties to how you can do it. That's the purpose of this lesson, to show you those additional ways and fine points.

For Windows, the primary way to convert e-mail messages to tasks is what you learned earlier—a simple drag and drop. This is best for e-mails without attached files. The second method, a modified drag and drop, is best for e-mails *with* attached files. And a third method, flagging mail (available in Outlook 2007/10), you will soon see is best used for tasks that represent deferred replies.

For the Mac, there are two methods: using an AppleScript to create a true Outlook task, and using flagged mail.

Note: *In their simplest form these methods maintain a copy of the original e-mail in the Inbox, which is what I recommend; more on that point later.*

Let's cover all these methods in more detail, starting with creating true tasks in Windows, and then on the Mac.

After that, I'll expand on the important 2007/10 and 2011 feature that allows you to convert an e-mail to a task-like entry in the tasks list by using Outlook's Follow Up flag. I don't recommend using that often, and there are some cautions to take when you do.

Converting E-mails to Tasks in Windows Outlook

Windows Outlook gets more coverage here because it has more options for converting e-mails into *true* Outlook tasks compared to the Mac, and that leads to a number of opportunities for refining the ways you manage tasks. For example, you can create tasks with or without attachments.

Creating Tasks Without Attachments

Here are the detailed steps behind the method I showed you in the Quick Start and at the end of Lesson 2. It creates tasks without attachments but does copy the e-mail text into the body of the task.

Once you decide that an e-mail contains a task that is important to you, if it has no attachment you want to include with the task, close the e-mail and follow these steps:

1. From within your regular e-mail *list* view, click the e-mail item and drag it to the Tasks folder icon or banner button in the Navigation Pane of Outlook. Depending on which version of Outlook you have and how you have configured it, the Tasks folder icon might be located in a folder list view, or located at the bottom of the Navigation Pane. See Lesson 2 for a complete discussion of where to find the Tasks folder icon or banner button.

2. A new task window containing the entire e-mail text opens, and the task name is the same as the subject name of the e-mail. That means you have very little typing to do to complete the conversion. But do the following steps immediately:

Note: *See note after step 2 on page 46 for how to fix odd Outlook 2010 behavior that causes the new task window to disappear.*

3. Change the title of the task so that it is in next-action format. This is an essential step; you must extract from the e-mail the core next action it implies and write that into the subject line, overwriting the old e-mail title. Lesson 6 covers next actions and how to write them.

4. Set a start date for this task. Set it to today or earlier if you want to see it in the TaskPad/To-Do Bar now, or defer it to a later date; do not leave the date at None. If you are undecided on the date, then set it to today. Allow the Due Date field to match the Start Date field (that's automatic); remember that the Due Date field is ignored in the MYN Outlook system due to the unfortunate linkages built into Outlook. Decide on and set the task Priority field per the principles in Lesson 4.

   Click Save & Close in the upper left corner of the new Task dialog box.

That's it! Your task has been saved in the task database inside Outlook. If the Start Date field was set to today or earlier, and you made Lesson 3 configurations, you can now see the new task appear in your TaskPad/To-Do Bar.

Note: *Outlook 2007/10 users may be wondering why I teach you to drag the e-mail to the Tasks icon or banner button and not directly to the To-Do Bar task list. Go ahead and try it and you will see it does not work; the e-mail will not be converted to a <u>true</u> task, rather, it will be listed as a flagged-mail task.*

Again, converting an e-mail to a task by this method does not save any e-mail attachments into the new task. Nor does it allow you to easily convert the task back into an e-mail (though there are *moderately* easy ways to do this). If you want to do either of these, follow the steps in the next segment.

Creating Tasks with Attachments

If your e-mails to be converted to tasks have attachments that you wish to save within the final task item, or if you may want to easily convert the task back to an e-mail someday (perhaps to reply to it after the task is done), do this: *right-click* the mail item to drag it to the task folder, instead of a left-clicking it. Make sure you right-click and *hold*, and then drag the item to the Tasks icon or banner button. When you release the mouse button over the task folder icon, a shortcut menu opens. From this menu, choose: Copy Here as Task With Attachment; this is the second item in the menu (see Figure 7.1).

Note: *This right-click operation can be a bit tricky for some people; if you do it incorrectly you will not see the menu in Figure 7.1, but a different, longer menu. So keep trying if it does not seem to work at first. Just make sure you right-click and <u>hold</u> the right mouse button down and then drag the item with that button still held down.*

After you select the correct menu choice, a new Task dialog box opens, showing the complete e-mail as an attachment inside the task; it appears as a simple icon in the task body (see Figure 7.2). Any attachments to the original e-mail are left intact nested inside this attachment. Immediately retitle the task to indicate the core next action, and set the start date and priority. (Also, see note after step 2 on page 46 for how to fix odd Outlook 2010 behavior that causes the new task window to disappear).

Later, when doing the task, to open the original e-mail simply double-click the e-mail icon inside the task item; the e-mail that opens is a fully operational e-mail with all its original attachments. And you are able to reply to this e-mail if you wish, which makes this right-click technique useful even for e-mails without attachments. Use it if acting on that task might also require replying to or resending the original e-mail.

Copying as task with attachment, by the way, is a great way to create follow-up tasks for important e-mail responses you are waiting for, discussed below.

Figure 7.1
Shortcut menu
when dragging an
e-mail to create a
task.

Note: *There is an obvious but minor disadvantage to this technique: when examining the task later, you need to double-click the e-mail icon inside the task to read the original e-mail, and some see this as an extra step. This trivial step is usually not a problem. But if you really want to see the text of the e-mail when you first open the task and have the attachments there too, do this: create the task using the text-only method described first; then open the original e-mail and drag the e-mail attachment from the e-mail to the newly created task window. This way you get both the e-mail text and the attachments visible when you open your new task. Even better is to install the ClearContext add-in software and use the special Task button provided, covered ahead. It creates a task that includes both text and attachments automatically.*

Figure 7.2
Result of creating a task with the e-mail saved as an attachment.

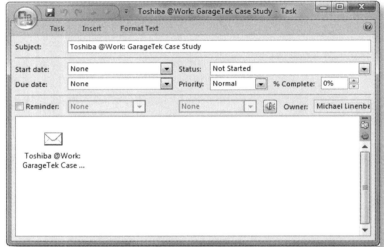

Figure 7.3
Outlook for Mac 2011 AppleScript menu to create a task from an e-mail.

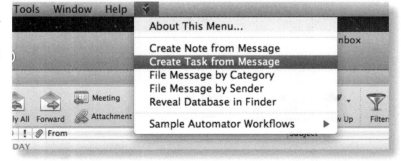

Converting E-mails to Tasks in Outlook for Mac 2011

In Outlook for Mac 2011, the drag-and-drop conversion features that have been in Windows versions of Outlook for years do not exist. So, to convert an e-mail to a true task on the Mac, you have to use an AppleScript utility provided in the script menu at the right end of the Outlook menu bar. Here's how.

Creating Tasks

1. With a message selected in Outlook for Mac 2011, simply open the AppleScript menu at the far right end of the menu bar (see the very top of Figure 7.3 — it looks like a small scrolled document) and choose Create Task from Message. Note: if the Create Task from Message command shown in Figure 7.3 is not present in your software, go to this link to fix that: www.myn.bz/MacScript.htm.

2. A new task window containing the entire e-mail text opens, and the task name is the same as the subject name of the e-mail. That means you have very little typing to do to complete the conversion. But do the following steps immediately:

3. Change the title of the task so that it is in next-action format. This is an essential step; you must extract from the e-mail the core next action it implies and write that into the subject line, overwriting the old e-mail title. Lesson 6 covers next actions and how to write them.

4. Set a start date for this task. Set it to today or earlier if you want to see it in the MYN task list, or defer it to a later date; do not leave the date at None. If your are undecided on the date, then set it to today. Allow the Due Date field to match the Start Date field (that's automatic); remember that the Due Date field is ignored in the MYN system due to the unfortunate linkages built into Outlook. Decide on and set the task Priority field.

   Click Save & Close in the upper left corner of the new Task dialog box.

That's it! Your task has been saved in the task database inside Outlook. If the Start Date field was set to today or earlier, and you made Lesson 3 configurations, you will see the new task appear in your MYN task list.

Note: *Step 1 above works both if the e-mail is selected in a mail list view and if the e-mail itself is open for reading; this is an advantage over Windows Outlook.*

What About Attachments?

Tasks in Outlook 2011 cannot hold attachments, which is a real shame. I am not sure why they cannot since e-mails can. I especially miss this feature when converting e-mails to tasks; often the e-mail has a file attached that I will need to refer to when I work on the action in the e-mail later. Or I may want to reply to that e-mail later and so I'd like to attach it to the task. This is one big disadvantage compared to Windows Outlook.

You can work around that, however. Assuming you save or file your mail as discussed in Lesson 5, you can use the search tool in Outlook 2011 (called Spotlight) to easily find that e-mail and its attachments later. Here's how:

When using the task later, just select and copy a unique phrase or sentence out of the body of the task (recall the task body came from the original e-mail). Next, activate the Processed Mail folder and paste the text into the Spotlight search box. Doing that search should allow you to find the original e-mail almost instantly; you can then either reply to it or access the attachments inside.

Note: If the e-mail is filed somewhere other than the Processed Mail folder, select All Mail at the left edge of the Search tab on the Ribbon to help you find it.

Other Tips for Converting E-mails to Tasks (Windows and Mac)

Header Information at Top of Task Body

In Windows Outlook, after you convert an e-mail to a task, you will notice at the top of the body of the task that Outlook has inserted some useful header info about the source e-mail. This includes the sender, the date of the e-mail, and the original e-mail subject line. Later, when you work the task, this provides you some context about the original e-mail that led to the task.

On the Mac that's not true; using the script above in Outlook 2011 does not insert that header information, and so later you may be left confused as to the context of the task. To fix that, here's a workaround. Before using the Create Task from Message command, first create (but don't send) a reply message to the original e-mail; then apply the command with that reply message window open. This creates the header and inserts it into the body of the new task giving you the context you need. Then delete the reply without sending it.

Converting Text Tasks Back to E-mails

In Windows, copying as a task with attachment is not the only way to enable replies to converted tasks. If you create a task as text and later decide you want to reply to the original e-mail, in Windows there are ways to convert it back to an e-mail. The easiest is to simply drag the task from the task list to the Mail banner button or Inbox icon. You'll need to edit the resulting e-mail and put an address on it. I give more details on that in Lesson 11.

The Mac does not allow this. However, if you are in the habit of using Spotlight to find the original e-mail as described above for attachments, that should be all you need to do; just find and reply to the original e-mail.

Dragging More Than One E-mail at Once

Let's say there are three e-mails in the Inbox that pertain to a task you want to create, and you want to save all three of them with a single task. In Windows you can create one task by pressing CTRL or SHIFT, and selecting the three e-mails in the list view, and then dragging them all at once. If you create a task as text, the text of all three e-mails is placed in the body of the task, one below the other. If you create a task as an attachment, three icons will appear inside the task body. Unfortunately, on the Mac this does not work.

Turn Off Message AutoPreview and Reading Pane

I find it easier to scan through messages and quickly convert e-mail to tasks if I turn off the message AutoPreview and Reading Pane features of Outlook.

Reading Pane is a Windows and Mac feature that allows you to see the contents of the currently selected message displayed in a separate segment of the Outlook window. AutoPreview is a Windows-only feature that shows you two or three lines under each message in the Inbox.

I find both of these distracting; they also reduce the number of e-mails I can see at once in the list. So I turn them off. I can move faster through my mail by scanning titles and sender information alone and only occasionally opening mail. Try this yourself and see what you think. Here is how you do that.

To turn off the Reading Pane, in all versions of Windows and on the Mac, go to the View menu or tab, choose Reading Pane, and from the submenu select Off (Windows) or Hidden (Mac).

To turn off AutoPreview in Outlook 2003 and 2007, go the View menu and find AutoPreview. If there is a check next to it, clear it by selecting it. In Outlook 2010, go to the View tab and select Change View at the far left. Then, click the icon that is labeled Single (it is located just to the left of the icon labeled Preview).

I think you'll now find that scanning e-mail to identify tasks is much easier.

Don't Convert Actions That You Can Do in One Minute

Needless to say, if you can actually do an action faster than you can convert an e-mail to a task, common sense says to just do it immediately. Typical for this would be a quick one-sentence e-mail note or reply. But be careful: if that act turns into a twenty-minute discourse, you've gone off the track.

Why You Should *Copy* and Not *Move* the E-mails (Windows)

Also note, when you right-click and drag a task, and then open the shortcut menu over the task icon, you'll see as in Figure 7.1 that the third item down in that context menu is the command Move Here as Task With Attachment; so you can choose to *move* the e-mail into a task rather than *copy* it. A move operation removes the e-mail from the Inbox. Some users may be eager to do that, thinking, "Hey, I processed that e-mail so now let's get rid of it."

I do not recommend doing that though. Why? Because there are *two* components of most action e-mails and both are important. There is the *action* component, which is what the task becomes, and there is also an *information* component that you might need to reference separately from executing the task. Most of us are used to looking in saved e-mail for this information. Years ago I used to *move* instead of *copy* during task creation, but not anymore, because I often spent hours looking in the wrong place (saved e-mail) only to recall that I had converted it to a task. Now I always *copy* when I create tasks from e-mails. There are just too many times I search my saved mail for things. If you are dragging all mail at the end of the day to the Processed Mail folder, it will soon be out of the Inbox anyway.

ClearContext Task Button (Windows)

The add-in software ClearContext has a Task button that I find very useful compared to the built-in Outlook tools for converting e-mails to tasks.

Here are some advantages of that tool.

▶ The Task button copies the e-mail as text and as an attachment into the task it creates. So it provides the best of both worlds.

▶ The Task button is located in several convenient locations, including within the e-mail itself. That means you can make the conversion without needing to close the e-mail first.

▶ You can configure the software to include all of the text or just the portion of the text with the task; the latter saves storage space for long messages.

▶ You can configure the software to automatically ask you to associate a project with a Task as you create it and optionally file the original message. This takes care of both components at once: the information as a filed mail, and the action as a task.

▶ On a more subtle note, when using the ClearContext Task button, e-mail *conversations* or threads are linked to the task via the ClearContext Dashboard — you can see in that view related messages received after the task was created in addition to the original e-mail message.

Creating Appointments from E-mails (Windows)

Everything I have described above for creating Outlook tasks also applies to creating Outlook *appointments* on the Outlook calendar. Just drag an e-mail to the Calendar icon or banner button. In addition to setting the date, you'll need to set the time, of course, but all else is similar.

The times you will want to do this should be obvious: whenever an action e-mail leads you to create a calendar appointment. For example, Ted Jones sends me a note saying a meeting is needed and asking me to set it up. His e-mail has details of what will be discussed. I just drag the e-mail to the calendar icon, an appointment item dialog box opens, and in that I set the date and time and change the title. If I have a second Outlook window open, I can drag directly to the intended date on the calendar; all I need to do is set the time.

Next, I send Ted an Outlook meeting invite generated from that item. Later, when I am about to go to the meeting, I can open the calendar item and all the original e-mail details from Ted about what will be discussed are right there.

Creating appointments from e-mails is needed much less often than creating tasks, particularly because many such e-mails arrive as an Outlook meeting invite already; all you need to do is accept it to place the meeting on your Calendar. But that said, this may come up occasionally. As mentioned before, however, do not get in the habit of placing all your tasks as appointments with yourself on your calendar. I will give more details why this is not a good idea later in this lesson.

In ClearContext there is also a Schedule button for creating appointments from e-mail; it has the same advantages as listed above for the ClearContext Task button.

Use of the Follow Up Flag Tool (Windows and Mac)

The Outlook Follow Up flag is a small (usually red) flag that sits at the right end of e-mails in a message list. It can be used for a variety of purposes but I recommend you focus your use of it carefully; that's because an Inbox full of flagged mail can become useless. In the pages ahead, I describe how to use the Follow Up flag correctly.

The Follow Up flag in Outlook 2007/10 and 2011 has changed dramatically compared to earlier versions of Outlook, so I describe those versions in their own section next. But first, let's learn how to use the Follow Up flag in Outlook 2003.

Setting the Follow Up Flag in Outlook 2003

The most complete way to add a Follow Up flag to a message in Outlook 2003 is to select the message in the mail list, right-click, and choose Follow Up from the shortcut menu. That menu opens a submenu in which you can choose various colors for the flag (see Figure 7.4). After selecting one, it leaves a flag of that color on the message in the list view.

A shortcut in Outlook 2003: if you always pick red as your flag color, merely click the flag icon in the right margin of the mail list window; that sets a red flag in one click.

When to Use the Outlook 2003 Follow Up Flag

In Lesson 5 I strongly encouraged you to empty the Inbox as often as possible. I have one exception to the rule of not leaving anything in the Inbox as you empty it, and that's this: if the action needed for an e-mail is simply to reply to it, but you know you don't have time to do it quickly in the moment (say because it will take more than a minute or two to compose a reply), it is

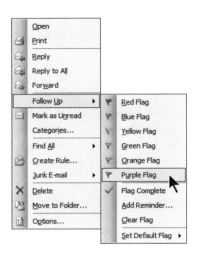

Figure 7.4
Setting the Follow Up in Outlook 2003 (right-click the e-mail in the Inbox).

silly to convert it to a task. Rather, I recommend you flag this message with a Follow Up flag. Later, when you collect and move your e-mails into the Processed Mail folder, just avoid the flagged items; leave them in the Inbox until you reply. Leaving such pending reply items in the Inbox ensures that you will see them often; they stand out prominently. It's either that or convert it to a High priority task, which takes a few more steps. You should, however, make a commitment to yourself to return to and reply to those messages before the end of the day or early the next. I try to reply to all mail within 24 hours; your organization may want to set a standard for maximum reply times. That said, delaying most long replies until the end of the day I consider a workday best practice, and I explain why in Lesson 11. Again, this is a good way to mark an e-mail for later reply. However, if the reason you are not replying is that some action is needed first, conversion to a task is usually much more appropriate.

When Not to Use the Follow Up Flag in Outlook 2003

There are a lot more things you can do with the Follow Up flag, including setting alarms to remind you of follow-ups. Some Outlook 2003 users utilize Follow Up flags as a form of a task list within their e-mail. I strongly recommend *against* using these capabilities because they get you in the habit of leaving tasks in your e-mail Inbox, and the Inbox is not a good location for tasks. Reason: once you collect more than five or six flagged e-mails they are difficult to keep track of. You cannot easily or may not want to change the title of an e-mail to a next action phrase, so if you leave tasks in your Inbox for very long you are constantly guessing what the flagged e-mails are really for. You then need to open each e-mail and reread it to figure out what the task actually is. You cannot sort them, prioritize them, defer them, and so on.

So even though the Follow Up flag may seem versatile, using it in Outlook 2003 as a way to mark *tasks* in the Inbox is really only a stopgap. Instead, the much better practice is to convert all action e-mails to tasks and use the Follow Up flag only for the limited purpose described above: to mark delayed replies.

Flagged-Mail Tasks in Outlook 2007/10 and 2011

One of the major changes in Outlook 2007/10 and 2011, compared to earlier versions, is the promotion of a flagged mail to near-task status. What I mean is this: when you activate a Follow Up flag at the right edge of an e-mail, a virtual copy of the e-mail is placed in the task list. It looks very much like a real task, so I call it a "flagged-mail task."

Why are these so important? As you know by now, my number-one assertion about how to get control of mail is to convert action mail to tasks (and then manage them in your task system). So anything that makes this easier I highly welcome. Particularly since this new feature will lead thousands of people who normally would never do this to start converting action mail to tasks.

But don't celebrate yet, because this feature will initially introduce some confusion for MYN system users, enough so that I recommend limiting the use of flagged-mail tasks. Why? Because these flagged items, even though they show up in the task list, are not true Outlook tasks and therefore behave differently. For example, once it is flagged, if you open a flagged-mail task from your task list, you won't see date fields, a priority field, or the reminder field as you would in a task; it's still an e-mail. You can find equivalents of those in various places (in the e-mail Ribbon menus and the flag shortcut menu), but setting them is inconvenient compared to a true task window. And I have identified a long list of other limitations (see sidebar: Why Flagged-Mail Tasks May Not Be Right for E-mail Tasks in MYN). These have led me to conclude that a more limited use of this feature is in order for MYN users. That said, it will play an important role, described next.

My Recommended Use for Flagged-Mail Tasks: Tagging Delayed Replies

Flagged-mail tasks are still useful though, because in one very good way they fit nicely into the MYN system: marking e-mail replies you want to delay for a few hours or a day. Let's say you read an e-mail and realize that to reply adequately would take several minutes, and that time is not available now. It is silly to convert it to a task; that takes several steps and it will be gone within hours. Rather, I recommend you flag this message with an Outlook Follow Up flag so you can find it easily later in the day to do the reply. When you collect and move your e-mails into the Processed Mail folder, just avoid the flagged items and reply soon thereafter.

Now, I know in Lesson 5, I strongly encouraged you to fully empty the Inbox as often as possible. But this is the one exception to the rule of not leaving anything in the Inbox as you empty it. Leaving such pending reply mail in the Inbox ensures that you will see it often. You should, however, make a commitment to yourself to return to and reply to those messages before the end of the day or early the next. I try to reply to all mail within 24 hours; your organization may want to set a standard for maximum reply times.

Flagging an e-mail item works quite well for delayed replies since it is quick, it leaves the e-mail intact as an e-mail, and it is very easy to reply to. See all

Why Flagged-Mail Tasks May Not Be Right for Converting E-mail to Tasks in MYN

Here are the major limitations of using flagged-mail tasks as a comprehensive way of converting action e-mails to tasks for MYN users:

► Recall that you should always change the e-mail subject to an action phrase once converted to a task. With flagged-mail tasks in Windows Outlook, you *can* change the subject without changing the original e-mail subject, which *is* good. However you need to go find the new task in the To-Do Bar and change it there, which is inconvenient. In contrast, during conversions of mail to true tasks, the window that opens upon conversion is the right place to change that wording, and it is right in front of you. It is a much smoother set of steps. And on the Mac you cannot change the title.

► You can't easily edit or add additional text to the flagged mail, say for describing thoughts about how to execute the task. There is a way to enable that in Windows, but as in the above point, you need to find the new task item, open it, and enable the editing there. Again, it is an awkward set of steps.

► As mentioned above, you won't see date fields, a priority field, or the reminder field when you open a flagged-mail task as you do in a true task; it's still an e-mail (though you can find e-mail equivalents by searching the e-mail Ribbon menus and the flag shortcut menu).

► If you connect handheld devices to your Exchange Server, flagged mail items on nearly all devices do not show up in their task lists. Update: at press time, there is one that does. The software called TaskTask for the iPhone and iPad can show flagged-mail tasks in its task list.

► In Windows, when working in the Tasks folder views, you need to select a special To-Do List folder to see flagged-mail tasks, and your existing Tasks folder custom views may not be visible there at first. This can be confusing at first.

► A flagged-mail task is a Search Folder item, so if you delete it, you delete the original e-mail as well. Awareness of that is needed as you handle these items.

the reasons in the sidebar Why Flagged-Mail Tasks Are Excellent for Tagging Delayed Replies.

So delayed replies are a great use for flagged-mail tasks and I encourage you to use them for that. Another good use for flagged-mail tasks in Windows is to create "flag on send" e-mails, covered later in this lesson.

Other Features of Flagged-Mail Tasks (Windows and Mac)

Here are some other features and implications of using flagged-mail tasks:

▶ On the Mac and Windows, you can set the start date and due date of a flagged-mail task by opening the item, choosing Follow Up from the

Why Flagged-Mail Tasks Are Excellent for Tagging Delayed Replies

Here is a complete list of reasons why flagged-mail tasks are especially well suited for delayed replies:

▶ After flagging a mail item, if you drag that e-mail out of your Inbox, the corresponding task remains in your task list. This is quite important because I often find that I am reluctant to empty my day's worth of mail when I recall mail items are in there that I intend to reply to. Now, after flagging them, I can select all mail in the Inbox and file it if I want, knowing my deferred replies are still neatly displayed and marked in my task list (however, I still recommend you leave them in the Inbox if you can).

▶ With default Outlook settings, when you create a flagged-mail task it sets the start date to *today* for you. That's good; you usually want to reply the same day. And due to our Lesson 3 task list configurations, it sorts the item to the top of the Normal priority section (nicely underlined in Windows).

▶ Flagged-mail tasks turn red in your Inbox the next day (assuming you chose the default date setting of Today). That's appropriate since I feel you should reply within 24 hrs to delayed replies; this reminds you to do that.

▶ A flagged-mail task puts a mail icon on the item in the MYN configured task list, so you can get in the habit of visually scanning for those first; replies are usually the first thing you should do (after must-do-today tasks), and this makes them easy to spot.

▶ In Windows, you can change the subject line to match the action name (with a little effort), and if you make that edit within the To-Do Bar list (not in the open flagged-mail task window), any later reply to that mail still carries the original subject line with it.

Ribbon menu at the top of the mail item, and then choosing Custom… from the drop-down menu (Custom Date… on the Mac). Or on Windows, right-click the flag at the right edge of the list view.

▶ In Windows, it's not just flagged *mail* that gets shown in the To-Do Bar. If you flag an Outlook contact item it will pop into your To-Do Bar as well. And with proper linkages, you can see tasks from SharePoint, OneNote, and Project Server.

▶ On Windows, with a minor configuration change, you can prevent mail you flag in the Inbox from showing in the To-Do Bar. If you flag a lot of replies each day, you may want to do that to keep your To-Do Bar task list uncluttered. See my instructions at this link: www.myn.bz/FlagFilter.htm.

Viewing Flagged-Mail Tasks in the Tasks Folder (Outlook 2007/10)

If you are going to start using flagged-mail tasks, know this: they do not show up in the standard Outlook 2007/10 Tasks folder that you might reach when you click the Tasks banner button or icon in your folder list. If you use flagged-mail tasks and you want to see them in the Tasks folder, you need to start using the mysterious To-Do List folder. Why do I call it "mysterious"? Because the logic behind its presence is confusing at first. I explain the logic fully near the end of Appendix A (see the section New to Outlook 2007/10: The Mysterious To-Do List Folder). For now, just know that if you want to see flagged-mail tasks when you click on the Tasks banner button in the lower portion of the Navigation Pane, make sure you subsequently select the To-Do List folder at the top of the Navigation Pane.

Create Follow-Up Tasks for Important Requests You Make by E-mail (Windows and Mac)

In Lesson 6 I showed one way to create a follow-up task when waiting for something promised you. The method there is best used if your request is made live with the person or if you think of it later. If your request is made by e-mail, there is a better way to do this, which I will show you now. During my seminars this is often the most popular section, so I know many people share this need. Some background first.

Problem

Before I created this process, I found I was often frustrated by colleagues and staff who failed to respond to simple requests I e-mailed to them. Often their one-minute effort to respond would have advanced my small project immeasurably.

The trouble is, to be polite I usually give staff or colleagues a few days to respond to the e-mail request, and by then I have forgotten that I am waiting.

I often only realize on the day my project is due that I received no response. It's too late by that time, and then the blame game starts ("Bill never got back to me; I would have completed this if he hadn't dropped the ball").

Many of the staff you send these requests to don't work for you, so they deprioritize your requests. And if you are juggling five or ten background projects, as many managers are, it is impossible to manage in your head all the loose-end requests that are hanging out there.

Solution

If you are on the hook for completing a multistep task or small project, and if a key interim step of that activity requires you to make an e-mail request for something, do the following. At the moment you send the e-mail request, create a follow-up task to yourself from the sent item telling you to remind that person later in case they don't reply. By using the sent item, you retain the original request. Set your task to appear on your Now Tasks list at some reasonable number of days into the future but well before the due date of your multistep task. That way, if they drop the ball on getting back to you, you are reminded to escalate this while you still have time to get your task done.

How to Create the Task

To create such a follow-up task easily in Outlook: immediately after you send the e-mail, open the Sent Items folder and find the item (it will be at the top of the date-sorted list); then convert it to a task. In Windows, use the right-click-and-drag method. In the popup menu that appears, choose Copy Here as Task with Attachment, as described near the beginning of this lesson. In the Mac create it the normal way using the AppleScript menu command.

Or instead of going to the Sent Items folder, BCC yourself when you send the message and convert it out of the Inbox.

In either case, set the start date to a reasonable day to send them a reminder. And set the subject text to start with *F:* to signify this is a follow-up task, such as F: Tim Jones-Request for Report Copy. A complete subject line annotation system is described in Lesson 10, on Delegation. If timing is tight, also set the priority to High to ensure that you make the reminder that day.

Effective Next Step: Send the Original Note Back

Here is why this operation is so useful. When the due date arrives and the follow-up task appears in your task list, if your request is unfulfilled, it's easy to find the original e-mail you sent and *resend it* as part of your escalation with the recipient; that saves the time needed to reiterate your request. In Windows you can open the message from within the task, and on the Mac you can search for it as I described in the section named What About Attachments?

Even better: when you open the original message, *Reply All* to your own message (adjusting the To: field back to the recipient only, by removing your name) and write a new sentence above the old note such as "Wondering if you received my e-mail below and had any thoughts." The reply action inserts a header above the old mail that clearly shows the recipient that the message was originally sent addressed to them and indicating the date it was sent, presumably some time ago. Showing this history (and the fact that a response is way overdue) is usually pretty effective at jogging some action.

Alternative to Waiting-For List

For those who may have used a "waiting-for " list in the past to track items like this, I find the above approach much better because the follow-up item does not appear until it has aged an appropriate interval. There is nothing worse than being bugged about a request without having been given time to work on it. This also eliminates the mental calculation of looking at a waiting-for list to decide whether action is needed on the items in the list. And it means you have only one task list to track; the follow-up task appears directly on your Now Tasks list and at just the right time and priority level.

Flag on Send Feature of Outlook 2007/10

This ability to create a follow-up task to e-mail that you send is built right into Outlook 2007/10, so you can do it in essentially one step. It's called flag on send. It's a nice feature and it's quite simple to use, but there are several reasons I do not recommend it compared to the method described above:

▶ It creates a flagged-mail task, not a true task; I list the many limitations of flagged-mail tasks above.

▶ You need to remember to set it before you send the mail; you'll often forget.

▶ The control to create it is a redesign of a previous control and you may find it to be a little confusing.

Let me explain these, starting with the third point first.

Retooled Control

In versions of Outlook prior to Outlook 2007 you may know that you could flag an outgoing message. Do not confuse this with setting a high-importance marking on the item; that is different. Rather, this was a true Follow Up flag, so that when the e-mail arrived in the Outlook Inbox of the recipient it already had an Outlook Follow Up flag attached to it and possibly a reminder alarm. It was a pretty cool capability, and honestly a bit intrusive. Why intrusive? Because it allowed you to control someone else's Outlook to pop up an alarm window on their computer against your e-mail deadline. I found that to be just a bit too pushy when others did it to me, so I rarely used it. Regardless, the way you set it was simple: you just clicked the flag symbol at the top of the outgoing e-mail before clicking the Send button (see Figure 7.5).

Outlook 2007/10 In-Message Flag Controls

In Outlook 2007/10 that flag button is still there but now looks different (see Figure 7.6), and it *works* differently. Its main purpose now is to create a flag on *your* copy of the mail, specifically, in your own Sent Items folder.

At first that may seem silly; why put a flag on a mail item hidden in the Sent Items folder that you may never see? But here's the key. This creates a flagged-mail task and so places a copy right in your Now Tasks list (To-Do Bar), along with all your other tasks. It's even marked with a special symbol indicating it is an e-mail follow-up (see Figure 7.7).

Figure 7.5
Setting the outgoing Follow Up flag,
Outlook 2003.

**Follow Up flag
Outlook 2003**

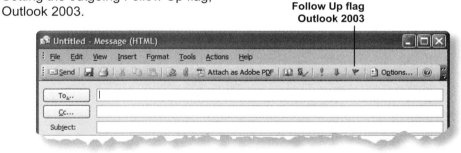

**Follow Up flag
2007 version**

Figure 7.6
Setting the Follow Up flag in Outlook 2007 (2010 is similar). This version creates a flagged-mail task.

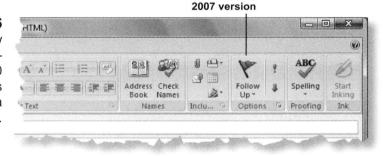

Figure 7.7
Special symbol on e-mail follow-up task created with Outlook 2007/10 flag on send feature.

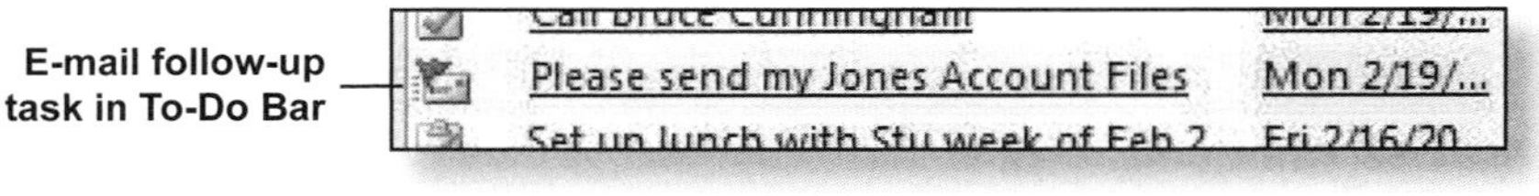

E-mail follow-up task in To-Do Bar

The net result: you have a tool that can create a follow-up task in one click.

Again though, it only creates a flagged-mail task. Since I encourage you to rely mostly on true tasks, not flagged-mail tasks, I do not encourage use of this tool very often; the ClearContext tool described ahead is a better choice.

More about Flag on Send: Setting Follow-Up Dates

When you use the flag on send feature to create a follow-up task like this, the Outlook 2007/10 interface also allows you to pick a follow-up time frame from the flag drop-down menu. This allows you to set the flag and pick the date in one step, which can be useful. Figure 7.8 shows how to pick various preset dates or a custom date; this menu looks very much like the flag shortcut menu accessible at the right edge of e-mails and To-Do Bar tasks, discussed near the end of Lesson 2. In 2007, one difference in this menu is the last item, Flag For Recipients... which I will describe next.

What If I Still Want to Set a Reminder Flag at the Recipient's Mailbox?

If you enjoyed the old pre-2007 way, where the outgoing Follow Up flag placed a reminder alarm in the recipient's mailbox, it is not gone. In Outlook 2007 it is an option at the bottom of the drop-down menu called Flag for Recipients...; see that choice at the bottom of Figure 7.8. And in Outlook 2010 you need to select Custom... from the Follow Up drop-down menu and then select the Flag for Recipients check box in the dialog box that opens.

One More Bonus of Flag on Send Tasks

There is one more bonus of using these flag on send tasks. If the recipient in fact replies to your original e-mail request, the Infobar at the top of that reply tells you that this is a reply to a flagged message. You can click that bar and automatically open the related flagged-mail task, and then mark it complete.

Note: An Infobar is the message bar sometimes displayed inside Outlook items, just below the Ribbon or menu; commonly it tells you things like "You replied on [date, time]").

Figure 7.8
Choosing a
follow-up date
when using flag
on send (Out-
look 2007).

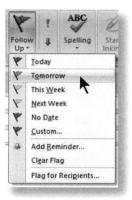

Creating Follow-Up Tasks with ClearContext (All Windows Outlook)

The ClearContext Outlook add-in software also has a one-button follow-up task capability built in, and it works on Outlook 2003 as well as 2007/10. It works better than the one I just showed you since it creates a true Outlook task as opposed to a flagged-mail task. Like the Outlook 2007/10 feature button shown in Figure 7.6, the ClearContext button is also right on the open mail message Ribbon or menu bar, but labeled differently, as shown in Figure 7.9. And like the Outlook 2007/10 feature, you need to remember to click that button before you send the message (though if you do forget, you can find the message in the Sent Items folder, and then apply the command via the ClearContext menu).

When the message is sent, a dialog box opens allowing you to set parameters on the follow-up task. One of those settings cancels the follow-up task automatically if a reply is received, removing the task from the task list. This is a nice tool.

Figure 7.9
The ClearContext
Followup Message
control (2007 shown,
other Outlook ver-
sions similar). This
version creates a true
Outlook task.

**ClearContext Followup
Message control**

Updated E-mail Processing Workflow (Windows and Mac)

In Lesson 5, I showed you a simple workflow for processing mail. With the additional material in this lesson, that original workflow plus all of the recommendations above now come together in a complete set of steps. There are many different ways to combine these tools, and you will develop a preferred method over time. Until you do, let me suggest an idealized workflow that incorporates all the elements of e-mail processing best practices into one step-by-step process.

The E-mail Workflow

The details of all steps below have been covered so far, except for step 6 (tagging), which will be covered in the next lesson; other than that, these steps will be mostly a review. This workflow is copied in the back of the book in Appendix C so you can tear it out and place it next to your computer.

Read Each E-mail, and...

1. **Delete it:** Decide if the mail has no action and no later value and should be deleted (junk mail, useless banter, and so forth). If so, delete it immediately. Don't spend much time on this. If you are uncertain, keep it and move on to the next step.

For All E-mail You Decide Not to Delete...

2. **Act on it now**: Decide whether the e-mail generates the need for an immediate action and if that action can be done quickly (completed in one minute); if so, just do it now. That action might be to reply to the e-mail, forward it, make a quick call, or send a new e-mail to someone else. Choose this option cautiously, however, because that one minute can easily expand to five, ten, twenty, or more.

3. **Mark it for reply:** If the only action needed is to reply to the e-mail but it will take more than one minute to do so, flag it with an Outlook Follow Up flag (right-click the message and choose Follow Up), and leave it in your Inbox until you can reply. These should be the only items left in your Inbox when you empty it. If you cannot reply immediately because some other action has to happen first, follow the next step instead.

4. **Convert it to a task:** If an action other than a simple reply is needed but cannot be done now, create an Outlook task and copy/convert the mail to a task using the steps described in the sections above.

5. **Set a follow-up task (optional):** If your action is to make a quick reply or send a new message, after you do so, consider whether you need to set a follow-up task for that message. If so, follow the instructions in the section above titled Create Follow-Up Tasks for Important Requests You Make by E-mail.

6. **Tag it (optional):** Tag the e-mail as appropriate, using the techniques in the next lesson. Or instead skip topic tagging in your workflow altogether, and rely on a search engine as described in Lesson 5.

7. **Move it to the Processed Mail folder:** In all cases except mail flagged for pending replies, the next step is to move the processed mail item out of the Inbox and into the Processed Mail folder (or immediately into individual file folders, if that is your method).

8. **Work your tasks from the MYN task list:** After you have converted mail to tasks and emptied the Inbox, work your highest-priority tasks from the MYN task list. That's the TaskPad/To-Do Bar in Windows; in the Mac it's the MYN Smart Folders within the Tasks folder. Use the principles taught in Lessons 4 and 6.

Try to Empty Your Inbox

Again, the only mail left in the Inbox should be mail that is flagged for a later reply. And commit yourself to processing those flagged replies within a day. If you know you cannot reply fully to someone for some time, immediately write a quick reply, "I will get back to you in a week," create a task for doing so, and process the mail out of the Inbox. Any mail that requires action later than a same-day reply should be converted to a task.

If after working through your Inbox it still contains messages (without follow-up flags), you are not finished; keep working until the Inbox is empty.

You'll gain a tremendously satisfying feeling once you have completely cleaned out your Inbox, so I urge you to work toward that goal. It clearly signals that you are completely done with that batch of e-mail. It frees your mind to move on to the next activities at hand. And it ensures that you do not drop or misplace any activities.

Thoughts About the Workflow (Windows and Mac)

Here are some fine points to consider when using this workflow.

Refrain from Working Your Tasks Until After the Inbox Is Processed

As I've stressed throughout the book, you need to get out of the habit of working a task the moment you see it delivered to you. Otherwise you'll never get to your High priority tasks. This principle is valid no matter how the action request is delivered to you, but especially with e-mail. When processing your Inbox, you are going to see a lot of things that seem to need immediate action. Make a pact with yourself that unless that action can be accomplished in a minute, or unless it is truly critical to do now, you will convert the action to a task in your MYN task list (or perhaps to an e-mail flagged for follow-up reply later in the day). Stick with this pact or you will never get through your Inbox. Only when you are done processing your Inbox and you have seen and prioritized the entire task list—only then start working the tasks from your MYN task list. Do that during time you set aside to work tasks. I provide some strategies for creating such time in Lesson 11.

Deleting and Archiving E-mails

You would think given the goal of reaching a near-empty Inbox, that the best thing you could do with an e-mail is delete it. True; if an e-mail is obviously junk throw it out immediately. But use some caution here: if it takes you more than few moments to determine that an e-mail should be deleted, don't bother. I have seen people torture themselves for minutes over whether to delete an e-mail, and this defeats the goal of becoming more efficient.

Rather, to keep your e-mail processing going quickly, I recommend you keep all e-mail that you have any doubt about. Disk storage is cheap these days, certainly cheaper than your time. And Windows Outlook has excellent AutoArchive features built-in. Appendix B includes strategies for Windows

Outlook for archiving and deleting aged mail and instructions for using Windows Outlook's AutoArchive features. I provide strategies for Mac archiving there as well.

How Often to Use This Workflow?

Use steps 1 through 5 whenever you read an e-mail, even if you have only a moment at your computer.

Try to do steps 7 (emptying the Inbox) and 6 (tagging, if you opt for tagging), at least once a day; I do it several times a day. The problem with putting steps 6 and 7 off too long is that when you come back to tag the e-mail days later you will have forgotten the contents of many of your e-mails; you may then need to open and reread each to classify them. More on this in Lesson 8.

Granted, between meetings, when you glance quickly at your Inbox for important messages, you will not have time to do a full processing. But commit to yourself that you will at least engage steps 1 through 5 *every time you read mail*; those steps are quick, and using them will have a remarkable impact on improving your e-mail efficiency.

If you are out of the office and miss a few days without processing, do not despair. I agree that returning from a day or two of travel and facing multiple screens' worth of e-mail can be demoralizing. However, I am continually amazed at how quickly several screens full of e-mail can be processed using the workflow. Even today I find myself surprised at how quickly I can empty a seemingly overloaded Inbox after many days of neglect. Because this workflow provides such a rapid decision-making framework, you will find that your mail processing goes much more quickly than in the past.

Getting Started with the Workflow

When you first start on this system, if you are like I once was, you probably have a huge Inbox containing months of historical mail. If so, you have two choices.

You may want to take a Saturday to process and empty your entire Inbox. Doing so will give you lots of practice on the workflow. It will also give you time to think about, set up, and experiment with using the tagging method of filing described in the next lesson, if you choose to do that. When you return to your normal busy workday you will be proficient at processing your mail and can fit the system in without issue. Note the section in Lesson 11 on automating assignment of categories; this method works equally well on e-mail already in your Inbox and so will speed your bulk-processing job.

If you do not have a large block of time available for dedicated catch-up e-mail work, or just don't feel like doing it, your other choice is this: follow the transition steps described in Lesson 5 (section named Transitioning), in which most mail is moved immediately to the Processed Mail folder, and catch-up processing is done over time, if at all.

These steps enable what is most important: that you empty your Inbox quickly, start extracting tasks, and start experiencing the benefits of an empty Inbox. They allow you to start and keep emptying the Inbox every day much more quickly.

Tape a Copy of This Workflow Next to Your Computer Screen

Again, there is a page in the back of this book with the workflow duplicated; copy it or tear it out of the book, and tape it next to your computer screen. After a while the workflow will become second nature and you will not need the list any more. But for now consider yourself in training and refer to it often.

Remote E-mail Access: Impact on Workflow

If you also read your mail when you are away from a full copy of Outlook, the above workflow requires a little modification. For example, if you use Outlook Web Access/App (OWA), or a handheld device like a BlackBerry, iPhone, Android, or a Windows smartphone, you cannot easily categorize or file. And most important, you generally cannot automatically convert e-mails to tasks.

Note: As mentioned in Lesson 6, there is one solution where you can convert e-mails to tasks on your handheld, and that's using the TouchDown app on an Android device.

Not being able to convert e-mails to tasks is by far the most critical problem of these non-Outlook tools because you do not want to allow tasks that arrive in your e-mail to remain unprocessed and scattered among your previously read mail. This leads to dropped tasks and the need to reread all your e-mail before you file it, frustrating the intentions of the new workflow. So my recommendation is this: when using remote e-mail readers, find some way to create a task by more manual means. Or somehow mark the mail to remind yourself to convert it later. In Lesson 6 I present some options for mobile scenarios, including using the Follow Up flag, or forwarding the task back to yourself with the word "TASK:" in front of the subject. See that lesson for more details.

In Summary: The Cure for Inbox Stress

Immediately converting e-mails to tasks as soon as you see an action in them removes the primary cause of an out-of-control Inbox. It is the cure for Inbox stress. If that is done consistently, the majority of your Inbox woes will evaporate.

Establishing a repeatable e-mail processing habit is essential for creating a successful task-management system, and essential for keeping your Inbox under control. It will prevent you from losing track of tasks that arrive by e-mail. It will increase the collaborative flow of productive work within your team.

You will be amazed at the sense of relief and control that you get once you have a sustainable e-mail workflow in place that allows you to stay ahead of your Inbox. Your attitude about e-mail will change dramatically. You will begin to appreciate fully the value e-mail brings to you as a work tool, and you will no longer experience that nagging feeling of unattended responsibilities every time you look at your Inbox. And, once mastered, it may even allow you to leave work at a reasonable hour without feeling that you have a stack of unfinished work left to do.

Exercises

Convert e-mails into tasks as described below.

1. Convert three e-mails to tasks as text only.

2. Convert three e-mails to tasks as attachments (Windows only).

3. Create a follow-up task for three items currently in your Sent Items folder; pick items you know you may need to follow up on later.

Next Steps

Now that you have learned how to convert e-mails into tasks, and you understand the e-mail workflow, you can learn how to topic-file e-mail with more powerful filing tools. That is the subject of Lesson 8.

Lesson 8:
Topic-Based E-mail Filing

Introduction

I consistently refer to many of my old e-mails as I work through my day, even mail many months old. So I appreciate having a good way to find my stored e-mail. If you retain your old e-mails too, you should not store them in your Inbox. Old e-mail stored there will clutter both your Inbox and your workday. You'll end up missing some important items in the clutter. And you'll unnecessarily rehash old mail as you look for things. So some filing system, even very simple, is needed to get old mail you are done with out of sight.

In Lesson 5, I showed you how to empty your Inbox into a single folder called the Processed Mail folder. I hope you tried that, or one of the variants, because I want you to have that incredible experience of emptying your Inbox daily.

There were two fundamental directions you could go from there to enable you to find individual mail later:

► Use a visual search for recent mail in that new folder; and use a search engine for the rest as described at the end of Lesson 5.

► Use topic-based filing in one of two ways. Moving mail into multiple topic-named folders is the old standby. Tagging mail with topics and using a view that shows your mail grouped in those topics is a newer way.

Many people combine these two approaches. They topic-file an important subset of their mail and use search engines on the rest stored in bulk.

In this lesson I review both of these methods but focus primarily on the second: tagging mail with topics and activating a view that shows your mail grouped in those topics.

Let me be perfectly clear, though: this lesson is purely optional. If you are content with how your mail-filing and searching needs were met as of the end of Lesson 5, then skip this lesson. It's long and a bit technical. And because topic-based filing takes so much time, if you can possibly avoid it, you should.

Mac users, this lesson is also for you; it fully applies to Outlook for Mac 2011.

Topic-Filing Your E-mail (Windows and Mac)

Some people, due to business requirements in their organizations, need to do topic-based filing. They need distinct collections of all mail associated with various dimensions of work. Here are some of the different dimensions people use when creating key words to file against.

- projects
- clients
- client groups
- cases
- initiatives
- persons

- business entities
- departments
- business process or function
- activities
- message type
- time periods

Sometimes the need to file is industry specific. Legal organizations usually need to create case files so there is a crystal-clear identification of all mail associated with a case. Organizations with distinct client groups often need to be able to trace all client mail. For situations like this, topic-based filing of e-mail may be the only way to go.

However, topic-based filing is not for everyone. It takes a lot of time. For many people, given the ratio of time actually using old mail compared to the time spent filing, the tradeoff is not worth it. For them, bulk filing as in Lesson 5 may be sufficient.

And by no means is topic-based filing a requirement for regaining workday control. Why? Because once you have extracted explicit or implicit tasks from incoming e-mail using the techniques in Lesson 7, what you do with it after that is, by comparison, low priority, as long as you get it out of your Inbox. Compared to taking action on e-mails or converting them to Outlook tasks, filing e-mails by topic is way down the scale of importance. And certainly if you are happy using the powerful Outlook e-mail search tools covered in

Lesson 5, topic-based filing is almost unnecessary; all you need to do is move the mail to another folder and apply the search tool.

All that said, if you determine that you definitely need topic-based filing, you have three choices to implement it:

▶   Move mail into multiple topic-named Outlook folders.

▶   Move saved mail into one folder and tag it.

▶   Use a combination of both.

Moving Mail into Multiple Topic-Named Outlook Folders

The most common way to file by topic is to create a series of custom Outlook topic-named folders and move your e-mails there. I suspect you have tried this before. This is not my favorite approach, but for those who need to do it, or like it, here is some advice to help you set it up.

Decide Where to Put the Set of Folders

In Appendix A, I discuss considerations to make when deciding where to store the Processed Mail folder. Use those same factors when deciding where to put your multiple file folders. If your organization is using Exchange Server, does it impose size limitations for your Inbox, and does your IT department provide file server storage in place of local storage? Do you have a backup system for your local storage? Based on questions like these, Appendix A can help you decide where to put your folders.

Decide How to Name (Categorize) the Folders

The naming or categorization system for your file folders can take several dimensions, as the list above shows. If your reason for using file folders is merely to empty your Inbox, date-based folders are a good solution. If you are truly looking for topic names, then use business priorities to guide you as listed above. Clearly, you should think about how these names will help you find the mail or use it later.

Decide Whether to Use Nested Folders

I really do not like nested folders (also called subfolders or hierarchical folders) because they greatly complicate filing and searching for mail. They also greatly increase the number of folders you have, which can make searching harder. But sometimes they are the only way to match the most logical filing system for your business needs. If you use them, try to keep their depth and count to a minimum.

Decide What to Do with Mail That Does Not Fit in a Particular Folder

How should you handle mail that doesn't fit into any of your existing folders? Should you just keep creating new folders or is there another approach? I strongly recommend keeping your folder count low; otherwise filing and searching will become very cumbersome. So create an Other or Miscellaneous folder for all mail that doesn't fit any other topic.

Consider Using Add-In Software to Help: ClearContext

The Outlook add-in software ClearContext has a number of tools to help with filing mail into multiple Outlook folders. For example, you can configure the tool so that once you file one member of an e-mail thread into a particular folder, all other items in that thread will automatically be moved into that folder. You can also auto-tag e-mail with topics as it comes in but not move it into the matching individual folders until later, when you are sure you are done reading the mail. And ClearContext has a good, simple rules engine for picking topics automatically. So if you like filing in multiple folders, take a look at this software as a way to speed your filing. See this link for more information: www.myn.bz/clearcontext.html.

Problems with Filing into Multiple Outlook Folders

I have mentioned several times that moving mail into multiple topic-named folders is not my favorite topic-filing method. This method never worked for me, and here is why.

▶ Whenever I tried this in the past, I regretted no longer having one view of all my collected e-mail. I often locate an e-mail by approximately how far in the past it arrived and by proximity with other events. I missed the ability to scan through my entire Inbox, sorted by date. Having my saved mail split among multiple folders precluded that.

▶ Along these lines, I often like to view all e-mails sent from one individual. Again, having my saved mail split among multiple folders precluded that. (There is now a workaround for these two problems, you can create a custom All Mail Search or Smart Folder, which I show in Lesson 11. It doesn't solve all the downsides to topic-filing, however, and it isn't available to users of 2003.)

▶ Sometimes it seemed that an e-mail item belonged in several different folders. Using folders required me to decide on one and only one folder to file it in. In my indecision, I'd leave the item unfiled or waste time and get frustrated with the process. Then, when I searched for the mail, I would often look in the wrong folder first.

▶ Once an item was filed, I would often forget which folder I stored it in and would become annoyed with having to hunt through multiple folders to find it.

▶ Because of how long it takes to file, I would often not finish filing for days or weeks at a time. Then, when I needed to look for mail, I would not know whether to look in the folders or in my Inbox and would waste time searching both.

> ▶   If I used a hybrid approach to filing (putting a small subset of my mail in topic folders and leaving the rest in a bulk folder for visual and search engine searches), I would often forget I filed away some recent mail and wonder why I could not find it in my visual search.

> ▶   I tried to set up an offline archive storage area into which I transferred my oldest saved mail. But when mail is split among tens or hundreds of folders, I found it harder to do that and still retain more recent mail locally.

For these reasons and others, I have given up on filing e-mail into a collection of various topic-named Outlook folders. Perhaps you have had similar problems. You'll see below that Outlook Category tagging, and putting tagged mail all in one folder, solves nearly all the above problems.

That said, many people have no problem with filing into multiple topic-named Outlook folders, and they are able to empty their Inbox nearly every day. If that is you, fantastic; keep doing what you are doing. However, if you go weeks at a time without filing or if any of the above symptoms sound familiar, read on and try these next approaches.

Better Filing Solution: Place Mail in One Location and Tag It (Typically Using Outlook Categories)

I feel there is a better filing approach: place the mail in one location (the Processed Mail folder created in Lesson 5) and tag it, using Outlook Categories or other tags. This solution provides the best of both worlds for finding important e-mails. It allows you to store your e-mail in a single date- or sender-sorted folder yet also view all mail in a folder-like structure grouped on tag names. You can tag one e-mail with multiple topics and see it in all topic locations. With this solution, all the shortcomings described above are eliminated and a fluid system of filing and finding e-mails is made possible.

I use the verb "tag" here loosely. A very specific concept of tagging as a way of organizing electronically-stored information has become popular in recent years on many search websites, with a specific set of rules on how this is done. The website delicious.com (originally del.icio.us) was in the vanguard of this movement. Yahoo followed, as did others. I am not advocating using tagging that way as the only way to go; only one of the tagging options I list below actually follows a similar tagging approach (using add-in software called Taglocity).

Rather, I use the term "tag" in a much broader context: simply attaching one or more keywords to an e-mail and finding the e-mail based on those keywords. Outlook had been using Outlook Categories for years to do this long before tagging became a web buzzword. And there are other Outlook approaches.

My recommended process is simple. You just add the keyword to the mail item in the Inbox using a variety of simple tools in Outlook, and then drag the mail from the Inbox to a single folder: the Processed Mail folder.

Tagging versus Separate Folders: Easier to Find Mail

Later, when you want to find an e-mail, you can take advantage of the tags. You just toggle into the view that groups mail by tag (see Figure 8.1 for an Outlook Categories example), scroll to the group you want, and then scan through the items in the group.

But perhaps even more important, since I have you store all mail in one folder in my approach, you can use three other nontag ways to find mail. That is the beauty of tagging in Outlook; you can store all the mail in one folder with all the advantages of that and still enjoy the advantages of seeing mail in folder-like groups using a category view.

Here is a list of the ways you can find mail using this MYN filing system. Since the three nontag ways are so simple, I will list them here, but I won't talk about them beyond what I covered already in Lesson 5. Only the fourth method in the list below uses tags and it is the focus of this lesson.

1. If you know approximately when the mail arrived, do a visual search in the Processed Mail folder of your chronologically sorted mail (as many of you do now in the Inbox).

2. If you know who sent it, sort on the From column by clicking the header of that column, scroll to the person's name, and visually search across titles and dates within the mail from that person (again, many of us do that already in the Inbox).

3. Use a search engine and direct it toward mail in the Processed Mail folder. I covered this in Lesson 5.

4. Tag mail and group your Processed Mail folder on category name as in Figure 8.1. This is probably new to you and is covered below.

Tagging versus Separate Folders: Faster When Filing

Even with the relative advantages described above, I am sometimes asked:

"Doesn't tagging take just as long as moving items into separate topic-named folders? After all, even though you can select multiple mail items and tag in bulk, you can do that when you drag mail to folders too. I will need to touch the same number of items in either case, correct?"

Well, that's true, but once you start using Outlook *rules* to automatically set tags, tagging comes out way ahead.

"Ah," the multiple-file folder user responds, *"but I can write rules for automatically filing into folders too!"*

Figure 8.1
Category
Groups in
Outlook.

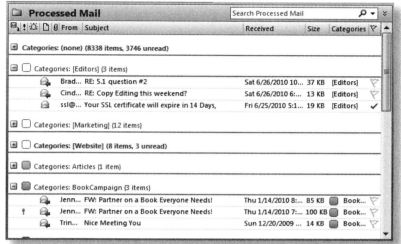

Yes, but wait. There is a huge difference between auto-tagging and auto-filing. With auto-tagging mail, the tagged mail stays in the Inbox until you drag it somewhere else. So, you can still read it day by day, hour by hour, as it comes in. With auto-filed mail (filed into folders), you never see the mail — you never have a chance to read new mail that day (unless you hunt through all your file folders several times a day, which I doubt you will do). That means you are very unlikely to use filing rules on important mail; most people I know who use auto-filing directly into folders do so only with mail they rarely read anyway (junk mail, newsfeeds, specialty mail subscriptions, and so on). So you will need to file most of your true business mail by hand, and that's why tagging comes out way ahead in this comparison. When I was actively tagging my mail, I reached a point where 70 percent of my *business-critical* mail was auto-tagged due to Outlook rules. I would then read as much of that mail as appropriate right in the Inbox, before I dragged it all to the Processed Mail folder. I show you how to create these rules in Lesson 11.

Note: *If you absolutely must use separate folders for each topic, Windows users should consider using a tool like ClearContext; it tags mail but leaves it in the Inbox — filing it later into separate folders when you click the File button. This lets you read your mail before you file it.*

Tagging versus Separate Folders: Solves Problem of Where to File

One of the other big advantages to tagging with Outlook Categories is it allows you apply more than one category to a mail item. This solves the common problem of not knowing where to file an item when it seems to fit in two or more folders. For example you get an invoice for the marketing project; do you file that in the Accounting folder or in the Marketing Project folder? With categories you can apply both and the item will appear in each of the groups, making it much easier to find. Outlook does not duplicate the item, it merely shows them virtually in both places.

In Outlook for Mac 2011 this works the same and then goes even further; it also shows an extra group for each combination. More on that ahead.

Tagging Mail Using Outlook Categories (All Outlook Versions)

I am starting this discussion of Outlook mail tagging with the original tagging engine: Outlook Categories. I'll mention other tagging methods after that.

Outlook Categories

Outlook Categories are simple keywords or phrases that you can quickly and easily tag to e-mail. Once you assign a category to mail in the Processed Mail folder, you can group your mail on that category by simply clicking the Category header. This creates a view showing folder-like collections of mail, all in the one Processed Mail folder (see Figure 8.1). And you can switch back to a date-sorted view by clicking the Received column. So you get the best of both worlds – all the advantages of a single-folder filing system, and all the advantages of seeing mail grouped in folders. Because of these advantages, this is definitely something you want to try out.

Also note, categories can be assigned to the multiple other data types used in Outlook: Calendar items, Contacts, Tasks, Notes, and Journal items. All these data types share the same master list of Outlook Categories to pick from when you tag. Microsoft made Outlook Categories available in all versions of Outlook covered by this book, but elevated the importance of Outlook Categories considerably in Outlook 2007 and later by adding more features.

How You See Categories in Outlook 2007/10 and Outlook for Mac 2011

If you have Outlook 2007/10 or 2011, it is hard to miss categories. Look at the right side of your Inbox and you should see the Categories column. You might even see mail with colored rectangles in that column (circles are used in Mac 2011). Note, the Categories column may be hidden if your Inbox mail list is too narrow. Widen it by minimizing the To-Do Bar or by moving the Reading Pane to the bottom (use View menu or tab, Reading Pane, Bottom).

Note: If the Categories column is truly missing for some reason in Outlook 2007/10, follow the instructions for adding it to Outlook 2003, immediately below.

Viewing Categories in Outlook 2003

In Outlook 2003 categories are a bit more subtle and you'll need to take a few configuration steps to make them visible in your list of mail. Specifically, you need to add a Categories column to your Inbox. Let's do that now.

Note: If you are using MYN-enabled ClearContext, this has already been done for you and you can skip these next steps.

To Add the Categories Column in Outlook 2003:

1. Open your Inbox, right-click any of your column headings, and choose from the bottom of the shortcut menu, choose: Customize Current View… (it may say Custom…).

2. I recommend you click the Reset Current View button. This is to clear out any odd settings you may have inadvertently made to the Messages view.

3. Then click Fields….

4. In the next dialog box (called Show Fields) click Categories in the list on the left to select it. Then click Add (in the middle of the dialog box) to add that field to the bottom of the list on the right side as shown in Figure 8.2.

If you have trouble finding the Categories field in the list on the left, try selecting All Mail Fields in the list box titled Select Available Fields From, and then look again at the scrolling field list. That should display it.

5. Click OK, and then OK again.

Once back at your Inbox, you may need to resize the width of the new Categories column to make it more readable. Do this by dragging the margin of the column heading.

You probably won't see anything currently in that column if you have not been using categories. But you might; Outlook Categories can travel with e-mail messages (pre-Outlook 2007), so if others are using Outlook Categories on their mail you might see them in your Inbox.

Now let's see how to tag mail with these categories.

Figure 8.2
Adding the
Categories
field.

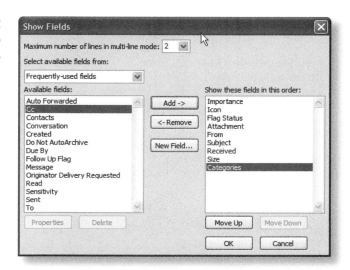

Note: *If you are currently using a multiple-folder filing system or no system at all and you would like tips on how to transition to this new category-based system, see the section at the end of this lesson called Transitioning to a Categories System.*

Note: *IMAP servers do not support Outlook Categories; the category lists shown in the sections ahead will be empty if using an IMAP server.*

How to Tag Mail with Outlook Categories, Outlook 2003

Here's the easiest way to assign categories to e-mail in Outlook 2003. Right-click any e-mail item in your Inbox list. From the shortcut menu choose Categories. A Categories dialog box opens, displaying whatever category list is currently populated in your system's list of available categories (see Figure 8.3). For test purposes, click one of the categories at random to assign it to the currently selected mail item, and then click OK. Now view the Categories column in your Inbox; you should see the assigned category listed at the right end of the selected mail item. Congratulations, you've just assigned your first category. You can go back into that dialog box to remove the category; just clear the check box.

It is likely that the default category list that ships with Outlook bears little resemblance to the list you want to use. Some of the default names are ridiculous for business purposes. Let's see how to add more meaningful categories.

As before, right-click an e-mail with no category assignments in the Inbox, and From the shortcut menu choose Categories. At the top of the Categories dialog box is an empty text box (see top of Figure 8.3). Type your new category in the box and click Add to List. Note that the new item drops down into the category list with the check box checked. Click OK and you are done. That item is now in your list for future use. Since you are back at the Inbox, note how the category you added also shows up in the category column.

Figure 8.3
Outlook 2003
Categories dialog
box where you can
assign one or more
categories.

How to Tag Mail with Outlook Categories, Outlook 2007/10 and Mac 2011

In Outlook 2007/10 and 2011, Microsoft added quicker ways to choose categories compared with all previous versions. In previous Windows versions it took four steps to assign a category to an e-mail. In Outlook 2007/10 and 2011 it now takes only two steps: right-click the Categories column (CTRL-click on the Mac) and select the category from the shortcut menu (see Figure 8.4). On Windows it can take as little as one step (just one click) for the default category if you have set one. More on that in a moment.

There are other ways to reach the menu in Figure 8.4. With the item selected in a mail list view, click the Categorize button in the Standard toolbar in Outlook 2007, or the Home tab in Outlook 2010 and 2011. In 2007 you can also reach the Categorize command by going to the Edit menu or the Action menu. And in 2011 the Categorize command is under the Message menu.

Figure 8.4
How to select Categories in Outlook 2007/10 (left) and Mac 2011 (right).

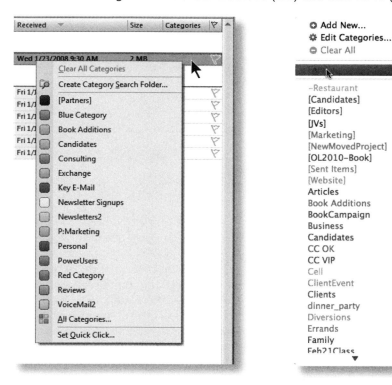

Figure 8.5
Category editing in
Outlook 2007/10,
above, and, Mac
2011 below.

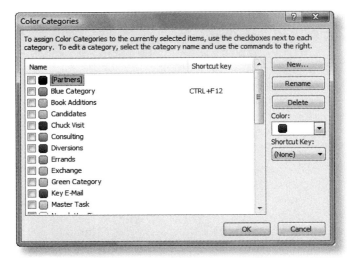

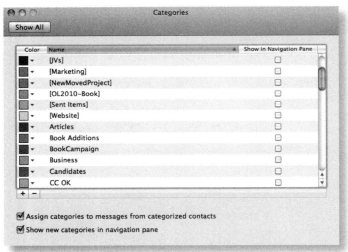

One caveat with using the drop-down menu on Outlook 2007/10 is that it shows only the most-used 15 categories; if you have more you'll need to open a more detailed window and scroll to the other categories. The way to do that is to choose All Categories… at the bottom of the shortcut menu (see bottom of the left side of Figure 8.4,). A dialog box called Color Categories opens with a scrolling list of all your Outlook Categories (see top of Figure 8.5); assign as many there as you like. This is also where you add, delete, or rename Categories. And you can set keyboard shortcuts here for up to 11 categories; note in the upper part of Figure 8.5 the control to set those shortcuts.

On the Mac, the shortcut menu in Figure 8.4 (right side) shows *all* categories; just use the scroll arrow at the bottom to reach any that have scrolled off the bottom. If you choose the Edit Categories... command shown at the top of Figure 8.4 (right side), you'll see the Categories window shown at the bottom of Figure 8.5. However, you cannot assign categories here like you can in the Windows Outlook equivalent; you can only rename, add, or remove them here.

The Six Special Color-Named Categories in Outlook 2007/10

If you upgraded from Outlook 2003, you will probably see a number of new categories in the list identified only by colors (Red Category, Green Category, and so on). These are the six colors from the Outlook 2003 Follow Up flags. They exist mainly to transition old mail to the new way Follow Up flags are used in Outlook 2007/10, where they can set an action date of a flagged-mail task and no longer carry those colors. Let me clarify. During upgrade installation of Outlook 2007/10, Outlook needs to make old 2003 mail compatible with the new flag usage. Since the six flag colors no longer exist, Microsoft did not want you to lose that color information on any old e-mails you may have flagged with various colors. So the color information is retained by transferring the color to the *category* of each e-mail. The new Red, Green, Purple (and so on) Outlook Categories exist mainly to enable that transition.

As part of that transition process, the first time you use one of these predefined color categories for a new assignment, Outlook will ask you if you want to rename it to something more meaningful, as shown in Figure 8.6.

Figure 8.6   Result of first use of a color-named category.

Since the color-named categories exist only for the transition, Outlook is giving you a chance to record what you intended when you used the colored Follow Up flags on mail items in Outlook 2003. If you do have such a specific meaning for each color, indicate it now in this dialog box by giving it a new name. If you do not care about the meaning of flags on old flagged mail, I would avoid using the color-named categories altogether and simply delete them.

Differences from Pre-2007 Versions

If you have used categories with previous versions of Outlook, some important differences have appeared in Outlook 2007/10 and 2011.

First, the separate Master Category List window of pre-2007 versions is no longer used, which makes editing your category list much easier.

You'll also see an emphasis on category colors in all newer versions on Windows and the Mac; nearly all categories are given a color by default when you create them. Associating colors with category names is useful because it allows you to see at a glance the meaning of tagged e-mail. And colors make category assignments easier to identify if the Categories column in the Inbox list view is narrow; colors are shown first, then the text.

Adding and Removing Multiple Categories in Outlook 2007/10 and 2011

As I said, there are now a few ways to assign categories to mail in your list view, one of which I mentioned is right-clicking the Categories column for the item (CTRL-click on the Mac). Note when using that right-click method, if you repeat the process on the same e-mail item, each newly assigned category is *additive*; it is added adjacent to any existing category rather than overwriting it. But what if you do want to replace it? You need to choose the existing category again from the drop-down, which removes it. Then go back and assign the new category. Or in Windows just click All Categories... and manipulate the check boxes in the Color Categories dialog box. On the Mac you could choose Clear All shown at the top of Figure 8.4, and then add your new categories.

Quick Click to Set Categories in Outlook 2007/10

I mentioned before a feature in Outlook 2007/10 that allows you to assign a default category to your mail when you make a normal left-click in the Categories column. Out of the box, mine was set to the new Red Category. I found this confusing at first, as I accidentally set categories every time I clicked. This default is called the "Quick Click" assignment and can be changed by

Figure 8.7
Setting the Quick Click choice in Outlook 2007/10.

right-clicking any e-mail and choosing Set Quick Click... from the bottom of the shortcut menu shown in Figure 8.4. This opens the dialog box shown in Figure 8.7.

If you have one category you tend to use a lot, this is a nice feature. If you do not have a favorite category, you probably want to turn Quick Click off to avoid accidentally assigning categories. Do this by choosing No Category from the drop-down list in Figure 8.7.

After I got used to Quick Click, I decided I liked this feature a lot. I created a category call Key E-mail, and assigned it a bright red color. Now, any e-mail that contains critical reference information I know I'll want to refer to later, I click and categorize this way. That now takes the place of how I used to use flags prior to Outlook 2007.

Adjusting the Master Category List in Outlook 2003

If you want to use the category method of tagging e-mail, you should go to the Master Category List dialog box first and edit it to match your needs.

Deleting Categories

The first step of editing your list is to remove the default categories that shipped with Outlook. Most are not useful for the business world. To delete categories, from within the Categories dialog box shown in Figure 8.3, click the Master Category List... button at the bottom right. This opens a dialog box where you can delete existing categories in the Master Category List (see Figure 8.8). Just select one or more categories, and click the Delete button at the upper right.

Figure 8.8

The Outlook 2003 Master Category List dialog box where you can delete and add categories.

After you delete categories from the Master Category List, to examine the edited list, close all open windows to return to your Inbox and then reopen the Categories dialog box; otherwise the results will look odd at first.

Another Way to Add Categories in Outlook 2003

I showed you earlier how to add categories in the 2003 Categories dialog box (Figure 8.3); you just type into the top empty box and click Add to List. Note that this does two things: it adds the category to the master list *and* it assigns it to the currently selected e-mail.

Well, you can also add categories inside the Master Category List dialog box (Figure 8.8) by typing the new name in the New Category text box at the top and clicking Add. This looks similar to what you did above except this time it does not actually assign the new category for the currently selected e-mail item. You must do that on your way out—in other words, when you click OK and return to the previous dialog box, stay there for a moment, find your new category, and select the check box next to it.

Some Points about Using Outlook Categories (All Versions)

Setting Category Standards. If multiple individuals in your organization intend to adopt this category-based e-mail filing system, and you are using an older version of Exchange Server, I recommend you consider adopting common category names for similar subjects. Reason: e-mail arriving from colleagues using this system may occasionally (pre-2007) display your colleagues' categories; you may need to change the category to match one of yours. You all will save time if you agree to use the same category names. See Lesson 11 for more discussion, including how to block migration of categories with e-mail.

The None Category. You may be tempted to create a category called Other or Miscellaneous to file e-mail that doesn't fit other categories. However, don't bother creating one of these catchall categories. The reason: Outlook automatically creates, assigns, and displays a category called None for all uncategorized e-mail. This is a great time-saver! I have more discussion of this below.

Category Hierarchy. There is no provision for using Outlook Categories to create a category hierarchy. If you are accustomed to using a nested folder filing system, sorry, you can't do the equivalent with categories. The ability to assign multiple categories to a single item somewhat makes up for this. Frankly though, I think hierarchical e-mail filing systems are too slow to use and too hard to maintain. I encourage you to try the single-level-category system for a while and see what you think.

Outlook 2003 Categories and Using Multiple Computers

One final point. In Outlook 2003, the Master Category List is stored in the registry of the computer you are making your edits on. That means if you use Exchange and more than one computer you will need to repeat any Master Category List edits on each computer you use for assigning categories. Let me be clear about this. I am only talking about edits to the Master Category List, not category *assignments* to e-mail. Any category assignments you make to e-mail *will* be retained no matter what computer you use; it's only the category *list* editing that must be repeated. Since you probably edit the Master Category List rarely, this should not be that big a problem.

This changed in Outlook 2007/10; in those versions the category list is stored with your main mailbox on Exchange, so you only need to edit the list once.

Note: One other constraint with using Outlook 2003 categories is that there is no quick way to rename a category once it is assigned to mail in Outlook 2003, at least not in one step. See Lesson 11 for instructions on how to do this.

Adjusting the Category List in Outlook 2007/10 and 2011

If you want to use the category method of tagging e-mail, you should first edit the default categories that shipped with Outlook. Most are not useful for the business world.

Editing the category list in Outlook 2007/10 is easy; just open the Color Categories dialog box shown in the upper part Figure 8.5 (use the All Categories command shown in Figure 8.4) and use the New and Delete buttons there.

Editing the category list in Outlook for Mac 2011 is also easy; just open the Categories dialog box shown in the lower part of Figure 8.5 (to open it, use Edit Categories… shown in right side of Figure 8.4) and then use the + and - buttons there to add or remove categories.

Tips for Using Categories (All Versions)

When You Adjust the Category List

The category list you adjust from the Inbox is the same category list used for Contacts, Tasks, and so on. So, as you delete categories, consider whether you are using them already in those data types and if you may need them there in the future. As you add categories, think of other ways they might be used.

If you plan to delete any categories you have already assigned to mail, study Lesson 11 for how to do that correctly.

When creating category names, don't forget the None category takes the place of a Miscellaneous or Other category (see inset box above).

Assigning the Same Category to Multiple Messages at Once

Prior to right-clicking an item in the e-mail list to assign a category, note that you can press SHIFT or CTRL (CMD on a Mac) to select multiple e-mails at once in an e-mail list. Whatever category assignments you make are then assigned to all the selected e-mail items. This is useful to speed category assignment to batches of e-mail, something I describe below.

Automatic Assigning of Categories Using Rules

As I described at the start of this lesson, you can easily create an Outlook rule that automatically assigns a category to all incoming mail from a particular sender, or to mail with particular keywords in the subject line or body of the message. For example, I have created a rule to assign the Personal category to mail from family members. If you create a number of such rules, categorizing in this way saves quite a few steps later. Instructions for doing this can be found in Lesson 11.

Note that if you are working in an organization that uses Exchange Server, there are limits to the number of rules you can create (also discussed in Lesson 11). Using the rules engine in an add-in tool like ClearContext can avoid those limitations.

In Outlook for Mac 2011 if you assign a category to a contact, then all mail from the contact will arrive with that category assigned—you don't need to create an Outlook rule. This is a great feature of Outlook for Mac 2011.

Should You Tag Sent Mail?

I get this question a lot: Should I categorize sent mail? I generally don't categorize sent mail, primarily to save time, but it is certainly useful. You can assign categories in the Sent Items folder after you have sent the mail using the usual Outlook tools. And you would think there would also be easy ways to assign a category to a message before you send it, but there are not. Rather, you need to perform three or four menu or button operations, and that's just too many.

So the best current option for assigning categories to outgoing mail is to install the Outlook add-in software ClearContext (Windows only) to make this an easy operation; by using its Projects button (and using the default association of Outlook Categories with ClearContext Projects), this is a one-click assignment. See the end of this lesson for more information on how to do that. You can also set ClearContext to prompt you for a topic on all outgoing mail if you need a reminder like that, and set the topic right in that reminder window.

Note: There are other ways to make tagging sent mail an easy part of your daily workflow. One is to BCC yourself and process the mail out of the Inbox with other mail, categorizing as you go. Another is to keep an extra window open showing the Sent Items folder. Then, each time you send a message, quickly click the sent item in that folder and categorize it.

Viewing Mail by Category (All Versions)

Now that you have learned how to tag mail with categories, you are probably curious how you are going to use those tags to find specific mail you have dragged to your Processed Mail folder. In nearly all cases, it's very simple and I already showed it to you earlier in the lesson. You merely click the top of the Categories column in the mail list view (2003 users see next section for a special case). Doing this gives you the virtual folder-like view of categories you saw back in Figure 8.1. That figure shows the Windows version of Outlook with some categories expanded and some collapsed; you control that by clicking the + or - buttons next to each category. The Mac is similar; there you click a small arrow to expand or collapse a group. In both versions, when you are done viewing the category groups, simply clicking on the Received column reverts the view back to a standard date-sorted listing.

As mentioned before, any mail item that has more than one category applied to it will be repeated in each category group. Outlook for Mac 2011 expands on this feature; you'll also see a group for each category name *combination*. So for example, if you have applied the two categories Accounting and Marketing to an individual mail item, you'll see a group called Accounting, a group called Marketing, and a third group with the phrase: *Accounting, Marketing*. This third combined group only lists mail that has both of those categories applied. In a way, this imitates the function of nested folders and so it is quite handy. But it also makes the number of groups you see in a Categories list a lot larger.

If you have a lot of categories, or a lot of mail in your category groups, it can be hard to scroll through them to find the start of specific category groups. To help with that, you can collapse all groups using a command with that name in the View menu or tab (in Windows). On the Mac, go to the Organize tab and then choose Arrange By, then Collapse All Groups.

Outlook 2003: Adding the Categories Column to the Processed Mail Folder

If you are using Outlook 2003, when you create the Processed Mail folder it will have no Categories column. So you will want to add it. The instructions below roughly repeat those given above for the Inbox.

To Add the Categories Column to the Processed Mail Folder, Do this:

1. Open your Processed Mail folder, right-click any of your column headings, and from the bottom of the shortcut menu choose: Customize Current View… (it may say Custom…).

2. In the dialog box that opens, click Fields….

3.   In the next dialog box (titled Show Fields) click Categories in the list on the left to select it. Then click Add (in the middle of the dialog box) to add that field to the bottom of the list on the right side.

If you have trouble finding the Categories field in the list on the left, try selecting All Mail Fields in the list box titled Select Available Fields From, and then look again at the scrolling field list. That should display it.

4.   Click OK and then OK again to return to the Processed Mail folder.

Once back at the list view, you may want to widen the Categories column in the Processed Mail folder to see it more clearly; just drag the edge of the column in the header of the view.

In Case You Get an Error in Outlook 2003

Once the Categories column is added, as I stated earlier you can group your mail by category by simply clicking on the Categories column header. That said, there are times in 2003 when clicking the Categories column header does not work; you may get an error message saying You Cannot Sort By This Field. Should you get that message, click OK, and then go to the View menu, choose Arrange By, and from its submenu choose Show in Groups. Then try clicking on the Categories column header again; it should work this time.

Using Search Folders to View Categorized Mail (Windows)

Search Folders are a Windows Outlook feature that allows creation of virtual folders in your folder list. The Macintosh has an equivalent feature called Smart Folders (discussed in a section ahead). Search Folders can be used to create category folders right in your Navigation Pane. They appear within and under the Search Folder group (see Figure 8.9). In this sample, eight Search Folders are shown. Using Search Folders is purely optional, but often useful.

Search Folders Defined

Search Folders are virtual folders that populate with an entry for every mail item that matches certain search criteria that are defined at the time the particular Search Folder is created. You create one folder for each set of search criteria. For our purposes, collecting mail that has a given Outlook Category assigned works best; but many other search approaches are also possible. Once created, clicking the folder opens a view of all matching mail in a folder view, as if it were a real Outlook folder.

Features of Search Folders

The advantage of using Search Folders to view categorized mail is this: they look and act nearly identical to regular Outlook folders. If you are accustomed to using a folder view in the Navigation Pane for manipulating saved mail, Search Folders create a very similar view for your collection of category-assigned mail. When you double-click a Search Folder, it opens just like any

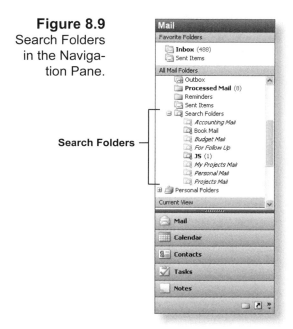

Figure 8.9
Search Folders
in the Naviga-
tion Pane.

Search Folders –

other folder, displaying the mail contained within. So there is a familiarity factor at work here, which many find appealing.

There are, however, two disadvantages. One is that you cannot drag mail items to the Search Folder, as you can with real folders. Rather, using our system, you need to assign categories as described above. Only then does the item appear in your Search Folder.

The other disadvantage of Search Folders is that you must explicitly create a Search Folder for each category you are using, and as you will see that takes a few steps. So if you consistently create a lot of new categories, Search Folders may not be for you.

Note: *There are two other limitations to Search Folders compared with regular Outlook folders: you cannot create nested Search Folders (no subfolders), and you cannot share Search Folders over a network.*

Even with those disadvantages, Search Folders have a certain elegance; their folder-like appearance right in the Outlook folder list is quite satisfying. If you have a relatively small and stable set of categories, you may prefer this approach. See my article to learn how: www.myn.bz/SearchFolders.htm.

Creating Category Smart Folders in Outlook for Mac 2011

The Mac's equivalent to Search Folders are called Smart Folders; they have been available for years in the Mac and they are also built into Outlook for Mac 2011. There they can be used to collect categorized mail just like the Search Folders described above for Windows Outlook. In Lesson 3 you learned how to create Smart Folders for tasks; the same principles apply in the Mail folder.

Luckily, you do not need to manually build these for categorized mail since Outlook for Mac 2011 will do this for you automatically. Here's how. In the bottom image in Figure 8.5, if you look at the right side, you will see a check box column titled Show in Navigation Pane. This does just what it says; it lists the indicated categorized mail in a group on the Navigation Pane (in the equivalent of a Smart Folder). This replaces a lot of manual work and I applaud Microsoft for this excellent design.

However, I could not get this feature to work on my installation (the folders never appeared), and I have heard other similar complaints from others. Give it a try; if it does not work I suspect it will be fixed in a future software update. In the meantime, follow Lesson 3 principles to create them manually.

Tips on Using Categories (All Versions)

Deleting a Search or Smart Folder

Search and Smart Folders are a virtual view of your mail. The actual mail sits in real Outlook folder(s) such as the ones you defined above as the source of your search (Processed Mail, most likely). So if you are done using a Search or Smart Folder, you can delete the *folder* and the mail itself is not deleted but is retained in the Processed Mail folder.

Deleting Mail in a Search or Smart Folder

However, when viewing *individual mail* inside a Search or Smart Folder *the opposite is true*. If you delete an individual e-mail item from within the folder, the actual mail item is *deleted* from its source folder (in this case, the Processed Mail folder). Any operations that you perform on individual e-mail items (delete, change category, or edit item, for example) within a Search or Smart Folder are made on the actual item wherever it is located.

Transitioning to a Categories System

Now that you are set up to start using Outlook Categories, here are some tips on doing that, particularly on how to get started.

From a Multiple-Folder-Based Filing System

If you are already using a multiple-folder-based filing system for e-mail, you may wonder what my recommendations are for transitioning to a category-based system. My primary recommendation is this: start fresh. As explained in Lesson 5, there is no reason you cannot add a Processed Mail folder to your existing multiple-folder system and start using the category system with mail that is currently in your Inbox. Retain your current system for the old mail you have already filed.

Or if you like, pick some date back in time a reasonable period and then categorize and drag mail newer than that from each of your folders to the Processed Mail folder. That way you have some continuity with recent old mail. Just be careful in an Exchange environment; if you are dragging mail from local folders into Exchange-based ones, you may immediately exceed your Exchange limits. See Appendix A for folder strategies to prevent that.

In any case, I am sure you know the following. The useful life of most old mail passes fast; in no time the only mail that you look at often will be the mail filed by category in your Processed Mail folder, and you will rarely touch your old folder-based filing system. At some point you will feel confident to archive that system and refer only to your category-based Processed Mail folder. And this is a good way to try out the Category filing approach. If you do not like it you can always drag the mail back to your old folders.

Note: *If you do combine with an old folder system, you may want to name your Processed Mail folder something like "_Processed Mail" (note the underscore at the beginning), so that it sorts to the top of your folders. Or store your older folders as subfolders of one other folder next to the Processed Mail folder, and call it "Before_MYN," or some such name.*

Transitioning From No Filing System

If you have no current filing system, you likely have many months of mail in your Inbox. So do you need to commit yourself to classifying all that old mail? My answer is no.

Again, as in Lesson 5, what I recommend is to take a fresh start. Pick a date one week ago and drag all mail older than that to the Processed Mail folder immediately. Mail newer than that (still in your Inbox) you should commit to processing into your Processed Mail folder immediately, extracting tasks and applying categories as you do so. Now you have an empty Inbox! Make a note of that process cutoff date. Then, as time allows, dip into the older mail in the Processed Mail folder and process it, doing at least one full day at a time, and note the date you stop again, so you can continue with unprocessed mail the next time you come back to this.

But processing that older mail is purely optional; it is likely that mail older than a few weeks has diminished in importance anyway. And since everything is in the one Processed Mail folder you can find mail by other methods if you must. What is important is that you empty your Inbox quickly so you can experience the benefits of doing so. And then keep maintaining it empty.

Should You Categorize Everything?

Is it necessary to categorize every piece of mail in your Inbox? Absolutely not. If you stare at a piece of mail for more than a second or two and no category jumps out at you, waste no more time on it. You need to balance the advantages of the system against its imposing on your time. One of the goals of this system is to get you out earlier at the end of each workday; you won't do that if you spend too much time using the system. I find I can assign categories to two full screens of mail in about five minutes or less. Once you get good at this, if it takes you longer than that, you are probably spending too much time choosing your categories. It may be better to leave more mail uncategorized (and/or reduce the number of your categories). Remember that mail in the automatic None category is still easy to search by eye or using search tools.

Integrating Categorization into Your MYN Workflow

The workflow presented at the end of Lesson 7 in which each e-mail is read individually, then categorized, and then filed, one at a time was, for simplification, an idealized one. In reality, I usually batch-process my e-mail by grouping the steps of that workflow. I read and take action steps for e-mail whenever I work my e-mail (steps 1–5 of the workflow in Lesson 7), no matter how short my time is. I place a particular emphasis on making quick replies and converting embedded tasks immediately into Outlook tasks. I'll later come back to that previously read e-mail and do steps 6 and 7 (set categories and drag to Processed Mail folder) on blocks of e-mail together. Steps 6 and 7 I may do hours later, or if I travel, even days later.

In reality, this matches how most of us process e-mails in normal life. When we have a few minutes here and there we read some e-mails, acting on those we can at the moment and deferring action on others. And every so often we try to go back and clean up the Inbox.

The difference with this improved workflow is a key one: as soon as you read an e-mail, before you close it, you should *immediately* make a decision—is this a task, a quick-reply-now, or a reply-later e-mail? And once you decide, make sure you act accordingly before you move on to the next e-mail: convert it to task, reply immediately, or flag it for later reply. In other words, *if an e-mail requires action, act or plan the actions immediately, when you first read it.* That way, when you return to your e-mail Inbox later to clean it up, your only needed action will be to optionally categorize the mail and then drag all mail to the Processed Mail folder. This removes nearly all tension you may feel about old mail sitting in your Inbox, because all actions have been taken or logged in your task system.

How Often to Categorize?

You can delay the categorization step if necessary because you have taken all the really needed actions, as described above. Try to categorize at least once a day. If you are very busy or traveling, this step can be put off for a few days, but any more than that and it will start to become painful.

The problem with putting off categorizing is that when you come back to it later, you will have forgotten the contents of some of your mail and you may need to reread them to classify them. Plus, this may discourage you from emptying your Inbox every day. So it is better to include the categorization step whenever you engage in an extended session of e-mail reading. Once you get ahead of your Inbox, looping back at the end of each e-mail reading session to categorize and completely empty your Inbox becomes easy. And the smaller the amount of mail you need to process at once the easier this becomes. When you do categorization just after reading and acting on a block of mail, there will be no need to reread any e-mails. Just quickly go through your Inbox and categorize in blocks, based on titles (see below). The crisp decision-making process and read-once policy are what makes this Inbox workflow so speedy.

But if you must skip categorizing, I still recommend you drag the e-mail (after extracting tasks) to the Processed Mail folder at the end of each day, per Lesson 5. Then, when you can, categorize the new mail in the Processed Mail folder later to catch up. Do not use categories as an excuse for not emptying the Inbox daily.

Speeding Up Category Assignments

One of the most common early complaints I hear from first-time users is this: "Assigning categories is harder than dragging to folders. It takes several steps to right-click the mail and pick a category from a dialog box, and this seems slow." If you do not use any of the tips below, this is true. But the tips below, if used selectively, usually clear up any objections.

Categorizing in Blocks

Categorizing e-mails in blocks is a way to make assigning categories go more quickly. For example, if I see a number of messages scattered about the Inbox that fit the Personal category, I will press CTRL to select the group (hold down the CTRL key and click noncontiguous items with the mouse; use the CMD key on the Mac), then right-click *one* of the items in the selected group, and set the Personal category classification. This operation sets the category for *all* the selected mail. Then, while the group is still selected, I drag the group to the Processed Mail folder. I then repeat this operation for other groups of categories I might see. After the obvious groups are done, I pick off and categorize the single items that are left in the list. This works for me; you will find your own preferred way of batch-processing your mail.

What may make this even quicker for you is this: try sorting on the From column before you apply your categories in batches. Often e-mails from the same person all categorize the same, so you can select adjacent items together (by holding down the SHIFT key) before setting the category. Also try sorting on the Subject column so you can batch-categorize e-mail "conversations."

Auto-Categorizing Based on Sender in Outlook for Mac 2011

On the Mac, if your intention is to categorize incoming mail based on sender, a built-in feature makes this very easy. You merely assign the category to the sender's entry in your Outlook Contacts list, and then check a box at the bottom of the Categories dialog box (see Figure 8.5), and it is all automatic. Again, you get to that box by CTRL-clicking any e-mail in its Categories column, and then choosing Edit Categories… from the shortcut menu.

Consider Creating Category Assignment Rules

In Lesson 11, I describe how to set rules in Outlook so that mail arrives in your Inbox precategorized. Once you have used the e-mail workflow and have been assigning categories to your mail for some time, I recommend you take a look at that section and give it a try. It takes a little work to set it up, but it will speed your Inbox processing tremendously. When I was using categories extensively (before I switched mainly to using Outlook 2007/10 Instant Search), nearly 70 percent of my filed mail was automatically categorized due to my frequent use of this feature.

Tagging Mail Using Outlook Add-In Software (Windows)

ClearContext

In Lesson 7, I recommended trying the software ClearContext because it provides useful tools to convert e-mails to tasks. The MYN Special Edition of ClearContext also pre-installs all the MYN settings in Outlook, so it can save you configuration time.

There are additional benefits to using ClearContext software if you choose to also use its optional approach to topic-based filing of mail. With ClearContext, you can tag and automatically file mail using powerful built-in tools.

ClearContext's original intention for this feature was to store all mail in multiple individual topic-named folders. But you can also use the software to simply tag topic names on e-mail like we just described with Outlook Categories, and to then file them in the single Processed Mail folder.

You can also tag *tasks* with topic names, and ClearContext adds a Dashboard view to show all mail and tasks associated with a given topic, together in one view. Because of this, and due to many other benefits, you may want to consider using this tool and this tagging approach.

ClearContext Projects and Outlook Categories

ClearContext calls its topic-tags ClearContext *Projects* and you can use them in ways similar to how you use Outlook Categories. In fact, once assigned to mail, the project name is displayed right in the Outlook Categories column.

However, ClearContext Projects and Outlook Categories are not the same thing. The main difference is that ClearContext uses a proprietary hidden data field on each e-mail to save its project name; because of that, you need to apply and edit projects using ClearContext controls. The controls are easy to use and include powerful automation. But you have to remember not to manipulate projects using category controls; otherwise the fields get out of sync and the software then becomes confusing to use.

There are advantages and disadvantages of using ClearContext Projects instead of Outlook Categories. Here are the pros and cons.

Advantages of Using ClearContext Projects with MYN Over Using Outlook Categories Alone

▶ Easy-to-use tools are added by ClearContext to Outlook to assign ClearContext Projects to e-mails and tasks. Many are automated. Most are easier to use than corresponding category assignment tools. This is by far the primary advantage to most users.

▶ Projects automatically assign to e-mail in the same conversation or thread. That means much of your mail will be already assigned for you.

▶ ClearContext makes it easy to assign project names to outgoing e-mail; this is much harder for categories.

▶ You can create nested (hierarchical) projects; you cannot do that with Outlook Categories.

▶ Projects take maximum advantage of the relationship capabilities of ClearContext, where all items related to each other can be identified using the Dashboard and manipulated in the Organizer. This is a bit more subtle but can be very powerful once you start using it.

▶ Projects do not import into other users' Outlook messages as categories can if using older Exchange Server software.

▶ There is no limit to the number of rules you can create to automatically assign ClearContext Projects. In Outlook run on Exchange Server, if you create rules to auto-assign categories, a rule limit is imposed by the server and it is easy to reach that limit if you have a large number of categories.

Disadvantages of Using ClearContext Projects with MYN Instead of Outlook Categories

▶ With Categories you can assign multiple Categories to one message. With ClearContext Projects you can only assign one. Many users will miss this capability dearly and in my mind it is the main reason to stick with Outlook Categories.

► With the project assignment prominently displayed in the Categories field in Outlook, many users are going to edit it directly there, not knowing that this will mess up many ClearContext features. Even once you become attentive to not editing the project assignment in the category field, there are many ways to accidently clear Outlook Categories, so I feel this makes the ClearContext approach a bit fragile.

► One result of the previous point is this: if you use a tablet or smartphone or other device that synchronizes with Outlook and takes advantage of Outlook Categories, ClearContext Projects will be visible in the category field on that device (good), but you will not be able to successfully edit the project assignment there (in fact, you will need to avoid editing it directly there).

For a complete description of how to use ClearContext with the MYN system, see this support page: MichaelLinenberger.com/BookTWCSupport.html.

Taglocity

I include Taglocity in this section on tagging Outlook e-mail because this product has won great reviews and maintains very close alignment with the pure web-centric concept of tagging as a way to organize and find scattered information in Outlook. I have not actually used the product though, so I cannot attest to it firsthand. If you are familiar with the web uses of tagging and like the typical tools used there like "tag clouds," give this software a try at www.taglocity.com.

Summary

Filing e-mail by topic is an optional activity you may want to do. Over the years, filing by using categories has proved to be an effective way to get e-mail out of the Inbox and into a place where you can find it easily later. Category groups, Search Folders, and Smart Folders are excellent ways to create folder-like structures from a collection of categorized e-mail. Once you configure Outlook appropriately and gain a little practice, using categories to file mail will become second nature.

Next Steps

Now that you have learned how to topic-file mail, it is time to go back to the workflows at the end of Lesson 7 and start putting it all together. This topic-filing skill is the very last step of that workflow. Your suite of e-mail tools is now complete. Start using them.

The next lesson revisits the theory underlying the MYN system and teaches you a few more core tools to help manage tasks.

Lesson 9:
Managing in the Now Horizon Using MYN Strategic Deferrals

Introduction

You've come a long way! You have learned powerful task and e-mail management tools. You are tracking critical tasks, and you are moving actions out of e-mails into your task system where they can be properly managed. Congratulations, your workday is coming under control.

If you have read this far you are probably eager for even more ways to fine-tune the techniques you have learned. That's what this lesson is all about. I build on the MYN Now Horizon theory presented in Lesson 1 to show additional task management tools that will allow your workday to be even better managed.

What's in This Lesson

In this lesson, first I cover how to use the Target Now portion of the Now Tasks list to indicate which noncritical tasks you want to target each day. That can be a powerful way to focus your work on specific nonurgent tasks, once you complete your Critical Now tasks.

Next, I show you how specific elements of the Now Horizon theory can be used to clarify how to keep your workload well balanced and under control.

And finally, building on what you learned about MYN Strategic Deferrals in Lesson 4, in this lesson I show the more advanced elements of that tool, specifically the Defer-to-Do and Defer-to-Review processes. If you are having trouble keeping your Now Tasks list short, or if the Low priority section of your task list is growing too large to review every week, now is the time to take this more advanced lesson.

All of these skills arise from the MYN Now Horizon theory presented in Lesson 1, so I'll start this lesson with a brief review of that and then provide a deeper study of some key aspects. If you skipped Lesson 1, I encourage you to read that before taking this lesson.

Review of the Now Horizon Work Model

Recall from Lesson 1 that the Now Horizon Work Model is best represented by an employee walking on the left end of a moving treadmill-like conveyor belt at a speed that just keeps him or her in place. The person's workday and workweek tasks approach on the belt from the right, and the person works those as they arrive, occasionally working ahead on the belt.

At the far right end of the conveyor belt is the limit of the work stream that the person can easily see coming; this is called the Now Horizon. Work beyond that point is out of sight and therefore out of mind, and so the person is not anxious about it. All this is shown in Figure 9.1.

Most knowledge workers report that horizon being about 1 to 1.5 weeks out. Nearly all attention is normally placed on work inside that horizon and inside that time frame.

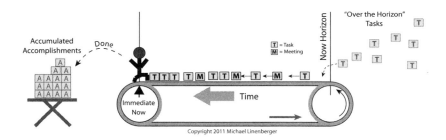

Copyright 2011 Michael Linenberger

Figure 9.1   Review from Lesson 1: the Now Horizon conveyor belt workload model. Ideal state.

If the rate of work entering the Now Horizon and exiting it completed is the same (as in Figure 9.1), the person feels good. If the person complains about being overloaded with work, he or she is most likely complaining about pileups of work inside the Now Horizon (see Figure 9.2 below). Even when overloaded, though, the person does not think much about work outside, or "over," the Now Horizon.

Review of Urgency Zones of the Now Horizon

In Lesson 1, I described the Now Horizon's four urgency zones—Critical Now, Target Now, Opportunity Now, and Over the Horizon; see Figure 9.2. I showed how the zones map to the Outlook configurations made in Lesson 3 (see figure 9.3 for Windows example). In Lessons 4 and 6, I showed how to manage your tasks by using these zones. Let's review them briefly.

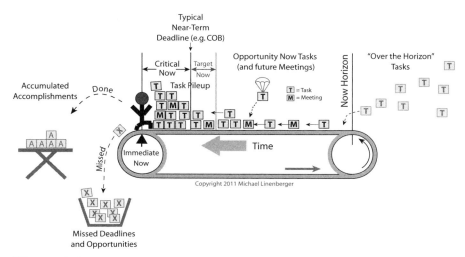

Figure 9.2　Review from Lesson 1: the Now Horizon model showing various "urgency zones," and an overloaded state.

Two Main Urgency Zones

Two of these zones you are already using extensively when you manage tasks in Outlook: the Critical Now and Opportunity Now zones.

Critical Now Tasks = High Priority in Outlook

Critical Now tasks are due within the typical deadline of close of business (COB). They are your must-do-today tasks. They probably have most of your attention and cause most of your feelings of urgency. It is here the typical task pileup occurs, leading to missed deadlines and opportunities. MYN users identify tasks in this zone by giving them a High priority in the Outlook MYN tasks list, configured per Lesson 3. They manage them by tracking them well and giving them extra attention throughout the day.

Opportunity Now Tasks = Normal Priority in Outlook

Tasks to the right of the Critical Now deadline but to the left of the Now Horizon are tasks that users are aware of and that need to be done as soon as is practical, but users will only do them *now* if the right opportunity arises. These map to the Normal priority section of the Outlook MYN tasks list, configured per Lesson 3.

Critical Now Tasks + Opportunity Now Tasks = Now Tasks List

One final reminder: these two groups together (High and Normal, or Critical Now and Opportunity Now) make up your Now Tasks list first described in Lesson 1. Now Tasks are those you either must do now or would *consider* doing now if you could. They form the list you review every day.

How these zones map to Windows Outlook shows in Figure 9.3 (repeated here from Lesson 1).

Two Other Urgency Zones

The other two urgency zones, which we covered only briefly in Lesson 1, are the Target Now and Over the Horizon zones. Drilling down on these reveals two more powerful task management tools you can use. Let's look at these zones now.

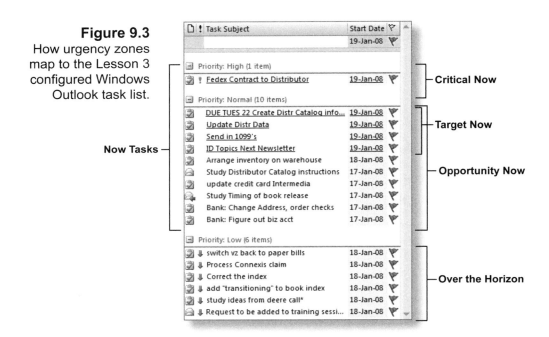

Figure 9.3
How urgency zones map to the Lesson 3 configured Windows Outlook task list.

New: Using Target Now Tasks

What follows is new material. I only briefly covered Target Now tasks in Lesson 1 and did not discuss how to implement this optional feature. Let me cover that here with some additional information, so you know how to implement it. Doing so is purely optional, as the Target Now zone does take some energy to maintain, but I think you will find it very useful.

Target Now tasks refer to noncritical tasks that you would *like* to do today but that are not urgently due. Getting them done now might make a client happy or ease the timing on downstream tasks. Or perhaps you are just very enthusiastic about the task. In essence, they are your most important Opportunity Now tasks. My recommended way to show these in Outlook is to *set a Normal priority task with today's start date* on it. This, per Lesson 3 configurations, causes the tasks in Windows versions of Outlook to be underlined and placed at the top of the Normal priority section, where they stand out nicely (see Figure 9.3 for an example). On the Mac they sort to the top of the Opportunity Now Smart Folder.

Optional Target Now Task Process

This leads to an optional process change to the Master Your Now! Outlook system, and it works as follows. Currently you might be setting tasks to today's date somewhat randomly as new tasks come in. Now do this instead: set new tasks to today's date only if you really want to do them today. Otherwise date them to the future or to the past (the latter will place them lower in your task list).

Then, each morning, identify which noncritical tasks on the Normal priority list you would like to target for today, and set the start date to today for those tasks, placing them at the top of the Normal section. If any items there are already set to today's date that you *don't* intend to do today, you should change the start date for those. Each day, you'll need to repeat the morning routine, because that section resets itself every day at midnight (more on that below).

That's it. These Target Now tasks will be your next action focus after you get your Critical Now tasks done.

Some Implications of Using the Target Now Task Process

This optional process fits nicely with many other processes you may currently be using in the MYN system and with Outlook. For example, if you defer a Normal priority task to a specific day you want to do it, when it arrives that day it pops into the Target Now zone of your task list, which is just what you want because you intend to complete that task today.

I also describe in Lesson 4 placing the word "TARGET" and a date in front of the subject of a task you want to start now and complete by a certain non-urgent target date. The two meanings of the word "target" correspond, since they both signify a task to be completed, nonurgently, on a particular day.

If you have a large number of Target Now tasks, in Windows you can show priority within that list by dragging individual tasks up and down. Outlook will reposition the tasks where you drag them, allowing you to create an ordered list inside that zone (such dragging only works on Windows, and only on tasks with the same date).

Maintaining the Target Now list takes a little attention, however, so you may decide you do not want to use this process. For example, you may be in the habit of setting all new tasks to a start date of today to get them on the Now Tasks list quickly. But stop and think about that: do you really want to target them for today? If not, set the date for, say, yesterday, which places it lower in the Opportunity Now list. That's a little less automatic. One shortcut is to type "yesterday" in the start date field when you create the task (this works on Windows Outlook only). You may want to make a habit of that so you do not water down the Target Now list.

And as stated above, you will quickly see that due to the MYN configurations you made in Outlook, this Target Now designation clears itself each morning and you need to choose your Target Now list again each day. This is good, since it ensures that your target list is fresh and matches you current priorities each day. This is similar to an old paper-based system where you had to rebuild your target list as you started a new page every day; it worked well then and it works well in this system. But it does take some energy to maintain and you may find yourself unable to keep up with it.

Note: *In Outlook 2007/10 and 2011, if you want to set the start date of a group of tasks to today (to place them all on the target list at once), press SHIFT or CTRL (CMD on Mac) and select them all, then right-click (CTRL-click on Mac) of one of them, choose Follow Up, and choose Today.*

Summary: Three Urgency Zones on the Task List

In Figure 9.3, I show all three zones mapped into an Outlook task list, configured as in Lesson 3. Naturally, your highest-priority attention is placed on the Critical Now tasks. If you have time after those are done you work the Target Now tasks next. And then if you have more time you would pick from the remainder of the Opportunity Now tasks, presumably starting at the top. You may of course mix up your order of attacking these.

Using the Now Horizon Model to Keep Your Workday Balanced

One advantage of having the model in mind is that it helps you get the most out of the MYN system to keep your workday balanced. It gives you a picture that helps you "see" how to use Outlook to keep urgency impact small enough, and at times visible enough, to prevent a chronic feeling of overload.

Here are some ways this model might influence how you manage your tasks to add balance to your day.

Which Tasks Go Directly to the Opportunity Now List?

When people first start using this system, they often ask, "What tasks should I put directly into my Normal priority task list? Should I pile every nonurgent task there and then just clean it later? That seems to be the process." Their concern is that the list will get too big if everything goes there and it is not cleaned constantly.

My answer is "Study the model." The model shows that you put tasks there that need to be in your current awareness. That's what the Now Horizon defines, and that's what the limit of the Normal priority section should be. We've stated that for most people the Now Horizon is 1 to 1.5 weeks out. So if a task does not need your attention in the next week or two, don't put it directly on the Now Tasks list. Rather, schedule it out for future attention, using one of the Strategic Deferral approaches shown in more detail below. This keeps the churn out of your list. And don't forget the 20-item limit there.

Too Many Critical Now Tasks?

Without this system, many people feel frustrated by fighting too many deadlines at the end of each day. The model shows that you should try to eliminate the pileup of tasks shown on the left side of Figure 9.2, inside your Critical Now; you want to prevent a constant state of near-term overload that can lead to unnecessary work anxiety. To do that, early in the day, make sure the list of items in your Critical Now really can be done today. If not, clean up the list so it is achievable and so you feel good about your day. You might have to do something early in the day to mitigate any blowback if you eliminate some tasks that you owe others, perhaps contacting stakeholders to get permission for delayed delivery. Then move the tasks out of the Critical Now section of the list to make that section reasonable again. Once that list is clearly defined and doable, your stress level will drop dramatically.

Review the Now Tasks List Often

You should review the entire Now Tasks list daily, if not more often. Since items in the Opportunity Now section are all moving toward you on the conveyor belt in the model, some items in this list, if they go uncompleted too long, can become overdue Critical Now items. And even if that doesn't happen, with a list too big to review, knowing you haven't checked your full list for a while can lead to discomfort about what you are overlooking. It is often the unknown or poorly defined urgencies that are most destructive to our sense of well-being. That's why you want to make sure that section is no larger than what you can easily grasp in a quick visual scan; you want to see these items coming every day. Again, I recommend reducing that list to no more than 20 items, keeping your workload well visualized and potentially stress-free. And then scanning the full list daily.

The overall review cycle that I recommend is to review the Critical Now section once an hour, the Opportunity Now section once a day, and the Over the Horizon section once a week.

Tossing Tasks over the Now Horizon

If the Opportunity Now section of the conveyor belt grows to larger than 20 items, and starts to pile up such that you cannot easily review it every day, you need to find lower-priority tasks that you can safely "toss over the Now Horizon." This is what I taught in Lesson 4, where you deferred some items and placed most excess items in the Low priority section. Over time, however, the Low priority section can become so large that you won't want to review it even once a week. Assuming you are experiencing that, now is the time to learn a more sophisticated version of that tossing. In the next section I will show you how to set a date on all deferred tasks that you toss over the Now Horizon (see Figure 9.4), using more advanced MYN Strategic Deferral tools. By doing that, you not only lower the number of tasks within the Now Horizon to a reasonable level but you also ensure that you have a reasonable way to track those deferred items. Let's go over the advanced MYN Strategic Deferral process now.

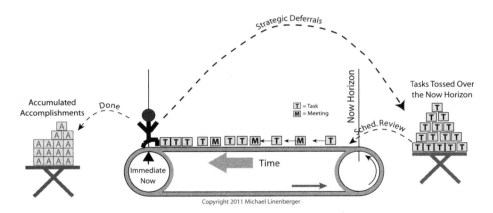

Figure 9.4 Using Strategic Deferrals: managing down the size of your Now Horizon tasks list by tossing lower priority-tasks over the Now Horizon and then scheduling reviews.

MYN Strategic Deferral

Use the CEO Approach

Sometimes you hear about CEOs who decide to postpone projects or products their company is currently working on. The CEO often states, "We are doing this to allow the company to focus better on primary current priorities," or maybe, "We need to return to our company's core competencies." The CEO is usually hailed as "strategic," "decisive," or "practical," or as being capable of "making the hard choices." The CEO is not usually called a "procrastinator."

Similarly, when you postpone focus on certain tasks in your list because you honestly have too much on your plate, take pride in your decision. Do not think of yourself as weak or procrastinating; rather think of yourself as making strategic choices. Just be sure to use the new MYN Strategic Deferral tools to do it in an accountable way. Specifically, use the scheduled review process for Defer-to-Review tasks. More on that below.

MYN Strategic Deferral Theory

MYN Strategic Deferral is a more intelligent and accountable way of handling tasks you cannot or won't do now, but that you can't delete or delegate either. These are the tasks that tend to build up over time. As a review, what MYN Strategic Deferral offers is this: if your Opportunity Now tasks list is larger than 20 items, take these steps to process the list down:

▶ Toss your lowest priority-tasks over the Now Horizon by setting the start dates to an appropriate time past that horizon. The key is to defer tasks always well past the Now Horizon. That way the tasks are far enough out that they do not impact your current perceived workload.

▶ Continue doing that until your Opportunity Now list is of reasonable size (well under 20 items) so that in your mind's eye your workload conveyor belt looks more like that in Figure 9.1. In other words, you feel reasonably comfortable with what's on your list.

▶ Then *manage* those tasks that are over the Now Horizon appropriately, taking a longer-term, scheduled approach. They are not forgotten.

Two Ways to Defer Tasks

When you defer a task to the future, past the Now Horizon, how you set the Outlook priority leads to a very important distinction.

If on that future-dated task you set the priority to High or Normal (medium), you've just created what I call a Defer-to-Do task. These are tasks you intend to *do* on the future date.

If you set a Low priority, you have created what I call a Defer-to-Review task. These are tasks you intend to *review* on the future date. Let's discuss both.

Defer-to-Do Tasks

Defer-to-Do tasks are tasks that you defer to a specific day *on which you really intend to do them*. On that future day, a Defer-to-Do task becomes either a Critical Now task or a Target Now task in your MYN task list. Using our definition mapping, in Outlook it appears as either of the following:

▶ A High priority task.

▶ A Normal priority task with the start date set to today (an underlined Normal priority task, at the top of the Normal section).

An example of a task that is a good candidate for this would be "Write monthly sales report," which you create on Tuesday and you intend to turn in Friday afternoon, and you know it won't take long to write. You know Friday is relatively open so you want to do it that day. To make this a Defer-to-Do task, you would set the start date to Friday and set the priority to either High or Normal (medium), depending how critical the item is. The task would disappear and then reappear Friday morning.

This is basically the same way I taught you to do deferrals in Lesson 4, but this time I want you to be very diligent about restricting the High and Normal priority deferred tasks to *only* those you really intend to do on the day they appear in your Now Tasks list. Once you enforce that limit I think you will find there will not be many of these.

Defer-to-Review Tasks

The Defer-to-Review process is the gem of this set of tools and is what you will use most of the time to manage down the size of your Now Tasks list. Because of that, the tool is slightly more complex than Defer-to-Do tasks and I will spend more time describing it.

Defer-to-Review Tasks Defined

Defer-to-Review tasks are tasks you merely want to put off for a while. You are doing this primarily because you have too much on your plate right now and want to get these out of sight. For various reasons you cannot or will not delete or delegate them. For Defer-to Review tasks, there is not a specific day in the future you intend to do them. Tasks like this are likely much more abundant than the Defer-to-Do tasks; for me the ratio is about 20 to 1.

These are the tasks you placed in the Low priority section in Lesson 4 but with little follow-up management. What I add in this lesson is the notion that you can estimate an approximate time frame for when you want to *reconsider* them or review them again. You will actually schedule that review. When you do review them again in the future, you will decide one of two likely possibilities:

▶ The tasks have become more urgent or more relevant and should be promoted to your Now Tasks list, or

▶ They should continue to be maintained over the Now Horizon.

Creating Defer-to-Review Tasks

Most Defer-to Review tasks start out as Now Tasks that you decide to deprioritize as your list gets too big. In the MYN Outlook system, once you identify which task you want to deprioritize:

▶ Set the Outlook priority to *Low*.

▶ Set the start date to a future *Monday* that is beyond your current Now Horizon. Set it as far in the future as is safe, practical, and appropriate.

▶ If the start date is more than a month away, try to set it to the *first Monday of the month* (I'll discuss why in a moment).

Processing Defer-to-Review Tasks: Four Options

To process Defer-to-Review tasks, you need to make the following two promises:

First, reserve the Low priority section just for these tasks; place nothing else there.

Second, every Monday you are going to see a group of these deferred tasks pop into the Low priority section of your TaskPad/To-Do Bar (see Figure 9.5). When they do, *process them out of there quickly*. Do not allow them to sit in the Low priority section more than a day or two. Completely empty that section.

Figure 9.5   Every Monday a new list will pop into your previously empty Low priority section. Process those out as soon as possible; keep that section empty.

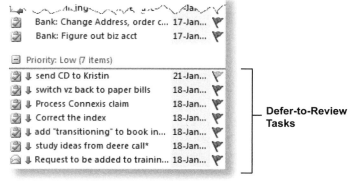

You have four ways you can process these tasks out of the Low priority section.

1. Set their start date to some other future Monday, thus deferring them over the Now Horizon again (as in Figure 9.4). Select a Monday as far in the future as is safe, practical, and appropriate. Since I have so many deferred tasks, this is my most common choice.

2. Set their Outlook priority to Normal or High so that they are promoted immediately to your current Now Tasks list. Do this if their importance has recently increased or if your workload has diminished enough to now get to them.

3. Do the task right now and mark it complete (if you have lots of tasks in the list, this is the less likely choice).

4. Delete or delegate the task. Often your older tasks can be deleted.

I find that 90 percent of my tasks make sense to defer to the future again (option 1 above). Some I might defer out one week; some six months or more. In fact, that is the beauty of this system—it gives you a way to apply appropriate deferral periods to each task, according to their built-in time frames.

Using this process, I can usually empty the Low priority section very quickly; I have never found this hard to do or a burden. In fact, it is almost a pleasure, since I often find things there I now really want to do, owing to more favorable circumstances. Or more likely, I find that the contents of my indistinct list of future to-do's, which can haunt my subconscious at times, are not so bad after all now that I see them again, and most can be deferred even longer this time. It is satisfying to do that since it feels so good to empty that section. It clears my psyche of concern about postponed items.

Create a Monday Appointment to Review Defer-to-Review Tasks

Even though it can be satisfying to review and empty the Defer-to-Review section of my task list every week, just to make sure I do this review I have an appointment for it scheduled on my calendar every Monday morning. I suggest you set up an appointment like that on your calendar.

Benefits of the Defer-to-Review Process

The Defer-to-Review process is what enables me to look at my short list of 20 Opportunity Now items (and up to 5 Critical Now items) and say, "This really *is* all I need to think about this week," and therefore feel my workday and workweek are well under control. It is one of the main ways to keep the conveyor belt in the model moving at a reasonable and doable pace with a reasonable task load. Here are some specific improvements over other ways you may have managed a long tasks list in the past.

▶ Compared to the simplified approach I taught in Lesson 4 and particularly compared to earlier editions of this book, it is a much more efficient approach. It prevents the top of your Normal priority task section from filling unexpectedly with high volumes of returning deferred tasks; it will now be easier to keep that section clean, well managed, and well prioritized.

▶ Compared to the simpler approach I taught in Lesson 4—dumping all other items into the Low priority section, which quickly becomes too large to review—it gives you a *scheduled* way to check a limited count of deferred Low priority items.

▶ It gives you a way to control which of these Low priority items to check in on soon and which to defer for a longer time. This is a huge benefit, since it makes the review process quicker and much more productive; you'll only be reviewing tasks that you predicted might be important that week (or month).

▶ And it gives these deferred items the low priority they really deserve until they arrive, keeping them out of your main focus until you are ready to conduct a review.

Defer-To-Review Tasks Replace Master Tasks Functionality

Those of you who used the first edition of this book may have realized by now that the Defer-to-Review process replaces the master tasks process for long-term tasks. Here's why I made that replacement. I have found that most people do not succeed with a scheduled review of a very large master tasks list. If you put an appointment on your calendar to review your master tasks and you're a very busy person, you'll skip that meeting every time. Why? Two reasons. First, the list gets too big too quickly, so it becomes discouraging to review. Second, most of the items you review do not need review every week and you feel the time is wasted. Once users start skipping those reviews, I find they are reluctant to place tasks on the master tasks list (for fear they will lose sight of them), and instead leave them on their main task list, overloading it. The main task list then becomes unusable.

Instead, the new Defer-to-Review process works much better, even for busy people. You know you will review deferred tasks because the process requires a commitment on when you will review each one. When that time comes, it puts that item right in plain view on the lower part of your TaskPad/To-Do Bar, a section you have committed to keeping empty. So even if you skip your Monday-morning review, the tasks are displayed prominently in the Low priority of your MYN tasks list anyway, encouraging you to do something about them. You are confident the only ones displayed there are tasks that you predicted might need review this week, so you are more likely to look at them. And you are reviewing a much smaller list each week, compared to a full master tasks list. The whole Defer-to-Review process just works better than any other process I know.

Note: *The first edition process of using the Low priority section of the Master Tasks view for tasks that you review very rarely is also incorporated into this new process. As you recall, that section held your ideas, inspirations, and long-term Low priority tasks, none of which you have any near-term intentions to act on. I now recommend you make Defer-to-Review tasks out of them too, and schedule their review out 6 to 12 months. You really should review everything eventually, and this enables you to do that.*

An Optional Tasks Folder View: Defer-To-Review Tasks (Windows)

You can manage these tasks right in the TaskPad/To-Do Bar. That's what I usually do. But you might also want to build a new optional Tasks Folder view that gives you a way to do some proactive management (see Figure 9.6). This suggested view groups tasks by their deferred-to Monday.

One benefit of this view is to see what week or month tasks are piling up in so you can avoid putting too many tasks into the same review period. Consistently using the first day of the week and the first Monday of the month as target dates is what makes this view work; it creates distinct groups that are easier to track and manage. You can even drag tasks from group to group in that view. I'll show you how to build that view in Lesson 12, when I cover optional custom Tasks folder views. This view is also delivered with the MYN-enabled version of ClearContext.

Figure 9.6   Optional Defer-to-Review Tasks folder view where all defer-to-review tasks are displayed grouped in their scheduled future review week (or month). Next-month's tasks are at the bottom; tasks at top are farther out.

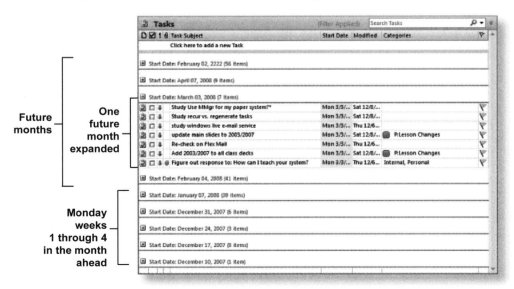

Summary of MYN Strategic Deferral Steps

MYN Strategic Deferrals are a way to reduce the size of your Now Tasks list to make it easier to use and better focused. Here are the basic operations.

▶ Set Defer-to-Do tasks: for any task that you intend to do on a specific future day, just set the start date ahead to that date. Leave the Outlook priority at either High or Normal as appropriate. Only do this if you really intend to do the task on that date.

▶ Set Defer-to-Review tasks: for any task that you merely want to put off for a while, set the Outlook priority to Low, and set the date ahead to some Monday in the future (beyond the Now Horizon) on which you want to review the task again.

▶ Every Monday, as Defer-to-Review tasks mature and appear in the Low priority section of your TaskPad/To-Do Bar, process them out immediately using the four options above, in the section Processing Defer-to-Review Tasks: Four Options. You will most likely defer the tasks again.

MYN Strategic Deferral FAQs

Q: Isn't this just procrastination?

A: No, absolutely not. You are proactively managing your dynamic and busy work life. Remember, you will always think of more things to do than you have time to do, so you need to prioritize and do the things that are right for the moment. You then need to come back to all those other creative ideas and tasks periodically to see if their time has come. This is merely a management tool to accomplish that effectively.

Q: Why hold on to tasks so long; why not just delete them when you first see they fall "below the line"?

A: You never know when the ideal time to revisit a good idea or moderately important task may come. Even though you may only reactivate a small portion of your deferred list, even if only one out of 20 offers high value later, you still come out ahead. Furthermore, what I find is that without this tool, I would never delete many of my Low priority tasks. I would not have the confidence to do so. I would be too concerned that they may in fact become important. If I retain them, my Now Tasks list would quickly get too big. This tool gives me a competent way to confidently move Low priority tasks off my Now Tasks list, thereby keeping that list well focused.

Q: Isn't the Monday review just another burdensome "should" I need to do and will probably skip?

A: Granted, that is a risk, but it is my experience that compared with all the other "shoulds" in the time-management world, this one is pretty darn easy to do and keep up with. As I mentioned above, it is almost a pleasure to do since it works so well. Plus, if you do skip it, the tasks sit rather prominently at the bottom of your list, urging you to do something.

Q: Over time, won't this list of Defer-to-Review tasks grow huge every month and become unusable?

A: No, and the reason is, as tasks get older you will in fact eventually delete them. Think about it. The only reason you maintain these tasks on the list is that they had some near-term relevance at the time. In my experience, the half-life of a task is relatively short. Business and personal priorities tend to move on and eventually the very old tasks on the defer-to-review list will stand out and you'll delete them.

Q: I used the previous version of this system, with the master tasks approach. In that system I was able to assign various levels of priority to master tasks. If everything is now a Low priority, how can I indicate various levels of priority?

A: The time frame settings are a form of prioritization. But if you are talking about core importance (regardless of time), use the intrinsic importance approach described in Lesson 12 for this.

Q: Isn't it possible that my entire collection of tasks with deadlines within the Now Horizon is so large that reducing that list to 20 Opportunity Now items (and up to 5 Critical Now items), by deferring them, is impractical?

A: Sure, that's possible. But I want you to study the exercise in Lesson 11 called Doing the Math on Your Workweek first before you decide that. If after that exercise you still conclude you are overloaded, yes, now you will have confirmed that and you need to do something about it. Strategies to correct the problem are discussed there. I suspect, however, that most people who think they are hopelessly overloaded really do have more options for remedy than they think, and Strategic Deferral is one.

▪ ▪ ▪

Summary

The Now Horizon model and MYN Strategic Deferral tools provide a way to reduce the feeling of workday overload and anxiety by giving you a practical tool to focus on your top tasks. They give you a clean and accountable way to toss tasks over the Now Horizon, where the perceived impact on your workday is minimal. Of the two MYN Strategic Deferral tools, Defer-to-Review is the most important for managing the Now Horizon because it is the tool you'll use most often when managing down the size of your Now Horizon workload.

How do you put this all together with all the other techniques you are using? The workflow is really pretty simple:

► Use the Critical Now, Target Now, and Opportunity Now sections of the MYN tasks list to list all tasks that you currently think are within your Now Horizon. Confirm this list often, preferably every day.

► If the entire Now Tasks list has more than 20 Opportunity Now items (or more than 5 Critical Now items) you will likely start to feel anxious about having too much to do, so reduce the list. Do that by deleting and delegating if you can, but primarily by using these two MYN Strategic Deferral tools.

► Once the list is maintained at or below 20 + 5, use the system as you were trained earlier: work your Critical Now tasks today, do as many Target Now tasks as you can do, and work Opportunity Now tasks if circumstances permit.

With this complete MYN task workflow in place, you will quickly reach the point where you do not feel overloaded or anxious about your work. You will then start to insert into your workday more and more of your important but not urgent items. So instead of being buried by and reacting only to urgent matters, you'll also be progressing your important projects and life priorities and probably making good headway in your career. You will develop a completely different attitude about your work, and possibly for the first time start to enjoy your job. That's what the MYN system can bring you.

■   ■   ■

Next Steps

You have now completed Part II of the book, focused on maturing the system.

Part III collects together mostly optional components of the MYN system that can make your work life easier, more efficient, and better focused, but that you can postpone implementing if you wish. The first lesson is on Delegation. If you have staff you delegate tasks to, I encourage you to take Lesson 10 now. Lesson 11 is on time management and various ways to save time with this system. Lesson 12 is a collection of optional techniques and custom Windows Outlook views that you may find useful. Feel free to jump around these next lessons and take them out of order if you wish, as they stand fairly independently of each other.

PART III

Mastering the System

Lesson 10:
MYN Delegation in Outlook

Introduction

Delegating tasks effectively is an essential means for clearing tasks off your list, which frees up time to focus on activities that are more important and more appropriate to your role. It is also good for the staff you delegate to because, as you assist them through increasing levels of skills, they learn; it can and should be a win–win arrangement.

However, many new and even experienced work managers have trouble delegating effectively. As a result, too many tasks that should be delegated end up remaining self-assigned.

Failures with delegation often stem from lack of good systems to assign, track, and follow up on delegated tasks. When a deadline arrives and the delegated task has not been completed, too often managers blame the delegated staff: "That person can't seem to get things done for me; if I need something done I'd better do it myself," and tasks end up back on the manager's list. It's highly likely that the failure was due to the delegation methodology, not due to the staff the task was delegated to.

Delegation of tasks can represent handoffs to subordinates or "requests" to colleagues. Both can be managed the same way.

Successful Delegation

It's amazing how much respect and attention staff will give you and the tasks you assign if you provide three elements in your requests:

► An honest and thoughtful discussion of the reasons the task is important and why this person may be the right one to work on it.

▶ Plenty of lead time on the deadline of the task.

▶ Consistent and reasonably spaced check-ins while waiting for the task to be completed.

It's when you fail to manage assigned tasks without providing these elements that tempers get short and staff feel overburdened.

It's no wonder managers are so bad at delegation. They have a large pile of their own tasks to manage, so how can they be expected to correctly assign and consistently track the task list of others? In the earlier lessons of this book, you have learned best practices for getting your own tasks under control; in this lesson you will learn best practices for delegating tasks to others.

The Task Delegation Approach

My approach to task delegation is a three-step process:

1. **Identify**: At the moment the task and the need to delegate arises, enter and annotate it in your task system as a task to be delegated and indicate to whom to delegate it. Do not actually communicate the task until the next step.

2. **Get Buy-In**: Use a face-to-face or phone meeting to gain buy-in and acceptance from the staff or colleague and to set a deadline for the task. Update the system to indicate acceptance (if achieved), and schedule your first check-in time frame.

3. **Follow Up**: At the scheduled check-in, follow up on the assigned task, provide help if needed, and set subsequent follow-up time frames. Escalate only after several follow-ups.

I like this approach because the staff manages the task in their own way, and I use my task system to initiate regular personal follow-up activities. This prevents me from forcing my task management approach on other staff, yet it allows me a personal touch in my follow-up. I cover logistics for each of these steps next.

Step 1: Identify and Annotate a Task for Delegation

In step 1, when I identify tasks that I intend to assign to others, I annotate the subject line of tasks in my task list. This helps me plan and initiate the assignment process. My assignment annotation system is simple: I place the initials of the staff member I intend to assign the task to in the very front of the subject line, followed by a colon, then the subject itself. So a task I intend to assign to Joe Smith to provide network performance resolution would have the subject line "JS:Resolve network performance." This is for my use only; I do not give the task list to Joe. I may give Joe a head's-up e-mail that something new is coming to be discussed in the next meeting; for big tasks, the more warning the better. And I set the start date to the day I intend to meet Joe to discuss the task assignment.

By using this annotation system, on the day I intend to meet with Joe I am reminded to make this assignment. Or if I meet with Joe early, I can sort the subject field alphabetically within the Tasks folder of Outlook (in Windows use the MYN All Now Tasks view described ahead in Lesson 12; on the Mac just use the unfiltered tasks folder), scroll down to Joe's initials, and collect the tasks that I propose to hand off in person.

Step 2: Gaining Buy-In for the Task

A Valuable Step

Assigning a task to someone without prior discussion is largely discouraged by management experts. An important element of delegation is achieving buy-in from the staff member you plan to delegate to. During one-on-one meetings, I spend time discussing the value of the task. I try to share the vision behind it. And if the task is an interesting one, I try to share my excitement. If the task is urgent I make sure the staff member shares my feeling of urgency and the reasons behind it. I then make a point of asking if he or she is interested in the task and feels it can be added to their list. And very important, can they complete it by the intended deadline? One hopes the answer is yes to all of those questions. If working this task may cause other delegated tasks to be late, now is the time to discuss that. You may have to make some trade-offs in your list of delegated tasks for this individual.

Gaining such buy-in is incredibly important. It builds your staff's respect for you and your management techniques. It creates a sense of ownership between the staff and the task. And it goes a long way toward ensuring the successful completion of the delegated task.

Skipping this step leads to bad morale and incomplete assignments. There are hundreds of ways to do this wrong. For example, dropping a task assignment in someone's Inbox without prior discussion is inadvisable.

Outlook's Assign Task Feature

This specific example is why, even though Outlook has an automatic way to delegate tasks, I recommend that you do not use that capability. Let me explain.

Figure 10.1
I avoid use of the Assign Task buttons.

If your organization has a Microsoft Exchange implementation, you can use Outlook to assign tasks electronically to other staff. Automatic assignment of tasks is activated by clicking the Assign Task button at the top of the task entry dialog box (see Figure 10.1). This feature is also available by right-clicking a task in the task list view.

When you use the Assign Task feature, your copy of Outlook actually sends a special e-mail with the task attached, asking the recipient to formally accept or reject the task assignment. If it is accepted, the task is added to the recipient's own Outlook task list, and you automatically get back a message saying the task was accepted. At that point your copy of the task is modified to show that a formal assignment has been made and to whom it was assigned. Subsequently you can request special Outlook-based status reports from those recipients (sent using the button just to the right of the Assign Task button shown above). And when you receive those status reports back, the status fields (Status and % Complete) will be updated in your own task list to reflect the progress of work that your staff has made on the task.

This is a great concept and a great implementation. However, every time I've tried to use it I've found that for various reasons, usually people-related, the team stops or never fully starts using this approach. There are two main problems:

▶ If not used carefully, it encourages the classic "dump and run" approach to delegating tasks. Dropping a task assignment in someone's Inbox is not consistent with gaining staff buy-in.

▶ Many of your staff may prefer not to use Outlook's task system to manage their tasks, or may not know how to.

That said, it is a well-implemented technology. One scenario where it could be used effectively is this: your entire staff is already using Microsoft Outlook to manage tasks per MYN principles, and you agree not to use the Assign Task button until *after* you've had your discussion with your staff about a task assignment. You may want to try that out. The following discussion assumes that you do *not* use Outlook's automated assign task functionality.

Step 3: Methods of Follow-Up (and Buy-In)

Meeting with Your Staff to Review Assignments

I have one-on-one meetings weekly with all my key staff to discuss and assign tasks and to check the progress of previously assigned tasks. But if the next one-on-one is too far off and the task urgent, I set a separate short ad hoc meeting to have the discussion. Before that meeting, I use the Tasks folder and, if on Windows Outlook, I use the MYN All Now Tasks view (see Lesson 12) to sort on tasks for that staff member. Mac users should just use their unfiltered Tasks folder. I review all tasks that are outstanding and all tasks that I intend to assign. I sort alphabetically on the subject line so that all tasks with that individual's initials sort together. I bring that list with me to the meeting for review. The best way to do this is to use a laptop or tablet and bring it with you to the meeting. Or you can instead print that list and bring the paper copy.

I discuss with the staff member tasks that they have not yet agreed to and, if needed, reprioritize and redate the outstanding ones to reflect newer priorities and meeting outcomes; I input those changes immediately or when I return to my computer. Again, this is even easier if you bring the laptop or a tablet with you to the meeting. Having a PC with you is an effective way to keep up with a rapidly changing landscape of assigned tasks — particularly if you have many staff. And assuming that during your discussion about the status of each task you may have changes to make to those tasks (for example, marking the subject for follow-up, extending the deadline, or marking the task as complete), you can edit the tasks right in this window, in the meeting. If you are not using any mobile devices you can mark up your paper printout of tasks and make the changes when you return to your computer.

Following Up on Delegated Tasks

Once the task is accepted, it is essential to schedule and engage in regular follow-up activities. Consistent and reasonable follow-up is the key, often-overlooked point. We are tempted to think that once a task is assigned, the recipient "should" do it. Even if we agree that check-ins are needed, it is easy to forget to do this well before the deadline. New managers are often afraid to disturb their staff about assigned work.

This is an essential step of task delegation. It is good management practice to track delegated task assignment progress regularly, well before the task is due. It is bad management practice to wait until the task is due for the first check-in.

The solution is to adopt a system whereby the next "fair" date for the check-in is negotiated at the assignment and clearly scheduled in your task system as an activity for you to do. And then you take a very proactive follow-up when that time arrives. Using Outlook tools, this is an easy operation; you simply create a dated follow-up task for each outstanding delegated item.

Creating the Follow-Up Task

Creating such follow-up tasks is made very easy if you do the following: convert your task entry for the intended assignment into a follow-up task at the time the task is accepted.

Here is how this works. Recall the task that I intended to assign to Joe Smith to resolve network performance issues. Remember that at the time I decided to assign it I marked it "JS:Resolve network performance." This notation indicated I intended to assign this task to Joe but that Joe had not yet accepted it. Once I discuss this assignment with Joe and he accepts it, I immediately modify the annotation of the same task as follows: "F:JS: Resolve network performance"; the added "F" stands for follow-up. That way, before or during my weekly one-on-one with Joe, I can sort separately on those tasks he's accepted already and on those that still need discussion to establish buy-in.

And at the same time I add the "F" for follow-up to my task I also change the Outlook Start Date field of the task to be the day I want to be reminded to check in with Joe (see sidebar text below for examples). I usually set the priority to High (Critical Now); this priority level ensures that I take action on the day the task appears on my Now Tasks list. Again, I avoid the use of Outlook reminders or alarms for tasks (I only use them for appointments). Rather, the

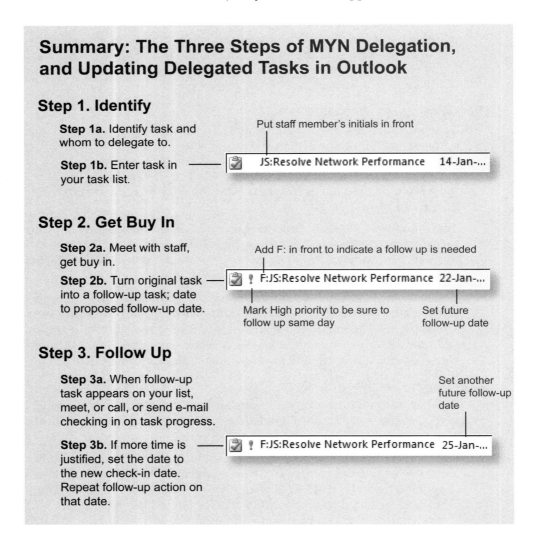

Summary: The Three Steps of MYN Delegation, and Updating Delegated Tasks in Outlook

Step 1. Identify

Step 1a. Identify task and whom to delegate to.

Step 1b. Enter task in your task list.

Put staff member's initials in front

JS:Resolve Network Performance   14-Jan-...

Step 2. Get Buy In

Step 2a. Meet with staff, get buy in.

Step 2b. Turn original task into a follow-up task; date to proposed follow-up date.

Add F: in front to indicate a follow up is needed

F:JS:Resolve Network Performance   22-Jan-...

Mark High priority to be sure to follow up same day

Set future follow-up date

Step 3. Follow Up

Step 3a. When follow-up task appears on your list, meet, or call, or send e-mail checking in on task progress.

Set another future follow-up date

Step 3b. If more time is justified, set the date to the new check-in date. Repeat follow-up action on that date.

F:JS:Resolve Network Performance   25-Jan-...

appearance of a brief check-in task at the top of my Now Tasks list nearly always leads to my taking action on that check-in the same day it appears. In fact, check-in tasks are among the quickest tasks to accomplish, so engaging them is a great way to knock a number of tasks off your list for that day, which always feels good.

Better Than Waiting-For List

For those who may have used a "waiting for" list in the past to track items like this, I find the above approach much better because the follow-up item does not appear until it has aged an appropriate amount. There is nothing worse than pursuing someone about a request that you just gave them without letting them have time to work on it; this keeps that from happening. And it keeps you from having to do a mental calculation every time you look at a waiting-for list to decide whether action is needed on the items in the list. Instead, the follow-up task appears on your action list at just the right time. Also, a separate waiting-for list is one more list you have to remember to check daily. It is so much easier if your follow-up tasks appear automatically in your single Now Tasks list on the day that they are due.

Assign Partial Deliverables for Check-In Points

You may also wish to negotiate a specific partial deliverable on a follow-up date. If the final task includes creating something tangible, a rough draft or first pass at the final product is a good target deliverable for the check-in. This keeps the check-in date from becoming merely an agreed-to reminder date. And you often discover a lot in creating a first draft. Requiring an early rough draft allows you to discover issues early enough to allow time to adjust plans. For this to be effective you need to convince your staff that you will be very lenient in judgment of that rough draft; otherwise, they will spend too much time polishing something that may be a false start.

I put the agreed-to final deadline of the delegated task either in the body of the text of the task or in the subject line if the delivery day is urgent (see Lesson 4 for a discussion of using the subject line for deadlines). If that day is approaching and the task is still not done, on my morning review of open tasks I convert it to a High priority (a Critical Now task).

A Follow-Up Task System That Really Works

This follow-up task system really does work. I find it is amazingly effective at clearing my subconscious of loose-end concerns about assignments and guiding me in appropriate follow-up activities. At any given time I can have 20 or more open assigned tasks that are neatly scheduled for follow-ups. They remain out of sight until exactly the right scheduled check-in point, freeing my attention for more important activities. Without a system like this I might forget to check in, and then the task becomes an emergency. I might even check in too often, which is unnecessary and irritating to staff. The system brings order and calm to an otherwise chaotic mess.

How to Follow Up on Delegated Tasks

When the start date of the follow-up task arrives (in reality, my informal reminder date) and the follow-up task appears at the top of my Now Tasks list, I then have a choice in how I follow up.

I may schedule it to coincide with the next regular one-on-one meeting. For that meeting, using the MYN All Now Tasks view, I sort on the task name and scroll to the task list for the individual.

Avoid Following Up in a Group

You may be tempted to make follow-ups part of a regularly scheduled departmental or team meeting. This is probably the most commonly used technique in the business world today. I recommend you avoid this unless team activity depends on that knowledge. In most cases not everybody needs to hear everyone's tasks and where they are on them. Such sessions lack positive energy and often lead to useless posturing. They usually do not optimize the time spent. Use your one-on-ones instead.

Many tasks, however, move too fast to wait for scheduled one-on-one meetings. Or you may need to cancel a scheduled meeting. You may not have regular one-on-one meetings with your staff. And you may make many assignments to staff who aren't your subordinates; you may not meet regularly with them. This is the beauty of having the scheduled follow-ups as individual tasks on your task list. They trigger and appear at the top of your Now Tasks list at just the right time, whether you look for them or not, and whether meetings are scheduled or not.

Following Up Outside of a Meeting

How to handle follow-ups outside of meetings can vary. If I'm really busy and the actual needed delivery date is not for a good number of days more, I may just shoot off an e-mail to Joe asking, "How are things going on the network performance issue? Let me know as soon as you can, the senior staff meeting is coming up in five days." If this is to a colleague, I would be much more politic: "Hi Karen, just checking in to see if all is okay on getting the product overview presentation together by Friday. Let me know if I can get you any additional information or help in any other way. Really appreciate you working on this. That report is going to make the BigCo sale a success."

If Joe is a member of my staff though, better yet is to call or walk over to Joe's desk. The personal touch and one-task-at-a-time nature of this check-in is usually effective at getting the task moving. And I am raising the reminder while Joe is at his desk, at his tools, where he can actually act when he gets the reminder and thinks, "Oh man, I forgot about this, I better move on it."

Setting the Next Follow-Up

Whether you follow up in meetings or between them, there is one more critical step that you must do. In case you don't or can't get an immediate answer to your follow-up, or the answer indicates that the task is not yet complete, decide and record immediately what day would be the appropriate next day to check in again. Immediately reset the start date on the follow-up task to that new date. This will cause the task to reappear on the task list on that day. If you send an e-mail or voice message as your follow-up action, then set the new date in the task at the moment you send the message (don't wait for a reply, otherwise you will forget). If your check-in takes place in person, enter the new negotiated date into your system as soon as you finalize it at your staff member or colleague's desk.

This is the key utility of using a system to boost your ability to get control of delegated tasks. Such tasks are too numerous and too fast moving to keep their status in your head. You need to keep the status of tasks up to date and in a system, and you need to make those updates immediately. Loose notes or memorized actions will not suffice; otherwise those tasks will fall through cracks. If you have a mobile device, you can do such a status reset right in your meeting with your staff. Whether that meeting is in the hall, in a conference room, or at your staff's desk, make sure you update the status immediately. Keeping tasks updated ensures a steady follow-up approach. It minimizes forgotten agreements and sends a consistent management message to your staff. If your staff learn from experience that you always follow up, they are less likely to relax on deadlines or take chances that you might not notice slipped deliverables.

Escalation

If the above reminder scenario repeats itself a number of times on the same task, however, you need to escalate management of this task beyond a simple reminder system. The weekly one-on-one meeting with your staff can be a good forum for this escalation because it allows time to brainstorm solutions to whatever is holding up completion of the task. Or if the deadline is too close, call an urgent ad hoc meeting to review the impact of the problem and together plan out a course of action. The latter only happens after a few check-in points, so all involved will feel the escalation is fair. The beauty of this approach is that you can stay ahead of assigned tasks and manage them in a timely and fair fashion.

Summary

The positive effects of a good delegation system are remarkable. Staff who previously seemed forgetful or even irresponsible suddenly start responding positively to your assignments. People are human and can forget promises they make. This is particularly true if they do not have a good task management system in place themselves. As the sponsor of a delegated task it is up to you to usher the task ahead and ensure its completion. A good delegation system combined with your good task management system is a winning combination for helping you succeed in delegating tasks.

You can succeed with delegation if you keep the following in mind:

▶ Effective delegation requires three important components: establishing buy-in, giving adequate lead time, and using effective follow-ups.

▶ You can implement an effective Outlook task nomenclature to accomplish successful delegation.

▶ Create follow-up tasks to ensure that you check in with delegated staff on a regular basis.

Next Steps

The next lesson explores a number of topics on time management and an array of time-saving suggestions. You may wish to work with the system for a few weeks before digging into that lesson. Or skim through it now and see if there are any techniques that you wish to start using immediately. You will find a wealth of time-saving ideas and insights there.

Lesson 11:
Time Management and
Other Time Savers

Introduction

Many people say they need to learn time management. However, what I think most people need to learn when they say that is *task* management. By following the task management principles in the MYN system, you will in fact meet most of your time management needs. You will find you use your time much more efficiently and effectively. You will find you sail through e-mail quickly. You will probably find that you are able to leave work without any nagging doubts about what has been left undone.

Beyond the task management principles taught in this book, however, a few simple time management techniques can be extremely useful.

What's in This Lesson

Some Key Time-Management Techniques

First, if your day is mostly full of appointments, you'll need to set some time aside to work your tasks. I encourage you to schedule general task time right on your calendar. That is discussed immediately below.

Second, you may need to make sure that time spent working your task list is kept well focused. In the sections below I provide a number of techniques to ensure that. For example, I provide a simple process for identifying clearly whether you really are overloaded with high-importance tasks or just working inefficiently; identifying this helps lead to a solution (see section below Doing the Math on Your Workweek). And in the section titled Cleaning Up Your Task Time you'll find tips to make sure you use your task time most effectively.

Time-Saving Tips

Finally, the second half of the lesson presents a number of time-saving tips for using Outlook with the MYN system, particularly for e-mail. These include the following:

▶ How to auto-categorize incoming mail.

▶ Quicker ways to maintain the list of Outlook Categories that you apply to e-mail.

▶ Creating an All Mail Search Folder or Smart Folder to find mail more quickly.

▶ How to make the e-mails you write more effective.

Since most of these techniques can stand alone, you may want to scan through this chapter and read only those that currently seem to offer you value. Then plan to return to this lesson after using the system for a while; you will find some sections will become more relevant to you over time.

Time Management: Finding Time to Work on Tasks

Just as important as deciding what tasks to do is ensuring that you have time to do them. Your task list is useless if you have no time to work the list.

Everyone's work patterns are different. Some of you have endless meetings all day long. Others of you may sit at your desk working assignments most of the day. Or you may have operational responsibilities scheduled throughout the day. Some of you may travel extensively. And I'm sure there is everything in between. So you will need to design an approach to making time for working tasks that is appropriate for your workday.

If you are at your desk all day and are not devoted exclusively to operational activities, you may not need to set aside dedicated task working time; your workday is your task day. If you are in meetings most of the day the opposite is true; you are going to need to identify periods of time when you will accomplish your task list, and schedule those periods on your calendar to block out that time.

Setting General "Tasks" Appointments

My typical day falls somewhere between the above scenarios. I am often 50 to 60 percent booked with meetings, so I usually have time between those meetings for working tasks.

During busy weeks when meetings are more prevalent, I need to schedule specific time for working tasks, and I have no problem doing so if I do it ahead of time. When needed, I place one- to two-hour appointments on my calendar labeled simply "Tasks." During those appointments, I work down my Now Tasks list trying to complete as many tasks on my list as possible.

There are other weeks when my meeting schedule is so intense that I find it takes some effort to schedule task time.

And farther down that scale, it is not unusual to meet executives whose every workday every week consists of endless meetings. After I teach them these task techniques, they conclude that they need to specifically schedule task time every day of the week, well ahead of time, to prevent the open slots from being claimed by appointment seekers. You may find this works for you too. It is something you should strongly consider because it prevents your only available task time from being after-hours time. Many of the meetings that subsequently cannot be scheduled probably were not critical anyway.

Scheduled Tasks versus General Task Time

Given the previous discussion, you may wonder when it is appropriate to schedule tasks individually on your appointment calendar in advance, as opposed to just listing them in your MYN task list and working them during general task time. My rule of thumb is to leave them on the MYN task list as much as possible. Only if a long-duration task (two hours or more) is coming due soon do I actually schedule it on the calendar, and that is only if I feel I may have trouble clearing time to do it.

Why not schedule most tasks right on your calendar? You might think this will prevent the accidental overbooking described above. You might think it will ensure task completion. "What gets scheduled gets done," right?

There are three reasons not to do this. First, since these are self-appointments usually based on nearly random decisions of when to work a given task, you are almost certain to ignore or change the task in that slot due to other priorities, time needs, and inspirations arising at that time. That means you'll need to reschedule it, and such constant rescheduling is cumbersome. There is too much overhead associated with making and moving calendar entries to make these constant changes worthwhile, so you will quickly start to ignore the appointed tasks, and possibly drop them.

Second, per Lesson 6 you are mostly listing next actions on your MYN task list and they tend to be small tasks. Small tasks are more efficiently worked off a list than off individual appointments. Trying to make tiny time slots for each task is tedious. And because our duration estimates for small tasks are usually off, this leads to inefficient completion; you will fill the allotted time even if less time is really needed. It is much more efficient to march down a list of small tasks and attempt to get as many done as possible within a large segment of general task time.

Third, the best time to attack a given task may vary and present itself naturally to you when you least expect it. You will find opportunities to work tasks synergistically with others. You will find that throughout the day priorities change and that you postpone tasks you thought you were going to do today and reprioritize other tasks first. Trying to keep track of that with individual appointments on your calendar will be nearly impossible.

For Large or Tough Tasks

All that said, occasionally you will come across a task that is accurately recorded in your Now Tasks list as a next action and yet it is clear that it will take several hours or more to accomplish. Or perhaps you have a task that has a hard deadline that you need to ensure gets done. In cases such as these, rather than using general "task time" on your schedule, it is better to schedule the specific task by name on your calendar, as I discussed in the Managing Deadlines section of Lesson 4. Doing so is a good way to make sure specific tasks have adequate time set aside for them. It also highlights the importance of a task. And it allows you to set an appointment reminder.

Converting Tasks to Appointments in Outlook (Windows)

To speed the operation of converting a task to an appointment, note that in Windows you can do this by simply dragging the task from the task list to the appointment calendar. The new appointment window pops up ready for editing. Also note that if you right-click before you drag you can choose to move the task rather than copy it. I do not recommend doing that. If you delete the task from the task list and the scheduled work time gets away from you due to distractions, the task is no longer on your list day after day reminding you to try again later.

■ ■ ■

Doing the Math on Your Workweek

The Problem

If after following the approaches in the book so far you still find that you're not getting your tasks done, you may need to focus on time management. The top recommendations from the best books on time management are these: avoid interruptions, manage the number of meetings you have, and schedule enough time to work on tasks. Generally, these are commonsense recommendations.

Note that at the base of the third recommendation is an implicit assumption that you also do a fourth thing: figure out the amount of work time really needed to get all your tasks done. Most of us rarely do this, and from time to time we need to. If week after week you are consistently falling short on accomplishing important tasks, you probably need to do a simple five-minute exercise that I call "Doing the Math on Your Workweek."

Discovery

Here is how I came across this technique. After changing jobs and digging into a busy set of new activities, one month I found myself well behind on my important tasks. I was confused because I had all the tasks prioritized correctly, I had deferred unimportant ones to review in the future, and I had scheduled ahead those that had specific best days to work. And I had set aside and consistently used what seemed like a considerable amount of task time. Yet a number of my most important tasks were not getting done.

I finally decided to do something I generally didn't do, which is to apply some of my routine project management techniques to the collection of tasks I had on hand. Project management techniques are usually not applicable to this system of ad hoc task management, but in this case they were. Let me explain.

In the project management world, when making a formal project plan, one of the first things to do after listing all the steps in a project is to estimate how long each of those steps will take. The project manager uses that information to estimate the total duration and effort of the project, schedule the tasks, and assign people to the tasks. And while estimates are usually just that — estimates — even with some inaccuracies the result of doing the exercise will usually get the manager to a fairly accurate plan.

So I applied the same technique to my list of tasks. I simply stepped through all the tasks on my list and estimated the duration of each, then summed them up. The results were surprising. Even though I thought I had a good picture of the amount of work on my plate, I found myself amazed at how much time the tasks I had signed up for actually added up to. My previous rough guess was low by a factor of three! Until I did the math, I had no idea how much work I had committed to.

Underestimating Time: a Common Problem

As I work with more and more people on task management, I find that this is a common problem. People consistently underestimate the total amount of time it takes to accomplish the sum of the tasks they sign up for. Individually, the estimates for each of their tasks are usually not that bad; it is just that they never stop to do the math and add up how much *all* their tasks really require in a given week. There seems to be a psychological block we all have toward doing this math accurately. Maybe the cause of this peculiarity lies in how the human brain functions, or, more likely, maybe it is just the result of our habit of optimism. I see this phenomenon again and again.

Part of the problem is the "heat of the workday." As the research cited in the Introduction points out, our brains function differently when under stress or during intense activity. As work stress increases, we lose accurate perspective on the various dimensions of our work, such as good prioritization and, apparently, accurate assessment of the time needed to accomplish work.

Easily Seen in Others

How often have you seen examples of this mistake occur with colleagues or your supervisor? For instance, your boss gets out of a stressful meeting with his or her boss, and in reaction to an urgent situation brought up in that meeting, assigns you a task to fix something. In your detached and calm perspective you estimate three days of work for this task. From your boss's emotional perspective he is amazed that it cannot be done in under a day. You both are experts in your field but you have amazingly different estimates of the effort required. The next thing your stressed boss usually does is accuse you of overengineering the solution. In the end, the estimate done by calm analysis is the accurate one.

You often do the same thing to yourself. Imagine yourself in a stressful work-week where day after day you are collecting tasks on your Now Tasks list and not getting as much done as you had hoped. As the week progresses and you see the list of uncompleted tasks getting larger, what happens? You become more stressed and do an even poorer job of estimating the time that you need to get your work done. You are most likely consistently underestimating the time needed.

The way we usually make up for these errors is to work late into the evening. If you do this only occasionally in reaction to unusual peaks in activity, this works. But if your high workload is consistent and you are pulling one late night after another, the cumulative stress and fatigue only exacerbate the situation. You do not regain your clear perspective but rather, like Don Quixote, you keep chasing your impossible dream, in this case, of *doing it all*. You are getting more and more detached from reality in the process.

The Solution

The solution to this is remarkably simple. You just need to sober up for a moment, take five minutes, and do the math on your workweek. You need to figure out how many hours of tasks you have on your task list in the week ahead and how that compares to committed time. And if in this objective analysis you find yourself overbooked, you need to take some measured and rational steps to account for that now, rather than hoping for a miracle to bail you out as the week progresses. Use this tool to identify that need, and consider using the results to show to your supervisor if you feel your pleas for relief are not being taken seriously.

How far out should you do this math? For ad hoc tasks such as those studied in this book, a week's planning horizon is a good balance between near-term commitments and unknown future changes in priority and available time.

You can make this exercise as simple or as complex as you wish. I prefer to make it simple by doing the following.

Step by Step

1. First, Windows users can optionally create and use a new Tasks folder view that displays tasks due in the next week. The details for this are in Lesson 12, in the section titled The MYN This Week's Task View. Should you not want to bother with that (or if you are a Mac user), you can also use your Tasks folder sorted on start date, it's just not as easy as the custom view.

2. Next, reconcile the tasks in your tasks list as follows: reset all High and Normal priority tasks that don't *really* need to get done in the next week as follows. Either schedule their start dates into a future week or set them to a Low priority (preferably using the Defer-to-Review process in Lesson 9). This removes lower-urgency tasks and leaves you with what *really* needs to get done this week; this is a reasonable activity if you are falling behind on important tasks.

3. Then simply go through all High priority and Normal priority tasks, studying each task with a start date before or inside this week for a moment (those are the only ones listed in the custom view). Do a rough estimate of the number of hours needed to complete each task. Don't worry about being terribly precise. I usually estimate in whole hours. Small tasks I usually list as 15 to 30 minutes each.

4. For each task, write the estimate for that task at the end of the subject line. For example: "Summarize staff meeting notes and distribute, 1 hr."

5. Then add the total hours of these tasks (you can do that in your head) and write it down.

6. Compare that sum to the number of hours you have scheduled for task time in the week ahead. I suspect, if you are finding your week has slipped out of control, you will discover that the total hours needed for committed tasks is two to three times greater than your scheduled task time. If so, read on.

7. If not, if the two are roughly equal, you are probably in good shape. But if you find repeatedly that you are estimating correctly and yet you are still not getting your tasks done, see the section below titled Cleaning Up Your Task Time.

You may at first balk at this exercise and think, "Estimating like this is very inaccurate; how can this really help?" My response: Sure, individual task estimates may be off a bit. In truth, however, inaccurate estimates for individual tasks are usually offsetting and the total is often not far from reality.

Another objection is this: "I always schedule more than I can accomplish, so this is not surprising; I'll just do what I can get done." If you really feel that way, go back to step 2 above, do it right, and repeat the process. Remember, only tasks that really *must* be done in the next week should be on your list for the purposes of this exercise.

Note: *If you know Windows Outlook well you probably know there are hidden fields for entering and tracking work hours on tasks; you could use those fields instead of entering the hours as text on the subject line. But I am purposely not getting fancy here. The point is to do a very quick estimate of what work is on your plate. Jotting hours onto the subject line and doing a quick summation by eye is fine for our purposes and ensures that you may actually do this check now and then.*

Resolution

So now what? Assuming you have discovered that you are overbooked, you now know you have a problem, and why. Like many problems in life, this is an important first step toward a solution. At least you now have a clear picture of the problem and can start doing something about it. And you can take some relief in the knowledge that no, you are not a bad or horribly inefficient worker who needs to work harder; rather you just really do have too much on your plate and you now need to fix that.

Clearly you have some corrections to make. Either you have to add a lot more task time, find others to delegate tasks to, or start renegotiating some of your commitments. Those next steps I leave to you. The beauty of this is, if you do this at the beginning of the week, well before tasks become due, you have time to start negotiating alternatives. You have time to seek permission rather than forgiveness.

The only thing more amazing than how simple this activity really is, is how rarely it is done. This seems so obvious and yet so few of us ever do it. We fail to recognize that we usually estimate low when mentally adding up the work we have committed to. It is a part of our human nature that we need to work around, consciously, by periodically stepping back and doing this math exercise.

■   ■   ■

Cleaning Up Your Task Time

Inefficient Task Time

Under the topic of time management I recommend one other thing: clean up your task time. Let me elaborate.

First, as mentioned above, I recommend for most of you setting aside dedicated time for doing your tasks. You should schedule this time on your calendar. Otherwise, if you only try to "work them in" you will be utterly disappointed; things are just not going to get done. Get this time assigned on your calendar early before others start placing appointments throughout your day. Honor those task-time appointments and do not set other appointments on top of them.

Then, if the analysis described in the section above titled Doing the Math on Your Workweek shows that you have enough task time yet are still not getting your tasks done, you have one more analysis step to do. You need to make sure you are keeping your task time "clean." What I mean by that is you need to ensure that you really work your tasks during your dedicated task period.

Relaxing into Your Task Time

Here is a common problem. Unfortunately, what people often do when the scheduled task time arrives is to relax into that time. If it is during the afternoon, it is often the first time of the day away from intense meetings or a constant stream of visitors. It may be the first time people can sit at their desk in a while. As a result, as they enter the general task period people tend to shift gears. They unconsciously start to unwind and often look for distractions to help them do so. They might visit cube mates. They might take a "quick glance" at the web, make a few personal phone calls, or go get a snack. Or they may go into information collection mode: reading e-mail, listening to voice messages, reconciling loose papers on the desk, and so on. Before they know it, the task time is gone and they have accomplished very little on their list.

So you need to consciously account for this requirement for taking breaks, socializing, reading e-mail, and other cleaning-up activities. One approach is to build in separate break and e-mail reading time into your schedule. For instance, I add about an hour or two a day to my task time to account for e-mail reading, paper shuffling, and ad hoc breaks. If your task time is in the afternoon, add the delineated break time just before the start of your task time, with a hard deadline for when you actually start on tasks. That way you are caught up as you enter your focused task period.

Another remedy is to schedule these task times for periods when you are fresh and not in need of unwinding, as discussed next.

Time Mapping

One technique highlighted by Julie Morgenstern in her book on time management, *Time Management from the Inside Out*, is something called time mapping. This expands upon a best practice recommended by nearly all the time and task management experts: identify the times of day that you are best at doing certain activities, and schedule those times throughout the week for their optimum usage (see Figure 11.1).

So, for example, if you like to do tasks in the morning when your mind is clear, make sure that your standing meeting for task processing is at the same time every morning of every day. If you like to keep open office hours

Figure 11.1 Time Mapping, idealized example.

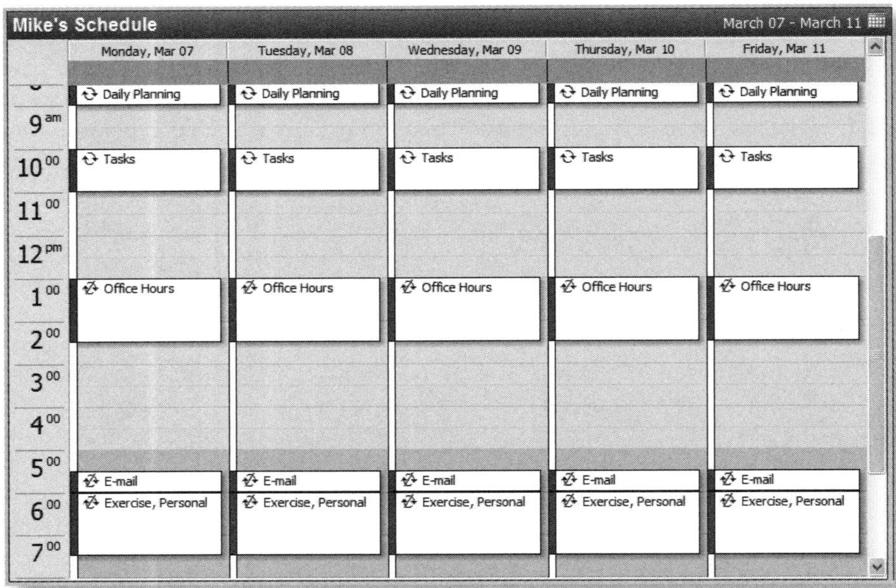

after lunch when you enjoy conversations with colleagues and subordinates, schedule a block of open time in your calendar every day at that time. In other words, map each day the same throughout the week. This is often difficult to pull off completely due to previously set standing meetings (Figure 11.1 is an idealized example), but to whatever degree you can, you will optimize your natural cycle and create a habit of doing the activity.

Write Your Long Replies at the End of the Day

Another way to clean up task time and make use of the time mapping approach is to save writing your long e-mail replies for the end of the day. Sure, if you can reply in less than a minute, go ahead and write a quick reply at any time. But if 30 minutes later you are still crafting and recrafting a carefully worded, politically correct message, you have just lost control of your time.

Better is to make longer replies your last action of the day. Why? You are less likely to get carried away. Your excess energy from your morning caffeine is spent by the late afternoon. Your initial emotional response has dissipated. And since your major intent at the end of the day is to wrap up and go home, you will more likely limit your reply to the minimum business words needed before you bolt out the door. So you will spend much less time on what for many is a major time sink. This also potentially minimizes the time spent on all-day e-mail threads; instead catch up at the end of the day and have the final word! Of course, if part of your job role is to monitor and reply quickly to e-mail support requests, then reply as fast as is fitting for your role. But most of us are not in such support roles and so delaying long replies to the end of the day can make sense.

It is also a shame to use the morning, which is often your most creative and productive time, on writing long low-priority e-mail replies. Try waiting to the end of the day for these replies for the reasons above and see if it works for you. As mentioned in Lesson 7, I recommend using the Outlook Follow Up flag tool exclusively for the purpose of marking these deferred replies (which works especially well in Outlook 2007/10 and 2011 since that also puts an entry in your MYN task list). I discuss the pros and cons of using that flag thoroughly in Lesson 7.

But note this: if the reason for not replying is that you need to take some action first, instead of deferring the reply with the Follow Up flag, convert the e-mail to a *full* task, per the instructions in Lesson 7.

Follow Up flag

Avoiding Interruptions

During the time you set aside to focus on tasks, you need to avoid outside interruptions. Commit to yourself that this is the purpose of this time and that you will discourage visiting, unneeded calls, and other distractions. You may even need to decide that you will not answer the phone, not take incoming e-mails when Outlook beeps at you, and most important, turn away visitors. This can be difficult. The social aspect of work is one reason people don't work alone. They enjoy interacting with coworkers. It feels good to help people who stop by for assistance. It feels good to get up from your desk and chat with others. But you need to solve this problem of interruptions to make your task time effective.

You might try some sort of physical change in your environment to delineate pure task time. This could be closing the door to your office if you have an office. Or if you work in a cubicle, either finding some other physical space you can escape to or putting a Do Not Disturb sign on the edge of your cube. Somehow you need to signal to others and yourself that this is a special time with a distinct purpose.

This is a very challenging problem and you may need to experiment to solve it. It is difficult to turn away visitors, difficult not to take phone calls. In the end, however, you need to find a way to isolate a period of pure task time in your day. You may want to brainstorm with your colleagues on agreed methods to accomplish this, so that you respect each other's private time.

Turn Off E-mail Notification

Another way to avoid interruptions during task time is to avoid reading incoming e-mails the instant they arrive in your Inbox. To help with this, turn off e-mail notification in Outlook—you know, that little message box that pops up briefly every time you get an e-mail (see below for a sample of the Windows version). In fact, I think notifications should always be turned off at work. Instead, I feel that you should choose or schedule a time to read your e-mail all at once, between blocks of work.

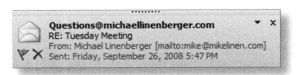

Why? Unless you work in a customer support role where e-mail is your main connection to customers, I strongly feel e-mail should *not* be an instant-response medium. The beauty of e-mail when used correctly is that you can batch up your communications into distinct time blocks and then keep your attention on uninterrupted work much of the rest of the day. Many studies have shown that it can take three to five minutes to reorient yourself to a work task after being interrupted. And the default settings for the desktop alert box in Outlook lead to an especially deep interruption. That's because they show just enough information about the e-mail to totally suck you into wanting to know more. They lead you to think about whether you want to consider the e-mail and to possibly open it, and that often completely drags your focus out of whatever task you are working on. With hundreds of e-mails coming in each day, the lost time and productivity adds up.

So I highly recommend you turn off the desktop alert notification and instead check e-mail only between blocks of work. Don't worry, you will still survive being out of e-mail touch a few hours at a time, and you will enjoy the focus and time you regain. And you can turn it on only for specific people.

How to Turn Off Notification

The controls to turn off notification are buried surprisingly deep in the Outlook 2003 and 2007 menus. From the Tools menu, select Options, and click the E-mail Options button and then the Advanced E-mail Options button. In the dialog box that opens, clear some or all of the four boxes as shown in Figure 11.2, depending on how much notification you want. At a minimum, clear the bottom box so the pop up alert box is suppressed; the other indicators are less invasive.

Outlook 2010 users should go to the File tab, select Options, and then select Mail on the left, and then use the same check boxes under the Message section.

Figure 11.2
Turning off e-mail
notifications
(Outlook 2003
and 2007).

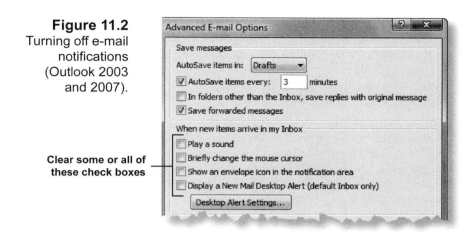

**Clear some or all of
these check boxes**

Outlook for Mac 2011 users should use the Outlook menu on the top menu bar, then Preferences, then in the Personal Settings section choose Notifications & Sounds. Clear the check box labeled Display an Alert on my Desktop, and then perhaps select the box Bounce Outlook Icon in Dock, should you want some minimal notification.

After general e-mail notification is turned off, you might want to be notified of the arrival of e-mail from specific people (say your boss). You can create an Outlook rule that will pop up the same desktop alert you just turned off, but only upon arrival of mail from those select people. Or create a similar rule to alert you upon arrival of mail with High importance. I discuss using Outlook rules a few pages ahead; see the Other Rules section after that for a link showing how to get alerts only for certain people.

Using the ClearContext Do Not Disturb Button Instead

Making the above configuration change requires a large number of steps, so you are not likely to toggle this on and off very often. If you only want to turn off notifications for a few hours (up to eight), use this one-step ClearContext button and choose your duration. Notifications return automatically after the time is up.

Identifying Deliverables

One more technique you may want to use to clean up your task time is to clearly identify deliverables you expect to accomplish in a given task time. Here is how this works. At the beginning of a scheduled task period, decide what tasks you intend to accomplish. If you have recently done the "Do the Math on Your Workweek" exercise described at the start of this lesson, the tasks in your daily list each have durations written next to them; use those durations to determine which tasks you can get done now. Then identify a deliverable, or end product, that must be created to signal the completion of each task. This might be an Excel document, a written report, or a memorandum. Copy that deliverables list right into the subject line of your task appointment in your Outlook calendar.

This is very effective. While working at your desk during the task time, each time you glance at your calendar to see what is up next you'll see those deliverable commitments staring at you. You will know they are due during the next hours, and you will refocus on the task at hand. It's a good way to get serious if you find yourself slipping off track. It's also a good way to manage interruptions. If someone stops by your desk with a request during your task

The War Room

Here is something to consider if important tasks or projects are not getting completed. The way many large project consulting companies accomplish task efficiency with their junior and midlevel staff working on projects is just the opposite of finding privacy for everyone; rather, they seek out team group work settings and use the peer pressure of the team to keep each other on track. This is commonly done in a "war room" approach: give a team of colleagues a common goal to reach with a challenging deadline, place them all in a single large conference room working on laptops, and have them work together to complete the tasks. Often the team members decide among themselves which tasks each team member is assigned. Through a combination of urgency, peer pressure, and teamwork, the tasks get done rapidly. In such a setting, since the team's success is measured as a whole, individual interruptions are not tolerated by peers, and staff who wander off on personal errands are met with glares upon their return. Weekly internal team assessments weed offending staff off teams, like "getting voted off the island."

At the consulting company Accenture, where I once worked, entry-level training consisted of several weeks of boot camp where newly hired staff were thrown into team settings solving hypothetical problems under urgent deadlines. The consultants who came out of such training were remarkably adept at knocking off tasks quickly on the real projects they were assigned to later.

If you and your colleagues are having trouble getting project tasks done individually, and you can pull away from meetings for a few weeks, you might consider such a war room approach. This works especially well if you are all working on parts of a larger project with clear deadlines. It can be remarkably effective.

time, you have the focus you need to be able to say something like "I'd like to help you, but I really need to get this memo done in the next half hour; let me talk to you later."

By the way, this deliverables focus is a common technique used in large-project-oriented consulting companies to drive project tasks to completion. The association of a distinct deliverable with a task is an effective way of adding structure and ensuring a task's completion.

■   ■   ■

Save Time by Auto-Categorizing Incoming E-mail (All Versions)

If you are filing e-mail using Outlook Categories, as described in Lesson 8, consider this. Probably the least enjoyable part of any e-mail organization system is filing. It takes time to decide how to file e-mail and assign categories or drag to folders. Wouldn't it be great if your e-mail were categorized automatically? Think how much time you would save. If e-mail arrived precategorized, all you would need to do after you read it is drag mail in bulk to the Processed Mail folder, which is what you do anyway.

While automatic categorization of *all* of your mail is not possible, you can do it with much if not most of your mail. The two primary ways to auto-categorize is to do it based on sender name or based on a keyword in the mail.

On the Mac, if your intention is to categorize incoming mail based on sender, a built-in feature makes this very easy. You merely assign the category to the sender's entry in your Outlook Contacts list, and then check a box at the bottom of the Edit Categories dialog box (see Figure 8.5 in Lesson 8), and it is all automatic. Again, you get to the Categories dialog box by CTRL-clicking any e-mail in its Categories column, and then choosing Edit Categories… from the shortcut menu.

Using Outlook Rules

On Windows, you do not have the handy Mac feature described above; rather, you enable automatic assignments based on sender by creating Outlook rules. And on both the Mac and Windows, if you want to automatically assign a category based on other criteria—like a keyword in the subject line—rules are the only way to go.

Rules are a bit complicated to create, but they do not take that long. The small amount of time it takes to create these rules pays off greatly in time saved during e-mail processing.

What do I mean by Outlook rules? Outlook rules are small logical statements that you create and apply against incoming (or outgoing) mail to cause the mail to be processed in a variety of ways.

For instance, a common use of rules is to cause mail, based on its contents, sender, or subject line, to automatically be filed in certain folders. Or you can use similar criteria to cause certain incoming mail to be automatically forwarded, display an alert, and so on. For the system in this book, the most valuable action is to assign a category automatically to incoming mail based on its contents or sender and then leave it in the Inbox so you can read it.

As mentioned earlier, I have an Outlook rule that assigns the category Personal to e-mail that comes from any of my family members. I have another rule that sets an e-mail's category to a specific project name whenever I receive mail from the project manager for that project. And mail associated with a number of other projects at my work are categorized using rules that search the e-mail subject line for certain keywords that are uniquely associated with those projects. Due to these and other rules, back when I used categories extensively, I enabled nearly 70 percent of my mail to arrive precategorized.

These rules are never foolproof; you should expect the logic of any rule that you write to misfire periodically, skipping or assigning the wrong category. But that doesn't matter. They *usually* work; and even if these rules work only 80 percent of the time, they will still save you great effort setting categories. Without these rules you would need to classify *all* of your mail, so even if you need to change a misclassified mail every so often, you come out way ahead.

Note: *There is a limit to the number of rules you can create in Outlook if you are running on Exchange Server. It is not count-based but storage-based, and that limit is easy to reach. Newer Exchange Server limits can be set by administrators to be much larger than older limits, but the default is low and usually left that way. If you start getting error messages when you create a large number of rules, it is probably due to that limit. If so, contact your administrator and ask them to raise it. If that is not possible or if it does not help, consider switching to ClearContext add-in software; it has a similar rules engine but with no limit on its rule count. Most IT departments do not like you to add software and they block that, but ClearContext is immune to most blocks; give the free trial copy a try and see what happens.*

So how do you create Outlook rules? Outlook provides a simple wizard to create these rules quite easily. I will show you how to use that wizard in a way that matches the MYN system for both Windows and the Mac. Use this guide to write three or four rules and, after that, you will be creating them on your own routinely, in seconds, without assistance.

Let's start with Windows Outlook first.

Initiating a New Rule (Windows)

Windows Outlook has a flexible (and complicated) wizard you can use to create your rules. Once you have thought through the logic with which you want to categorize some mail, do this:

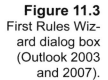

Figure 11.3
First Rules Wiz-
ard dialog box
(Outlook 2003
and 2007).

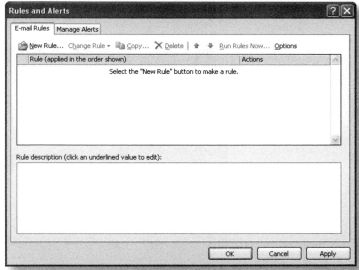

1. Since you are interested in e-mail that is entering your primary Inbox, you must first select that folder. Note: Exchange users need to be online with your mail server to create these rules.

2. Next, **Outlook 2003 and 2007 users**, from the Tools menu, choose Rules and Alerts… and the dialog box in Figure 11.3 appears.
Outlook 2010 users, on the Home tab choose Rules, then Create Rule.

3. **Outlook 2003 and 2007 users**, click the New Rule… button. In the dialog box that opens, click the second option button, Start from a Blank Rule (in Outlook 2007 just locate that section of the dialog box), and then go to step 4.
Outlook 2010 users click the Advanced Options… button and then go to step 5.

4. Select Check Messages When They Arrive. Then click Next.

5. In the window that opens (similar to Figure 11.4), with the heading Which Condition(s) Do You Want to Check? select one of the check boxes. In **Outlook 2003 and 2007** it is likely one of these two check boxes:

   From People or Distribution List
   With Specific Words in the Subject

   In Outlook 2010 the appearance of the top two selections vary depending on what e-mail was selected in the Inbox when you clicked the Rules button; but you will likely pick one of the top two.

Figure 11.4
Setting the search criteria in the Rules Wizard.

All users, once you select one of these, it is added to the rule statement being built in the lower portion of the dialog box (labeled Step 2), which you can edit for specificity.

In this example, let's assume that the rule you are creating is a Specific Words rule for the word Legal, to be located in the subject line of the e-mail message. So select the check box next to With Specific Words in the Subject. Note that this inserts a phrase in the lower portion of the dialog box, which you now need to edit to enter the word Legal. Here's how.

6. In the lower part of the dialog box labeled Step 2 (similar to Figure 11.4), click the underlined phrase (it may say specific words, or it may have a phrase from your Inbox in there).

7. That opens the Search Text dialog box (not shown here). Type the keyword or phrase (in this example "Legal") in the upper text box of this dialog box, and click Add. You will see the keyword appear in the Search List box at the bottom. You may need to remove any existing keywords in the lower list.

    If you have more than one keyword, you can add them now. After all words or phrases are added, click OK. This returns you to the previous Rules Wizard window, and it now appears exactly as shown in Figure 11.4.

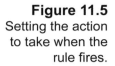

Figure 11.5
Setting the action
to take when the
rule fires.

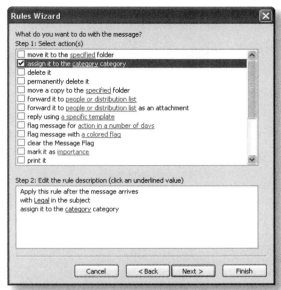

Note that the chosen keyword(s), "Legal" in this example, have been added to the rule phrase in the bottom of the dialog box. This concludes setting the criteria.

You now need to identify the action Outlook will take on the e-mail if the criteria are met.

8. In the Rules Wizard window (Figure 11.4) click Next; the window in Figure 11.5 appears.

9. Select the second check box, Assign It To The category Category. Doing this places this portion of the rule into the lower portion of the Rules Wizard window shown in Figure 11.5.

10. In the lower portion of the window labeled Step 2, click the underlined word category to set a value for it. That will open a dialog box that should look familiar to you; it is the standard Categories selection dialog box. Select one or more categories that you want auto-assigned to e-mail that meet the earlier criteria; in this example I chose Attorney. You can create a new category if you like here. Refer to Lesson 8 if you need help with creating or assigning categories. When you are finished, click OK.

You have now completely assembled the rule. Examine the rule in the lower portion of the Rules Wizard. You need to take a few more steps to finalize and save the rule.

11. Click Next, and you will be presented with a dialog box that allows you to create an exception phrase for your rule. I always skip past this

Figure 11.6
The Finish Rule
Setup dialog box.

Exception dialog box because it is usually not needed for setting categories on incoming e-mail.

12. Click Next again, and a screen with the heading Finish Rule Setup opens, as in Figure 11.6.

13. Now you can name the rule. The default choice is shown in the upper text box of this dialog box, and it is often too vague; I recommend you rewrite it to indicate what this rule is doing. That way, when you start cleaning up an overly long list of rules later, you'll know what this one does.

14. Leave the check box Turn on This Rule selected.

15. If you have an Inbox full of e-mail that you would like to auto-categorize, select the check box Run This Rule Now on Messages Already in "Inbox" in Figure 11.6.

16. Outlook displays the full rule in the lower portion of this window; you can edit it if you see an error; otherwise click Finish.

17. If you are in an Exchange environment, you will see a message telling you that this is a client-side rule. This reminds you that rules like this are run from your Outlook client (some other types of rules are run on the Exchange Server). This means that if you use more than one computer to read, classify, and file your mail, you may need to create the rules at each computer. Or if you are working with OWA or a mobile device, the rules will only run when Outlook is also running at your main computer.

18. **Outlook 2003 and 2007 users**, you then return to the dialog box shown in Figure 11.4, this time with the new rule listed there. If you are about to create more rules in this same session, click the Apply button before you do. That saves the rule you just made. Reason: even though rules are auto-saved when you click OK in this dialog box, if by chance you subsequently start creating a new rule and then change your mind and click Cancel, it will delete all the earlier rules you created in the same session. Clicking Apply after you create each rule prevents that.
Outlook 2010 users, you will briefly see the very first rules dialog box; then it will disappear and you are done.

Your rule creation is now complete. **Outlook 2003 and 2007 users**, you can start another rule or, if you are done, close this dialog box. Click OK to do so if you just created a rule.

Note: *Outlook 2007 users may see a rule delivered with Outlook 2007 called Clear Categories on Mail. This strips categories off incoming mail. It exists to keep other people's categories from clogging your e-mail (see section below Dealing with Categories in Mail Sent to You, for more discussion). If you decide to keep that rule active, you should ensure that any category assignment rules you make per the steps above appear below that rule in the list of rules. The reason for that is rules trigger in the order they occur in the list, top to bottom; it would be a shame to add a category to an e-mail and then strip it right back out again. Use the Move Up and Move Down buttons to place the rules in the proper order and prevent that.*

That's it. From now on, Outlook will automatically categorize incoming mail that meets the criteria of these new rules. This will occur as you see the mail appear in your Inbox.

This may seem like a lot of steps, but after creating a few of these, the above steps will become second nature and you will not hesitate to create rules for nearly all of your categories.

Initiating a New Rule (Mac)

On the Mac there is no need to create a rule if your intention is to auto-categorize based on sender name, as mentioned at the very start of this section. However, for any other type of auto-categorization (most likely categorizing based on a keyword in the subject line) you will need to create a rule.

Creating rules on the Mac is much easier than on Windows, but you lose a bit of flexibility compared to Windows Outlook. For this example, let's say you want to create a rule based on a keyword in the Subject field.

1.   Since you are interested in e-mail that is entering your primary Inbox, you must first select that folder. Note: Exchange users need to be online with your mail server to create these rules.

2.   Next, from the Home tab click the Rules button and click Edit Rules....

Figure 11.7   Sample Mac Edit Rule dialog box.

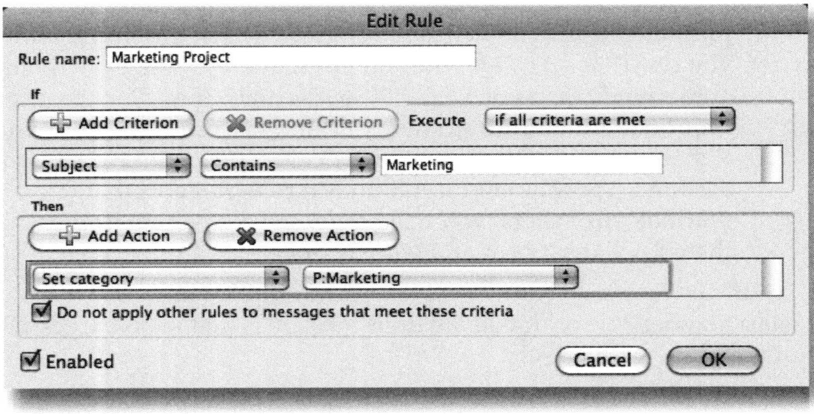

3. If you are using Exchange, then in the window that pops up, select Exchange from the top of the list presented. Otherwise select POP (or IMAP if by chance you are using that type of server). Then click the plus sign at the bottom of the window.

4. In the Edit Rule window that pops up (Figure 11.7), type a rule name at the very top; then edit the rule elements as indicated next.

5. Edit the first If statement (initially labeled All Messages) to read Subject. In the next box to the right adjust it so it reads Contains. And in the third box to its right, type a keyword or phrase as appropriate. In Figure 11.7, I typed the keyword Marketing.

6. In the Then section in the bottom half of the Edit Rule dialog, two actions may appear by default and you need only one. If two are there, delete the first action by clicking it once (so it is selected and surrounded by a faint blue box) and then click the Remove Action button.

7. Then edit the remaining action; ensure the first box is Set Category, and then choose the category name in the next box at right.

8. Consider whether you want to clear the box that says Do Not Apply Other Rules to Messages that Meet These Criteria (examine your other rules, if any, that may affect these messages). And leave the Enabled check box selected. The complete example is shown in Figure 11.7

9. Click OK.

You are now done creating the rule. From now on, Outlook will automatically categorize incoming mail that meets the criteria of these new rules. This will occur as you see the mail appear in your Inbox.

Other Rules

Use these principles to create other rules to improve your efficiency in Outlook. The other rule I typically make is to show a desktop alert when mail from certain senders comes in (after turning off e-mail notifications, per my earlier instructions on that). See this link: www.myn.bz/Alerts.htm.

. . .

Maintaining Category Names Quickly and Efficiently (All Versions)

In Lesson 8 I showed how to use Outlook Categories to tag and file mail. And in this lesson I've shown how to auto-assign categories. In Lesson 12, I will also show how to use categories to create a projects view of tasks and a goals view of tasks. By now you can see that Outlook Categories are very useful in this system. Getting the category list right, and maintaining it, will become important.

However, this is one place using folders can be easier than using Outlook Categories, because it can be confusing to change and delete category names. As a result, you will want to use some tricks to make your category maintenance easier and faster, particularly in Outlook 2003. The category maintenance approach in Outlook 2007/10 and 2011 is easier.

The first lesson to learn about category maintenance is that the list from which you assign categories in all Outlook versions is really just a pick list from which to make category assignments. Depending on the Outlook version, if you change or delete a category name in those lists, doing so may have little influence on categories already assigned to mail—the old assignments will be retained there.

This acceptance of categories not on the master list also occurs in mail sent by other users should the category name get through your Exchange filters. In older Outlook and Exchange installations, as you receive e-mail from colleagues who may also be categorizing e-mail, the mail, once in your copy of Outlook, can retain the category names from your colleagues (see section below titled Dealing with Categories in Mail Sent to You). If so, Outlook, in its ever-accepting mode, will treat these categories almost as though they are your own. As a result, your category-grouped mail will include even those imported ones (sometimes tagged with a note saying Not in Master Category List).

This set of behaviors is good and bad. It is good because it gives you a historical trail; you do not lose previously assigned categories in old mail. It is bad because it seemingly leaves Outlook cursed to accept and retain all categories, old and new, at times when you expect a change to be fully retroactive.

Complications with Changing Category Names in Outlook 2003

Changing category names in Outlook 2003 is a prime example of where you need to take special care. Occasionally an old category term needs to be refreshed. Perhaps you discover another term that fits the intention of the collection better. Or a project name changes. Your goal is that all mail collected under the old name should now be filed under the new name. With folders, all you would need to do is edit the folder name. But with Outlook Categories, recall that the category tag exists inside each message. That leads to complications in Outlook 2003.

In Outlook 2003, if you change the name of a category within the Master Category List dialog box, filed mail with that category name will not automatically be changed. You will see the new category when you go to make new assignments, but any existing mail with that old category assigned to it will retain the old assigned category. You *will* see this change: when you see the old category in category-grouped mail, it will be tagged with a note Not in the Master Category List. Otherwise it is treated as if the category fully exists. All new mail assigned to the new category name will behave correctly, however.

So in Outlook 2003 you need to follow a special set of steps to fully change category names, which I show below.

How to Rename a Category Name in Outlook 2003

1. Open the Master Category List dialog box in 2003, and add the new category; then click OK to close the dialog box (see Lesson 8 for more about finding and manipulating these dialog boxes).

2. Go into your Processed Mail folder and group on Categories by clicking on the Categories header. Scroll to the category group you want to change.

3. Select (highlight) all of the mail in that group.

4. With that mail selected, right-click under the Categories column and choose Categories to open the category selection dialog box. Then clear the check box next to the old category. Then select the check box next to the new category.

5. Click the Master Category List... button and in that dialog box delete the old category. Exit the dialog boxes by clicking OK on each.

That's it; all mail in the Processed Mail folder has been reassigned to the new name. If you have other mail stores (say, another .pst file or archive file) you will need to repeat these steps with each.

How to Rename a Category Name in Outlook 2007/10 and 2011

Renaming a category in Outlook 2007/10 and 2011 is much simpler. On the Outlook 2007/10 Color Categories dialog box select the category and then find the button called Rename; click it and then type over the name. On the Mac's Edit Categories dialog box you simply click the category name a few times and by the second or third click it becomes editable; then type over the name. Changing the name like this causes Outlook to find all the places the old category exists and change it to the new name, *even in other data files in your folder tree* (which is pretty amazing). And the old name now no longer exists in the category list.

Deleting a Category Name (Windows and Mac)

In all Outlook versions, if you delete a category name, the name will be removed or altered in the category pick list, but the assignments will not be changed in the mail itself.

So first consider carefully why you want to do this. Do you want to remove a category but not its assignments? Or is your intention to also clear the assignment from all mail messages? Or is it really to reassign them to a new category name? If it's the last, follow the steps above under Renaming a Category Name.

But if you really do intend to remove that category from all mail, the steps are these:

1. Go into your Processed Mail folder and group on Categories by clicking on the Categories header.

2. Under the category you want to delete, select all of the mail.

3. With that mail selected, open the category selection mechanism appropriate to your version of Outlook (right-click or CTRL-click under the Categories column and possibly open a scrolling list of category names) and clear the check box next to the category you wish to delete.

4. Then delete the category. You do this in Outlook 2003 by opening the Master Category List dialog box (see Figure 8.8 in Lesson 8); in Outlook 2007/10 by opening the Color Categories dialog box (see upper portion of Figure 8.5 in Lesson 8); and in 2011 by opening the Edit Categories dialog box (see lower portion of Figure 8.5 in Lesson 8). In the latter that means using the minus sign at the bottom of the dialog box.

Dealing with Categories in Mail Sent to You (2003, and some 2007/10)

If your colleagues are using categories too, you may start to receive mail that has categories already assigned before it arrives in your mailbox. Newer Exchange Servers are designed to prevent this, but some category assignments may slip through in older installations. This will cause Outlook to group your mail in your category-grouped mail list under categories that are not of your invention. In Outlook 2003 these will stand out with a Not in Master Category List phrase appended to them.

How should you deal with this? If this is happening consistently, you may want to agree with your colleagues on a standard naming convention for categorizing mail. That way, as e-mail arrives, it will be precategorized in a category that is already in your list.

If you cannot get colleagues to align their category names with yours, all is not lost; you merely need to recategorize the e-mail when you set your categories in your Inbox. The Category or Color Categories dialog box allows you to clear the check box next to those unwanted categories. Then just continue by selecting the categories you want. It is a bit annoying; you need to consciously clear the check box on the old or wrong category before assigning the new category, but it really only takes a split second of extra work. The imported category disappears once all references to it are removed. If this happens consistently you can also create an Outlook rule that swaps categories (old and new) automatically.

As I said above, Microsoft realized importing others' unwanted categories was an issue, so, as a result of changes they made in the 2007 suite, this problem no longer exists in organizations that have standardized on Outlook 2007 and Exchange Server 2007 or later. These versions now strip out categories on incoming mail. How? First, the newer Exchange Server is set by default to strip these out at the server level. Second, in case a newer Exchange Server is not in the sending path, an Outlook rule is created when you install Outlook 2007 to do the same on incoming mail at your computer. It is called Clear Categories on Mail and is turned on by default.

Unless you know you are working with Exchange Server 2007 or later, take care with the terms you use when creating Outlook Categories; someone may see yours in the mail they get from you.

■　■　■

Finding Mail Quickly: Creating an All Mail Search Folder (Outlook 2007/10) or All Mail Smart Folder (Outlook 2011)

In Lesson 8, I showed you how to create Search Folders to display categorized mail. And in Lesson 3, I showed you how to use Smart Folders for tasks. Well, you can also use Search Folders and Smart Folders for other purposes. Here is one perfect example—a way to display all your mail from various folders in one long list.

Why might you want this? Well, have you ever looked for a recent e-mail by visually scanning your Inbox or Processed Mail folder, but not been able to find it on the first pass? If so, you ended up having to look through your Sent Items folder next, and then maybe in several other folders, opening and scrolling through each one at a time. Sometimes the mail you want is part of a send-reply conversation and you are not sure if the mail you seek is something that you sent (so in Sent Items), or something they sent to you (so in the Inbox or Processed Mail folder). You could of course use Outlook's search engine; but for recent mail, scanning a folder visually is sometimes the best way to find something.

The Search Folder and Smart Folder I show below creates a virtual folder that allows you to easily view one long scrolling list of all your "recent" mail—even up to years' worth—no matter where the mail is actually stored in Outlook (with one caveat discussed below). It will make it much easier to find your mail when you are not sure where to look. It's virtual, so it does not duplicate any mail; it just gives you a very convenient single-folder view of all your mail, collecting it from all the folders it may be distributed in. I call it the All Mail Search Folder and using it is a fantastic way to find mail.

The All Mail Search Folder and Smart Folder is Useful Because:

▶ You can easily do a visual search of all your recent mail in one list, even after it has been filed. You can view and scan messages chronologically if you wish, just like in the Inbox. Or you can click on the From header and easily see all your mail from a single sender; again, no matter where it is actually stored.

▶ If you are still filing mail into multiple topic-named folders, this custom approach allows you to see all that mail in one long list too—no matter how you split your filed mail across your actual folders.

▶ If you have not filed out of the Inbox for a while, and so are not sure whether to search there or in your files, using this approach allows you to visually search for it all in one place.

▶ Using Instant Search in Outlook 2007/10 in this folder automatically searches all mail on your mail store; you don't have to do two passes and click "Try searching all mail items" on the second pass to add other folders.

▶ You can see full conversations, including mail in your Sent Items folder. That makes finding mail in long send-reply conversations easier.

One Caveat. Search Folders in Windows Outlook only consolidate mail from one mail store, and that's an important limitation for a few of you. A mail store either means a mail server (Exchange) or a local mail file (a .pst file). That's not an issue if you are using my recommended folder configurations where all recent saved mail is on your main mail store (e.g., in the Processed Mail folder on Exchange or on your primary local file for non-Exchange installations; see Lesson 5 or Appendix A). However, if you split your recent mail across mail stores (e.g. you place your Inbox on your Exchange Server but you place your recent saved mail in a personal folders file—a .pst file), then this search folder won't include mail in that local file; nor will it include archived mail. But for most of us, that's not an issue when looking for recent mail.

On the Mac, Smart Folders present none of these problems since they search over all mail stores.

By the way, using this custom Search Folder somewhat changes my Lesson 8 objection to using multiple topic-named folders. Recall in Lesson 8 I asserted strongly that using many topic-named Outlook folders to file mail can be a major waste of time. But this new Search Folder changes that somewhat. I still regard filing into many multiple topic-named folders to be limiting due to having to choose only one topic; I also think it's too slow to be practical for most people (unless you use add-in software like ClearContext). However, I now admit that finding mail in those folders can be greatly improved with this new Search Folder.

How to Create the All Mail Search Folder (Outlook 2007/10)

1. In the Navigation Pane folder list, right-click the Search Folders header, and select New Search Folder....

2. In the New Search Folder window, scroll to the very bottom and double-click the "Create a custom Search Folder" item at the bottom of the list.

3. In the Custom Search Folder window that opens, click the Browse... button.

4. Clear the check box in the very top-level item, and then add check marks to all the next-level folders where you store your mail—that's most likely your Inbox, your Sent Items folders, the Processed Mail folder, and maybe more folders if you use several. Make sure "Search Subfolders" is selected at the bottom—that way you do not need to open each checked folder and select all their subfolders—they'll be included. Click OK.

5. Back at the Custom Search Folder window, in the Name field type All Mail.

6. Click OK, and then click Yes at the error dialog saying that you have not specified any criteria (we don't want to). Then click OK at the New Search Folder window, and you are done! You can now see the All Mail Search Folder in the Search Folder list.

How to Create the All Mail Smart Folder (Outlook for Mac 2011)

Smart Folders are created by doing a search first, and then saving the search criteria as a new Smart Folder. Here's how to do that for all mail such that you see all folders (except the ones you would want to exclude like Junk E-mail).

1. Click in the Search This Folder box at the top right of your Outlook Window.

2. Click the All Mail button at the left end of the Search tab in the Ribbon.

3. Click the Advanced button at the right end of the Search tab in the Ribbon.

4. When you do step 3, an Item Contains button and field appears below the Ribbon. Click the Item Contains button and choose Folder at the bottom of the shortcut menu.

5. An Is button appears to its right; change that to Is Not.

6. Click the None button to its right and select Choose Folder… at the bottom and type Junk at the top of the next dialog box that opens and then select the Junk E-mail folder in the list that forms below, and click Choose.

7. Click the plus sign (+) at the right end of that line and repeat step 6 as many times as needed to include all other folders that you would like to exclude as well—that's most likely your Deleted Items folder, and any other Deleted Items and Junk E-mail folders you may have for other accounts or local mail.

8. Click the Save button near the right end of the Search tab in the Ribbon. A new Smart Folder appears with an untitled title selected; type over that so it reads All Mail.

Next Steps

Since the All Mail Search folder or Smart Folder is selected by default after you first create it, you'll now see its contents in the main mail list window at the right of the folder list. Note that Windows Outlook may churn a while as it builds this folder's contents from your various folders, but that only happens the first time you create it; you will not need to wait like this again in the future—it is updated automatically from now on.

Also, in Windows, the folder initially opens with mail grouped by source mail folder, which is not very useful; so click on the Received column to see an Inbox-like date-based sorting.

From now on, if you are looking for an old mail item and you are not quite sure where it is, click on the new All Mail Search or Smart Folder in your folder list, and do your search there. You are much more likely to find what you are looking for—and much more quickly.

Place it in the Favorite Folders Pane (Windows)

Since the Search Folders group is located a bit low in your folder list, and since your folder list may be large, the new All Mail Search Folder may be hard to locate quickly. So I recommend, after you create it, you drag a link to this new Search Folder to your Favorite Folders pane; that way it's easy to get at quickly. The Favorite Folders pane (called Favorites in 2010) is the little subpane at the top of the Navigation Pane. By the way, if you do not yet use this Favorite Folders pane, then you should try it—it makes finding key folders in your folder list much easier. I drag a link to all my main folders there including my Inbox, Sent Items, Processed Mail, and even Deleted Items; you may want to do that too.

If that subpane is not visible at the top of the Navigation pane, then go to the View menu or tab, then to the Navigation Pane submenu, and then select Favorite Folders at the bottom of that menu (Favorites in 2010).

That's it! Start using this new All Mail Search Folder today.

■　■　■

More Outlook Time-Saving Tips

Speeding Task Creation (Windows)

Here are some tips related to out-of-the-box Outlook functionality that will save you some time when you create tasks or appointments.

Typing "Today" or "Yesterday" in the Task Start Date Field

When you manually create a new task in the TaskPad (Outlook 2003), the Start Date field is by default None (see below).

This is too bad, since in most cases you are creating a dated task; in fact, often you want to set it to today. So you are required to manually enter a date. While you cannot change this default behavior, you can use a shortcut: After typing the subject, *tab* over to the date field and *type* the word "today" (see below) and press ENTER. Outlook then converts this to a real date.

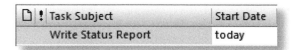

This saves a little time and may prevent selecting the wrong date. By the way, in Outlook 2007 Microsoft changed this behavior and made today's date the default entry in that field.

You can also type "yesterday" in the Start Date field.

Note: You may want to type "yesterday" fairly often. In Lesson 9, I pointed out that as an optional addition to the MYN system you can reserve Normal priority tasks with today's start date for the Target Now urgency zone — these are tasks you really hope to do today (but not on a deadline). Since many new tasks you create you do <u>not</u> intend to do today, you can avoid clogging the Target Now list by typing the word "yesterday" in the start date field of most new tasks. See Lesson 9 for more details.

Typing Other Words in the Task Start Date Field

You can also type the word "now" and reach the same results as "today." And you can type the day of the week if you want to set a date a few days ahead, even using abbreviations like mon, tue, wed, thu, and fri. You can type intervals such as "2 weeks" to set the date to two weeks from today. You can do the same with months and years. If you type only a number in the field, it will be read as the day of the month, and Outlook will fill in the rest of the date for you when you tab out or press ENTER. You can even type holiday names into the field, but only if they are in the future in the current calendar year.

Save Time by Using Recurring Tasks (Windows and Mac)

Recurring tasks are a type of task in Outlook that allows you to create a task once, and then have it recreated automatically after a designated time interval. You can make any existing task into a recurring task by simply using the Recurrence button at the top of the task window.

An example of why you would create them might be a Monday status report that is due each week. You can cause that task to recreate itself automatically every Monday morning in your Outlook tasks list. Unlike repeating appointments, however, future instances of recurring tasks are not placed in your task list immediately; rather, the next one shows up only after the previous one is marked complete or deleted. So they are a convenient way to keep a repeating task on track without burdening your task list with a long list of future tasks.

Outlook's implementation of recurring tasks is quite well done. It provides a lot of flexibility and power. However, there are some subtleties to using recurring tasks with MYN. I have a complete write up about this online; I encourage you to study that article by going to this link: www.myn.bz/Recur.htm.

Save Time by Converting Text-Tasks Back to E-mails (Windows)

In Lesson 7 you learned how to convert e-mails to tasks. Sometimes (say, after a task is complete) you may want to write back to the original sender and include the original e-mail as a reference. I recommended using Convert as Attachment for any task you thought you might want to reply to later. But sometimes when we create the task we do not know we might want to reply later, and we create the task as text, only to discover later we *do* want to reply to the original e-mail.

When you want to reply to those tasks, you can look for the old e-mail in your Processed Mail folder, but that takes time. Instead, save time by converting the task back to an e-mail. Here are two ways to do that.

From the List View

If you are viewing the task in a list view, simply drag the task to the Mail banner button or to the Inbox. That opens an e-mail window with the text of the task inside it. Remove the task header information at the top of this text, and then add any message you want above the remaining original e-mail text. You will need to address the To field and perhaps adjust the Subject field. Then click Send.

Figure 11.8
Outlook 2007
Move choices.

From an Open Task

In the open task dialog box of that task, find the Copy to Folder command.

In Outlook 2007 it is called Move, and it is inside the Office Button, that large round orange button in the upper left corner of the Task dialog box. First click the Move command button, then select Outbox. See Figure 11.8.

In Outlook 2010 click the task, then from the Task tab select Move, then select Other Folder and then select Outbox.

In Outlook 2003 the command is under the task's File menu instead. Choose Copy to Folder, and a dialog box opens showing your folder tree. Find your Outbox folder and select it.

For all versions, follow the instructions above for editing the resulting e-mail window before clicking Send.

Save Time by Writing Clearer E-mails (All Versions)

Using Clearer Subject Lines

A pet peeve of mine is getting an e-mail whose title makes it seem merely informational, but then inside the e-mail I find an important request. Indicating that request in the subject line would help my business life immeasurably as I try to identify action mail to do or convert to tasks.

With that in mind, I figure the least I can do is set an example for my colleagues and indicate action requests in the subject lines of e-mail I write. Doing so also helps me; it helps ensure that my request will get done. If I am requesting that my staff or colleague take some action, I put it right in the subject line. For example, if the action is *required*:

> Action Required: Update Sales Report

If it is an *optional* action, or I want to soften the message, I use the word Requested or something even more innocuous:

> Action Requested: Feedback on Conference
>
> Your Response Appreciated: Survey Enclosed

And if there is a deadline, I put it right in the title:

> Action Required by Fri 2nd: Update Sales Report

Writing Clearer E-mail Text

A related problem is this: not getting to the point quickly in an e-mail. Sometimes a request for action is buried at the bottom of a long problem statement in the e-mail. This causes the reader to have to dig through the mail to find out whether an action is requested and what it is. Instead, summarize the request right at the top of the e-mail by creating these headings and statements in the beginning of the e-mail text:

> **Who**: All members of the Go-To-Market Sales Team *(write this in case the distribution list is large and readers may think they were wrongly sent the mail; this clarifies exactly who the mail is intended for)*.
>
> **What**: Budget Justification Write-up.
>
> **Action Needed**: Create draft report and send to me *(describe clearly the next action you are requesting; you might be able to combine this and the above into one Action Needed statement)*.
>
> **When**: By Friday February 2nd.
>
> **Details**: *(if needed include your discussion of why this is required or details of what the result should look like, and so on)*.

Repeat this information even if some of it is in the subject line, as sometimes people skip over or quickly forget the subject line.

■   ■   ■

Summary

This lesson discussed a large number of optional time management and time-saving tips, including the following:

▶ Making time to work on tasks and, if needed, setting aside dedicated task time, including an exercise to determine if you really are overloaded at work.

▶ How to clean up your task time if it tends to be ineffective.

▶ Several ways to improve your use of Outlook Categories when filing e-mail.

▶ A number of Outlook time-saving tips.

▶ How to write clearer e-mails.

Next Steps

I suspect you skipped over many of the items in this lesson, and that's fine. Consider reviewing it again after using the system for a while to see if any sections become more important or relevant to you.

The next lesson is a similar collection of optional system components that Windows users may find valuable (sorry, they are not applicable to Mac users). I suggest you scan the section headings to see if any resonate with needs you are experiencing in your current workday. In particular I suggest you look at the Intrinsic Importance section, as it shows a way to focus on not just the urgent but also the important.

Lesson 12:
Advanced Topics for
Windows Outlook

Introduction

I promised at the beginning of this book that I would focus first on getting your workday, e-mail, and tasks under control and then later rise up a level and teach you more ways to improve your work life. By now I hope you *do* have your workday under control using what you have learned so far. So let's take a little of your extra time to look at some advanced perspectives that you can apply.

Unfortunately, these ideas can only by applied in Windows Outlook, not in the Macintosh version of Outlook. That's because they all rely on added task view features available only in Windows Outlook.

What's in This Lesson

In this lesson I am going to discuss extensions of the MYN system you may want to add to your daily ritual. Here are some of the specific items covered.

► Tasks that link strongly to your goals and values are said to have high intrinsic importance. I describe the concept and offer a column you can add to your TaskPad/To-Do Bar to track such tasks.

► I show a number of ways to track goals and projects and several methods that link them to tasks.

► I show you how to add a column to your TaskPad/To-Do Bar that displays task deadlines.

► If you have Outlook 2007/10 and work with a narrow monitor, I demonstrate how to add back the compact layout to the To-Do Bar, thus saving space on your screen.

▶   I show how to configure a large number of Outlook task views and view changes to round out your suite of MYN tools.

Consider this entire lesson as graduate level work in the MYN system. It is not a set of prescriptions that you must do; rather it is a list of independent suggestions to consider. So feel free to scan through and pick and choose among the tools and views, finding items that you feel meet your needs.

As an introduction to these advanced concepts, let's start with Intrinsic Importance, which can be a very important optional add-on to your MYN system.

Intrinsic Importance

Beyond Urgency Management

In today's over-clocked business world, we are more often driven by urgency and recentness of attention than by the core importance of tasks. I call the core importance of tasks their *intrinsic* importance, and it is easy to over-look. When you have way too much to do, you tend to wait till something is urgent to do it. You then get in the habit of only doing the critical stuff, which means important but not urgent things are often passed by. We say to our-selves, "Hey this can wait, it's not about to boil over," and then we get almost addicted to focusing only on the urgent. An entire book has been written on this topic, *First Things First*, by Stephen R. Covey. There are ways to move beyond this limited focus.

This sounds pretty important, so why did I wait to the last lesson to introduce it? My contention is that while urgency focus is unfortunate, managing urgent items is necessary. Urgency often comes from sources out of your control, so you can't just make a decision that you are no longer going to pay attention to it and focus only on core importance instead. You really do need to be good at managing urgency and the high volume of work that often leads to it. That's where most of us fail, and that's why much of this book is about dealing with lots of tasks and about identifying various levels of urgency of tasks on your list, and managing them appropriately.

By this point in the book you have done that. You have brought order to chaos and your workday is generally under control. You know how to man-age high volumes of tasks and e-mail, and you can now afford to step back and take a higher perspective. I now want to introduce you to a way to man-age and promote *intrinsically important* tasks within your Now Tasks list.

Intrinsic Importance Defined

What do I mean by intrinsically important tasks? These are tasks that link strongly to your values or goals. So for example if you had a high-value goal such as "I will have great health and vitality," then tasks such as *go to gym* or *schedule annual physical* should have a high intrinsic importance. But in an urgency-based world you might easily skip over tasks like these.

No system can make you do these tasks. All you can hope for is a way to call them out so you at least acknowledge their importance. I am going to show you a small TaskPad/To-Do Bar change you can make that gives you a way to acknowledge tasks with high intrinsic importance. With this in place, you are more likely to notice these tasks and less likely to defer them without thinking. You are more likely to make them a priority.

Adding Intrinsic Importance to the TaskPad/To-Do Bar

Here is how to implement this intrinsic importance feature in the MYN system. You are going to add a new column to the TaskPad/To-Do Bar called "II" (short for Intrinsic Importance). Once added, you will examine the tasks in your TaskPad/To-Do Bar and put a 0 through 9 score in that column for how high you think their intrinsic importance is. The question is, Do these tasks link strongly with important goals or values you have? Enter a 9 if they link extremely strongly or 0 if there is no link at all. You may want to use a narrower range if you like, say 0 through 5 or even 0 through 3; it's up to you; I use 0 through 9 in these instructions.

Figure 12.1
Optional intrin-
sic importance
(II) column.

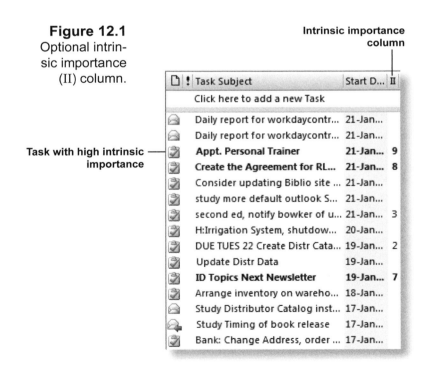

Assuming you are using 0 through 9, you are then going to add a custom formatting rule that says any value of 7 or above will cause that task to be boldfaced in your task list.

Figure 12.1 shows how the task list looks once that column is added; note the values chosen on the right and the three bolded tasks in the list. Clearly these tasks now stand out.

Once this feature is in place and tasks are scored, you'll use this in several ways. As you consider which tasks to do on a given day, you might favor any tasks that are bolded. And as you periodically clean your list you can avoid deferring tasks that are bolded. You can also occasionally sort on the Intrinsic Importance column, putting all high-importance tasks at the top. You might promote some of those tasks to your Target Now tasks list by setting their start date to today.

This approach won't necessarily get those tasks done first, but it provides you additional data as you make intuitive decisions on which tasks you will do when. As you glance at your list it is good to be reminded which tasks have high core value to you.

How to Add the Intrinsic Importance Column

Here's how to add the Intrinsic Importance column and formatting.

Note: The view change below is NOT prebuilt in the MYN-enabled version of the Outlook add-in software ClearContext. You'll need to add it yourself.

1. Right-click anywhere in the TaskPad/To-Do Bar task list heading bar (with the heading TaskPad or Task Subject).

2. Choose Customize Current View… from the shortcut menu. It might say Custom… instead, and in Outlook 2010 it might say View Settings…. The following dialog box will open (the title may vary). You are going to set a few of the view attributes in this dialog box.

3. Click the Fields… button (called Columns… in Outlook 2010), which opens the following dialog box.

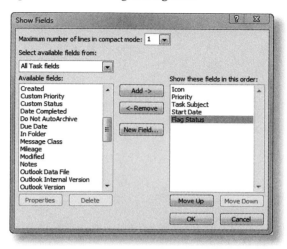

4. Click the New Field… button (called New Column… in 2010), in the middle of that dialog box. The New Field/New Column dialog box opens (see below). Type "II" in the Name field (that stands for Intrinsic Importance). Set the Type field equal to Number and the Format field equal to All Digits.

Click OK to add the field to the right-hand field list in the Show Fields/ Columns dialog box.

5. Reposition the field so it is below the Start Date field. In Outlook 2007/10 that places the field second from the bottom, as shown below. In Outlook 2003 it will be right at the bottom. Click OK.

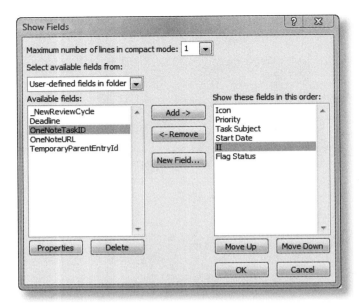

6. Back at the large stack of buttons, click the Automatic Formatting… button (called Conditional Formatting… in Outlook 2010). In the resulting dialog box, click the Add button, and in the Name field type the title "High II" (you'll see in a moment why to use that title).

7. Click the Font button, and in the Font window that opens, choose Bold from the Font Style list in the upper middle. Click OK.

8. In the formatting dialog box again, click the Condition button. The Filter dialog box opens. Click the Advanced tab.

9. Click the Field button in the middle left of this dialog box.

10. From the Field list, choose User Defined Fields in Folder, and from its submenu choose II.

11. From the Condition list choose Is More Than.

12. Type "6" in the Value box.

13. Then click Add to List to place this condition in the criteria list at top middle of the dialog box. Here is how that should look.

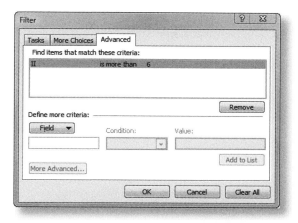

14. Click OK to accept this, then click OK on the formatting dialog box, and OK in the large stack of buttons window. This will bring you back to the TaskPad/To-Do Bar.

You should see the II field appear in your TaskPad/To-Do Bar. Resize the field width so it is just wide enough to show one-digit numbers.

Using the Intrinsic Importance Column

Since this is a user-defined field, the only way you can enter the II value is in the TaskPad/To-Do Bar column; you will not be able to add that field to the Task dialog box. But that's okay, it still works.

Scan through your current list of tasks and enter scores for any tasks that seem obvious. Try, if you like, to enter a score for everything in the list. After using this a few days or weeks I predict that you will only enter the Intrinsic Importance score on tasks that have a high score. There is little value in comparing the relative importance of a task scoring a 4 versus a task scoring a 2. But the upper scores do delineate well; so a 9 probably is more important than a 7 and you might do it first. In my practice I only enter scores on tasks with a 7 or above, which means all my tasks with II entries get bolded; I then end up with a 3-level rating system for important tasks, which works well for me. You'll find what works for you over time; the system is flexible.

And now, in the days ahead, consider this score as you pick which tasks to target for the day.

You might wonder, shouldn't we just leave the Now Tasks list sorted on the Intrinsic Importance field, placing the high scoring ones always at the top of the list? Definitely not. I have concluded that sorting tasks only on Intrinsic Importance does not work; our lives do not function that way. For example, which is more important, *Go to gym* or *Attend office after-work party*? The gym might meet a goal, but the party might be just what you need that day. Intrinsic importance is only one factor in determining what tasks we will put at the top of our list. And it's often not the highest factor. That's not a bad thing, it is just reality. So instead keep the list *date* sorted and use the FRESH Prioritization approach described in Lesson 4. Then factor in the intrinsic importance value using your intuition to decide which tasks to do next.

Note: *If a task with high intrinsic importance is really time-critical as well, consider placing it on the calendar instead of just putting it on the task list, and set aside enough time to make sure it gets done. This is discussed in Lesson 11.*

■　■　■

Tracking Goals and Projects in Outlook

Moving to another topic, how do you track goals and projects on your task list in Microsoft Outlook?

First of all, starting with goals, I deliberately do not say much about creating or tracking goals in this book. Not because they are not important, but because most people's problems with tasks and e-mail are not related to a shortage of goals or inattention to the ones they have. Instead, most people's problems are in dealing with the barrage of incoming e-mail and action requests at volumes that seem to defy an eight-hour workday. This dilemma is not solved by merely having and working goals.

The same is true of projects. Unless you are managing relatively large projects, I don't see lack of project management skills as being the main cause of an out-of-control workday. Again, mastering management of the daily deluge of e-mail and tasks should come first.

That said, after successfully using MYN to conquer the disarray of your e-mail and tasks, it is fitting to take the next rung of the achievement ladder and yes, *do* start focusing on your goals and projects. Again, this is graduate-level MYN.

By the way, in my book *Master Your Workday Now!* I write extensively about goals—how to write them and how to achieve them. So check out that book. In the pages ahead I will focus mainly on how to track them in Outlook.

Tracking Goals

By now the distinction between goals and tasks should be clear, but if not let's just say this: a task is *actionable*, and a goal is *plan-able*. Specifically, tasks, when you glance at them in the middle of your workday, should be something you can *do*, that you can *act* on. Goals should be something you can plan tasks against to achieve the goal.

This means you should not place goals on your Now Tasks list. For example, if you have a goal to lose weight, don't write "Lose weight" on your Now

Tasks list. Why? Because in the heat of a busy workday if you see that item pop up on your list you won't know what to do with it. What you *should* write on your Now Tasks list is an action (task) toward that goal: "Call Sam the personal trainer." Or "Go to gym today." This is essentially the next-action concept that I discussed in Lesson 6, and it is an important element of getting your tasks done.

So if not on the Now Tasks list, where *do* you place your goals in order to plan against them? Note that you should record them *someplace*, because you want to continue to refer to them often and create actions against them. I suggest you create a goals list, and Outlook is a good place to put it. I show you some options for that in a moment, options that work well also with projects.

Tracking Projects

There are two ways this system can help you with projects. First, as with goals, you might want to list your projects somewhere in Outlook so that you can periodically identify next-action tasks and place them on your Now Tasks list. And, as with goals, you should not list them in your Now Tasks list itself because they are too big to place there. Second, projects tend to have a sequence of dependent tasks. I'll show you a few ways to track these tasks together in Outlook.

But not all projects are usefully tracked in Outlook the same way. That really depends on how complex the project you're talking about is. Let me list the two extremes of project types and then show how the MYN system can help.

Types of Projects

Large Formal Projects are multiweek, multimonth, or multiyear activities, usually worked independently of your operational duties. They often include some fully dedicated staff. Such projects are large enough to warrant their own set of planning and follow-up meetings and should be managed using formal project management techniques, not the Outlook Task system. The discussion below does not really apply to these. That's because you need to separate project planning and management steps from the execution of individual tasks, and Outlook is not a large-project planning and management tool. Instead use a tool like Mindjet's MindManager and Microsoft Project to identify and schedule the long string of dependent tasks that result.

That said, if you are assigned a number of individual tasks from a large formal project, you could put those on your Outlook task list and use this system to help you execute them.

Background or Miniprojects fall well below the large size and intense focus of a formal project. I define these as work units that require multiple associated or linked tasks but that overall are not large enough to be managed as a formal project. These may be spin-offs from a larger project, or they may stand alone as simple multitask activities. Your attention on these projects is usually part time; it starts and stops throughout the week as you try to fit these into your other operational duties. A lot of what you do at work probably falls in this category. The MYN system can be useful for executing and even managing these small projects, if the task list for the project is small and not complicated. The best way Outlook can help is to create a list of these projects, as you do with goals, and periodically identify next-action tasks and place them on your Now Tasks list. Ways to do that are listed below. But even better is, after creating tasks, to actually track tasks in context with the project, and solutions for that are also discussed below.

Outlook MYN Solutions

Ways to List and Manage Goals and Projects in Outlook

There is a large range of possible approaches on where to record goals and list projects, and I don't feel any one of them is the best. I think this varies by individual and the number and size of goals or projects. Let me throw out a few approaches that you can pick from, most of which use Microsoft Outlook. For the Outlook-based ones below I'll provide implementation details later in this lesson.

1. Create Outlook Categories with your goal or project name, and then assign those categories to tasks that help achieve those goals or projects. Put a G: or P: designator in front of the category name (G:LoseWeight; P:LandscapeFrontYard); that way all project or goal items clump together in the Outlook Categories list and you can scan them there. Then you can configure an Outlook view in your Tasks folder that groups tasks by each goal or project, to help plan your steps to achievement. I'll cover that ahead. Use this approach only for a small number of projects and goals, otherwise the category list can get quite cluttered. So you might want to reserve them for the largest and most important.

2. Enter each goal or project as an individual task in your master tasks list (covered ahead). You can then periodically glance at that list and, if appropriate, create new Now Tasks against some of those goals and projects. You can brainstorm and record future actions in the Notes text field of each master task for later reference. Again, put a G: or P: designator in front of the master task name (G:Lose weight; P:Landscape front yard) and sort alphabetically on that view. I'll show how to create that ahead. This is suitable even for very numerous projects and goals.

3. Recognizing a natural Goal→Project→Next Action hierarchy, some people create nested Outlook task folders using the goal and project names and then store next actions as Outlook tasks in the lowest-level folder. The advantage is that it lets you create hierarchical relationships if you need that. One disadvantage is that in pre-Outlook 2007 versions it makes using the TaskPad as a place to list all your daily tasks difficult, if

they are tucked away in other folders; this can work well, however, with Outlook 2007/10. More on this ahead.

4. Or just list your goals or projects in an Outlook Note data type, and don't make any attempt to link them to tasks. Ultimately, having a place where you can record and review your goals and project names is often enough.

5. Use some application other than Outlook. I really like the software Mind-Manager, by Mindjet. I use it for brainstorming many things, including my goals and projects. And there are many other software titles available that can help; just do an Internet search on goal setting software and project management software.

6. Use paper. Tape a printed goal list or project list (or graphic representation of it) to your wall next to your computer monitor. If you have one main project, paste the printed project plan in clear sight. Paper is actually an excellent approach; sometimes we try to be too clever with technology and lose sight of good old-fashioned paper. The advantage to this is that your goals and projects are always in sight, and you can format the list in any way that helps you to understand and focus on them, say using hierarchies, pictures, maps, and so on. And you will see them daily, which many experts say is essential if you hope to realize your goals and move your projects forward.

What to Do with a Goals or Projects List

The key to all these approaches is to refer to the goal or project list often, and then periodically toss into your TaskPad/To-Do Bar next-action tasks. In fact, I feel strongly that once you get e-mail and tasks under control using MYN, and you can finally relax enough to consider your higher work objectives, you should then commit to this: every day complete at least a few tasks related to your key goals and maybe even projects. Otherwise you can get so accustomed to just knocking tasks off your list that you forget to specifically target important ones (as opposed to merely doing the urgent or easy ones).

Series Tasks

One reason to consider a project tasks perspective in Outlook is series tasks. With these tasks, once you complete one, the next one is eligible for doing, and then the next one, and the next. These are also called linked tasks or dependent tasks and they are typical in project environments where a complex stream of activity is required to meet the end goal. They are also common once you start using next actions (Lesson 6) because after you break down a task to identify its very next action, you are likely to end up with other steps to reach the final desired outcome.

How do you designate this in Outlook? Should you attempt those linkages in Outlook?

Well, if this truly is a large complex project with complicated dependencies, use a good project management tool like Microsoft Office Project. Every time I have tried to find logical ways to link across a large number of tasks in Outlook, too many exceptions arise that make it too complicated; instead use a tool built just for that. Mindjet MindManager recently released a new version that allows you to display linked tasks as well.

If it is a simple miniproject with a relatively small number of tasks, it *can* be useful to make some linkages in Outlook. Why? Because when you complete one task it is nice to know which ones need your attention.

So how to do this? One thing you should *not* do is copy all the dependent tasks into your Now Tasks list. Recall that the Now Tasks list is only for tasks that you could consider working on *now*, and dependent tasks don't pass that test. You should write only next actions on the Now Tasks list, otherwise it becomes cluttered with nonactionable items and slowly becomes unusable.

I would also avoid entering a series of future-dated tasks with *estimated* start dates. Even though hidden from view, those estimated dates will come back to haunt you as soon as the project timing changes. The tasks will either show up too late or too early.

Instead, there are two better ways to handle linked tasks.

First, use any of the options listed above where multiple actions are associated with a project and are reviewable. Then, when you complete one project task, remember to come back and review the project list to decide which next action to activate in your Now Tasks list. In the list above, both the project categories approach and the master tasks list approach will work for this (items 1 and 2).

While this list review can work well, the weakness is that as you complete a given project task you may forget to look again at the associated project list to find the next. Then the sequence stalls out.

The MORE or PigPog Method

Another solution helps solve the problem described above and works especially well with the multiple steps arising from next-action decomposition. There are a number of variants of this solution. The common element of each is this: you place the next action of a larger series of tasks in the Subject field of a single Outlook task item, and then indicate in the Subject field somehow that more tasks are associated with this next action. Here are the variants:

▶ Use the MORE method that I mentioned in Lesson 6 where you place the first task of a sequence as a task item in your Now Tasks list and at the end of the Subject field put the word "… MORE." For example: "E-mail Ted about proposal… MORE." Then in the task text box (the body of that task), list the subsequent tasks. When you complete the first task, seeing the word "… MORE" reminds you to open the item and look for subsequent tasks. When you do, change the Subject field of the task to the next task in the list. Keep doing that until the sequence is complete. This idea was contributed to me by Don Morgan.

▶ Do the same as above but instead of "…MORE" put a project name or outcome name after the task subject, in brackets. For example: "E-mail Ted about proposal {Newco Sale}." Seeing brackets around the project name will remind you to look inside. And having the project name in the Subject field reminds you why you are doing this task. This is called the PigPog method and was created by a number of people in the GTD Palm Yahoo! Group, and documented by Michael Randall. See this link for more information: www.pigpog.com/node/1031.

▶ Mark Ashton contributed the following idea. Do the same as above but put a → at the *beginning* of the subject line. This is to ensure that you do not accidentally delete a series task after partial completion, when long task names cause the word MORE (or the project name in brackets) to scroll out of sight at the right. You might try other codes at the front, a P: for example.

▶ In some descriptions of this technique, listing next steps inside the task is described as optional. I think you should do it and even feel free to include date information in that text if it is pertinent, say deadlines or start dates.

This technique is best suited for either very small projects or large tasks that have relatively few steps to complete; I would not use it as your only way to track a large project with many steps.

Some small projects may have parallel work streams, each with its own series of dependent tasks. In those cases create a MORE task or PigPog task for each work stream.

Using ClearContext for Tracking Project Tasks

The Outlook add-in software ClearContext that I highlight throughout this book has a nice set of features for tracking project tasks. Its Dashboard view can be used instead of the project views I show ahead, and offers much stronger integration with the other elements of Outlook that may be related to your projects (e-mail, contacts, appointments, and more). Take a look at it.

■   ■   ■

Custom Tasks Views for Projects, Goals, and More

Let's get busy now and build some of these views. In Lesson 3 you customized the TaskPad and To-Do Bar to match Master Your Now! system principles. So by now you know how to create custom views. The custom view capability of Windows Outlook separates Outlook from many of its competitors. It separates it from the Mac version of Outlook too. It gives Outlook great power for creating custom solutions.

In this section I am going to show you 10 custom views or view changes that you can use; nearly all are mentioned either above or elsewhere in this book as being optional but perhaps useful to you. I've collected them all together here because you may want to create them all in one sitting; they use similar skills to create. And since they all are optional it makes sense to list them together.

I have also placed here the configuration of the Master Tasks view, which has been optional in all editions of this book except the first edition.

Before showing you how to build the views, I want to talk a bit about Tasks folder views in general, the Task folder itself, and Outlook folders in general. It will help you understand what you are doing when you create and use these new views.

Tasks Folder Views

First, you should know by now that you access the Tasks folder by clicking the Tasks icon or banner button at the left side of your Outlook window. All major folders in Windows Outlook, including Tasks, come with preinstalled views that allow you to vary the way you see your data. The default Tasks folder view is called Simple List. It is basically a list of all tasks in the system with only the task subject name and the due date displayed. It is this view that opens when you click the Tasks folder icon or banner button the first time (see Figure 12.2).

Even though it is not configured for MYN, the Simple List view is very useful. For example, it displays completed tasks (designated with a strike-through dimmed font); I use this view if I accidentally mark a task complete in the TaskPad/To-Do Bar and want to find it and make it active again. I also sometimes use it to find future-dated tasks, though a custom view described ahead is better for that (called MYN All Now Tasks)

You can display a number of other optional Tasks folder views. For example, Outlook 2010 ships with 11 Tasks folder views you might want to use. Think of these views as filtered or selected subsets of your entire task list. Let's say you want to see a list of your tasks without viewing the completed tasks. To do that you would choose the view labeled Active Tasks. The views also vary by showing different task information columns.

Figure 12.2   Simple List view in Tasks folder.

☑	Tasks	Search Tasks	🔍 ▾
▯ ☑	Subject	Due Date	▽
	Click here to add a new Task		
▨ ☑	Chk air in tires	Fri 8/17/2007	✓
▨ ☐	Appt. Personal Trainer	Mon 1/21/2008	⚑
▨ ☐	F:JS:Resolve Network Performance	Fri 1/25/2008	⚑
▨ ☐	figure out deadlin for corp filings	Mon 1/28/2008	⚑
▨ ☑	Call this inquiry Beumer Corporation	Thu 1/24/2008	✓
▨ ☐	F: Study timing of book release	Fri 1/25/2008	⚑
▨ ☐	ask hong: delta insurance?	Tue 1/22/2008	⚑
▨ ☑	try torn edge in photoshop	Thu 1/24/2008	✓
▨ ☐	F: Harrison Medical Center	Mon 2/11/2008	⚑
▨ ☐	Russian Publisher Rights-Reconsider	Mon 2/11/2008	⚑
▨ ☑	Fedex Contract to Distributor	Sat 1/19/2008	✓
▨ ☐	find this wine	Mon 3/3/2008	⚑
▨ ☑	move itunes library	Fri 1/18/2008	✓
▨ ☑	contact 1099 folks	Fri 1/18/2008	✓
▨ ☐	F: Tuscon Fire Dept Training	Mon 2/11/2008	⚑
▨ ☐	buy cooking pan	Mon 1/21/2008	⚑
▨ ☐	F: Am I in NBN System Yet?	Fri 1/25/2008	⚑
▨ ☐	DUE TUES 22 Create Distr Catalog information	Sat 1/19/2008	⚑
▨ ☐	F:Watch for Data instructions, NBN	Tue 1/22/2008	⚑
▨ ☐	Update Distr Data	Sat 1/19/2008	⚑
▨ ☑	FedEx Contract	Thu 1/17/2008	✓

Choosing Between Optional Task Views

Multistep (All Versions)

In all Outlook versions you can select views from the View menu or tab. Open the View menu or tab, then in Outlook 2003 choose Arrange By and then in 2003 and 2007 choose Current View. Outlook 2010, on the View tab click Change View (at the very left end of that tab). All versions: once you do that, all available views for the currently selected folder are displayed, ready for you to choose from. In Outlook 2010, because this control displays view *icons* rather than a scrolling list of view names, it can be hard to find some custom views. To make that easier, click Manage Views… and select your views from the scrolling list displayed there.

Advanced Toolbar (Outlook 2003 and 2007)

Outlook 2003 and 2007 give you a better way to see at a glance which view is open and to select others; it is unfortunate that it was removed in Outlook 2010. It requires that you add another toolbar called the Advanced Toolbar; here is how you do that. Go to the View menu and click Toolbars; then choose Advanced on the submenu. You will see a new toolbar added to the top of your Outlook window (see below).

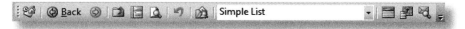

In that toolbar you will see a box that lists names of task views, with most likely the view named Simple List shown by default. This is the Current View

Selector. You use this tool to select other views that may be available for the currently selected folder. For instance, click now on the drop-down arrow at the right edge of that list and choose Detailed List. Note that the task view now changes to a new view (one very similar to Simple List but containing a few more columns). Select Simple List again from that box to return to the default view.

Always Choose the Folder First

One important lesson to learn about choosing views is this: you always need to choose the folder your view applies to first, before trying to choose the view from the view list. So if you are trying to open one of the task views, make sure you first click the Tasks folder. Only then will the list in the Current View Selector open what you want.

Another Current View Selector in 2003 and 2007

For completeness, note that Outlook 2003 and 2007 have an additional way to select views right on the Navigation Pane. Unfortunately, this is not available in 2010. With it you can select views by choosing from the Current View Selector on the left side of the screen (see Figure 12.3). That tool should appear after you click the Tasks banner button; however, if you have lots of task folders you might need to scroll down the middle pane of the Navigation Pane to see it.

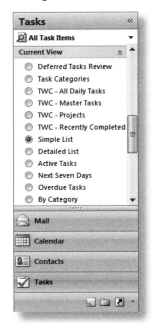

Figure 12.3
Selecting views in Navigation Pane.

If this Current View Selector control is not visible at all, activate it as follows. For Outlook 2003, from the View menu choose Arrange By, and from the Arrange By submenu select Show Views in Navigation Pane. For Outlook 2007 do this: from the View menu choose Navigation Pane, and select Current View Pane from the submenu.

This setting applies only to the current data type being viewed, so you need to repeat these steps if you want to see this pane with Contacts or Calendar, for example.

Outlook 2007/10 To-Do List Tasks Folder

Before you start creating custom views, note that when creating views in Outlook 2007/10 it is important to understand the new To-Do List "Tasks folder." I encourage you to read the Appendix A section New to Outlook 2007/10: The Mysterious To-Do List Folder, for a full discussion. In the meantime, know this: many of the Task view creation instructions you will follow below ask you, if using Outlook 2007/10, to select the To-Do List Tasks folder when creating the view. Be sure you do this, and then be sure to select the To-Do List Tasks folder when you *use* the view. Why? Because it is the only way to see flagged-mail tasks.

You will also see one other thing that is related to this in the instructions below. Views you create in the To-Do List folder in Outlook 2007/10 that hide completed tasks should usually have two filter conditions in the Advanced tab of the Filter dialog box:

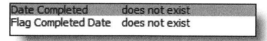

I call these "Outlook 2007/10 transition filter conditions," because that's what they do; they fix an odd behavior in how some Outlook 2007/10 views treat flagged-mail tasks created from pre-2007 mail. You will notice that these two conditions will always appear by default in any new view you create within the To-Do List folder, so be sure to leave them there for all views that *filter out completed tasks*. Remove them for any view in which you want to see completed tasks.

Outlook 2007/10 Tasks Subject Field versus Subject Field

As you build the views below, you will notice another distinction made between 2007/10 and earlier versions, and that is the use of the Tasks Subject field in Outlook 2007/10. In earlier versions, a similar field called Subject was always used. With the introduction of flagged-mail tasks, Microsoft added the Task Subject field to all tasks and uses that field in any view that shows flagged-mail tasks (such as the To-Do Bar task list). Make sure to use that field in any views below where it is called out.

Why the different field? This is a bit subtle, but here goes. It is to enable users to change the title of a flagged-mail task without changing the Subject of the original e-mail. So on creation of a flagged-mail task, Outlook copies the e-mail subject name into the new Task Subject field. Notice that if you edit the Task Subject field of a flagged-mail task in the To-Do Bar, the Subject of the corresponding e-mail in the Inbox will not change. This is true even though these two items really are the same entity. It's this new field that enables that.

This is a good feature because it supports a key tenet of the MYN system: tasks should be titled with an action phrase. So once you create a flagged-mail task from an e-mail, you can change the task name to an action phrase without disturbing the original e-mail. And that's important, because what if you later reply to that e-mail? The recipient may be confused about why the e-mail conversation titles no longer match. So get used to this new field called Task Subject.

One downside to using Task Subject is you cannot sort on it. In Lesson 10, on delegation, I instruct users to sort alphabetically on the Subject field, so if you need to do that, feel free to use the Subject field instead of the Task Subject field when building any view ahead where that might matter. The MYN All Now Tasks view is one such view.

Using Multiple Windows, or Side by Side

With the creation of these new views below, you may at times want to open one next to your TaskPad or To-Do Bar so you can plan your Now Tasks list. You cannot do that normally in Outlook 2003, but there is a trick. Something even many experienced users of Outlook do not realize is that you can open multiple windows within Outlook showing different views in each one. This makes it possible, for example, in Outlook 2003, to keep your Calendar folder with TaskPad open in one window and your goals and projects view open in another. To do this, right-click the icon or banner button for the data type that you want to open in the second window, and choose Open in New Window from the shortcut menu. If you have a very large monitor, you can display both windows in different parts of your screen. If you have a smaller monitor and the windows overlap, you may wish to use the keyboard shortcut, ALT + TAB to move between the windows.

If you use multiple windows like this and you want to have the same windows reopen automatically the next time you start Outlook, be sure to use the File menu's Exit command to exit rather than clicking the Close button on the windows. Using the Exit command reopens the multiple windows on next use of Outlook.

In Outlook 2007/10 you can open the To-Do Bar next to any data-type view. So once you create a goal or project list as below, you can open the To-Do Bar next to it and view your Now Tasks at the same time. This is very useful to do as you plan how to complete goals and projects.

■   ■   ■

Category-Based MYN Goal and Project Views (All Windows Versions)

Now that you understand custom views better, let's create some. Let's start with the goals and projects views.

These first two parallel views are now my favorite approaches to tracking goals and projects. They assume you will create your goals and projects as entries in the Outlook Categories list and that you will link tasks to these Categories. These Tasks folder views enable you to view a list of all tasks for a given goal or project grouped with the goal or project name, so that you can plan ahead, pick next actions, defer longer-term associated tasks, and so on.

Some Background

To make this work, you should only use this approach for less numerous (probably larger) goals or projects. For those who use David Allen's Getting Things Done system, or who used my system in the first edition of this book, a little discussion is needed to describe why that's important and how this differs from the first edition of this book.

In the past I did not use categories to list projects, because my project lists tended to be long; I tended to create a lot of project names. Why? Because one premise of the first edition of this book was that any time you have a multi-step activity you should identify it as a miniproject and put it on a project list (in the Master Tasks view). That's also a teaching of David Allen's Getting Things Done approach. The idea is, after you complete the current next action you can review the project list and determine if additional next actions are needed for these miniprojects.

But I found I gradually stopped reviewing that long project list. Many of those miniprojects were for next actions I had deferred out a ways, so I did not need to review the corresponding miniproject weekly. And that approach does not make sense now that I am using the Defer-to-Review method (Lesson 9). So I skipped reviews a lot, and the whole project list approach for all multistep activities no longer worked for me.

So I now no longer recommend converting all multistep activities into projects. Instead I now recommend using the MORE approach for linking tasks (described above in the section Series Tasks). Using that, you don't need to create a miniproject for every multistep activity.

One outcome of this is that the project list gets much smaller and only lists "real" projects— those that might have long time frames and substantial collections of related tasks. With a much shorter project list, using the Outlook Categories capability to list projects is much more practical now. The advantages of using Outlook Categories for listing projects are that you can link individual tasks to project names using category assignments. Then you can create views that show all the tasks associated with a given project. Those

Figure 12.4   MYN Projects view, based on categories.

🗒 Tasks	(Filter Applied)	Search Tasks	🔎 ▾	⌄
🗋 ! 𝕀 Subject		Start Date ▾	Categories	⟙
Click here to add a new Task				

⊟ ⬤ Categories: P:Lesson Changes (11 items)

	Subject	Start Date	Categories
🗒	fix Prework*	Mon 2/11/2008	⬤ P:Lesso... ⟙
🗒 ⬇	Re-create full day class slide set	Sat 2/2/2222	⬤ P:Lesso... ⟙
🗒 ⬇	improve section on filing. People did not get it*	Sat 2/2/2222	⬤ P:Lesso... ⟙
🗒 ⬇ 𝕀	correction to one of last e-mails in lesson chain*	Sat 2/2/2222	⬤ P:Lesso... ⟙
🗒 ⬇	Update half day slides for 2003	Sat 2/2/2222	⬤ P:Lesso... ⟙
🗒 ⬇	clean up class material per eval comment from attendee	Sat 2/2/2222	⬤ P:Lesso... ⟙
🗒 ⬇	Add to movie: convert to calendar item	Sat 2/2/2222	⬤ P:Lesso... ⟙
🗒 ⬇	update main slides to 2003/2007	Mon 3/3/2008	⬤ P:Lesso... ⟙
🗒 ⬇	Add 2003/2007 to all class decks	Mon 3/3/2008	⬤ P:Lesso... ⟙
🗒 ⬇ 𝕀	Add changes from Ariz Fire Chief	Mon 2/25/2008	⬤ P:Lesso... ⟙
🗒 ⬇	Add slide to courseware: task management workflow	Mon 2/4/2008	⬤ P:Lesso... ⟙

⊞ ⬤ Categories: P:Marketing (10 items)

⊞ ⬤ Categories: P:Website Redesign (14 items)

views are useful for planning projects and identifying next actions. They also help during execution, as you may find related components to the project are done more easily together; the project tasks list helps you plan that out.

Using P: and G:

As you will see, both the projects view and the goals view use the same logic with category names. For these views to work, you need to put a P: in front of project names and a G: in front of goal names in the category list. The view filters look for these character strings. I find using this nomenclature works well when picking projects or goals out of the Outlook Categories list because they group together in the list.

Figure 12.4 shows how this view will look when it is completed (in Outlook 2007; other versions are similar). One of the project categories (P:Lesson Changes) is expanded.

How to Build the Category-Based Projects View

Note: The views below are included with the MYN-enabled version of the Outlook add-in software ClearContext, available from my website.

1.   **Outlook 2003** users, go to the Tasks folder;
Outlook 2007/10 users click the Tasks banner button and then select the To-Do List folder near the top of the Navigation Pane.

2.   **Outlook 2003 and 2007**, in the Advanced toolbar's Current View Selector, scroll to the bottom of the views and select Define Views.
In 2010 go to the View tab, then Change View, then Manage Views….

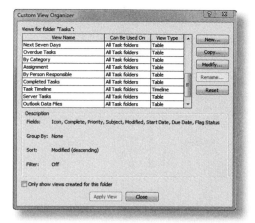

3. Click the New… button in the upper right corner, and name the view "MYN Projects" as shown below. Leave Table selected, and select the All Task folders option button at the bottom and click OK.

The Customize View: MYN Projects dialog box opens (called Advanced View Settings in 2010; we'll call it "the large stack of buttons" from now on).

4. Click the Fields… button (called Columns… in 2010). Use the same skills you used in Lesson 3 to build a field list for this view, shown below. Reminder: if you have trouble finding any of the field names in the list on the left of that dialog box, try selecting All Task Fields in the list box titled Select Available Fields/Columns From, and then look again at the scrolling field list. Task Subject and Flag Status can only be found under All Mail Fields.

In Outlook 2007/10 build the list shown below.

> Icon
> Complete (optional)
> Priority
> Attachment
> Task Subject
> Start Date
> Categories
> Flag Status

In Outlook 2003, build the following list instead:

> Icon
> Complete
> Priority
> Attachment
> Subject
> Start Date
> Categories

5. Click OK.

6. Back at the large stack of buttons, click the Group By… button.

7. Clear the check box in the upper left corner that reads: Automatically Group According to Arrangement, then…

8. From the Group Items By list, chose Categories. Select Ascending to the right of that list box, and click OK.

9. Back at the large stack of buttons, click the Sort... button, and set up as shown in the figure below. Sort items by Priority, Descending, and then by Start Date, Descending. Click OK.

10. Back at the large stack of buttons, click the Filter... button, and in the dialog box that opens, click the Advanced tab. Using the skills you learned in Lesson 3, add the following conditions.

▶ Outlook 2007/10 users, retain (or insert if missing) the Outlook 2007/10 transition filter conditions:

Date Completed	does not exist
Flag Completed Date	does not exist

▶ All versions add these conditions (see figure below for pre-2007 style):

Categories	contains	P:
Status	not equal to	Completed

11. Click OK. Back at the large stack of buttons, click the Automatic Formatting... button (called Conditional Formatting... in 2010) and ensure that the Overdue Tasks rule is not selected. Then click OK.

12. Click OK to close the large stack of buttons. Click Apply View.

Using the Category-Based Projects View

From now on, in Outlook 2003 and 2007, you can activate and use this view by selecting it from the Current View Selector on the Advanced toolbar. In Outlook 2010 activate it by going to the View tab, then Change View, and if you can read the title in the icon, click it. Otherwise go to Manage Views... and select it from the scrolling list of views, and then click Apply View.

You now should start creating Outlook Categories that match your project names (see Lesson 8 if you need to review how to create and assign Outlook Categories). Put a P: in front of each category name; make sure there is no space between the letter "P" and the colon. Then start assigning those categories to tasks that are associated with that project. Some thoughts on this:

▶ **Share categories with e-mail**. Recall that these category names are shared with e-mail, appointments, contacts, and all other Outlook data types. So plan to label project e-mail and project tasks with the same project's category name.

▶ **Renaming categories**: If you are already using Outlook Categories as project names and you want to use this new view, you'll need to rename that category so it now contains a P:. In Outlook 2007/10 a renaming effort is trivial. But in Outlook 2003 it is much harder. See Lesson 11 for instructions.

▶ **Dating dependent tasks**. One thing this view will do is encourage you to start brainstorming future tasks needed to complete a project. You can drop those into that Projects view anytime. That's good; however, stick to the rules: do not try to create a list of project tasks with start dates of dependent tasks estimated into the future; this gets complicated fast, especially when dates of early tasks change. Instead, use Microsoft Office Project or Mindjet MindManager if you want to create a true schedule of dependent tasks. For use in Outlook, label all future dependent tasks with the date 2/2/2222. Why? This future date prevents these tasks from dropping into your TaskPad/To-Do Bar (your Now Tasks list) randomly. You want them to appear there only after they graduate to next-action status. The date 2/2/2222 ensures that. It is easy to type, and it's a very long way into the future and so a good way to keep tasks out of your Now Tasks list. One day, when you are reviewing the project list for this project, you'll decide one of these tasks is now ready to activate as a next action for the project, and then you will change the date to the date you want to start it. That said, feel free to enter fixed-date, independent project tasks with their true future start date. That's the same as entering a Defer-to-Do task as described in Lesson 9.

► **Project work streams**. Many projects have parallel and independent work streams, each with its own string of dependent tasks. For example, a house painting project might have separate crews painting the main house and the detached garage, and their paths never cross. They work separate schedules and their tasks are not dependent on each other. You will want to identify the next action for *each* work stream, and place it on the Now Tasks list.

► **No hierarchy**. There is no provision in this process for hierarchical projects or for displaying relationships with goals. See section ahead for one approach to handle this.

Periodically, open this view and do some project planning. The most important planning action is to identify any tasks that are now eligible for action and to move them out to your Now Tasks list, as a next action, by giving them a near-term date. Remember to write these tasks in next-action language per Lesson 6.

Project tasks tend to be large, so chances are when you start to activate a task, you will turn it into a MORE series task. You will likely do this once you identify the true next action of each (see section above titled Series Tasks).

How to Build the Category-Based Goals View

Please follow all the steps above where you built the MYN Projects view, except for two changes.

► In step 3 name the view "MYN Goals."

► In step 10 replace **Categories contains P**: with **Categories contains G**:

All else is identical. This view is available in MYN ClearContext.

Using the Category-Based Goals View

Once you create the view, you now need to start creating Goal categories with a G: in front of their names (see Lesson 8 if you need to review how to create and assign Outlook Categories), and then start assigning those categories to tasks that are associated with that goal. Some thoughts on this, similar to those above for the Projects view, are repeated here in case you skipped that section:

► **Share categories with e-mail**. Recall that these category names are shared with e-mail, appointments, contacts, and all other Outlook data types. Take advantage of that if possible.

> ▶ **Renaming categories**: If you are already using Outlook Categories as Goal names and you want to use this goal view, you'll need to rename that category so it now contains a G:. In Outlook 2007/10 that is trivial. But in Outlook 2003 it is much harder. See Lesson 11 for instructions.

> ▶ **No hierarchy.** There is no provision in this process for hierarchical goals or displaying relationships with projects. See section ahead for one approach to handle this.

As with projects, study this view periodically and adjust dates on tasks to best help you achieve that goal. Add new tasks that you think might advance each goal. If new goal-based tasks are already next-action tasks (they could be done now if time and priorities allow), give them a near-term date now. Dependent tasks are less likely with goals, but if you encounter any, use the 2/2/2222 date approach described above for projects, to keep them out of sight on most Now Tasks types of views.

Adding a Category Column in the TaskPad or To-Do Bar

When using these Category methods on goals and projects as described above, you may want to be able to see what category a task is assigned to right in the TaskPad or To-Do Bar. You can display a category in a narrow column at the right end of your TaskPad or To-Do Bar without hogging screen space. Then you can zero in on goal- or project-based tasks at a glance. This is another place Outlook 2007/10 is nice because those small color category squares take little space. But even earlier Outlook versions are good using a narrow category column in the TaskPad because the "G:" or "P:" will stand out in the category name. In Lesson 3 you learned how to add columns to views, so I leave this to you to experiment with. If you do add this column to 2007/10, note that it will make the To-Do Bar much more sensitive to stray clicks on the header bar; be careful not to click the Categories column header.

Assigning Other Categories to Tasks

In the category-based goals and projects views above, you assign goal and project categories to tasks. There are other ways to use categories with tasks. One nonproject or goal category I commonly assign to tasks is the category "Errands." I assign that to shopping items or other out-and-about type activities. That way, when I am out doing errands, I can filter my tasks by the category Errands on my mobile device, and see my shopping list or errands list. See Lesson 6 for more about using mobile software that syncs with Outlook tasks. Also see Lesson 6 for a discussion of using MYN with Getting Things Done (GTD). There I mention how categories can be used on tasks to assign GTD Contexts.

● ■ ●

The MYN Master Tasks View (All Versions)

About the Master Tasks View

In the first edition of this book the Master Tasks view was a very important part of the system. If you read that edition you may recall that tasks were divided into two types: daily tasks and master tasks. Master tasks represented long-term tasks you were not yet ready to work on (as well as the place to list project and goals). The master tasks concept is common to many task systems and books, including FranklinCovey and the long-famous book *The Time Trap*, by Alec Mackenzie.

Starting in the second edition of my Outlook book I have stopped using master tasks as a storage place for long-term tasks. It's not that there is no need for long-term tasks; there still is. It's just that I decided the master tasks list does not work well as a way to manage individual long-term tasks. I discuss why in Lesson 9, and discuss there as well why the new Defer-to-Review process solves this problem so well.

But there could still be a place for a master tasks list, and that's to use it solely to list projects, goals, roles, agendas, and so on, assuming you choose not to use the category-based project and goal views defined above.

Note: *If you followed the first edition but have recently reconfigured your TaskPad/To-Do Bar per Lesson 3 of this book, you should delete your old Master Tasks view as it will no longer work with the new TaskPad/To-Do Bar settings. Reason: these new settings no longer filter out tasks with no dates. If you still want to use the master tasks approach, create the new folder and view described below.*

Master Tasks View versus Category View

You can use this new Master Tasks view as an alternative to the category-based project and goals views described above. Why might you want to do that? If you like to identify all multistep tasks as projects and so have a long list of projects, this Master Tasks view will work better for you because it will prevent clogging your Outlook Category list with too many project names. And if you have no need to link individual next-action tasks to higher-level goals or projects, the new Master Tasks folder and view is simpler to use.

How This View Works

Very simply, the way this new master tasks list and view works is this: you list a project as a task entry by placing a task with a P: in front of the name there. Add as many as you like. List goals by placing a G: in front of the task, and so on (see Figure 12.5).

And one other very important point: this view is applied in a brand-new Tasks folder. In the old system you shared your current primary Tasks folder for this use, indicating master tasks as tasks with no dates. But no longer; you

Figure 12.5 New Master Tasks folder and view.

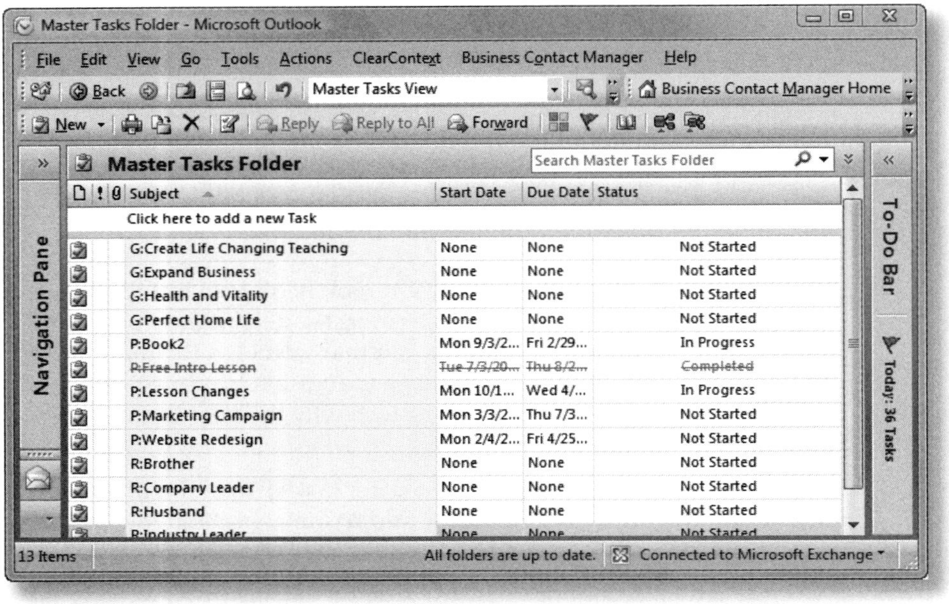

are now going to create a whole new Tasks folder and call it Master Tasks. Let's go through the steps.

Create the Master Tasks Folder and View

Note: The view and folder below is NOT included with the MYN-enabled version of the Outlook add-in software ClearContext. You'll need to create it following the steps below.

1. Make sure the full Folder List mode is activated in the Navigation Pane. Click the Folder List button at the bottom of the Navigation Pane if not.

2. Right-click the primary folder group name in your Outlook Folder list. That's the top of the folder group that your Inbox currently resides in.

3. Choose New Folder from the shortcut menu. You will see the dialog box below.

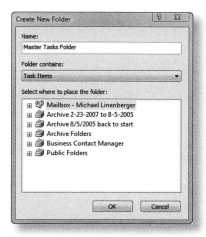

4. In the Name field type "Master Tasks Folder."

5. From the Folder Contains drop-down list, choose Task Items.

6. In the Select Where to Place the Folder box, again select the name of your main folder group. Then click OK.

7. You should now see that new folder appear in your Folder List, as below. Again, make sure you activate the full Folder List view, or you will not see it; click the Folder List icon at the bottom of the Navigation Pane to do that.

   The new folder should have an Outlook tasks icon next to it (a clipboard with a check mark). Select that folder now so it opens in your main Outlook window. It will of course be empty. Now you will create the view in that folder.

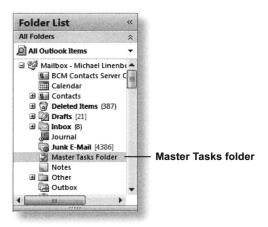

Master Tasks folder

8. Outlook 2003 and 2007, in the Advanced toolbar's Current View Selector, scroll to the bottom of the views and select Define Views. In 2010 go to the View tab, then Change View, then Manage Views....

9. In the view lists dialog box, click the New... button.

10. Name the view "MYN Master Tasks View." Leave all defaults as is. Click OK.

Note: Notice that I did not select All Task Folders in step 10. This is because I only want this view applied to this specific tasks folder. It might be confusing if I saw this view in other task folders, as it is not applicable.

11. Back at the large stack of buttons, click the Fields... button (called Columns... in 2010).

12. Create the following field list:

> Icon
> Priority
> Attachment
> Subject
> Start Date
> Due Date
> Status

13. Click OK, and then OK again. Then click Apply View.

Your new folder and view is complete. There is one more step, however, if you are using Outlook 2007/10.

Filter Master Tasks Out of To-Do Bar in Outlook 2007/10

If you are using Outlook 2007/10, you will need to add one more filter to the To-Do Bar, to keep these master tasks from appearing in the To-Do Bar. Here is how:

1. Right-click anywhere in the To-Do Bar task list heading bar (with the heading Task Subject).

2. Choose Customize Current View... from the shortcut menu. It might say Custom... instead and in Outlook 2010 it might say View Settings.... The dialog box with the large stack of buttons will open.

3. Click the Filter... button, and then click the Advanced tab.

4. Click the Field button on the left, select All Task Fields, and from the (very long) submenu, select In Folder.

5. Select the condition Doesn't Contain.

6. Type the phrase "Master Tasks" (with quotation marks) in the Value box. Make sure this wording exactly matches the first two words of your new Master Tasks folder name.

7. Then click Add to List. If you scroll down the criteria list you will see this new entry:

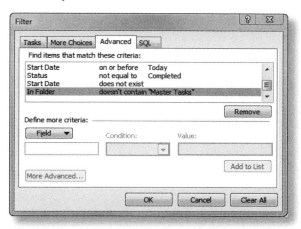

8. Click OK, and then OK again to get back to the To-Do Bar.

Using the Master Tasks Folder and View

In the future, after selecting this folder, you may need to activate the view as follows: in Outlook 2003 and 2007, select MYN Master Tasks View from the Current View Selector on the Advanced toolbar. In Outlook 2010 activate it by going to the View tab, then Change View, then select the icon named MYN Master Tasks View or click Manage Views... and select it from the scrolling list of views.

This is a very simple view. The way to use it is this: place an entry for each project by creating a task for each one and naming the task P:Project name, e.g., P:Landscape front yard. Do that now for all your projects.

The idea is to review the complete project list periodically and make sure Now Tasks are created that advance each project. Open each project, and in the text field for that project list future tasks that someday may become next-action tasks. When they do, move them to the Now Tasks list. You now need to commit to review this list periodically to make those determinations. You may also want to write in the text field a short narrative of the expected outcome of this project, and perhaps a short vision statement.

You can make similar entries for your goals. In that case you will be placing a G: next to each entry instead.

Note: *Readers of the first edition of this book, if you have created this view because you want to continue your previous practice of storing most lower-priority tasks here, you now have a new process for doing that. In the first edition, you set the date fields of a daily task to None to move it to the Master Tasks view. With this new approach, to convert a Now Task to a master task, you'll drag the task from your Now Tasks list to this new Master Tasks folder. Drag the other direction to promote a master task to a Now-Task. Again, though, I highly recommend using Strategic Deferrals instead.*

Start Date, Due Date, and Status Fields in Master Tasks Folder

Note that the start date, due date, and status fields are optional but useful. They are especially useful for projects; unlike next actions, projects do have start and end dates and may exist on various levels of status. So use these fields in their traditional ways.

I also left off the Priority field since it is less useful in this view, but feel free to add it if you feel you need it. And I do not filter out completed projects or goals; those I feel you want to admire for a while. You can delete them later.

One other thing: in the first edition of this book, I placed very low-priority tasks, tasks that you may or may not ever get to, ideas, whimsies, low-priority interests, all in the Low priority section of the Master Tasks view. I reviewed that section on a very long cycle and often skipped that review. My new thinking on this is that no matter how low priority a task may seem, you ought to glance at it periodically to see if your interest in it has increased, and each item may have a different appropriate schedule to review on. So these types of tasks are now made part of the Defer-to-Review process, with generally long review periods assigned (say six months or more), which are determined individually for each item. See the Defer-to-Review section of Lesson 9 for more information on this.

■   ■   ■

Adding the Concept of Roles to All the Above Views

All of the above views, whether category based or master-task based, can be expanded to include the concept of roles. Stephen Covey in the book *First Things First* talks about periodically reviewing the list of roles and responsibilities you have in your life, and making sure tasks related to those are routinely added to your daily activities as well. Roles like spouse, parent, committee chair, and so on, require more than reactive actions; they require proactive and thoughtful consideration of new activities you might take in the weeks ahead. Around each of these roles it helps, for a brief moment, to consider creative ideas, leadership needs, stakeholder expectations, and perhaps even, if the relationships are personal, random acts of kindness — all in support of that role.

Proactive planning like this separates a leader from a mere doer. Without proactively placing specific activities on your Now Tasks list or appointment calendar to support these important but nonurgent roles, leadership activities toward these roles and responsibilities will likely get no attention in the heat of a busy week. When making these entries in your master list, consider using the code "R:" for roles and responsibilities, "R:Team Lead" or "R:Husband" See the bottom of figure below, where this approach was applied within the Master Tasks view.

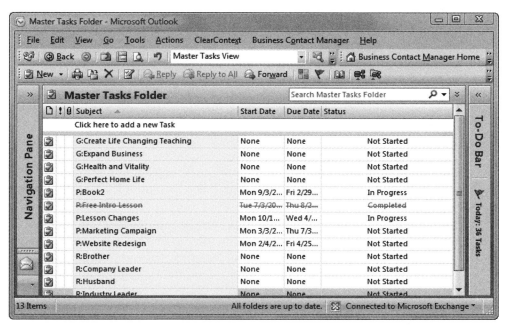

Hierarchical Goal, Project, and Task Folders (Outlook 2007/10)

If you consider goals, projects, and tasks it won't take you long to realize that there is a natural hierarchy present that goes something like this: from our goals we create projects, and from our projects we create tasks. So we should be able to trace many tasks back to a project and then to a goal. In fact some people say *every* task we do we should be able to trace back to a goal.

The logic in this is undeniable; however, the utility of doing much work on it is debatable. Every time I spend much time creating goal→project→task hierarchies I don't seem to get much value out of it compared to the time it takes to create the hierarchies and maintain them. But that's just me, and a large and vocal group of task system users feels very strongly about using such hierarchies in task systems.

So to that end, let me show you one way to do this that works relatively well in Outlook 2007/10. I would not try it in other Outlook versions and I'll explain why in a moment.

Outlook has a strong capability to create hierarchical folders. I am going to use that capability to create a goal→project→task hierarchy. In fact I can make these hierarchies as deep as I want; for example, I could add subgoals or subprojects in the middle of the hierarchy. One thing I cannot do is create a subtask and expect the task above it to also show up in my To-Do Bar; but that's okay. I just use various levels of projects to enable that, and only declare tasks at the bottom level.

Here is an example that you can use as a guide for your own implementation. I create a Goals tasks folder in my main data store (my Exchange Mailbox), and under that I create three goal entries as task subfolders. Under each of those folders I create task subfolders that I call projects, and under some of those, task subfolders I call subprojects. Finally, within the bottom folders I create actual tasks. Those actual tasks will show up in my To-Do Bar task list. The reason this only works in Outlook 2007/10 is that in earlier versions tasks created in folders other than the primary task folder did not show up in the TaskPad; but in Outlook 2007/10, due to the Search Folder–like nature of the To-Do Bar task list, the tasks *do* show up there. So Outlook 2007/10 is perfect for this job.

In Figure 12.6 you can see my Goals task folder halfway down the list, with three subfolders that are named after my three goals. I put G: in front of each to make that clear. I create the Goals folder simply by right-clicking the first folder group and choosing New Folder…, and then creating a Task folder called Goals.

Once that is created I right-click it, choose New Folder… and create my first goal (G:Create insightful teachings) as an Outlook Tasks folder as well. Then I create two more goals. I right-click the goal G:Expand business (see Figure 12.7) and enter projects (as Task folders with P: at the beginning) and subprojects (as Task folders with SP: at the beginning) and then actual tasks under the subprojects. Figure 12.7 also shows how the rest of this looks, with one subproject (SP:Delivery) selected; examine carefully the bottom half of the Folder List.

The tasks on the right side of Figure 12.7 are contained within the subproject folder SP:Delivery, since that is what is selected. These tasks will appear in the To-Do Bar (if the start date is on or before today). Notice I set the start date to 2/2/2222 for most tasks to keep them out of the To-Do Bar; they are dependent tasks and not yet ready to be worked as Now Tasks.

The Outlook 2007/10 folder system and To-Do Bar offers quite a bit of flexibility for creating hierarchical relationships among tasks. I encourage you to experiment with this capability should you want this kind of approach to tasks.

Figure 12.6
Hierarchical
Goal folders.

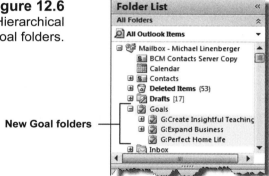

Figure 12.7
Hierarchical
project and
subproject
folders.

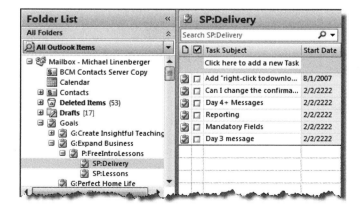

The TaskPad/To-Do Bar Deadline Column (All Versions)

Let's move away from projects and goals and again focus on tasks.

A Review of Using Task Deadlines

As discussed in Lesson 4, hard deadlines are not common in next-action tasks. You don't want to create fake deadlines because that will lead to disrespect for any deadline date. Instead, you should use the Target-Now or Defer-to-Do approach (Lesson 9) for tasks that you have strong feelings about completing but that don't have true deadlines.

If you truly have a hard deadline, use the DUE [date] designation in the subject line, as described in the Lesson 4 Deadlines section. I also mention there the option of creating a second task with the start date set to the deadline date and set to a High priority; that's for a bit of insurance.

I mentioned that you cannot use the task Due Date field that already exists in Outlook for use as deadline field. That's because it is self-populating; whenever you enter a start date on a task a due date is automatically entered. This defeats the purpose of highlighting only those tasks with true deadlines. So entering DUE [date] in the subject line is a good compromise way to handle the occasional deadline task.

This DUE [date] in the subject line technique works if you have an occasional deadline task. If you tend to have a lot of true deadline tasks, that approach can get tedious, especially if you decide to make duplicates as described above. So for those people who have a lot of true deadline tasks, here is a better way to do this.

Create a New Deadline Column

As with Intrinsic Importance above, you can create a new user-defined Outlook field and place a corresponding column in the TaskPad/To-Do Bar. In other words, you will have a dedicated column just for deadlines. That way deadlines stand out and you can view them easily. You can sort on the Deadline column to see all upcoming deadline tasks together; just click on the Deadline column title in the header. You can even create a rule that

will highlight a task in red when the deadline is due (that rule is included in these configurations).

Only add this column if you really need this, only if you really have a lot of true deadlines. I state that caution because this field will occupy a considerable width of scarce screen real estate in the TaskPad/To-Do Bar. I advise users to avoid adding extra columns to the TaskPad/To-Do Bar unless they really need them.

One more point. Like the Intrinsic Importance (II) column defined earlier in this chapter, because this is a user-defined field, the only place you can enter the deadline value for a given task is directly in the TaskPad/To-Do Bar column. You will not be able to show or enter that field within the Task dialog box. You can of course add it to other Tasks folder custom views if you so choose.

Adding the Deadline Column to the TaskPad/To-Do Bar

Here's how to add the Deadline column and formatting.

Note: The view change below is NOT included with the MYN-enabled version of the Outlook add-in software ClearContext. You'll need to create it yourself.

1. Right-click anywhere in the TaskPad/To-Do Bar task list heading bar (with the heading TaskPad or Task Subject).

2. Choose Customize Current View… from the shortcut menu. It might say Custom… instead and in Outlook 2010 it might say View Settings…. The dialog box with the large stack of buttons will open. You are going to set a few of the view attributes in this dialog box.

3. Click the Fields… button (called Columns… in 2010); the following dialog box opens.

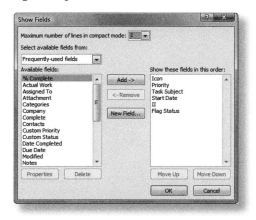

4. Click the New Field… button (New Column…) in the middle of that dialog box. The following dialog box opens.

5. Type "Deadline" in the Name field. Set Type to Date/Time and set Format as shown below (note the format only, the date will be different).

6. Click OK to add the field to the right-hand field list in the Show Fields/ Columns dialog box. If this doesn't work, from the list box in the upper left (Select Available Fields From), select User-Defined Fields in Folder. Then find the Deadline item in the new list that appears on the left, and add it to the list on the right using the Add button.

7. Reposition the Deadline field so it is the second from the bottom, as shown below for Outlook 2007/10. For 2003 make it the very last field. Click OK.

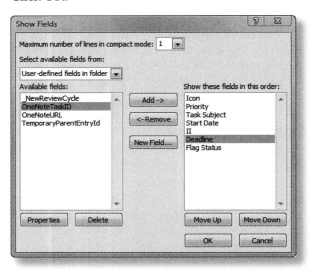

8. Back at the large stack of buttons, click the Automatic Formatting… button (called Conditional Formatting… in 2010).

9. In the formatting dialog box, click the Add button, and type the title "Deadline Due."

10. Click the Font button; the Font window opens. Choose Bold from the Font Style list in the upper middle. Set the color (lower left corner) to Red. Click OK.

11. In the formatting dialog box again, click the Condition button, and click the Advanced tab in the Filter dialog box that opens. Build the following filter:

    Deadline   on or before   Today

    Note you will need to choose User Defined Fields in Folder under the Field button to find the Deadline field.

12. Click OK to accept this, and then click OK on the formatting dialog box, and OK on the large stack of buttons. This will bring you back to the TaskPad/To-Do Bar.

You should see the Deadline field appear in your TaskPad/To-Do Bar. Resize the field width so it is just wide enough to show any dates you enter.

Using the Deadline Column

Again, the only place you can enter the deadline value is in the TaskPad/To-Do Bar column; you will not be able to add that field to the Task dialog box. Also note, in some versions of Outlook, you will need to tab over and *type* the date into the field; the date drop-down list will not work. I am not sure why.

Use this field only for true deadlines. When the deadline arrives, the task name will be displayed red and bolded. At that point you should immediately move it up to your Critical Now section (by dragging or by resetting the priority to High), since it now meets that definition.

It only makes sense to use this field if the deadline is in the future. If the deadline of a new task is today, placing the task in the Critical Now section accomplishes the same goal: showing the task is due today.

■   ■   ■

Adding the Compact Layout Back In (Outlook 2007/10)

If you have added the two optional fields described above (Intrinsic Importance and Deadline), the To-Do Bar is starting to get a bit wide. Unless you have a nice wide-screen monitor, this may begin to impinge on other Outlook columns. So you might want to add the compact layout setting we removed in Lesson 3 back in, albeit somewhat modified, so that you can see more of the other columns if you ever need to resize your Outlook window narrower. Figure 12.8 shows how the previous To-Do Bar looks in compact layout.

Recall what compact layout does: it hides fields and merges others together; it also removes the field names from the header bar. In the example in Figure 12.8 the compact layout hides three fields: Start Date, II, and Deadline. And it merged the Priority field into the end of the Task Subject field.

Notice that while three fields are now missing, most of the information you need is shown. You don't really need to see the start date, since the sorting gives you the info you need on that. And if you need to change the start date, you can right-click the flag and use some presets, or double-click the task and edit the start date in the Task dialog box. If the II value (intrinsic importance) is above six the task will be bolded. And if a deadline is today the task will be bold and red. So really, your most important information is still visible.

One key bit of information you cannot see is a deadline in the future if you only marked it in the deadline column; there is no way to see that when in compact mode. And you cannot set that field until you widen everything again. But these shortcomings are not so bad if you only use this layout occasionally, say when working on your laptop while on the road.

Figure 12.8 Compact layout.

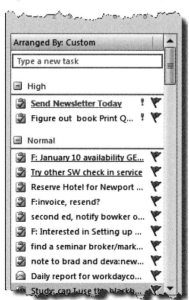

Should you like to enable the compact layout again, here is how:

Note: The view change below is NOT included with the MYN-enabled version of the Outlook add-in software ClearContext. You'll need to create it; but the changes are minor.

1. Right-click anywhere in the To-Do Bar task list heading bar (with the heading Task Subject).

2. Choose Customize Current View… from the shortcut menu. It might say Custom… instead and in Outlook 2010 it might say View Settings….

The dialog box with the large stack of buttons will open. Click the Other Settings… button.

3. At the bottom of that window, in the Other Options section, select the Use Compact Layout in Widths Smaller Than option, and then type "40" in the box. I feel 40 is an appropriate threshold given our field count, but feel free to experiment with other values.

4. Click OK, and then OK again.

Now try dragging the left edge of your To-Do Bar narrower and notice how at some point it switches over to the compact layout. If you want to change the width at which that switch occurs, repeat the above and change the number 40 to some other value.

Once this compact layout is displayed, be mindful of using the controls at the top of the task list. If you click the header and change the Arranged By setting, you will lose the MYN grouping and sort settings and you cannot get them back by clicking something else. You will need to go back into the large stack of buttons dialog box and reset the Priority field grouping and the start date sorting by hand.

■   ■   ■

Modify the Simple List View (All Windows Versions)

Normally, I don't recommend changing existing Tasks folder views that ship with Outlook; instead I have you create new ones. But here is one case where I do recommend changing a default view; the Simple List view.

You should make two simple modifications to the Simple List view in all Tasks folders. That's to add the Start Date column and to add the Modified Date column.

As discussed in Lesson 4, the start date is now your main task management date; that's why you are adding the Start Date column. The reason for adding the Modified Date column is less obvious; here's why to add it. The primary use of the Simple List view, at least for me, is to find misplaced tasks — tasks I accidently marked deleted, or tasks I marked to a future date and want to confirm, and so on. Usually I do such a search right after I take the (possibly wrong) action on the task. So by having the Modified Date column and sorting on it, I can see the last task I modified right at the top of the list.

You also may want to add columns commonly used in the TaskPad/To-Do Bar such as Priority and, if you use them, Categories, II, and Deadline, so you can edit them in-line. The last two may be especially important since you cannot edit them when you double-click the task.

Use skills from Lesson 3 to add all these columns.

■   ■   ■

MYN Defer-to-Review View (All Versions)

In Lesson 9 you learned how to use Defer-to-Do and Defer-to-Review MYN processes to defer tasks and keep your Now Tasks list short. You were shown how every Monday a group of Defer-to-Review tasks might pop into your Low priority section, and how you should process those tasks out of there as soon as possible.

You can do all your management of these Defer-to-Review tasks right in the TaskPad/To-Do Bar. But a new Tasks Folder view you might want to build gives you a way to do some proactive management. It allows you to see all future Defer-to-Review tasks in a nicely divided collection grouped by week and then by month into the future (see Figure 12.9). Using this view, as you scan each group and see any tasks that you need to reassess sooner, or later, you can simply drag the tasks from one group to the next. One benefit of this view is to see what week or month tasks are piling up in, to avoid putting too many tasks into the same review period.

The view is pretty simple to create. You are going to group by Start Date and set the filter to show only Low priority uncompleted tasks. Also turn off the overdue tasks rule in that view—the one that marks old tasks red. I also like to show the Modified Date column—that's so I can see when I last reassessed a particular item. Here are the details of how to implement those features.

Note: The view below (without the optional II column) is included with the MYN-enabled version of the Outlook add-in software ClearContext, available from my website.

Figure 12.9
Defer-to-Review
view.

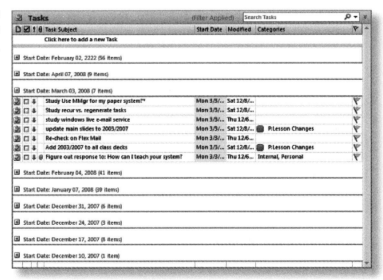

Building the Defer-to-Review View

1. **Outlook 2003** users, go to the Tasks folder;
Outlook 2007/10 users, click the Tasks banner button and then select the To-Do List folder near the top of the Navigation Pane.

2. **Outlook 2003 and 2007**, in the Advanced toolbar's Current View Selector, scroll to the bottom of the views and select Define Views.
In 2010 go to the View tab, then Change View, then Manage Views....

3. Click the New... button in the upper right corner.

4. In the dialog box that opens, type "MYN Defer-To-Review Tasks" into the Name box. Select All Task Folders at bottom. Click OK.

5. Click the Fields... button (Columns... in 2010). Use the same skills you used in Lesson 3 to build a field list for this view, as shown below. Reminder: if you have trouble finding any of the field names in the list on the left of that dialog box, try selecting All Task Fields in the list box titled Select Available Fields (Columns) From, and then look again at the scrolling field list. Task Subject and Flag Status can only be found under the All Mail Fields category.

In Outlook 2007/10 build the field list shown below.

> Icon
> Complete (optional)
> Priority
> Attachment
> Task Subject
> Start Date
> Modified
> (optional: add the II user-defined field from above)
> Categories
> Flag Status

In Outlook 2003, build the following field list instead:

> Icon
> Complete
> Priority
> Attachment
> Subject
> Start Date
> Modified
> (optional: add the II user-defined field from above)
> Categories

6. Click the Group By... button and group by Start Date, Descending; you may need to clear the check box in the upper left corner to activate the Group By drop-down menu. Click OK.

7. Click the Sort... button and sort on Start Date, Descending. Click OK.

8. Click the Filter... button; the Filter dialog box opens. Click on the Advanced tab.

   ▶ Outlook 2007/10 users, retain (or insert if missing) the Outlook 2007/10 transition filter conditions:

Date Competed	does not exist
Flag Completed Date	does not exist

   ▶ All versions add:

Priority	equals	Low
Status	not equal to	Completed

9. Click OK.

10. Click the Automatic Formatting... button (called Conditional Formatting... in 2010) and clear the check box next to Overdue Tasks rule. Then click OK.

11. Click OK to close the large stack of buttons.

12. Click Apply View to open the new view.

Later, you can activate the view as follows: in Outlook 2003 and 2007, select it from the Current View Selector on the Advanced toolbar. In Outlook 2010 activate it by going to the View tab, then Change View, then Manage Views... and selecting it from the scrolling list of views and clicking Apply View.

When using this view be careful not to click on the Categories column heading, as that will blow away the custom grouping and you will need to reconfigure the view to get that back.

That's it. Again, use this view to plan out future task reviews, as described above.

▪ ▪ ▪

MYN All Now Tasks View

This view is formatted the same as the task list in the TaskPad/To-Do Bar list, except it shows all *future* Now Tasks as well. So this view is useful for studying future commitments or for confirming or editing future dated tasks you may have just entered. Note that the Low priority section shows all Defer-to-Review tasks as well; if your purpose is to study and manage Defer-to-Review tasks, however, I recommend instead using the MYN Defer-to-Review view described immediately above. By the way, this view replaces the All Daily Tasks view used in the first edition of this book.

Just like the TaskPad/To-Do Bar list, this view groups on Priority and sorts on Start Date. And it filters out completed tasks. The Intrinsic Importance and Deadline fields described above are optionally added.

Note: *The view below (without the optional columns) is included with the MYN-enabled version of the Outlook add-in software ClearContext, available from my website.*

1. **Outlook 2003** users, go to the Tasks folder;
   Outlook 2007/10 users, click the Tasks banner button and then select the To-Do List folder near the top of the Navigation Pane.

2. **Outlook 2003 and 2007**, in the Advanced toolbar's Current View Selector, scroll to the bottom of the views and select Define Views.
   In 2010 go to the View tab, then Change View, then Manage Views....

3. Click the New... button in the upper right corner.

4. In the dialog box that opens, type "MYN All Now Tasks" into the Name box. Select All Task Folders at the bottom. Click OK.

5. Back at the large stack of buttons, click the Fields... (Columns... in 2010) button. Use the same skills you used in Lessons 3 to build a field list for this view, shown below. Reminder: if you have trouble finding any of the field names in the list on the left of that dialog box, try selecting All Task Fields in the list box titled Select Available Fields From, and then look again at the scrolling field list. Task Subject and Flag Status can only be found under the All Mail Fields category.

   In Outlook 2007/10, build the list shown below.

   > Icon
   > Complete (optional)
   > Priority
   > Attachment
   > Task Subject (optional: use Subject so you can sort on it)
   > Start Date
   > (optional: add the II and Deadline user-defined fields from above)
   > Categories
   > Flag Status

In Outlook 2003, build the following list instead:

Icon
Complete
Priority
Attachment
Subject
Start Date
(optional: add the II and Deadline user-defined fields from above)
Categories

6. Click OK.

7. Click the Group By... button, and group by Priority, Descending; you may need to clear the check box in the upper left corner to activate the Group By drop-down menu. Click OK.

8. Click the Sort... button, and sort on Start Date, Descending. Click OK.

9. Click the Filter... button; the Filter dialog box opens. Click on the Advanced tab.

   ▶ Outlook 2007/10 users, retain (or insert) the Outlook 2007/10 transition filter conditions:

Date Competed	does not exist
Flag Completed Date	does not exist

   ▶ All versions add:

Status	not equal to	Completed

   Click OK.

10. Click the Automatic Formatting... button (called Conditional Formatting... in 2010) and clear the check box next to Overdue Tasks rule. Click OK, and OK again, and then click Apply View.

You can activate the view at any time as follows: in Outlook 2003 and 2007, select it from the Current View Selector on the Advanced toolbar. In Outlook 2010 activate it by going to the View tab, then Change View, then Manage Views... and selecting it from the scrolling list of views; click Apply View.

Again, use this view for studying future commitments or for confirming or editing future dated tasks you may have recently entered. And this is the view you will use most with Lesson 10 on Delegation; Outlook 2007/10 users make sure you use the optional Subject field in step 5 for that purpose.

■　■　■

The MYN This Week's Tasks View

I described in Lesson 11, in the section Doing the Math on Your Workweek, a method to figure out how much work you have on your plate by totalling the minutes and hours of tasks due this week. I said you could create a special Tasks folder view to help you with this exercise. Well, here are the instructions for creating that view.

There are really two approaches to creating the view needed for the Doing the Math activity. You can use one or the other, or both, according to your needs. The first approach identifies all tasks due in the next seven days. If you are doing this exercise on a Wednesday, it will list all tasks scheduled through Tuesday of the following week.

Note: *You already have a Tasks folder view delivered by default with Outlook called Next Seven Days; this view is not configured correctly for our needs, so do not use it.*

This seven-day view may or may not be what you want; many workers use Friday as a natural deadline for a week's worth of tasks. In this case, if you are doing the exercise on a Wednesday morning, you want to see only tasks for the next three days. For this you need to instead create a view that displays all tasks in a given calendar week. The following steps show both of those views.

Note: *Both views below are included with the MYN-enabled version of Outlook add-in software, ClearContext, available from my website.*

Creating the Views

1. **Outlook 2003** users, go to the Tasks folder;
    Outlook 2007/10 users, click the Tasks banner button and then select the To-Do List folder near the top of the Navigation Pane.

2. **Outlook 2003 and 2007**, in the Advanced toolbar's Current View Selector, scroll to the bottom of the views and select Define Views.
    In 2010 go to the View tab, then Change View, then Manage Views….

3. Click the New… button in the upper right corner, and name the view "MYN This Week's Tasks." Choose the All Task folders option at the bottom and click OK.

4. The dialog box with the large stack of buttons opens.

5. Click the Fields… button (Columns… in 2010). Use the same skills you used in Lesson 3 to build a field list for a view, using the specific items shown below. Reminder: if you have trouble finding any of the field names in the list on the left of that dialog box, try selecting All Task Fields in the list box titled Select Available Fields/Columns From, and then look again at the scrolling field list. Task Subject and Flag Status (Outlook 2007/10) can only be found under the All Mail Fields category.

In Outlook 2007/10 build the list shown here.

Icon
Complete (optional)
Priority
Attachment
Task Subject
Start Date
Categories
Flag Status

In Outlook 2003 build the following list instead:

Icon
Complete
Priority
Attachment
Subject
Start Date
Categories

6. Click OK.

7. Click the Group By… button, and group by Priority, Descending; you may need to clear the check box in the upper left corner to activate the Group By drop-down menu. Click OK.

8. Click the Sort… button, and sort on Start Date, Descending. Click OK.

9. Click the Filter… button; the Filter dialog box opens. Click on the Advanced tab. With the skills you learned in Lesson 3, use this dialog box to build the following filter conditions.

   ▶ Outlook 2007/10 users, retain (or insert if missing) the two Outlook 2007/10 transition filter conditions:

Date Competed	does not exist
Flag Completed Date	does not exist

   ▶ All versions, if you want to view the Friday week, add:

Status	not equal to	Completed
Start Date	this week	
Start Date	on or before	today

   (note: the "this week" filter actually includes Saturday as well)

   ▶ All versions, if you want to view the 7-day week, instead add:

Status	not equal to	Completed
Start Date	in the next 7 days	
Start Date	on or before	today

10. If you did the above correctly, 2007/10 users will end up with five conditions; users of other versions will end up with three conditions.

11. Click OK.

12. Click the Automatic Formatting… button (called Conditional Formatting… in 2010) and clear the check box next to Overdue Tasks rule.

13. Click OK, then OK again, and then click Apply View.

From now on, in Outlook 2003 and 2007, you can activate and use this view by selecting it from the Current View Selector on the Advanced toolbar. In Outlook 2010 activate it by going to the View tab, then Change View, then Manage Views… and selecting it from the scrolling list of views; then click Apply View.

See the Lesson 11 section titled Doing the Math on Your Workweek to study how to use this view.

■   ■   ■

Summary

We covered a lot in this lesson. Here are the main points:

▶ I described how you should consider adding the Intrinsic Importance column to your TaskPad/To-Do Bar to track tasks that link strongly to your goals and values.

▶ If you plan to track goals and projects, I described many optional methods to do so, including a new version of the Master Tasks view.

▶ I covered series tasks (MORE and PigPog method) to ensure that a series of small dependent tasks are tracked together.

▶ I showed how you can list your primary roles—such as team lead, spouse, parent—on the Master Tasks view and use that list to create tasks that support your various roles.

▶ I demonstrated how to add the Deadline column to your TaskPad/To-Do Bar. This is recommended if many of your tasks have hard deadlines. Only do this if you have a relatively wide monitor, as it takes up significant screen real estate.

▶ I described one solution to narrow screens if you have Outlook 2007/10, which is to add back in the compact layout.

▶ The lesson ended with a number of optional Outlook views and view changes you should consider adding or making, to round out your suite of MYN tools.

■　■　■

Next Steps

It is likely that you selected a small subset of the items above to actually implement right now, and that makes sense. Over time, however, other tools described above may become important to you. So do this: put a task on your task list timed for one month from now to reread this lesson, to see if anything you previously skipped looks useful to you.

■　■　■

Wrapping Up Total Workday Control

This is the last lesson. The journey is now complete. You have learned the best task management system available, one based on the most effective practices in the industry. You have learned how to move tasks out of your e-mail and into your task system, thus removing the most common source of out-of-control e-mail. You know how to empty your Inbox and file your mail, helping to keep your workday clear and focused. You have worked through all the principles and applied them in Outlook.

Next is only practice. Review the steps at the end of Lesson 4 on how to manage tasks. Also follow the e-mail workflow summary presented at the end of Lesson 7. Both of those summaries are copied at the end of Appendix C so you can tear them out and place them next to your computer if you like. Use these steps and workflows and all strategies in this book only as a starting point, and then adapt them to fit your work style.

Plan, a few months from now, to skim through the book again, rereading selected lessons. The book is packed with suggestions, many of which may not sink in until you have used the system awhile. Your use of the system will evolve over time. Rereading will suggest ways of using this information that become apparent to you as you use the system. In particular, Lessons 1, 4, 6, 9, and 12 contain much rich information that subsequent reads can bring to your notice.

But most of all, use the extra time you achieve from this system wisely. You have now mastered something few are able to do: getting everything important done, keeping easy pace with your e-mail, being in control of your workday. This is important stuff. Go home from work on time for a change and spend time with your family. Do some strategic thinking and planning. Think big. You are ready for the next level, so start planning to be there.

One last thing. If you find this system is as powerful as I expect at getting your workday under control, consider introducing these concepts to your colleagues. Raising the efficiency of your whole organization is a worthy goal. Note this, however: while you may be proficient at learning from a book, many people are not. So consider the webinar and in-person training options you can find at the author's website: www.MichaelLinenberger.com. While there, sign up for the free monthly e-mail newsletter so you are notified of system updates and enhancements.

Appendixes

Appendix A:
Understanding Outlook
Folders in the MYN System

Introduction

Most Outlook users work for years in Outlook without ever really under-standing its built-in folder system. For example, few Outlook 2003 and Outlook 2007/10 users realize that an expanded Folder List pane is available. Most do not really understand the file setup behind the mail folders. And a majority of users do not know the difference between an Exchange-based Outlook configuration and a local file-based one. While this level of under-standing is sufficient for simple Outlook usage, a whole expanded set of capabilities is available to those who are willing to dig a little deeper.

A deeper understanding of folders will particularly help you get the most from this book. For example, it is worth figuring out whether you are using an Exchange Server or not (I discuss that here), because having Exchange gives you access to mobile solutions not possible when using Internet POP mail in Outlook. If you are using a Processed Mail folder as in Lesson 5, you may benefit from creating a more intelligent Processed Mail folder placement—I discuss that here as well. The Navigation Pane in Outlook 2003, 2007/10, and 2011 can be a mystery to use; that mystery is unlocked at the end of this appendix. If you save a lot of e-mail, you need to understand folders to set up an effective archive system; you can learn those folder details here—and you should—before moving on to Appendix B, Archiving Your Mail in the MYN System.

Let's explore the topic of Outlook folders and their underlying data sources to create the groundwork for a deeper understanding of using the MYN system with Outlook.

Outlook Folders Explained (Windows and Mac)

By Outlook folders I am referring to the hierarchical structure of Outlook data optionally displayed in the Navigation Pane on the left side of Outlook.

Note: *Lesson 2 provides an introductory discussion of the Outlook window layout including the Navigation Pane and folders, along with details on how to manipulate the folder views. If you have not read that yet, I recommend doing so now.*

Viewing Folders

The Navigation Pane on the left side of the Outlook screen nearly always displays folders. Figures A.1, A.2, and A.3 show an examples of the Navigation Pane with the mail folders open.

If for some reason you do not see the Navigation Pane, open the View menu or tab and click Navigation Pane to activate it (2007/10 users also choose Normal from the submenu). To see the list of mail folders, click the Mail banner button near the bottom of the Navigation Pane.

The Navigation Pane often shows only a partial list of folders. To see a *full* list of Outlook folders in Outlook 2003 and 2007/10, click the Folder List icon at the very bottom of the Navigation Pane (it looks like a folder); or on the Go menu (2003 and 2007), choose Folder List. Either action displays the full folder structure across all data types. Try that now; when you do you should be viewing your complete list of all Outlook folders on the left side of your screen. The Mac does not have an equivalent capability.

Note: *Later in this appendix you can find a full description of the Outlook Navigation Pane and the many ways to use it to manipulate folder views.*

Similar to Operating System Folders, But Not the Same

The complete Outlook folder collection you opened above may remind you somewhat of your computer's folder and file list as displayed in Microsoft Windows Explorer or in the Mac Finder. The reason they are called folders is because if you open any one of them you are likely to see a collection of individual matching items contained within, just like physical file folders. For example, the Inbox folder contains a collection of e-mail items; the Contacts folder contains a collection of contact items, and so on. As with operating system folders, you can drag items from one folder to another (if they hold similar data types) to organize them better. The actual graphics for these folder icons do not look like traditional operating system folder graphics, however; rather the artwork represents some reference to the type of data contained within. Nonetheless, they act like the hierarchical folders you have become accustomed to in the Microsoft Windows or the Mac Finder file interface.

These Outlook folders are not really operating system folders. They do not correspond one-to-one to actual folders in your computer's file system. Rather, they are *virtual* folder structures visible only from within Outlook. In

Figure A.1
Navigation
Pane in Outlook
2010.

Figure A.2
The Navigation
Pane in Outlook
2003 (2007
similar).

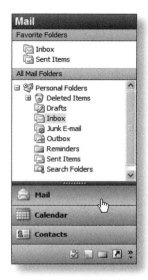

Figure A.3
Outlook for
Mac 2011
Navigation
Pane

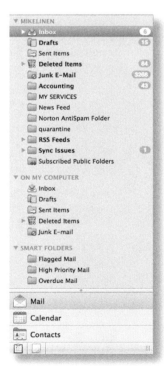

fact, in Windows Outlook, other than the folders in your Exchange mailbox (if you use Exchange Server), a given group of Outlook folders are usually stored together, invisibly, within a single Microsoft Windows file; knowing about this file and its name will be helpful to you later in this discussion when I show how to create additional folders. It will also be useful when you think more carefully about where to put your Processed Mail folder in Windows. It is similarly helpful when you learn how to archive your mail.

In contrast, Outlook for Mac 2011 uses one file per e-mail message and Outlook folders there are completely virtual.

Since all Outlook folders are solely owned by Outlook, all your folder creation and manipulation activities must take place from within Outlook's menu system.

Up To Four Major "Buckets" in Outlook

The folder list within your copy of Outlook may have just one group of folders as in Figure A.2, or it may have multiple groups of folders as in Figure A.1. Each group represents a different "bucket" of information and in fact corresponds to different Outlook data files. Each group might have similar-looking items in it (there may be an Inbox within each group, for instance), but each default group or bucket of information has a distinct and different functional purpose within your usage of Outlook. Furthermore, the files corresponding to these buckets may be stored in different locations: some on a server, some on your local hard drive.

In fact, Outlook can use up to four different buckets or types of information that correspond to these groups of folders (three on the Mac)

▶ Exchange Server Mailbox

▶ Local Folders (usually called Personal Folders on Windows; called On My Computer on the Mac)

▶ Archive Folders (not present on the Mac)

▶ Public Folders (optionally present if you use Exchange)

Note: If you use Outlook add-in software, such as Business Contact Manager, you may see additional types of folder groups. And you may see RSS feeds and other informational "folders."

Exchange Server Mailbox

The first type, the Exchange Server Mailbox, is the most common data type in large companies. The folders displayed in this group represent data stored on a central Microsoft Exchange Server. Server-based data like this enables several advantages; more discussion on this ahead.

Local Folders

The local folders groups represent mail stored on your computer or locally-networked file system that act similarly to data stored on the Exchange Server, but they are somewhat limited in their capabilities. If you are using Outlook at home, or in a small business without an Exchange Server, this will be your only choice for storing Outlook data. Even if you are working in a company with an Exchange Server, adding local folders is a good way to store local copies of your Exchange Server–based data. You might have several local folder groups. You may have additional POP e-mail accounts here.

In Windows local folders are usually call Personal Folders, but they may be labeled differently (in 2010 new ones are labeled My Outlook Data File). On the Mac local folders are called and labeled as On My Computer folders.

Note: In addition to Exchange and local folders/Internet mail, there is IMAP server-based mail that acts similar to Exchange but has fewer features. And there are HTTP accounts like Hotmail that also behave differently. I do not cover IMAP or HTTP accounts in this appendix.

Archive Folders (Windows)

The third type of data folder you may have if you use Windows is the Archive Folders group. The Archive Folders group is really just another personal folder group, with the added feature of automatic copying of data into it. In Outlook 2010 they are labeled Archives. You can optionally use these in the MYN system; see Appendix B for a full discussion of archiving, the Archive Folders group, and how to archive in the MYN system.

Public Folders (Windows and Mac)

The last of the major data buckets in Outlook that you may see in your folder list is Public Folders. You will see these folders only if you are working within an Exchange Server environment. They are usually configured by your Exchange administrators and show up automatically in your folder list. These are shared Outlook accounts that multiple users can read and in some cases contribute to. The most common use of public folders in the companies where I have consulted is to display public calendars containing the schedules of shared resources in the company (conference rooms, equipment, and so on). These do not play a role in the MYN system.

Folder Group Contents

Each of these four types or buckets of folder groups can, within them, hold one or more Mail folders, Calendar folders, Contacts folders, Tasks, Notes, and so on. While a single bucket is really all you need (as shown in Figure A.2), you may want to use more than one bucket to help organize your information; the additional groups of folders allow you to create alternative structures to separate your information logically. They also provide optional data archiving structures. And depending on your work environment, you could actually be required to use certain types of these folder sets; you may have no choice. Let's explore these concepts.

Exchange Server Mailbox

Determining If Your Copy of Outlook Uses an Exchange Server

The most important thing to know about these groups of folders is whether your copy of Outlook is set up as part of Microsoft Exchange Server. Many large corporations (and even many medium-size and small businesses) use an Exchange Server as part of their Outlook deployment. In contrast, if you work with Outlook from a home business, you most likely do not use an Exchange Server (but you can; see the Hosted Exchange Accounts inset box).

There are a number of ways to determine whether you are using Exchange.

First, ask your technical staff; they should know. But, if you want to check for yourself, do this:

▶ Within Windows Outlook 2003, go to the Tools menu>E-mail Accounts… and click View or Change Existing E-mail Accounts, then click Next… and look for the word Exchange under the Type column.

▶ In Outlook 2007, go to File menu>Data File Management>E-mail tab, and look for the word Exchange under the Type column.

▶ In Outlook 2010 go to the File tab>Account Settings>Account Settings… >E-mail tab, and look for the word Exchange under the Type column.

▶ On the Mac go to the Outlook menu>Preferences>Accounts (under Personal Settings) and select your default account. Look for the word Exchange on the right, at the top.

If you are in an Exchange environment, the key distinction is that your primary e-mail, appointments, contacts, and tasks folders are stored on a central mail server shared by others in your company. If you are not in an Exchange environment but are solely using personal folders (Windows) or On My Computer folders (Mac), your primary folders are instead stored within a simple file structure on your computer. Their content is periodically updated, most likely by accessing an Internet mail service called a POP mail service (again, I don't cover IMAP in this book, which is typically the other option).

Why Use an Exchange Server?

You may wonder: Why do companies often use Exchange? What does an Outlook user gain by using Exchange Server over just local folders with a POP mail server or other types of servers?

The advantages include features, costs, and security.

Hosted Exchange Accounts

By the way, even if you work from a home office or for a small business that has not installed an Exchange Server, you can gain the extra benefits of Exchange by signing up with a hosted Exchange service. This in an Exchange mail service you reach over the Internet that provides an experience nearly identical to having Exchange in your organization, without any of the server maintenance headaches. Most companies that provide such hosting allow you to purchase either an individual account (if, say, you work alone at home) or a set of accounts (if you own a small business with multiple employees), and accounts go for as little as $5 per user. While you reach these servers over the Internet, this is not your typical Internet e-mail account (usually called a POP mail account), but a full Exchange account with all of its benefits. Search the Internet on the term Exchange Hosting to find such a provider. Microsoft offers them, as does GoDaddy. My company uses an Exchange Server hosting service called Intermedia.net. See Appendix C for links.

Exchange Server Feature Advantages

The primary advantage of using Exchange is the wide set of features that Exchange offers to Outlook users—like seamless integration with other Microsoft Office applications, intelligent meeting scheduling, shared e-mail distribution lists, ability to recall messages, Out of Office Assistant, public folders, integration with SharePoint, and voting capabilities, to name a few. One favorite advantage of working with Exchange Server is the ability to add wireless synchronization with a smartphone device. Because of these extra capabilities, many companies opt for Exchange Server.

Note: Other than mobile connectivity, most of these features are not pertinent to this book. Knowing whether you are on an Exchange Server, however, is necessary for making some decisions later in this appendix regarding Processed Mail folder placement options.

Exchange Server Cost and Security Advantages

The other advantage can also be a lower cost to the business. The usual alternative to Exchange Server, when using Outlook as a client, is Internet-based e-mail. This is usually cheaper if you have few users, but at high user counts, Exchange may be cheaper. Why? With Exchange Server, your company hosts the e-mail accounts "internally." The mail is stored on *your* Exchange Server and the costs for all users can be spread across your internal server investment, and so can be cheaper (but not always). Also, many companies like the idea of having their e-mail on their own internal servers—for security reasons.

Other Exchange Server Advantages

Another advantage when using Exchange is that, like browser-based e-mail, you are essentially looking at the live contents of a server, not a local copy of your latest mail download (although Outlook does cache server mail so you can work offline). Because of being server based, compared to using local folders only as described below, you can usually move from computer to computer within your organization and, with a few setup steps, access all your mail.

Local Folders

Local folders are Outlook data files stored on your local hard drive (and possibly on a corporate file server). They are used as your primary data storage if you are using an Internet-based POP mail account. And they can be used for secondary "offline" storage; more on that ahead. On Windows they are often labeled Personal Folders; on the Mac they are labeled On My Computer.

Personal Folders (Windows, also called My Outlook Data File in 2010)

Windows Outlook users, if you know that you are *not* working in an Exchange Server environment, then you are likely storing your primary e-mail, appointment, contacts, and tasks folders in an Outlook personal folders file. What does this mean? It means that your primary Outlook data is probably stored on your local computer. When you open your Inbox, for example, you are looking at a list of mail stored within a file on your computer. You must periodically synchronize that Inbox with your Internet e-mail provider to keep it up to date (this is probably set to happen automatically). Many Exchange users also add a Personal Folders group to Outlook so they can move mail to it from their Exchange mailbox.

On My Computer (Mac)

Outlook for Mac 2011 shows its local files in its On My Computer folders, and you may see that term in various places on the Navigation Pane (see Figure A.3). On My Computer folders are usually there because you are using an Internet mail account. But even with Exchange they may appear in the Navigation Pane depending on settings in your Outlook Preferences; either as an additional Inbox, or as an entire ON MY COMPUTER section lower in the Navigation Pane, as it is in Figure A.3. I discuss how to make those settings in the section ahead called Viewing and Creating Local Folders on Outlook for Mac 2011.

Outlook Calendar, Contacts, Tasks Are Usually Not Known to Internet Mail

Looking beyond your Inbox, the other folders visible in Outlook—Calendar, Contacts, Tasks, and so on—are also only on your local personal folders file if you do not have Exchange. In fact, these other folders usually have nothing to do with your Internet mail provider; they are concepts known only to Outlook and only stored locally when using local folders as your main mailbox. That greatly limits your mobility and is why, especially if you use Outlook tasks, I recommend you get an Exchange account.

Mixing Local Folders with Exchange Folders

While local folders are *required* if all you have is an Internet e-mail account, local folders can be *optionally* used or added if you have an Exchange account. If used, they exist in addition to the Exchange mailbox set of folders. Figure A.1 above shows such a situation in Windows. The top group of folders represents the Exchange folders, and the bottom group represents a local set of personal folders. Same with Figure A.3 for the Mac. In some MYN e-mail storage scenarios (described below), if you are an Exchange user you will want to also use local folders in your mail filing strategy.

Local Folders as Locally Saved Mail or Archives

A more significant reason for using a set of local folders along with an Exchange Outlook configuration is this: the mailbox on Exchange Server tends to fill up quickly and, in companies with hundreds or thousands of users, these mailboxes consume considerable central server storage. Excess Exchange Server storage can slow mail performance. Your IT staff does not like this, so they put size limits on the amount of mail you are allowed to store on Exchange Server; it is likely that you will reach those limits well before your interest in the old mail stored there has passed.

So you need to find a place to store your old mail, either as a place where you can get at it quickly, or for long-term archiving. Local folders created on your local computer (or elsewhere) are perfect for this. They look just like folders on Exchange Server but are accessible separately from Exchange. Therefore, as your mail ages, you can manually drag it from your Exchange mailbox to your local folders, thus freeing up the Exchange space and providing long-term storage of your older mail.

Note: *This, by the way, is one advantage of having an Internet account over a typical space-restricted Exchange account. With an Internet account and a local folders–based Inbox, you have complete control over your primary Inbox and can let it fill up with much more mail before needing to invoke space management techniques (but don't forget to add a backup capability).*

Local Folders as a Filing System

Another reason for using local folders is this: within a local folders group you can create multiple folders and nested folders with names that match filing classifications or for mail archiving. For example, as you finish reading mail in your primary Inbox you can move that mail to a variety of intelligently named folders and folder groups where it will be easier to find later if needed. This is a very common technique used by many Outlook users to help organize their massive amounts of mail, and to save space on their servers.

Creating multiple personal folders for filing works whether you use Exchange or an Internet mail server.

Note that you do not have to create these custom folders within local folder groups; you can create your own named folders right within your Exchange Server folder group if you want, and still file out of the Inbox. That is what you did in Lesson 5. If you store those new folders on Exchange you may be limited by server storage, so keep that in mind. I address that issue below.

In all cases, you can add as many additional folders as you like. You can nest folders within other folders to create as deep a folder hierarchy as well.

Local Folders as a Possible Place to Put the MYN Processed Mail Folder

In the MYN system, as we saw in Lesson 5, you file at the end of each day by dragging all mail from the Inbox to a *single* folder called the Processed Mail folder. From there you can use various filing strategies (described in Lesson 8). In Lesson 5, I showed you one way to set up that Processed Mail folder, but you can actually use a few different scenarios for setting that up. Internet mail users will of course store that folder in a local folder group—you have no choice. If you use Exchange, and if you have storage limits on your Exchange mailbox (most Exchange users do), two optional setup scenarios allow you to store that Processed Mail folder in a local folders group, which you might like. I will cover that below.

Local Folders and Outlook Web Access/App or Mobile Devices

While local folders are a great way to get mail off the Exchange Server, there is one aspect of their use along with Exchange you need to consider. Local folders you create outside of Exchange are not visible to Outlook Web Access/App or to your mobile devices that synchronize wirelessly through Exchange Server. The synchronization process does not see them.

Note: *Outlook Web Access (Called Outlook Web App if using Exchange Server 2010) is also referred to as OWA. It is the Internet web browser version of Microsoft's Outlook e-mail. If when away from the office you access your company's Outlook e-mail through Internet Explorer or some other browser, you are probably using Outlook Web Access/App.*

Normally, using OWA or a mobile handheld or tablet device with Exchange is not a problem since most people do not empty their Inbox for weeks or months at a time and so can easily see older mail; it is all still on Exchange. In the MYN system, however, I encourage you to empty the Inbox daily. In Lesson 5, I instruct you to place the Processed Mail folder in a place that is still on Exchange; if you do that, all still works. But ahead I suggest you consider alternative scenarios that place the Processed Mail folder in a local folders group. So if you want to use OWA or a synchronized mobile device to read older mail (mail moved out of the Inbox), that will be a factor when deciding if those alternatives will work for you. You'll see all that when you get to the next section. But note this for now: if all you do with OWA or a mobile device is check *brand-new mail*, you are fine with Lesson 5 configurations; the new configurations described ahead are only important if you use these devices to work with mail older than a day or so. Again that's because, in the MYN system, you will move that mail out of the Inbox.

Considerations When Creating Personal Folders on Windows

As stated earlier, local folders on Windows Outlook are called personal folders, and you will usually see these in groups. A Personal Folders group is one collection of personal folders that contains one or more individual personal folders. In the Navigation pane this group is titled Personal Folders if it was created in Outlook 2003 and 2007, and titled My Outlook Data File if created in Outlook 2010. It is important to know the distinction between folders and groups, because each Personal Folders group represents a separate file. Let me explain what that means and why that may be important.

The .pst File

If you decide to change your Processed Mail folder setup as described in the sections below, or if you choose to set up an archive plan in Appendix B, then you may be creating a Personal Folders group and file. In case you have never created a Personal Folders group before, note that adding a Personal Folders group is a two-step process. First, you create a special Outlook data file (which by the way is stored within the Windows operating system). That adds the new Personal Folders group to the folder list in Outlook; you will see the new group appear on the left side of your Outlook window. Second, you add logical Outlook folders to that group.

It should be clear now that each group of personal folders in your folder list corresponds to one Windows operating system data file that you (or your IT staff) added. If you were to look at that file in Windows, you would see that it is named by default either Outlook.pst or PersonalFolders(n).pst, or, in Outlook 2010, My Outlook Data File(n).pst (where n is an incremented number that starts at 1 and gets larger as you add additional personal folders files). Note the file extension ".pst"—that is unique to the Outlook personal folders data file. You will see references to .pst files elsewhere in this book and in other Outlook books. Knowledge of this data file becomes important for several reasons. The first is for deciding what file format to use when creating new Personal Folders groups.

The New Personal Folders File Format in Outlook 2003 and 2007/10

In the steps below, when creating a new personal folders file, you may be asked to select which personal folders file format you want to use. Let me explain the background behind that because the choice is very important.

With Outlook 2003 (and continuing with Outlook 2007/10) Microsoft introduced an optional new personal folders file format that allows a much larger personal folders file size. Where the technical limit of the older format is 2 GB, the technical limit of the new format is 20 GB.

If you use the newer format when you create your Processed Mail Personal Folders group, it provides a number of advantages when planning your folder strategy. The primary advantage is that since its capacity is so large, in many folder scenarios archiving old mail out of that folder group is needed much less often (perhaps years between each archiving).

The only slight disadvantage is that this new file format may not be backward-compatible with Outlook 2002 or older mail you may have stored prior to upgrading; you may need to keep these two data types separate. If you have just upgraded from 2002 or older (to either 2003 or 2007/10) and are trying to mix your older mail into a new Personal Folders group, you may see Oultook errors. Rather, to be safe, stay completely with the old format or use the new file format only for new mail.

The steps below specify clearly how to choose the new format. You just need to decide if you are happy with segregating old Outlook 2002 (or older) mail storage. My recommendation is to do that segregation; leave the old mail in its own old file and always go with the new file format when creating new personal folders files.

Why is this so important? As I said above, the older format is officially limited to 2 GB of storage, which may seem like a lot. However, in my experience, and the experience of others, when the file gets larger than 500 MB it can become unstable and unusable without warning. I know many users who have lost entire mail collections as a result. And with high mail volumes or large attachments, many users can reach 500 MB in well under six months.

That said, many IT departments using Outlook 2003 or 2007 still choose the older format by default when they help their staff create personal folders, either out of ignorance or because they are concerned about compatibility with older mail. That's why in the steps below to create the Processed Mail folder, even if you already have a Personal Folders group in place in your folder list, I want you to create a new group. That way you can ensure that you use the new larger file format.

Note: *Outlook 2003 and 2007/10 users may be wondering how you can determine whether a .pst file currently in use in your copy of Outlook has the new or old format. Here is how. From the File menu, Outlook 2003 and 2007 users choose Date File Management... Outlook 2010 users from the File tab select Account Settings and Account Settings again. Outlook 2007/10 users, then click the Data Files tab. All users then select the file of interest in the list of data files, click the Settings... button, and in the window that opens, examine the Format field. If you see Personal Folders File (97-2002) in that field, that .pst file is in the old format.*

Note: *The .pst file approach is being replaced. In Exchange 2010 a new server-based Personal Archives option was introduced. See: www.myn.bz/PersonalArchives.htm.*

Deciding Where to Store the Personal Folders File

The first step when adding a new Personal Folders group is to consider *where* to store the personal folders data file. If this is a home or very small business computer, the default location proposed by Outlook as you start to create the file is probably the correct location; it is usually on your local hard drive. Just make sure you are backing these files up.

If you work in a larger organization, the choice might be more complicated. Ask your IT department. If your IT department has no policy on where to store Outlook personal folders files, read below to help decide where to put these new files.

If Your Company Uses File Servers for Local Files

Some companies require or recommend the use of central file servers for all "local" files; this is to enable easier automatic backups and easier movement of employees between multiple computers. In this case you will probably want to store the personal folders file on that central file server instead of on your hard drive. For instance, a company I consulted with recently had such a central file server available and encouraged its staff to store their local files there. It issued file server space to all of its employees and mapped that space to a logical drive called the "P: drive" ("P" stood for "Personal"). Other organizations may use a different letter like H: or S: and so on. At this company, in their standard configuration, the Windows My Documents folder was also mapped to this server space; so all "locally" saved files were actually saved to this file server, which was backed up nightly. If you work in a company with a similar arrangement, this automatic backup service is quite valuable and something you will probably want to take advantage of when deciding where to store your Outlook personal folders file. Storing your personal folders on the server also enables you to get at your personal folder stored mail if you are logging on from another computer on the corporate network, or if you are working remotely over a wide area network connection or VPN. So if your company uses file servers for local files I recommend you store the personal folders file there.

If Your Company Does Not Use File Servers for Local Files

If your company does not use file servers for local files, determine if your company provides over-the-network backup services for your desktop computer, and which drive on your desktop computer is normally backed up. That's where you want to put your personal folders file. This is not a common IT service, however, so it is unlikely that you have this.

If no over-the-network backup is available, determine if you have multiple hard drives or partitions in your desktop computer and see if one is dedicated to data storage, and plan on using that one; you may need to ask your IT department about that. It is probably called the D: drive, but it might be something else. If you only have one drive or partition, probably the C: drive, use that; most likely Outlook will default to it.

If you do use your computer's hard drive, I would also ask your IT department if they can arrange a backup solution for it. I consider saved mail important data and would insist on some sort of backup plan.

Viewing and Creating Local Folders on Outlook for Mac 2011

As stated earlier, local folders on Outlook for Mac 2011 are called On My Computer folders. To ensure you can see your On My Computer files in the Navigation Pane, Go to File>Preferences>General and clear the check box next to Hide On My Computer Folders. Also, to make the list of local folders more clear, in that same General settings dialog box, clear the check box next to the setting: Group Similar Folders, Such as Inboxes, from Different Accounts. I discuss this control more later in this appendix, but leave the check box cleared for now.

Next, look in the Navigation Pane; if you have an Exchange account, you will see the folders associated with Exchange at the top. Below that you will see a section called ON MY COMPUTER with (if Mail is selected) a set of five folders below it by default.

These default folders in this lower section start out empty; they are local storage areas that you can use to offload data from your Exchange Server.

Note: Unlike Windows Outlook, local folders in one group on the Mac are not stored in one Mac OS file. Rather, they are a collection of Mac OS files (one per e-mail message).

You can use the predelivered mail folders under ON MY COMPUTER to store mail moved from your Exchange account. Or you can add more folders there by selecting the ON MY COMPUTER label and CTRL-clicking it, and then choosing New Folder—perhaps adding a Processed Mail folder. Or you can add subfolders to the existing five folders. Note that you cannot delete or rename the original five folders; they are part of the system.

Of course, if you have no Exchange account, the ON MY COMPUTER section will be your only section.

· · ·

Strategies for Setting Up Your Processed Mail Folder

All the above can help you in defining a strategy for setting up your Processed Mail folder. If you were directed here from Lessons 5 or 8 to enhance your Processed Mail folder configuration, now you are ready. First, some review of how the Processed Mail folder is used in the MYN system.

In Lesson 5, I described a simple filing system of dragging mail from the Inbox to a single Outlook folder called the Processed Mail folder. The main goal was to empty the Inbox daily, after you extracted tasks. Once mail was in the Processed Mail folder, you were invited to leave it there and search it in bulk when needed, preferably using one of the new fast search engines available. In Lesson 8, I took filing to the next step; if you wanted topic-based filing, you applied Outlook Categories or other tags to mail in the Processed Mail folder. Or if you preferred multiple file folders, you could distribute your mail from the Processed Mail folder into those folders later, when you had time.

So, central to the MYN system filing approach is the Processed Mail folder. It is what makes daily emptying of the Inbox possible. It is what makes Outlook Category or other tag-based filing so useful. And it can be a staging area for later multifolder filing.

Refining the Processed Mail Folder Configuration

In Lesson 5 you created the Processed Mail folder as a subfolder of the Inbox. That placement is the most flexible and it is a nice quick solution for the early stages of using the MYN system. However, you now may want to refine that setting. First, I want you to answer a few questions; after the answers are explained, you may decide to keep your original Processed Mail folder configuration, or extend it, or replace it.

▶ Which do you use: Exchange-based mail or Internet-based POP mail?

▶ Is there a significant size limit on your Exchange mailbox?

▶ Are you using Outlook Web Access/App (OWA) or a mobile smartphone or tablet device synchronized with Outlook to view mail older than a day or so?

Your answers to the above questions will lead to one of three Processed Mail folder configurations (A, B, and C). The bullets below help you decide which configuration to choose, and the table below summarizes the same information. After that, full descriptions of each configuration and how to implement them follow. Here is how to determine which of the configurations is for you:

▶ If you are using an Internet-based POP mail service in Outlook, use Configuration A, which is simply to leave the settings as they were in Lesson 5, with the Processed Mail folder as a subfolder of the Inbox.

▶ With Exchange, if there is no size limit (or it is very large, say six months' worth or more), do the same as above, use Configuration A; that is, leave the settings as they were in Lesson 5, with the Processed Mail folder as a subfolder of the Inbox.

▶ If your Exchange implementation *does* impose a significant size limit but you are *not* using OWA or a mobile smartphone or tablet device synchronized with Outlook to view older mail, use Configuration B, which is to create a local folder group and to place the Processed Mail folder in there. This prevents "Your Mailbox Is Full" messages and possible inability to use mail. I'll describe how to set that up in a moment.

▶ If your Exchange implementation does have a significant size limit and you *are* using OWA or a mobile smartphone or tablet device synchronized with Outlook, use Configuration C, which is a combination of Configuration A and B; that is, leave the Processed Mail folder as a subfolder of the Inbox and *add* the Configuration B local folders group as a place to move your oldest Processed Mail folder mail, every few days. This allows you to see your old mail on your OWA or mobile device and it gives you a place to put the oldest mail when you get the "Your Mailbox Is Full" message.

All this is summarized as a table in Figure A.4, next:

MYN Processed Mail Folder Configurations	Restricted size limit on Exchange Inbox	No limit or generous size limit on Exchange Inbox (or using Internet mail)
Using OWA or mobile device to view older mail	Processed Mail Configuration C	Processed Mail Configuration A
NOT using OWA or mobile device to view older mail	Processed Mail Configuration B	

Figure A.4 Processed Mail folder configuration options.

Processed Mail Folder, Configuration A (Windows and Mac)

This configuration is for those without significant size limits on their Inbox. You might be an Exchange user lucky enough to be in an organization that does not impose limits, or you might be an Internet mail user. The action in this configuration is simply to just leave the settings as they were at the end of Lesson 5, where the Processed Mail folder is made a subfolder of the Inbox. In case you did not do that yet, go to the Lesson 5 section titled Emptying the Inbox step 1, and follow steps 1 through 4 there.

Once that is done, your folder should be indented as shown here.

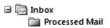

Processed Mail Folder, Configuration B (Windows and Mac)

If your Exchange implementation *does* impose a restrictive size limit but you are *not* using OWA or a mobile smartphone or tablet device synchronized with Outlook to view older mail, use Configuration B, which is to place the Processed Mail folder in a local folders group. This prevents you from exceeding your Exchange limit because, per MYN processes, you are constantly dragging mail out of your Exchange Inbox into your local folders. So you will probably never again get the "Your Mailbox Is Full" message.

The steps below show how to create this setup. But Windows users, before proceeding, be sure to read all the prior sections of this appendix so you fully understand how personal folder files work and how to create them. You will need this understanding for the next steps, and you should decide before you start where you are going to store the new personal folders file.

Mac users have it easier; you simply create a folder in the ON MY COM-PUTER section.

The steps for Windows are covered first, followed by instructions for the Mac.

Configuration B in Windows Outlook

1. Open the File menu and choose Data File Management… (2010 users open the File Tab, choose Account Settings, and, again, Account Settings…).

The following dialog box will open in Outlook 2003.

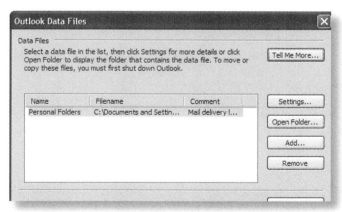

The Outlook 2007/10 equivalent is below; make sure the Data Files tab is selected (your list of files may be shorter).

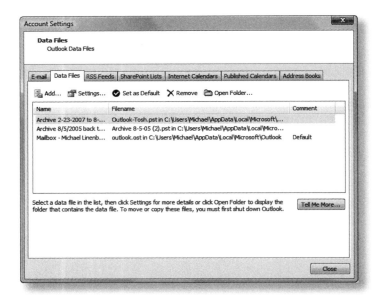

2. Click Add…. The following dialog box opens.

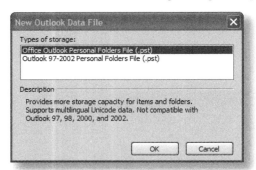

The list inside the dialog box varies with Outlook version. The file type you want is labeled as Office Outlook Personal Folders File (.pst) in 2003 and 2007, and as Outlook Data File (.pst) in 2010.

3. After you select the data type in step 2 above and click OK, a Create or Open dialog box appears where you can name the file and tell Outlook where to put it. In most cases you would simply click OK on this dialog box to accept the default file name and default file location. Home or small office users will probably do that.

You may have decided, though, when reading the section Deciding Where to Store the Personal Folders File, to use a different location; your IT department may require a specific location. You change locations by using the controls in that dialog box to navigate through your file system. If you have no idea how to do that, ask a knowledgeable colleague or your IT department for advice (there are so many possible locations, being more specific is beyond the scope of this book). Once you have navigated to the correct location, click OK on the above dialog box.

4. Whether you use a local location or a network location in step 3 above, the following dialog box opens in Outlook 2003.

Here is the same dialog box in Outlook 2007/10:

In the Name field type "Filed E-mail" or something similar. This will be the name of the new Personal Folders group in your folder list, so name it in a way that distinguishes it from your other folder groups. In 2003 you are also able to choose the file encryption type, and in all versions, to assign a password to the file. I recommend the default choices—

compressible encryption and no password; in other words, after typing the name, simply click OK. (You might consider using a password if this file is stored in a location accessible to others.)

5. This returns you to the Outlook Data Files dialog box shown in step 1 above. There you will see that your new data file has been added. Click OK to close that. More important, if you look in the Navigation Pane, you will see that a corresponding new Personal Folders group has been added, with the name you entered in step 4.

6. Next, you will create the new folder within that new folder group. Do this by right-clicking the folder group in the Outlook folder list (in the Navigation Pane), then choosing New Folder from the shortcut menu, which opens a dialog box. In the Name box type "Processed Mail" and leave all the other settings alone. Click OK, and you should see the new folder appear in your Navigation Pane, within that group, ready for immediate use.

7. If you are collecting all your sent mail in the Sent Items folder, then I also recommend you create another folder, called Saved Sent Mail, within the above folder group. Use this to periodically drag mail from the Sent Items folder. This also helps you avoid exceeding your Exchange limits. Repeat step 6 to do that, just changing the folder name to Saved Sent Mail.

Configuration B in Outlook for Mac 2011

If you are using Exchange with Outlook for Mac 2011, you can use the On My Computer Inbox as a place to create your Processed Mail file. You can either create it at the same level as the other existing five folders there (my recommendation), or perhaps make it a subfolder of the Inbox; but I see no advantage to the latter. To do the first, select the ON MY COMPUTER group, CTRL-click it, and choose New Folder; then rename the new folder Processed Mail.

Once created, this Processed Mail folder is where you will place mail dragged from your Inbox every day. Similarly, use the existing Sent Items folder there to store older sent mail. Or create a new folder and call it Saved Sent Items, to prevent confusion.

Processed Mail Folder, Configuration C (Windows and Mac)

If your Exchange implementation *does* have a size limit and you *are* using OWA or a mobile device to view older mail, use this Processed Mail folder configuration. This is simply a combination of Configurations A and B. This allows you to see your old mail on OWA or a mobile device, and it gives you a place to move the oldest mail when your Exchange mailbox fills up.

Note: Windows users, this scenario, of the three, will benefit most from using Windows Outlook AutoArchive recommendations in Appendix B. If you decide to do those, only do step 1 below (which you may have already done), and then move to Appendix

B and use AutoArchive Scenario 2 there. However, only consider doing that if you have a half day to read and follow those instructions; they are complicated. If you do not have that time, continue with step 2 below for now, in which case you are building a form of manual archiving into the configuration. You can always come back to Appendix B AutoArchive steps later.

Here are the steps for Windows and Mac:

1. Per Configuration A, leave the Processed Mail folder as a subfolder of the Inbox (as in Lesson 5) or follow Configuration A steps above to create it now.

2. Next, follow the Configuration B steps above (Windows or Mac as appropriate). There is one small and optional modification to the steps above. Name the folder Older Processed Mail, or something similar. That way you do not get it confused with the Processed Mail folder in the upper part of the Navigation Pane.

Here's how to use the folder created in step 2. The next time you get a "Your Mailbox Is Full" message from Exchange, drag the oldest mail from the Processed Mail folder under your Inbox to the folder created in step 2. Or do that every few days just to stay ahead of those messages. One way to stay ahead is to check the folder group size of your Exchange mailbox and compare it to known limits; I show how to do that next. And when you do move mail, do not forget to drag mail from the Sent Items folder periodically to the folder you have decided to place saved sent mail in.

Note: *The above instructions correspond to the Scenario 2 manual-archiving setup in Appendix B.*

■ ■ ■

Checking Outlook Folder Sizes

Configuration C has you move mail from your Exchange mailbox into local folders, once your Exchange mailbox gets close to its limits. So it is good to know what your mailbox limits on Exchange are (ask your IT staff; they know). That way you can monitor the size of the Exchange mailbox and start moving mail once it gets close to the limit. You can of course wait until you get a message saying it is full, but that usually happens at the worst possible time and often shuts down your ability to send or receive mail.

Here is how to check your folder size. On Windows you can use this both on Exchange Server folders and on local folders. You may want to check local folders as well since, at least on Windows, they have limits too, as discussed near the beginning of this appendix. On the Mac you can only check the size of Exchange-based folders using the method below.

No matter whether you are checking an Exchange folder or a local folder (the latter on Windows), you will always check the size of the highest-level folder or group as a whole.

Steps to Check Folder Size

1. Right-click (CTRL-click on Mac) the Exchange mailbox group in the Navigation Pane (or the personal folders group if checking local folder sizes on Windows). Always select the highest level of the folder group hierarchy.

2. Choose Properties (Folder Properties on the Mac) on the shortcut menu (it might say "Properties for…" or "Data File Properties…" and then, if given a choice, the group name).

3. On Windows, in the dialog box that opens, click the button in the lower left titled: Folder Size. On the Mac select Storage. The following dialog box opens (or something similar).

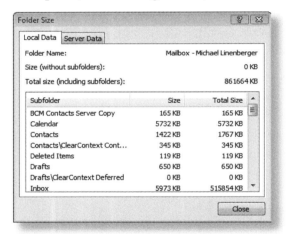

Note the third line down is titled Total Size, and to the far right of that label is a number in KB. This is the number you are looking for. Of course, you should divide by a thousand to get MB; divide by a million to get GB. If you see that it is getting close to your known mailbox limit, it is time to move mail out of this folder group.

In the example above, this file contains approximately 862 MB. If the folder group you chose were from a Windows personal folders file in the old pre-2003 format, I would say it is well past time to freeze this file and start a new one, or time to move mail out of the folder group. If it were larger than 15 GB and you were using a newer format file, I'd say it was time to replace it.

If this is an Exchange account, 862 MB is also way over the Exchange storage limits of most corporate systems and you would have had messages by now telling you that. My Exchange account in this example has a much larger limit than that in most corporations, so I am fine.

You can also examine the sizes of individual folders within the folder group by studying the scrolling list at the bottom of this window. This is useful if you are at or close to your limit and you want to move mail; you can use this to identify which folder you need to drag items from. Depending on the MYN configuration, it is usually either your Inbox, your Processed Mail folder, or your Sent Items folder that is too big.

Note: In Outlook 2007/10 with Exchange Server 2007 or 2010, you can also access the Folder Size dialog box from within the "Your Mailbox Is Full" alert window (called Mailbox Cleanup). Just click the View Mailbox Size… button at the top of that alert window.

Again, on the Mac, this technique only works on Exchange Server folders. You cannot use it to check the size of local folders because an Outlook for Mac 2011 folder group does not correspond to a file like it does on Windows; rather, it maps to a database entry that points to individual files on your Mac (one per mail message). So your real limits on the Mac are your hard drive limits, and you can check space remaining for local files by referring to your Mac Finder.

.   .   .

Outlook's Navigation Pane (Windows and Mac)

I am going to switch direction here and present a large section discussing how to understand the folder access that the Outlook Navigation Pane provides. The Navigation Pane has some subtle designs to it. I know many users who have used the Navigation Pane for years but still do not really "get" how it works. I am going to spend some time on this because knowing these details will help you understand why in fact it is a great design, but with a few shortcomings. If you think you fully understand it, feel free to skip the rest of this section and move on to the section titled New to Outlook 2007/10: The Mysterious To-Do List Folder.

Understanding the Navigation Pane

The Three Functions of the Navigation Pane

The Navigation Pane in Windows has three main functions on both the Windows and Mac versions; these will seem fairly obvious. First, the Navigation Pane is used to select or locate Outlook folders so you can see what's inside. Once you select a folder, its contents are displayed in the main window to the right of the Navigation Pane. Second, you can drag Outlook items directly to folders displayed in the Navigation Pane, to file intelligently. Third, you can rearrange folders and change properties of folders in this pane.

And depending on your Outlook version, there are three other features that may be there that are less obvious. In Windows you can drag items within the Navigation Pane to convert them into other data types. In Windows 2003 and 2007 the Navigation Pane provides controls to change the folder data *views* you see on the right side of the screen. And in Windows 2003 and 2007 the Navigation Pane sometimes presents commands to change the structure of the pane itself, or to control Outlook Instant Search.

The Three MODES of the Navigation Pane

Locating and manipulating Outlook folders is the Navigation Pane's primary function. To fully understand how to use the Navigation Pane to locate folders, and this is the part most users do not get, you need to know that the Navigation Pane can exist in one of *three modes.* You activate each by clicking buttons at the *bottom* of the Navigation pane. Outlook Windows offers all three; Outlook for Mac 2011 offers only the first, but it does have two variants (see next section).

▶ **Data-Type Mode (Windows and Mac).** When in this mode, one and only one of the six Outlook data types (Mail, Calendar, Contacts, Tasks, Notes, and in Windows, Journal) is highlighted, and all folders of that data type are displayed no matter where they are stored. Click one of the six data-type banner buttons (or icons) near the bottom of the Navigation Pane (see Figure A.5) to enter the data-type mode for that type. The Mail data

Figure A.5
The Navigation Pane in Outlook 2007 (2003 similar).

type shows a folder list tree. All others display a mostly one-dimensional list of folders of their type. Note that Journal is not displayed by default in this list, but you can add it in Windows.

▶ **Folder-List Mode (Windows Only).** The folder list mode emphasizes data location and displays together all data types in a each location. By location I mean which server or local folder group. This is the folder view you may remember from pre-2003 versions of Outlook. When in this mode, a folder tree is displayed that highlights data storage locations at the highest level, and then the multiple data types within each location. For example mail, calendar, tasks, and contacts folders on your Exchange Server are shown first, then below that mail, calendar, tasks, and contacts folders on your first .pst, and then the same on the next .pst, and so on. This is by far my favorite mode since data locations are to me a powerful indicator of an item's context and importance. To reach this view, use the Folder List icon (looks like an like an image of a folder, as shown at the bottom of Figure A.5) or the banner button with the Folder List label in it (as shown in Figure A.6, a few pages ahead).

▶ **Shortcuts Mode (Windows Only).** Only folders you have specifically created shortcuts for are displayed when this mode is active. To select this mode, click the Shortcuts icon (looks like an upper-right-pointing arrow in a box as at the bottom of Figure A.5) or click the icon or banner button labeled Shortcuts (as shown at the bottom of the Navigation Pane in Figure A.6, a few pages ahead). I rarely use this mode; that's because the Favorites pane at the top of the Navigation Pane is an equivalent for mail, which is all I set shortcuts for.

Selecting one of these three modes from the bottom of the pane (and switching between the six different data types within the first mode) dramatically changes the appearance of the upper part of the Navigation Pane. The Navigation Pane reconfigures itself to manage the selected mode only.

Once you understand the existence of these three modes, a lot of the mystery of the Navigation Pane goes away. Most of the complaints I hear from people who do not like the Navigation Pane stem from lack of knowledge of these three modes. After a brief discussion of the variants in the Mac's Navigation Pane, I cover two of these modes and the six data-types in more detail.

The Mac's Two Navigation Pane Variants

Outlook for Mac 2011 offers an innovative two-way variant within its Data-Type mode. It allows you to group folders within each data-type mode either by folder type or by account. For example, when in the Mail data type, you can group all the Inboxes from various accounts together at the top of the Navigation Pane, then all the Sent Items, then all the Drafts folders, and so on. Or instead you can choose the other perspective, where you group all folders from a given account together in its own account group. We saw earlier how to toggle between these two modes; you go to the Outlook menu>Preferences>General, and select or clear the check box next to the setting: Group Similar Folders, Such as Inboxes, from Different Accounts. I recommend leaving that check box cleared; I think it gets too messy otherwise.

Data-Type Buttons (Windows and Mac)

The banner buttons and icons that correspond to the six Outlook data types (Mail, Calendar, Contacts, Tasks, Notes, and Journal on Windows) I call collectively *data-type buttons,* as they determine which one data type the Navigation Pane is displaying when in the data-type mode.

The first time you click a data-type banner button or icon near the bottom of the Navigation Pane, you open the *default* folder for that data type in the main Outlook window to the right. So for Mail, you open the Inbox. You also expose panes in the upper two-thirds of the Navigation Pane; these allow you to open other folders of the Mail data type, such as the Sent Items folder, or any local folders of the Mail data type you might have created.

If you are new to Outlook and have not created many other folders, then not many other folders will be exposed in that pane at the top of the Navigation Pane. The Mail data type is likely to be the only data type that exposes multiple folders in that upper pane; Contacts and Calendar initially only show one folder each, for example (the Mac is slightly more complex). However, if you have been using Outlook for years and have collected many years' worth of folders and data stores, or if you are in an organization that has many servers with different Outlook data, you may see many folders in the upper part of the pane for all data types. In those scenarios, the pane becomes a convenient way to find similar data types across multiple data stores. So in summary, clicking a data-type button essentially shows you all folders associated with that data type and *only* folders associated with that data type.

Note: *There is one exception to this segregation of data. The Deleted Items folder only shows up when you select either the Mail data-type button or Folder List, yet it is the collection point for all items that you delete from any of the data types.*

Also note, for data types other than Mail, the upper pane is more *list-based* rather than *folder–based.* For example, click Contacts. You will probably see one or two contacts folders displayed at the top, in a list (on the Mac they will have check boxes next to them). But whether it displays a list or folder tree, that upper pane still accomplishes the same thing: it shows other folders of that same Outlook data type you have currently selected, and you can display the contents of those folders, one at a time, by clicking the them. If check boxes are present, clicking more than one of them lets you merge data from the various folders on the left into the display on the right; this is especially useful for combining various calendars into one view.

In Outlook 2003 and 2007, clicking a data-type button can also expose the Current View Selector in the middle of the upper pane (depending on whether it has been activated for that data type). I discuss the Current View Selector in Lesson 12 in the section titled Another Current View Selector in 2003 and 2007. I especially like this feature in the Tasks folder, and am unhappy it was removed in Outlook 2010 and 2011. In Windows the upper pane can also show a variety of type-specific tools like mini-calendars, short-cut groups, and even menu commands; I won't cover those here. Outlook 2007 Instant Search also uses a small portion of this upper pane, as described at the end of Lesson 5.

Default Folder Can Change

Once you use the upper portion of the Navigation Pane to open another folder for a given data type, it "sticks" and becomes the default folder when you return to this data type. So, for example, after clicking the Mail banner button, if you select the Sent Items folder in the pane above, it becomes the default. If you navigate away from the Mail type, say by clicking the Calendar data-type button near the bottom of the Navigation Pane, when you click the Mail data-type button again later, the Sent Items folder is what will open first. This often confuses new users, so you might try that sequence of steps now to get used to how it works.

One more point. You can also use the Go menu on the main menu bar of Outlook 2003 and 2007, and in the View menu of 2011, to switch between the data types and modes just as you do using the buttons or icons near the bottom of the Navigation Pane. Outlook 2010 does not have this menu.

Summary of Using the Data-Type Buttons

Let's summarize what we've just covered. There are three modes to the Navigation Pane (one on the Mac) and the main one is the Data-Type mode. Clicking one of the six data-type buttons near the bottom of the Navigation Pane causes the Navigation Pane to enter that mode, and opens the current default folder for that data type in the main Outlook window to the right. And it also opens detailed controls for that data type in the upper portions of the Navigation Pane. Once those controls are open, you can pick from various other folders that may exist for that data type, opening their contents in the Outlook window as you click them. Whichever folder is last opened for a given data type will reopen as the default when you return to that data type.

So as you can see, the first step when navigating among folders is to always start with the lower buttons to first pick your mode; then use the upper folder pane to accomplish your Outlook navigation in the Navigation Pane. This two-step requirement is important, and many people lose track of where they are in the Navigation Pane if they do not understand this.

Folder List Mode Advantages (Windows Only)

As mentioned, the Folder List mode, the second of three modes in Windows Outlook, is very useful. You enter that mode by clicking the Folder List icon or banner button at the bottom of the Navigation Pane. Back in Outlook 2002, the Folder List was the primary way to navigate among Outlook folders. Once opened it never went away, which I liked. But, unfortunately, in these later versions, this full Folder List is hard to keep around. It disappears as soon as you click one of the other data-type buttons. In a way, that is unfortunate; the more segmented, one-data-type-at-a-time focus of later versions can feel restrictive and confusing. Many of us prefer to consistently use this more complete and simpler Folder List approach so we can consistently view how folders relate by data store. Why? First, because seeing the data location adds context in how the various data-type folders relate to each other. But mainly, because with the complete Folder List *all* folders are in view at once, so opening one is a one-step process. With the segmented data-type modes it is a two-step process: you need to click the data-type button at the bottom to activate that data type, and then you need to find the folder and click it. That can be slightly slower and confusing. And with the Folder List view, the folder-tree data-store location information is intuitive for many of us. Once used to it, you feel like you are missing information when you see just a list of folders of a single data type.

One solution that helps to keep the Folder List mode in view is this: if, after you open the Folder List, you make a point of not clicking any of the data-type banner buttons or icons at the bottom, you'll be able to keep that Folder List tool open and use it exclusively. But I usually forget that and end up losing it by clicking one of the other banner buttons.

Data-Type Mode Advantages

All that said, there are times when the Folder List is not the best navigation approach, and the data-type mode is better. First, if you have many storage locations, it can become tedious to scroll through a long folder tree looking for a particular folder; it is often nice to see only single data-type folders together in one list. Second, there are some folders you cannot see in the Folder List mode. For example, when navigating Tasks folders in Outlook 2007 you need to enter the Tasks data-type mode to see the To-Do List folder; it is not visible in Folder List mode. Third, there are some special new Outlook capabilities that become active only in the data-type mode. For example, using the Calendar data-type mode allows you to overlap appointments from multiple Calendar folders on one calendar display (by selecting multiple check boxes in the Navigation Pane). So there are many advantages to using the Navigation Pane data-type modes, and you should learn them well.

Configuring Banner Buttons versus Icons in the Navigation Pane

I mentioned earlier that you can configure whether to expose a data-type button (or other mode button) near the bottom of the Navigation Pane as a banner button or as an icon. Figures A.6 and A.7 shows the two extremes; figure A.6 shows all banner buttons, and Figure A.7 shows these buttons mostly as icons.

Four Ways to Configure

Here are four ways to configure whether you see a particular data type as a banner button or an icon; only the first of those ways works on the Mac.

First, you can enlarge the banner button area by clicking and dragging the boundary at the top of the banner button area. As you drag up, Outlook will convert the small icons at the bottom of the banner button area into full-sized banner buttons, one at a time (see Figure A.8).

Alternatively, in Windows you can click the small Configure Buttons drop-down arrow in the very bottom right corner of the Navigation Pane (it's a

Figure A.6
Full banner
button list.

Figure A.7
Partial banner button list
(mostly icons), Win-
dows; Mac is similar.

Figure A.8
Dragging the boundary up
adds more banner buttons.

Figure A.9
Click the Show More Buttons com-
mand to add more banner buttons
(Windows only).

small, faint triangle, located to the right of the icons). This will open a shortcut menu that allows you to show more or fewer banner buttons in the Navigation Pane. Once that shortcut menu opens, click the Show More Buttons command (see Figure A.9).

As you repeatedly click this menu item, you will sequentially convert the small icons from the very bottom row to banner buttons. Click the Show More Buttons command as many times as needed. The Show Fewer Buttons command reverses this.

The third way to modify these buttons, also Windows only, is to use a control to choose which data types and modes to show as banner buttons in the Navigation Pane. For example, by default, the Journal is not included in the list of buttons or icons, but you can use the control to add it here. To select these, click the Add or Remove Buttons command on the Configure Buttons shortcut menu shown in Figure A.9.

A fourth way to modify the button configuration, again Windows only, is to click the Navigation Pane Options command (using the same Configure Buttons shortcut menu) to change that list. Unique to this method, you can change the *order* of the list as well. So if you want the Tasks banner button just below Mail, or even at the top, use this method.

Minimizing the Navigation Pane (Outlook 2007/10)

One last thing to say about the Navigation Pane. If you lack screen space or just do not like seeing the Navigation Pane, in Outlook 2007/10 you can minimize it but still show the major data-type buttons. To do that just click the left-pointing chevron (2007) or left-pointing arrow (2010) in the header of the Navigation Pane, or use the Minimize function reached from the View menu or tab, and then the Navigation Pane submenu.

■   ■   ■

Outlook 2007/10: The Mysterious To-Do List Folder

This lesson is primarily for Windows users since the To-Do List folder only exists in Outlook 2007/10. But note Mac users may want to read this as well; it helps clarify how your Tasks folder works.

I mentioned in Lesson 7 that if you start using flagged-mail tasks and you want to see them in the Tasks folder, Windows users will need to start using the mysterious To-Do List folder. I directed you here for more information on that. Why do I call it "mysterious"? Because its presence in the My Tasks portion of the Navigation Pane seems out of place; that subpane is suppose to list task folders, but where is this task folder? And why is it there in addition to the Tasks folder that carries over from previous versions of Outlook, since they seem to show essentially the same information? But do they?

You should know by now, it's all about flagged-mail tasks — the To-Do List folder shows them, and the normal Tasks folder does not.

By the way, in Outlook for Mac 2011 there is no To-Do List folder. That's because the Tasks folder on the Mac acts just like the To-Do List folder in Windows — it always shows both tasks and flagged mail tasks. What's missing is a separate folder that does *not* show flagged mail tasks on the Mac.

There are of course more details to this, and before I cover them, first let me say that, Windows users, if you follow my recommendation in Lesson 7 to use flagged-mail tasks only for delayed replies, you can ignore the distinction. You should be able to handle those completely in your To-Do Bar, so visibility of flagged-mail tasks in the Tasks folder views will be irrelevant in those circumstances. But if you plan to skip that recommendation and use flagged-mail tasks more extensively, or you just are curious, then you'll want to learn more about this To-Do List folder and how it works.

First, in case it's not clear yet, let me demonstrate how the To-Do List folder displays flagged mail tasks, and how the Tasks folder does not.

1. Navigate to the Tasks folder by clicking the Tasks banner button or icon near the bottom of the Navigation Pane.

2. Then, click the To-Do List folder choice at the top of the Navigation Pane in the My Tasks section (see top of Figure A.10, the item with the flag on it).

Now, any e-mails you may have flagged (flagged-mail tasks) will appear within the task list at the right, along with all your ordinary tasks; they'll be mixed together. This is similar to the To-Do Bar task list by the way, just filtered and sorted differently. Hopefully you've created a few flagged-mail tasks so you can see these in there. If not, do that now from the Mail folder, then return to the Tasks view and the To-Do List folder.

To confirm the difference, just below the To-Do List folder in the My Tasks pane is the standard Tasks folder. Try clicking back and forth between the Tasks folder and the To-Do List folder, within the My Tasks subpane, to see how flagged-mail tasks are shown and not shown (you may need to sort on a date field to see your new flagged-mail tasks).

So again, the main reason to use the To-Do List folder in Windows is so you can see flagged-mail tasks mixed into your tasks list. On the Mac they are both mixed into any tasks folder.

Note: *The additional functionality of the To-Do List folder and the To-Do Bar tasks list go well beyond just showing flagged-mail tasks. For example, the single To-Do List folder will also display tasks from other task folders elsewhere in your folder list if you have them — every task in any tasks folder will show here. They also display flagged Contacts. And with proper linkages, you can see tasks from SharePoint, OneNote, and Project Server. So be aware this list can get very busy. If you find these features*

Figure A.10
Locating the
To-Do List
"folder" in the
Navigation
Pane.

To-Do List "folder"

Tasks folder

Click the Tasks
banner button or
icon first to see
above items

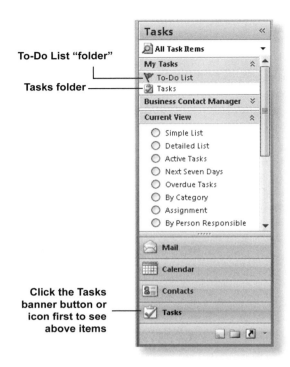

*useful, these are other reasons to become proficient with the To-Do List folder. They
are also reasons to be cautious with the To-Do List folder — it can get confusing.*

Okay, so now you know *how* to show your flagged-mail tasks when viewing
the Tasks data-type folders, but do you understand *why* this special To-Do
List folder is needed? I sure didn't at first. I was confused because this To-Do
List folder is not really a separate data folder. To confirm that, click the Folder
List icon at the very bottom of the Navigation Pane and view the entire
Outlook data folder hierarchy. You will see true Tasks folders there, but not
the To-Do List folder (see Figure A.11). And why can it display tasks from so
many other locations?

The Story behind the To-Do List Tasks Folder

So what's going on here? The underlying story is a little complicated; it starts
with the introduction of the To-Do Bar in Outlook 2007/10. In order to show
flagged e-mail (flagged-mail tasks) in the To-Do Bar, the tasks list there is
implemented using a modified Search Folder technology (see Lesson 8 for
more information on Search Folders). This means that it is a virtual folder
view of items resulting from defined search criteria; in this case the search criteria is hard-coded in Outlook. Since the task nature of flagged-mail tasks in
the To-Do Bar is accomplished virtually this way, Outlook 2007/10 also needs
to use a Search Folder approach when viewing these flagged-mail tasks in a

Figure A.11
Note that the
To-Do List
"folder" is not
a "real" tasks
folder.

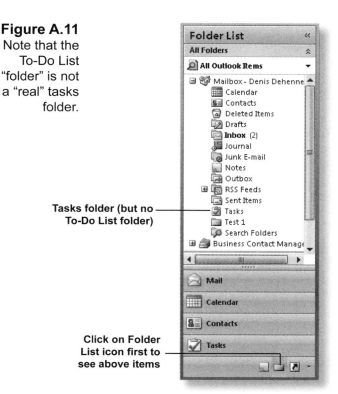

Tasks folder (but no
To-Do List folder)

Click on Folder
List icon first to
see above items

folder view. So the To-Do List folder in the My Tasks pane of the Navigation
Pane was created to fill that need. Like the To-Do Bar task list, the To-Do List
is a Search Folder. In other words, the To-Do List folder *is not a real Outlook
folder*. It is a virtual view.

So why didn't Microsoft just *replace* the Tasks folder icon with this To-Do List
Search Folder? After all, it shows all the ordinary tasks too. The answer is this:
Search Folders are very limited tools. They do not have all the features of a
true folder: you cannot share them, you cannot drag items to them, and you
cannot create subfolders in them. So if you want these functionalities in your
Tasks folder, you need to use the original task folder (and lose access to the
flagged-mail tasks). That's why Microsoft is showing *both* these folders in the
My Tasks pane of the Navigation Pane, to give you the option.

Note: *In the Outlook for Mac 2011, Microsoft bit the bullet and did replace the normal
Tasks folder with the equivalent of the To-Do Bar — it's just still called the Tasks
folder. The Mac's default Tasks folder does show flagged mail tasks along with normal
tasks. And, as a Search Folder, it has some of the disadvantages listed above. For
example, unlike all other folder types on the Mac, you cannot create a subfolder in it
(if you try to, it gives you another tasks folder at the same level, but one that does not
show flagged mail). But it does appear sharable and it does appear that you can drag*

*items to it. So in my mind, the Mac design team did this right by removing the confu-
sion of two types of folders and merging them into one simple folder. That said, creating additional tasks folders reintroduces the distinction and perhaps the confusion.*

A couple more points on this To-Do List folder in the Navigation Pane:

▶ Just like the To-Do Bar task list, this To-Do List folder collects tasks from
all data sources: Exchange, personal folders, and so on. That's another
reason it does not show up when the Navigation Pane is in Folder List
mode, because that tree of folders is data-store-location structured at its
highest level, and the To-Do List shows tasks across all data stores; there
would be no place to logically put it in that folder tree.

▶ What if you enter a new task when in this To-Do List folder—where is it
actually stored? It's stored in your primary Tasks folder, the one that is in
the same folder group as your primary Inbox.

▶ While the To-Do List folder is a Search Folder, it is not a ordinary Search
Folder since it does not show in the Search Folders folder in the Folder
List and it displays multiple data types. So it is a *special* Search Folder
created by Microsoft just to help us with viewing flagged-mail tasks (and
other special items). It does act like a real folder in many ways, though.
For example, you can define custom views for it as I show in Lesson 12.

That's it. I hope this explanation has helped you understand better the new
To-Do List folder, why it exists, and how to use it. In nearly all cases, I advise
you to use it whenever you visit the Tasks data type to view your tasks in specialized views. In fact, in Lesson 12 all custom Tasks folder view instructions
guide you to select this To-Do List folder option as you create those views
(except one, which is avoided on purpose).

·   ■   ·

The Daily Task List under the Outlook 2007/10 Calendar View

I am going to diverge from the topic of folders for the last section in this
appendix. Instead I am going to talk about a whole new tasks structure available in Outlook 2007/10. It is called the Daily Task List.

I used the term *daily tasks* extensively in the first edition of this book. They
were tasks that showed up on your TaskPad, once configured per that book;
essentially they were tasks with dates. I don't refer to *daily tasks* in the later
editions; instead I use the term Now Tasks for TaskPad/To-Do Bar tasks and
that term refers to a very specific subset of dated tasks.

Microsoft has adopted the term *daily tasks* in Outlook 2007/10 with a new
definition and a new view for showing them. Essentially they are tasks with
a due date (or start date) on a given day (or in the past if that day is today).
Microsoft has created a new place to view such tasks: underneath the day

column in the Calendar folder view (Day and Week views only). See the bottom of Figure A.12. This new structure is not bad and could have been useful to MYN users. Unfortunately, though, this list is not designed very well to support the MYN system's use of dated tasks, so I recommend in general staying away from this structure. But there is still some usefulness here. Let me explain.

First of all, here is how this task display works. If you focus on today's date (in Figure A.12, it is Sunday, January 20), the list below the calendar for that date shows all tasks with a date of today or earlier. This is much like our TaskPad/To-Do Bar filter, which does the same. So you might think this is another way to view your MYN Now Tasks. Unfortunately, though, this view always sorts the *older* tasks to the top of the list (the opposite of the MYN system), and that sort order is not configurable, including no way to sort on priority. So assuming you are allowing 15 or 20 near-term tasks to move forward from day to day, as I teach in the MYN system, the *least* important of those tasks may be at the top of today's list in this display and the most important scrolled off the bottom. In MYN we want High priority tasks always at the very top (no matter what their age), and the newest Normal priority tasks just under those, which this view cannot do. So the configuration of this new task

Figure A.12   The new Daily Task List in Outlook 2007, Calendar folder (Day and Week views only).

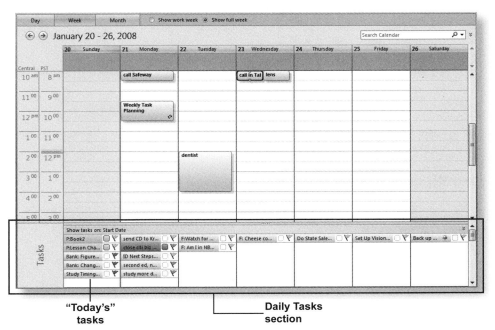

display makes the today's list portion of the new Daily Task List not very useful for MYN users.

Do not give up on this display yet. What is useful to MYN users is to look at the days *after* today on the week calendar. There you can see tasks that you have deferred to those days. For example, in Figure A.12 I have deferred a task to Friday (by setting the date to Friday), and I can see it clearly in this view on that day. I have always wanted a way to view deferred tasks, a way to look ahead and see what's coming, right in the main views. You can also drag tasks to various days as a way to set that defer date. So this view does have some usefulness to MYN users, as long as you know to ignore the today's list portion of it.

And by the way, this display also has a nice feature of showing which tasks you completed in past days of the week.

One other thing. While Due Date is the initial filter in this display for deciding which tasks to show on which days, you can also set the filter to use Start Date. You select this by right-clicking the header of the list; a menu opens as shown in Figure A.13. You will want to do that for the MYN system. The same action can be used to turn off the completed tasks display.

Unfortunately, these are the *only* configurations you can make on this display. So again, it is of limited use for MYN system users. You can hide this section if you like and make more room on your Calendar view by doing this: from

Figure A.13
Configuring the
Outlook 2007
Daily Tasks list.

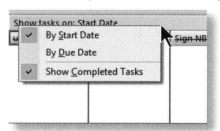

the View menu or tab, choose Daily Task List, and click Off in the submenu. Or you can adjust the height of the view by dragging its top edge.

Next Steps

Now that you understand the details behind using folders in Outlook, you are ready for Appendix B. There I show you how to use those folders to archive old mail.

Appendix B:
Archiving Your Mail in
the MYN System

Introduction (Windows and Mac)

If you use a Windows version of Outlook, you may periodically get messages from Outlook offering to archive your old mail. New installations of Windows Outlook are configured to display these messages automatically. This feature is called AutoArchive. If you were like me, you quickly canceled out of those messages and perhaps scratched your head wondering what they really meant. You probably wondered where the mail went after you archived and if you would be able to see old mail again easily. Or perhaps you actively accepted those messages and are using the AutoArchive features of Outlook, but you don't really understand the process. Few people take the time to figure out what is really going on.

And you might have come to this appendix solely to learn how to turn Auto-Archive off so you no longer get those nagging archive invitations. That is one of the first things I cover in the AutoArchive section below.

And whether you use Windows or the Mac, you are probably wondering what options there are for archiving old mail in Outlook.

Many people archive their mail manually, by dragging it to other storage folders, but have wondered if there are better ways to archive mail, either manually or automatically. Due to Exchange Server limits you may be forced to archive mail often and feel there ought to be better ways to automatically keep folders below those limits.

All of these things, and more, are covered in this appendix. I pay particular attention to the Processed Mail folder and how to archive mail from it. Where you put the Processed Mail folder strongly guides whether you need to archive and how to do it. For that reason, this appendix works hand in hand with Appendix A, where distinct Processed Mail configuration scenarios are identified; I match those scenarios with corresponding archive strategies here.

Understanding Archiving (Windows and Mac)

From here on, when you see the word archiving in this appendix I am referring to archiving in general, whether done with Outlook AutoArchive (in Windows) or by manually dragging mail (in all versions).

Archiving is a difficult topic, especially when learning to use Windows Outlook's AutoArchive feature. Most users trying to use it end up with a jumble of folders and difficult-to-find mail. Corporate support departments have a tough time teaching a uniformly applicable approach, so users are often left on their own to figure this out.

One of the first steps to solving this confusion is to get the terminology straight, so let's do that.

Archiving versus Filing

In Lessons 5 and 8 you learned ways to file e-mail. Many users get the terms *filing* and *archiving* confused, and for good reason; the distinction is subtle. How is filing mail different from archiving mail? Filing is usually done with the intention of fast retrieval. Archiving, in contrast, usually implies a deeper storage, storage that may be harder or slower to search through or retrieve from. These days, though, with lots of local storage available, that distinction is less important.

Filing also usually involves identifying distinct folders or topics to store messages in so you can find them quickly later. Archiving usually refers to moving older mail to another location, regardless of topics or search strategy. This latter definition is the one I will use.

Archiving versus Backing Up

Let's put another terminology confusion to bed. Since archiving is sometimes done onto external drives, some people confuse *archiving* mail with *backing up* mail. These are very different activities. Archiving mail *moves* mail from one location to another, thereby removing mail from the first location. Backing up mail, in contrast, makes a *copy* in the second location, but does not remove it from the first. Archiving solves a storage problem while backing up is preparation for disaster recovery. So just to be clear, in this discussion we are not talking about backing up mail (though that is important too).

Archiving Due to Age versus Storage Limits

There are two schools on why you should archive. One says you should archive when your documents become less important, usually due to aging. In some cases this is true. For instance, staff on a project or a legal case that comes to an end may collect all the related mail and archive it in separate storage, out of the way, but still reachable in case old issues arise. And others package up *all* mail older than, say, one year and archive it into a date-named storage space.

For most people, though, it is not an aging or project-end trigger but rather a storage-limit trigger that drives them to archiving. Archiving is what they do when their most convenient file cabinet (e.g., Outlook's Inbox) fills up and they want to get the oldest stuff out of the way to make room for more of the new.

The filled-up Outlook Inbox might be an Outlook Exchange mailbox reaching its limit. Or it could be a local file filing up, which is possible if you are working with an Internet POP mail server in Windows Outlook—in this case the .pst file described in Appendix A can get too large. But a filled-up Inbox is most likely an issue in an Exchange-based mail setting since the policy trend among corporate IT departments has been to keep individuals' Exchange Inboxes very small. Because that policy leads to constant messages saying "Your Mailbox Is Full," archiving is more important than ever for corporate Exchange users.

Will the MYN System Avoid Storage Limits?

You might think that since, in the MYN system, you are dragging mail from the Exchange Inbox every day, and with ample local hard disk space available as a place to store that mail, archiving could be avoided. But if you study Lesson 5 and Appendix A you will see that in one scenario that is not true. The main culprit is if you make the Processed Mail folder a subfolder of the Inbox. If you do that on Exchange, the server mailbox will continue to fill. So you will need to move mail again—to keep the Processed Mail folder from driving through your Exchange limits—and archiving is the best way to do that. You will see that solution among others described ahead.

If You Have Mail Retention Policies

Many companies these days have mail retention policies where mail older than a certain number of days is automatically deleted from the Exchange Inbox. In some cases you are allowed to store that mail in local Outlook folders before it is deleted. In other cases, no local storage is allowed. If you are in the first case—if you are allowed to save old mail locally—this appendix is for you, so read on. If you are in the latter case, well, there is really nothing to be done—you can't store old mail, and archiving is a moot point. In this case you may want to export very important e-mails as text files on your computer, but I offer little advice on how best to do that.

Archive versus AutoArchive (Windows)

Let's get back to AutoArchive, which is the Windows Outlook feature at play when you get those messages asking if you would like to archive your mail.

You may ask yourself, Is this form of archiving different from manually moving mail into another folder or hard drive? Where does this mail go? How do I retrieve it? Is this the only way to do archiving in Outlook?

Archiving can be done either way, manually or automatically, and the outcome is the same; the mail is moved from one folder to another folder. This is confusing to new users so I'll say it a different way. Once mail is moved automatically by Windows Outlook AutoArchive, the mail is no different than if you had dragged it there manually. You can open and read and use that mail just like any other mail. The source of this confusion is that with default settings, AutoArchive seems to hide your archived mail in an arbitrary location (and sometimes it does). But it doesn't have to. And the naming of the Archive Folders group may make you think it is special, but it's not. In fact, you can set AutoArchive to place the mail in practically any Personal Folders group you want, and once it is there, you can continue to use that mail as you would regular saved mail. So mail stored by AutoArchive is no different from mail you archive manually.

The power of AutoArchive is that it is a highly configurable way to move mail *automatically*. There are user-controllable settings that control *which* mail goes, *where* it goes, and *when* it goes. You can change those settings folder by folder. These settings can make AutoArchive a very useful tool for you.

Out of the box, however, Outlook comes with default AutoArchive settings that are one-dimensional, a bit confusing, and not suited for the MYN system. But with a little instruction you can learn how to improve on those settings and make them do what you want. We'll get to those instructions later in this appendix.

Outlook for Mac 2011: No AutoArchive Per Se, Other Solutions

Outlook for Mac 2011 does not have AutoArchive built in like Windows does, so you'll probably be using the instructions below for *manually* archiving mail. That said, there are ways to create AppleScripts and to use Apple's Mac OSX scheduling tools to accomplish virtually the same thing as Window AutoArchive—but programming those is beyond the scope of this book.

You may want to look at third-party tools as well. At the time this book went to print, Outlook 2011 was a very new product and few solutions were available. Keep your eye on my newsletters and other Mac online sources to see if an automated archive solution is released. One product I saw that was released at press time, but that I have not tested, is Outlook Exchange Accounts Optimizer. It is designed to do essentially the same thing on the Mac that AutoArchive does on Windows Exchange e-mail (but it appears to lack the folder-by-folder control offered in Windows AutoArchive). It does look like it could work for MYN. See www.softhing.com/oeao.html.

Should You Use Windows AutoArchive or Manual Archive?

I mentioned above that Windows Outlook AutoArchive can be very useful, so you might be itching to try it. Before I show you how to use AutoArchive, I want you to think long and hard as to whether you really should set it up and use it.

Setting up and using AutoArchive is not for the faint of heart, particularly the way I recommend you do it in MYN. AutoArchive, if you choose to apply it just right, can get complicated; the steps ahead are a bit extensive. You probably should set aside about two hours to work through the configuration steps. If you feel overly challenged by these steps and yet feel strongly about saving old mail, stick with the alternative *manual* methods described below. In the long run the manual methods take more work and are inherently more risky, but they require less up front configuration and understanding. You can always *start* with manual archiving, then move to using AutoArchive once you get the hang of archiving and feel the need for some automation.

That said, there is one case where I do recommend using AutoArchive immediately if you are using the MYN system, and that is the case I described earlier: you are in an Exchange Server environment and are consistently using OWA or a mobile device to view *older* mail and have strict storage limits on your Exchange account. If this describes you, I recommend configuring and using AutoArchive right away when using MYN. More on that ahead.

Archive Solution Scenarios (Windows and Mac)

I'll cover how to do both manual and automatic archiving. First I want to show you the typical Outlook and MYN configuration scenarios where you will *need* archiving (and point out scenarios where you clearly do not need it). Then for each of those scenarios, I'll show you how to archive manually (Windows and Mac) and then by using AutoArchive (Windows only).

Note: *This appendix assumes you are using my recommended MYN filing method of storing all mail in the Processed Mail folder. I do not specifically include archive scenarios for mail moved into multiple topic-named folders; there are just too many possible combinations of setup to cover that option here. Users in that situation may still want to read this appendix to learn more about archiving and how you might design a solution to fit your needs, because the same principles apply.*

Now let's get started.

In Appendix A, I went over local folders on Windows and Mac. I also covered the difference between the old Windows .pst file format and the new one. I went over Exchange-based mail versus Internet-based mail and how to tell the difference. And I covered the impact of using OWA or a mobile device on how you set up your Processed Mail folder. The combination of these variables makes a big difference in what kind of archiving I recommend you do and whether to do it at all, so please be sure you have read those sections and understand them.

Figure B.1 ahead condenses these variables into four scenarios, each with recommended archive approaches. These are not the same configuration scenarios described in Appendix A (though they do overlap a bit), so be sure to study the ones below as well. Then I'll explain how to do those four archive scenarios both manually and, for Windows, using AutoArchive.

Using the Archive Scenario Table

Using Figure B.1, identify where your Outlook usage fits on the chart. The column headers show where you store your Inbox and whether you use OWA or a mobile device to read old mail.

Make sure you have identified your scenario before proceeding; if needed, restudy the pages above and relevant portions of Appendix A to identify where your Outlook usage fits.

Some notes on Figure B.1:

► "OWA/MD" stands for using Outlook Web Access (Outlook Web Access in Exchange 2010) or a mobile device (MD) for reading older mail (mail older than today).

► "Limited Exchange" means you are in an Exchange environment and have typically small storage size limits on your Inbox, and/or a fairly restrictive age-based mail retention policy that allows off-server storage.

1) Limited Exchange *without* OWA/MD 2) Using Internet Mail	Limited Exchange *with* OWA/MD	Exchange with essentially no limit
Solution Scenario 1	Solution Scenario 2	Solution Scenario 3

Figure B.1 MYN Archive Scenarios.

Note: *As mentioned in Appendix B, the Windows .pst archiving approach is being replaced in Exchange environments. In Exchange 2010 a new server-based Personal Archives option was introduced. It is not in widespread use yet, but most likely will be within a few years. For more information, see: www.myn.bz/PersonalArchives.htm.*

The What and Why of the Three Archive Solution Scenarios

First I will discuss *what* these three solution scenarios are and *why* you will use them. In the subsequent section I will tell you *how* to use them.

Solution Scenario 1

You got to this scenario because you are using Exchange for your Inbox (with restrictive size limits, or with retention policies that allow off-server storage). And per MYN you have probably created one Processed Mail folder within a local folder system that has generous space. By local folder system, I mean you are using a newer .pst file in Windows Outlook or using an On My Computer folder on the Mac. And you are not using OWA or a mobile device to read old mail. By the way, this describes Configuration B in Appendix A. Alternatively, you are using Internet mail with a local folder system to store the Inbox, which is Configuration A in Appendix A.

Archiving is rarely needed in this case, since the Processed Mail folder is stored in a very large data store and you are keeping your Inbox relatively empty per Lesson 5. However, you may want to limit the number of years' worth of mail you see in a given Processed Mail folder to reduce clutter. And some people report slower Windows Outlook performance with a very large local .pst file; you may eventually reach the 20 GB limit of the .pst file on Windows. If you think you are reaching that limit, feel free to do manual archiving as described in the Scenario 1 steps ahead, perhaps once a year. And be sure to back up your mail files often.

For the Mac, since there is no single file that may get too large, you are limited only by the size of your hard drive, or perhaps sluggish performance. With today's large hard drives, it is unlikely you will reach that limit very soon. And if it does get overloaded, you really do not have another Outlook-based storage option. Because of all this, Outlook archiving is not needed and not an option for you. You may want to move mail into different date-named local folders just to keep clutter down. If you eventually do start to reach Outlook limits on your local files, your only option would be to drag the files to a Mac OS folder located on another hard drive.

Solution Scenario 2

You get to Scenario 2 because you are using Configuration C in Appendix A. That means you are using Exchange for your Inbox, with typical restrictions on its size, and you are using OWA or a mobile device to read older mail. Because you want to see older mail while mobile, you have a Processed Mail folder on the Exchange Server that you copy into every day. But because of the Exchange size limits, you have placed another Processed Mail folder on a local folder system to archive mail into periodically. Since this scenario corresponds to Configuration C in Appendix A, per instructions there you may already be doing the manual archiving steps described below.

This is the one scenario most in need of archiving, which is why manual archiving was built into the Configuration C setup instructions in Appendix A. It is probably the most likely scenario that readers who need archiving will fall into, since Exchange limits and mobile mail are common. It is also the scenario most ripe for AutoArchive.

The reason it is ripe for AutoArchive is that, in this scenario, it is to your benefit to keep the Exchange-based Processed Mail folder as full as possible. Why? Because, when you eyeball search for mail there, you want to see as much recent mail as possible; that way, your mail searches in that folder are most productive and you can avoid looking in older archive files. Therefore you do not want to archive too much at a time.

For example, you would not want to empty the entire Exchange-based Processed Mail folder during archiving since the next time you used OWA or a mobile device to search for mail you would not see any mail older than a day or so. Ideally you will only archive a little of the oldest mail at a time and keep that Processed Mail folder just below the Exchange storage limit.

AutoArchive is perfect for this. You can set it to run every day, taking just a little mail out each time. Your Exchange-based Processed Mail folder stays nearly full, and you don't reach your Exchange limit.

So I commonly recommend AutoArchive for this scenario. That said, you still can use manual archive if you want to avoid the AutoArchive setup steps. Both options are described ahead.

Solution Scenario 3

This scenario is for Exchange users with nearly unlimited mailbox sizes. This corresponds with Configuration A in Appendix A.

In some organizations, the Exchange administrators never get around to setting a limit on user mailboxes. This is especially true for new installations, where the server hard drives have not started to fill yet, or in small companies with few employees. With nearly unlimited storage, you can get by (for now) with no archiving. Just make sure your Exchange administrators are backing up your Exchange Servers (nearly all do).

However, for these cases, even though your Inbox is currently practically unlimited, it is likely that eventually your Exchange administrator will chase you down and complain about your storage. So you might want to get ahead of this by following the manual archive steps below for Scenario 2 and save your oldest mail to another storage area. Just use a larger threshold or an age-based approach. For instance, you might decide in step 3 below (in the Scenario 2 manual archive instructions) to drag all mail older than, say, two years to your archive storage—or older than three years—you be the judge of where to draw the line. Again, you might as well start doing this now before you are asked on short notice to "clean your mailbox." You may not be as prepared as you are now to think this through. And your IT staff will appreciate it.

How to Do Archiving: Manual Archiving, All Scenarios

Okay, now let's talk about *how* to do archiving, and let's start with manual archiving. It is what most people do, it requires the least study, and it certainly requires the least *up-front* investment in time. Manual archiving means dragging mail manually from one overflowing data store to a less full one. Let's cover manual archiving for each of the scenarios.

Scenario 1 and Manual Archiving (Windows Only)

Remember, this scenario is for Windows only, and it assumes you are using a local .pst file for your Processed Mail folder. You have a limited size Exchange Server without OWA/MD. This is essentially Configuration B of Appendix A. Or you are using Internet mail with the a local file (in which case OWA is not an option), which corresponds to Configuration A in Appendix A.

Manual archiving works fine for this scenario. You will need to do it very rarely, and it is fairly straightforward. You are simply going to drag a large chunk of old mail from the bottom of the date-sorted Processed Mail folder to another Processed Mail folder in a local folder group. See Figure B.2 for the Exchange view of this, and Figure B.3 for the Internet mail view.

Scenario 1: Timing of Manual Archive (Windows Only)

In Windows Outlook, if you recently created your Processed Mail folder in a brand-new personal folders file when you first set it up, this folder will not fill up for some time, say several years. I would set a task, now, to appear in

Figure B.2
Manual Archive Scenario 1 (Exchange-based Inbox).

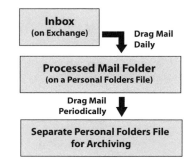

Figure B.3
Manual Archive Scenario 1 (Internet Mail variant).

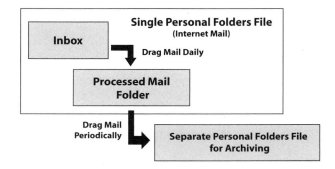

perhaps 12 months, to check the file size of the folder group containing your Processed Mail folder. Once it starts reaching 15 GB, I would start doing the manual archiving described next. Internet mail users, start checking size now since you may already have lots of mail in your local file.

Note: *Why 15 GB? Well, if you recently added a new .pst file, I assume you used the newer file format per Appendix A. That format has a size limit of 20 GB, but I recommend you never allow it to reach the absolute limit. Files in the older file format performed poorly and were often corrupted if they got near their absolute limit, and I have to assume files in the newer one could be too. So I have arbitrarily picked 15 GB. Feel free to try more, but backup often.*

Scenario 1: Manual Archive Steps (Windows Only)

1. You are going to periodically check the size of your main Processed Mail folder group (say once a year), and if it gets close to or over 15 GB, go to step 2. Instructions on how to check a folder group size are in Appendix A.

2. Create a new personal folders file using the instructions in Appendix A, section titled Processed Mail Folder, Configuration B. Set it up with a Processed Mail folder as described there; however, use the name Older Processed Mail.

3. Open the original Processed Mail folder, sort by date with newest on top, select the bottom (oldest) third of mail, and drag it to the new folder called Older Processed Mail that you created immediately above.

4. In three months or so repeat steps 1 through 3. You may want to set a task to remind you.

5. After three or four of these copy routines in step 4, check the file size of the file containing the Older Processed Mail folder. If it is at or over 15 GB, you'll want to replace it. At that point rename the folder group with a descriptive date-range name (like Archive-Jan07-Jul09). Use steps 1 to 3 of the instructions later in this appendix in the section Renaming a Folder Group to do so.

6. I also recommend you rename the personal folders file underlying this folder group using the same naming convention. This is a little cumbersome but doing so will help avoid confusion later. Follow instructions in the section later in this appendix titled Renaming Your Active Archive.

7. Now repeat step 2 above to create another Older Processed Mail folder as a place to periodically drag mail.

Be sure to make the archive files created above a part of whatever backup routine you have for your computer.

Figure B.4
Manual Archive
Scenario 2.

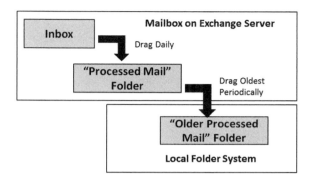

Scenario 2 and Manual Archiving, Overview (Windows and Mac)

Remember, in this scenario you have a constrained Exchange Inbox and are using OWA or a mobile device to work your mail while out of the office. This corresponds to Configuration C in Appendix A. If you recall from Appendix A, to set up this archive you create a local Older Processed Mail folder to store your oldest mail moved frequently from the Exchange-based Processed Mail folder. Figure B.4 is how that process would look.

Scenario 2: Manual Archive Steps (Windows and Mac)

1. Continue to drag mail from your Inbox to your Processed Mail folder as you process mail and empty your Inbox daily. When you are starting to get size limit errors from your Exchange system, go to step 2.

2. You probably already did this step in Appendix A. But if not, you now need to create a new local folder using the instructions in Appendix A, section titled Processed Mail Folder, Configuration B. That mean creating a new .pst file on Windows, or creating an On My Computer folder on the Mac. Set it up as described in Appendix A; however, use the name Older Processed Mail.

3. Open the original Processed Mail folder, select the bottom (oldest) third of mail, and drag it to the folder called Older Processed Mail folder.

4. Repeat step 3 the next time you start to get size limit error messages. This may be in as little as a few weeks.

5. Keep doing this for a long while. On the Mac, you probably will have no maintenance to do unless your hard drive fills up. In Windows Outlook, since newer .pst files have such a large size limit, you may not need to do the file replacement in step 6 for several years.

6. Windows Only from here on. After a year or so (set a task to remind yourself), check the file size of the file containing the Older Processed Mail folder. If it is near full (say at or running over 15 GB; see note in previous section) you'll need to replace it. At that point rename the folder group with a descriptive date-range name (like Archive-Jan07-Jul09); use steps 1 to 3 of the instructions later in this appendix in the section Renaming a Folder Group to do so.

7. I also recommend you rename the personal folders file underlying this folder group using the same naming convention. This is a little cumbersome but doing so will help avoid confusion later. Follow instructions in the section later in this appendix titled Renaming Your Active Archive.

8. Now repeat step 2 above to create another Older Processed Mail folder as a place to periodically drag mail.

Be sure to make the archive files created above a part of whatever backup routine you have for your computer.

Scenario 3 and Manual Archiving

Scenario 3 archiving is optional. In this scenario the Processed Mail folder is stored on the Exchange Server, probably as a subfolder of the Inbox. With no Exchange limits (or very large limits), the Processed Mail folder will essentially never fill up.

If you do decide you want to archive (say to reduce clutter), you can do it rarely, say every six to 12 months. Just select a large subset of your oldest mail at the bottom of your Processed Mail folder and drag it to a locally stored folder. The process and diagram in Scenario 2 should be used here.

Wrapping Up Manual Archive

That is it for manual archiving. As you can see, it is relatively simple but just a bit time-consuming. And in Scenario 2 it can become tedious, so next, I will cover AutoArchive and how to apply it to Scenario 2.

・ ・ ・

Using AutoArchive Intelligently (Windows)

Again, the sole value of AutoArchive is to automate the movement of older e-mail between folders (or deletion of old e-mail, which I describe ahead). Assuming you are emptying your Inbox almost every day per Lesson 5, Scenario 2 is the only candidate for using AutoArchive. Using manual archiving in this scenario, you may find you will get size limit errors every week or so, and so will need to drag mail that often. This can get tedious. Even worse, if the folder size jumps fast due to arrival of a big attachment one day, you can actually get locked out of sending e-mail (assuming your Exchange Server administrator has implemented that policy). What if you are on the road using only your mobile device when that happens? AutoArchive can be a real life saver for Scenario 2, not just a convenience.

If AutoArchive is so desirable, why didn't I just skip the manual archive lesson in Scenario 2 and take you right here? Because using AutoArchive is complicated. And unless you use the default settings (not recommended for MYN users), it takes a while and a lot of steps to set it up. Some people just would rather not deal with it. So read ahead and see if this is for you.

The AutoArchive controls have not changed over the full range of Windows Outlook versions covered in this book, so everything in the following section will apply to all Windows Outlook versions.

Turning Off Outlook AutoArchive Completely (Windows)

If your sole reason for coming to this appendix is to learn how to turn off Outlook AutoArchive completely, to eliminate those pesky "would you like to archive your mail" requests every couple weeks, here is how to do that.

Out of the box, Outlook ships with some folders configured for AutoArchive and some not. You could go to each folder and turn AutoArchive off if it is on. An easier method is one that turns it off for all folders at once. Here is how:

1. Right-click your Inbox folder, choose Properties, and click the AutoArchive tab; you will see a dialog box similar to the one below:

2. Click the second option button, Archive Items in This Folder Using the Default Settings.

3. Click Default Archive Settings….

4. In the dialog box that opens, *clear* the first check box at the very top labeled Run Archive Every. Click OK and OK again to close all dialog boxes.

That's it; that will turn off AutoArchive and prevent the periodic messages asking for permission to archive.

Preparing to Use AutoArchive

If you are using Scenario 2 and you decide that Outlook AutoArchive is for you, you will need to dig into the configuration screens and set AutoArchive up intelligently. Rather than just turning it on, it is worth taking the time to set it up right so that you can work with it for months and years ahead.

And again, you would not normally use AutoArchive with Scenario 1 or 3.

Realize that you can set up AutoArchive in a number of different ways, depending on your goals. The goals of the steps ahead are to keep both your Processed Mail folder and your Saved Sent Mail folder at a safe but reasonably large size, without the need to periodically empty them manually. And the steps assume that, per the system in this book, you will be manually dragging mail from the Inbox (and in some cases the Sent Items folder), so you will not set AutoArchive on those.

For this system, three main operations need to be set up to use Outlook Archive:

▶ Determine the "Older Than" setting.

▶ Set up and configure AutoArchive.

▶ Run your first archive manually and fine-tune your settings.

What follows are detailed steps for these operations.

Note: *I recommend you read Appendix A before embarking on using Outlook AutoArchive; it will give you the understanding of Outlook folders that you need to be successful.*

Determine the "Older Than" Setting

AutoArchive works like this: when it runs, all mail older than a certain number of weeks or months from today (the "Older Than" setting) is removed from any folder that has AutoArchive activated for it and placed in a folder of the same name, stored in the Archive Folders group (a personal folders file group). That Archive Folders group, along with the matching file folders within, is created automatically the first time AutoArchive runs.

Note: *If desired, items can instead be deleted during AutoArchive. I'll show cases of doing that at the end of this appendix.*

All mail younger than the Older Than setting is retained in the original folder. So the Older Than setting is the maximum age of mail you would like to keep together in the folder you are archiving from. The Older Than setting is a value that you enter in the AutoArchive configuration screens (described ahead) before you allow AutoArchive to run the first time. Getting it right is essential to preventing those pesky "Your Mailbox Is Full" messages. How do you choose the correct value?

For Scenario 2, your limiting factor is your Exchange mailbox storage limit. Calculating the Older Than setting is fairly simple. Just wait until the next time you get a mailbox-over-limit message. At that point stop and check how old the oldest message in your Inbox/Processed Mail folder is, and use approximately that age period, minus four or five weeks (for safety), as your Older Than setting. This is not an exact determination, but it should be close enough. If in the steps ahead you still get a "Your Mailbox Is Full" message shortly after running archive with that value, shorten the age period some more and rerun archive; repeat until you stop getting the messages.

Set Up and Configure AutoArchive

There are many different ways to configure AutoArchive. The easiest way is to set the default settings (while configuring the first folder) and subsequently apply those to multiple folders.

Here is how you configure your first folder and create the default Auto-Archive settings.

1. Right-click your Processed Mail folder, choose Properties, and click the AutoArchive tab; you will see a dialog box similar to the one below:

2. Click the second option button, Archive Items in This Folder Using the Default Settings.

3. Click Default Archive Settings…; a dialog box similar to the one below opens:

Configuring Default Archive Settings

To configure this dialog box:

1. Set all the check boxes as shown above, except as noted below.

2. Change the 14-day interval default to one day. With the small sizes of most Exchange mailbox limits, you will want to clean the oldest mail from your Processed Mail folder every day.

3. Set the Clean Out Items Older Than setting to the value you determined above. Make sure you studied that section carefully and have the correct value.

4. Next, click the option button labeled Move Old Items To. This tells Outlook where to place the archive.pst file, which is the file that holds all your archived items. Use the same considerations you used when deciding where to create your personal folders files. See Appendix A for a full discussion of that. Use the Browse... button to locate it.

5. Click OK, and then OK again.

You have completed settings for your first folder, and the AutoArchive default settings have been created. Note that the Archive Folders group will not show up in your folder list until after the first AutoArchive session is run (as described below).

Configuring Sent Mail and Saved Sent Mail AutoArchive Settings

Next, configure your Sent Items folder to be archived as well:

1. Right-click your Sent Items folder and choose Properties, then click the AutoArchive tab.

2. Click the second option button Archive Items in This Folder Using the Default Settings. Since you have already set the default AutoArchive settings, there is no need to define them again for this folder; no other configuration is needed.

3. Click OK, and OK again.

Clear AutoArchive Settings for the Inbox

Once you turn on AutoArchive in Outlook, it runs the default settings against all folders, all folder groups, and potentially all data sources in your folder list. Most folders other than those listed above you do *not* want to archive in the MYN system. So you need to explicitly remove archive settings from each of those excluded folders, one at a time. If you have a lot of old folders, this can be tedious but it must be done. And it must be done at all levels of a hierarchical folders list.

You will first turn off archiving for your Inbox folder and the Tasks folder. Why? Since you manually drag your Inbox mail to your Processed Mail folder daily as you empty it, archiving the Inbox is not needed or desired.

And in general I do not recommend archiving Tasks. Instead of archiving tasks, I recommend you clean out your completed tasks periodically; see the very last section of this appendix, in the subsection titled Purging Old Completed Tasks, for a discussion.

So to turn off AutoArchive, do this.

1. Right-click the Inbox, and choose Properties, then click the AutoArchive tab.

2. Click the first option button, Do Not Archive Items in This Folder.

3. Repeat steps 1 and 2 for the Tasks folder so it is not archived either.

4. Follow the same steps on Drafts, Junk, Deleted Items, and any other system folders that do not make sense to archive.

Clear AutoArchive Settings for Any Other Personal Folders You May Have

Repeat the above steps for any other personal folders that may have been left over from your previous mail-saving systems. You want to clear the settings so as to not disturb these folders during archiving; otherwise these folders may lose much of their mail, and you will unnecessarily move it to the Archive Folders group. Remember, once you turn on archiving in the default settings, it runs again *all* folders, *all* folder groups, and potentially *all* data sources in your folder list, unless you make settings at each folder to prevent that. So be thorough in clearing existing archive settings from all old folders. Of course, if you are using a hybrid approach and filing out of the Processed Mail folder into multiple other folders, you may want to leave these folders with archiving turned on, so you can control their size as well.

Note: If you have multiple hierarchical folders, here is an important point: settings made to a parent folder are <u>not</u> inherited by child folders. You need to apply or remove Auto-Archive settings to all the folders individually, at every level of the hierarchy. Yes, this can take time.

Do the First Archive and Fine-Tune Your Settings

You next need to run a first AutoArchive manually to create the new Archive Folders group and to fine-tune and confirm the settings of your AutoArchive configuration.

Normally AutoArchive is an automatic process and you would not run it manually. While configuring your settings for the first time, however, run it manually once so that you can see the effects of your settings and confirm that they are correct. Here's how:

1. Check to see if you already have an archive file in use. Have you been accepting Outlook's periodic archive requests in the past? If so, or if you accidentally did once, you already have an archive file created. Look for a folder group with the name Archive Folders (Archives in 2010). You'll need to rename the file behind that group so that you can start fresh. Follow steps 1 through 4 in the section titled How to Swap Your Archive Files later in this appendix to rename the underlying archive file.

Note: This file might not be visible as a folder group in your folder list pane, so to accurately determine if an archive file exists, do this: in Outlook 2003 and 2007, from the File menu, choose Data File Management…; in Outlook 2010 from the File tab choose Account Settings and then Account Settings… and then click the Data File tab. In all versions, in the dialog box that is now open, if you see archive.pst in the file name list at the right, you currently have an archive file in use. If so, you will need to rename it following the instructions referenced at the bottom of step 1 above.

2. Before running Archive for the first time, open your Processed Mail folder, sort by date, and write down the date of the oldest mail in that folder. You will need that date in a moment.

Note: To be most accurate, you should add the Modified field to the Processed Mail folder view and write that down, because AutoArchive actually uses the modified date rather than the received date when deciding whether to archive an individual piece of mail.

3. You are now ready to start the first archive. In Outlook 2003 and 2007, from the File menu, choose Archive…. In Outlook 2010 choose the File

tab, then Cleanup Tools, then Archive.... The following dialog box will open:

4. Select the first option button at top, as shown above.

5. Click OK. This starts AutoArchive, using all the settings in all the folders you have configured above.

6. You will see a message in the lower margin of your main Outlook window stating that Archive is in progress.

7. Archiving runs in the background while you do other work; if you have a lot of aged mail, it may take five to ten minutes or even more.

8. When it is complete, you will see a folder group appear in your Folder List named Archive Folders. In 2010 it will be named Archives.

Note: *If you do not see the Archive Folders or Archives group appear in your folder list, go back to Configuring Default Archive Settings earlier in this appendix and confirm that you selected the Show Archive Folder in Folder List check box in the AutoArchive dialog box.*

Examine Archive Folders to Confirm Success

A number of things can go wrong with your archive settings, so now is the time to check results.

Checking That Mail Was Moved

The first thing you should confirm is that a Processed Mail folder now exists in the new Archive Folders group (called Archives in 2010). When Archive runs the first time and creates the Archive Folders (Archives) group, inside that group it creates copies of the folders it is copying from. So you should find a Processed Mail folder inside this new folder group.

Open the new Archive Folders (Archives) group and find the Processed Mail folder and open it; is there mail in there now? If yes, skip to the subsection below titled Mail in Archive Folders Group.

If No Mail in Archive Folders Group

If there is no mail in the Processed Mail folder, inside the Archive Folders group, the first thing to check is the age of the oldest mail in your Processed Mail folder, the one that you wrote down a moment ago before you ran Archive. Was your oldest mail younger than the Older Than setting you used when you set up AutoArchive?

Note: *You may need to add the Modified field to the Processed Mail folder view to confirm this and the next test, because AutoArchive actually uses the modified date rather than the received date when deciding whether to archive an individual piece of mail.*

If yes, then no mail *should* have moved and everything is fine. In fact, you probably didn't need to set up AutoArchive yet. In this case, there is not much to confirm yet, so figure out how many days before your oldest mail will reach that Older Than setting and then come back to this section at or beyond that time to do the rest of the confirmation steps.

If on the other hand your oldest mail *was* older than the Older Than setting, mail should have been moved to the Archive Folders group and something is wrong. Don't forget to examine the modified date, not the received date, per the note above. If it looks like it should have run, but didn't, you may need to go through the configuration steps again.

Mail in Archive Folders Group

If there *is* mail in the Processed Mail folder in the Archive Folders group, check the date of the youngest mail there. Compare that to the Older Than setting. It should roughly correspond. Don't forget to examine the modified date, not the received date, per the note above. If the dates look right, so far so good.

Too Many Folders with Mail in Archive Folders Group

If you see folders other than the Processed Mail folder inside the Archive Folders group, and they have mail in them, and you did not expect this, it is probably because you failed to remove archive settings from some of your source folders. Find those folders now and turn off Archive for them. Copy the archived mail back to the original folders.

Assuming you got this far, all is working so far. Now for a few more steps.

Setting the Order in Your Folder List

Over time, if you collect multiple Archive folder groups with named date ranges, you may want to order the groups within the Navigation Pane in date order. In Outlook 2010 you can simply drag them to where you want them. In earlier versions that does not work—they sort alphabetically. So you will want to rename them to distinguish the order of various date ranges. Follow the steps below.

Renaming a Folder Group

Here is how to rename a Personal Folders group:

1. Right-click the top level (the group level) of the new Archive folder.

2. Choose Properties. The name looks editable here, but it isn't.

3. Click Advanced….

4. In the Name box, type "Z - " in front of "Archive Folder" (or another letter or word that will place it in the order you want, alphabetically).

5. After you click OK and OK again, you should see the new name in your list, and the modified order.

Periodic Archive File Swap

The archive.pst file will fill up eventually, perhaps over a year or two, and you want to catch it before it does and swap it out for a new one. As it fills up you probably won't get an error message, rather, you may experience data corruption, which is not a good thing. So you will want to monitor its size using the instructions in Appendix A on how to check a folder size. I recommend you examine your Archive Folders group size about a year after you create it, and then, if not yet full, perhaps every two to three months after that so you can catch it when it is full. You may want to set a recurring task to do this. If it is larger than 15 GB, do the file swap as instructed below.

How to Swap Your Archive Files

Swapping archive files is a two-step process.

First, you need to rename the current active archive file and corresponding folder group to something else, which removes it from the current archive process. Doing this also makes the archive.pst file name available for use in a new archive file, which will be created next.

Then run AutoArchive manually. Since no archive.pst file now exists, when AutoArchive runs, it will create a new blank archive.pst file and corresponding Archive Folders group. This becomes your new target archive store. You now are left with your retired and renamed archive file and group (which you can view your old mail in) and a new near-empty archive file ready for your continuing batch of archived mail.

Here is how to do each of those two operations.

Renaming Your Active Archive

The AutoArchive process we have defined always writes to a data file named archive.pst. This file is linked to the current Archive Folders group displayed in your Navigation Pane (called Archives in 2010). The file and group start with the same name (Archive or Archives), but you can name them differently. To swap archive files you must find that data file and rename it. Then rename the corresponding Archive Folders group in the Navigation Pane to something else. Preferably you rename both with names representing the date range of the retired archive group. And finally, since renaming a data file breaks the link to the folder group, you need to relink the two. Here are those steps:

1. Find the archive.pst file wherever you stored it during the initial configuration. To do this, in Outlook 2003 and 2007, open the File menu and choose Data File Management…; in Outlook 2010 open the File tab, then choose Account Settings, and then Account Settings …. click the Data Files tab. Select the archive.pst entry in the file name list that opens, and click the Open Folder button. This opens the Windows folder that contains that file, with the file selected.

2. With that Windows folder open, but without yet renaming anything, exit Outlook (you cannot rename an Outlook data file while Outlook is running).

3. In the open Windows folder, which will still be present after you exit Outlook, rename the archive.pst file to something like Archive-Jan09-Jun10.pst (using dates as appropriate for the month and year range it represents). Keep that window open because you may need to refer to the file path in step 4 below.

Note: *In some instances, even if you exit Outlook, the file system does not let you rename this file, stating that it is still in use. In such cases you will (unfortunately) need to restart the computer to fully release Outlook's control over that file. After restarting your computer, rename the file before you start Outlook again. To make this easier, before you restart your computer, write down or save the path of the open folder so you can find the folder again after you restart.*

4. Once the file is renamed it will break the link to the original folder group, so you must recreate that link. Here is how:

5. To do this, when you restart Outlook, click OK to accept the File Not Found error message that appears (you may need to click the old folder group to generate it). A file dialog box opens showing the contents of

the folder where the archive files are stored. In that dialog box select the newly named file and click Open. This will relink the folder group to the file.

6. Exit and restart Outlook one more time to test that you did all this right and clear out any remaining old links. Open the folder group corresponding to the file that you just renamed to confirm that you have relinked it correctly (it should open without error).

7. If needed, now rename that Archive Folders group using steps 1 to 3 of the renaming technique in the section titled Renaming a Folder Group, earlier in this appendix. Rename this to something similar to the file name you just used, like Archive-Jan09-Jun10. It does not have to match the file name, but it makes sense to make it match because if you ever need to reinstall Outlook, you'll need to add these files manually and you'll be happy you gave them names.

Creating the New Archive Store

You next need to run AutoArchive manually to create the new Archive Folders group and corresponding archive.pst file. The steps below accomplish this.

1. Run AutoArchive manually using instructions above in the section Do the First Archive and Fine-Tune Your Settings. This recreates a new archive.pst file. You'll see a new Archive Folders group appear in your folder list.

2. Set a task to check your folder size again in 12 months or so.

This is all you need to do when swapping files. Your previous archive settings for all folders are retained, and your previously scheduled AutoArchive sessions will continue, but will now move old e-mail to the new empty archive.pst file.

Now you have old saved mail stored in frozen and renamed archive files. I call them frozen because you have no reason to ever modify these again; they are for search and view only. You can view mail in those old files and search them with Outlook 2007/10 Instant Search (running in the background, it may take a day or so for indexing to complete on the new files).

Backing Up Your Archive Files

These frozen archive files are valuable files so you should add those files to your backup strategy. Take this requirement seriously. If you work in a big company, your best backup strategy is that described earlier, where your archive files are originally saved and updated to a networked file server that is part of a regular corporate backup plan; many corporate IT departments have this available.

Note: *If you are not in a corporate environment, but rather work in a small office or from home, purchase a high quality external hard drive and backup software, and ensure these files are included.*

As these frozen archive files build up, the space these files require on that server may exceed your allocated file server limit. In that case, or if you have no backup scheme at all, do this: store these files on your hard drive and then burn a copy to a CD or DVD for backup. This is a reasonable backup approach since these files are now frozen (no longer modified). Label and store the CD or DVD in a safe place.

But even better is to have an overarching backup strategy that you simply add these files to. You need one anyway. Ask your IT department to advise you on how to set one up. If you have no network backup available, the software I use for local backup is called ShadowProtect Desktop; it creates a full-disk image and makes incremental backups. However, adding this is an option only if you are allowed to install software on your computer in your organization.

Wrapping Up AutoArchive

That completes the instructions for configuring your AutoArchive settings to best serve the system described in this book. As you can see, it is a bit complex to set up and maintain. Everything AutoArchive does you can do manually, so use manual archiving if you wish to avoid the complex setup scenarios. However, even if you can successfully archive your personal file folders manually, you will find that the AutoArchive approach, since it is automatically done more often, will allow you to keep the maximum amount of mail in your Processed Mail folder.

Note that AutoArchive can assist with a variety of other special requirements for saving and purging old mail and other Outlook data. The section below describes a number of these features.

·   ·   ·

Other Uses of Windows AutoArchive to Prevent Exchange Mailbox Size Limit Messages

Even in this system, where the Exchange Inbox is kept well maintained through our filing and archive steps, you will still find your Exchange mailbox group periodically overrunning your corporate limits. Remember, no matter what Outlook version or Inbox archive scenario you are using, if your organization has imposed a limit on your Exchange mailbox size you will get "Your mailbox is over its size limit" messages when the sum of all Outlook data in the folders within the Exchange mailbox gets too large. With the Inbox emptied daily, and Processed Mail folder now under AutoArchive control, error messages will be due to four other folders filling over time: Deleted Items, Sent Mail (Scenario 1), Tasks, and Calendar. Let's go over these one at a time and discuss maintenance strategies and how AutoArchive might help.

Emptying the Deleted Items Folder

Your Deleted Items folder, as it fills, may help drive your Exchange mailbox over its size limit. Rarely do you want to save deleted items more than a day or two. Yet I often forget to empty it. You can use AutoArchive to do that for you. To configure this, right-click the Deleted Items folder, choose Properties, click the AutoArchive tab, and configure the settings to look like those shown in Figure B.5.

Cleaning Out Old Sent Mail

In Scenario 2 the Sent Items folder is well controlled in the AutoArchive scheme above.

For Scenario 1 users, however, your Sent Items folder, as it fills, can drive your Exchange mailbox over its size limit. What I do when I see the size limit warning message is this: open the Sent Items folder, sort descending by date, select approximately the bottom half of the messages, and drag them to the Saved Sent Mail folder (created in Appendix A). This works for me.

There is unfortunately no easy AutoArchive configuration that works well in the MYN system. Rather, I stick with the manual approach of periodically dragging my sent mail to the Saved Sent Items folder.

Purging Old Completed Tasks

Completed tasks can start to build up and impact your Exchange Server storage space. You can manually purge those old completed tasks by going to the Tasks folder and opening the Completed view (I show you how to find and open Task folder views in Lesson 12 in the section titled Custom Tasks Views for Projects, Goals, and More). Then scroll to the bottom and delete your oldest completed tasks using the DELETE key (you may want to save some recent ones to review for status reports, and so on). Outlook 2007/10 users, make sure you are using the Tasks folder and not the To-Do List folder; otherwise you will also delete old mail that was once flagged. Instead, you can clear such completed flagged mail from the To-Do List folder without deleting the e-mail by right-clicking the flag and choosing Clear Flag.

You can also use AutoArchive to automatically purge old tasks. Luckily, AutoArchive archives tasks based on the Completion Date, which is exactly the behavior we expect. As with Deleted Items, there is no reason to save the archived tasks; you just wish to delete them.

To configure this, right-click the Tasks folder, choose Properties, click the AutoArchive tab, and configure the settings so they look like those shown in Figure B.6.

Calendar

Your Calendar is probably the least likely source of an overloaded Exchange mailbox, but it can contribute, particularly if you create appointments with file attachments. To use AutoArchive for the Calendar, follow the instructions above for Deleted Items, using a much larger Older Than setting. Many people like to be able to look back in their calendar over the past year to see when certain meetings were held, so 12 to 18 months may be a reasonable setting for the Older Than setting.

■   ■   ■

Figure B.5
Settings for
AutoArchive of
Deleted Items.

Figure B.6
Settings for
AutoArchive of
Tasks folder.

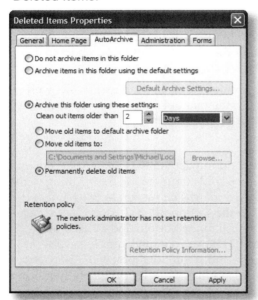

Appendix C:
Resources and Quick Guides

Websites for this Book and Michael Linenberger

www.MichaelLinenberger.com
Sign up for the monthly newsletter there to get book updates and useful tips.

www.masteryourworkday.com/blog
Michael Linenberger's blog.

www.facebook.com/masteryourworkdaynow
Michael Linenberger's facebook page for tips related to the MYN system.

www.twitter.com/mikelinenberger
Michael Linenberger's twitter page.

Some Useful Books

▶ *Master Your Workday Now!* by Michael Linenberger. Released in 2010, this title includes a paper-based approach to MYN, as well as a discussion of goal and career achievement.

▶ *Total Workday Control Using Microsoft Outlook, 2nd. Ed.* by Michael Linenberger. Use the older second edition if you need support for Outlook 2002.

▶ *Seize the Work Day: Using the Tablet PC to Take Total Control of Your Work and Meeting Day,* by Michael Linenberger. This older book is largely out of date; but many concepts in it can still be applied to today's Tablet PCs.

▶ *Getting Things Done,* by David Allen

▶ *First Things First*, by Stephen R. Covey, A. Roger Merrill, Rebecca R. Merrill

▶ *The 7 Habits of Highly Effective People*, by Stephen Covey

▶ *To Do... Doing... Done!*, by G. Lynne Snead and Joyce Wycoff

▶ *The Time Trap*, by Alec Mackenzie

▶ *Time Management from the Inside Out*, by Julie Morgenstern

▶ *Microsoft Office Outlook 2003 Inside Out*, by Jim Boyce

▶ *Microsoft Office Outlook 2007 Inside Out*, by Jim Boyce

▶ *Microsoft Office Outlook 2010 Inside Out*, by Jim Boyce

▶ *Microsoft Outlook 2003 Bible*, by Rob Tidrow

▶ *Special Edition Using Microsoft Office Outlook 2003*, by Patricia Cardoza

▶ *Special Edition Using Microsoft Office Outlook 2007*, by Patricia Cardoza

▶ *The Unofficial Guide to Microsoft Office Outlook 2007*, by Marc Orchant

Software and Product Links

ClearContext

▶ ClearContext Windows Outlook Add-in, special MYN version: www.MichaelLinenberger.com/clearcontext.html

Non-Outlook Tasks Solution: ToodleDo

▶ ToodleDo, all about: www.myn.bz/ToodleDo.html

▶ ToodleDo MYN special edition: www.myn.bz/TD.htm

▶ ToodleDo iPhone & iPad App: www.toodledo.com/info/iphone.php

▶ ToodleDo Android App Got To Do: www.myn.bz/GotToDo.htm

Accessing Outlook Exchange Tasks on Mobile Devices

▶ iPhone & iPad TaskTask: www.myn.bz/TaskTask.htm

▶ Android TouchDown: www.myn.bz/TouchDown.htm

▶ BlackBerry: www.myn.bz/TDM.htm

▶ Windows Mobile 6 Pocket Informent: www.myn.bz/PI-Config.htm

Exchange Hosting

▶ Intermedia: (3 mailbox minimum)
www.intermedia.net/exchange-hosting/exchange-hosting.asp

▶ Microsoft: (5 mailbox minimum)
www.microsoft.com/online/exchange-online.aspx#

▶ GoDaddy: (1 mailbox okay)
www.godaddy.com/email/hosted-exchange.aspx

Microsoft Outlook Links

▶ Microsoft Office Outlook, main product page:
office.microsoft.com/en-us/FX010857931033.aspx

▶ Outlook 2007/10 add-in, Calendar Printing Assistant for Microsoft Office Outlook:
www.microsoft.com/downloads/en/details.aspx?FamilyID=e7bab4eb-d032-46cd-908e-a7a6af2ef404&displaylang=en

▶ Microsoft Office Web Apps:
office.microsoft.com/en-us/web-apps/

Search Engine Software

▶ Windows Search (useful if you have Oultook 2003):
www.microsoft.com/windows/products/winfamily/desktopsearch/default.mspx

▶ X1 full product list: www.x1.com

▶ Google Desktop: desktop.google.com

▶ Xobni: www.xobni.com

Voice Mail to E-mail Services

▶ CallWave: www.callwave.com/landing/mobile/SelectService.aspx

▶ GotVoice: www.gotvoice.com

▶ Ribbit: www.ribbit.com/

▶ eVoice: home.evoice.com/

▶ PhoneTag: www.phonetag.com/

▶ Google Voice (also includes single-number routing of calls)
google.com/voice

▶ 3Jam (similar to Google Voice): www.3jam.com

► Jott: www.jott.com

Data Backup and Archiving Products

► ShadowProtect backup software (my current favorite):
www.storagecraft.com/shadow_protect_desktop.php

► Acronis True Image backup software:
www.acronis.com/

► Retrospect backup software for small to medium size businesses:
www.retrospect.com/products/software/retroforwin/

► Outlook Exchange Accounts Optimizer, software for archiving mail in
Outlook for Mac 2011: www.softhing.com/oeao.html

Master Your Now! System Quick Guide: Outlook Task Management Principles

(See Lesson 4 for a full discussion of these principles.)

Configure your MYN Task List per Lesson 3, then:

1. Assign to the High and Normal priority sections of your MYN task list only tasks you must do or would consider doing now. These are your Now Tasks. Give must-do-today tasks a High priority (your Critical Now tasks), and all other tasks a Normal (medium) priority (your Opportunity Now tasks).

2. Set the Start Date field of all tasks to the day you would like to start seeing the task on your MYN task list. If it is in the future, the task will not appear on your list till that day. Do not leave any tasks with a start date of None.

3. Do not set Outlook reminders on tasks. Do set them on appointments.

4. Set to a High priority any task due today; that means any task you would not leave work today without completing. Set the start date to today. Work those tasks early. If a future deadline, set the start date to that day.

5. If a task has a future deadline, but you'd like to start work on it before that deadline, set the start dater earlier, use a Normal priority, and enter DUE and the deadline date in front of the task title. Consider creating a duplicate High priority task with the start date equal to the deadline. Or use the Deadline field taught in Lesson 12 instead of either of these.

6. Complete all your High priority (Critical Now) tasks by end of day. Review your Normal priority section (Opportunity Now tasks) at least once a day to find appropriate additional tasks to do.

7. When reviewing your Normal priority (Opportunity Now tasks) section, if you find tasks near the bottom of the list that are important and need to be emphasized, set their start dates to a date near today. That will move them to near the top of the list. This is the FRESH Prioritization approach in action.

8. Keep the Opportunity Now section of your MYN task list no larger than about 20 items. If it gets much larger than 20, first try deleting or delegating. If that is not possible, set some tasks to a future date, or better, move tasks to the Low priority section by setting their Outlook priority to Low; this is the same as tossing them over the Now Horizon as described in Lessons 1 and 4. Review your Low priority tasks section once a week (or less often), in case any tasks there become more important over time. If the Low priority section becomes too large to easily review, start using the full Strategic Deferral system taught in Lesson 9.

Master Your Now! System Quick Guide: E-mail Workflow

Read Each E-mail, and...

1. **Delete it:** Decide if the mail has no action and no later value and should be deleted (junk mail, useless banter, and so forth). If so, delete it immediately. Don't spend much time on this. If you are uncertain, keep it and move on to the next step.

For All E-mail You Decide Not to Delete...

2. **Act on it now**: Decide whether the e-mail generates the need for an immediate action and if that action can be done quickly (completed in one minute); if so, just do it now. That action might be to reply to the e-mail, forward it, make a quick call, or send a new e-mail to someone else. Choose this option cautiously, however, because that one minute can easily expand to five, ten, or twenty.

3. **Mark it for reply:** If the only action needed is to reply to the e-mail but it will take more than one minute to do so, flag it with an Outlook Follow Up flag (right-click the message and choose Follow Up), and leave it in your Inbox until you can reply. These should be the only items left in your Inbox when you empty it. If you cannot reply immediately because some other action has to happen first, follow the next step instead.

4. **Convert it to a task:** If an action other than a simple reply is needed but cannot be done now, create an Outlook task and copy/convert the mail to a task using the steps described in Lesson 7.

5. **Set a follow-up task (optional):** If your action is to make a quick reply or send a new message, after you do so, consider whether you need to set a follow-up task for that message, following the instructions in the Lesson 7 section titled Create Follow-Up Tasks for Important Requests You Make by E-mail.

6. **Tag it (optional):** Tag the e-mail as appropriate, using the techniques in Lesson 8. Or instead skip topic tagging in your workflow altogether, and rely on a search engine as described in Lesson 5.

7. **Move it to the Processed Mail folder:** In all cases except mail flagged for pending replies, the next step is to move the processed mail item out of the Inbox and into the Processed Mail folder (or immediately into individual file folders, if that is your method).

8. **Work your tasks from the MYN task list:** After you have converted mail to tasks and emptied the Inbox, work your highest-priority tasks from the MYN task list, using the principles taught in Lessons 4 and 6.

Cut out here, or go to www.myn.bz/MYN-Guides.htm for a printable page.

Index